KU-997-134
R'324.2(7)/C09
America, South
AUTHOR
COGGINS
HOUSE OF COMMONS LIBRARY

POLITICAL PARTIES
OF THE AMERICAS AND THE CARIBBEAN

POLITICAL PARTIES OF THE AMERICAS AND THE CARIBBEAN
A Reference Guide

Editors: John Coggins and D. S. Lewis

Deputy editor: Giovanna Milia
(Central and South America and the Caribbean)

Other contributors:
Marc Cole-Bailey (USA); Joanna E. Peberdy (Canada)

POLITICAL PARTIES OF THE AMERICAS AND THE CARIBBEAN

Published by Longman Group UK Limited, Westgate House,
The High, Harlow, Essex CM20 1YR, United Kingdom.
Telephone (0279) 442601
Telex 81491 Padlog
Facsimile (0279) 444501

Distributed exclusively in the United States and Canada by Gale Research Inc.,
835 Penobscot Building, Detroit, Michigan 48226, USA.

ISBN 0582 096464 (Longman)

A catalogue record for this publication is available from the British Library.

Printed in Great Britain by BPCC Wheatons Ltd, Exeter

Table of Contents

Introduction

The aim of this volume is to provide accurate and detailed information on the political parties currently operating in the Americas. The book is divided into country-entries, arranged alphabetically and including essential background information on the constitutional structure, franchise and electoral system of the country concerned. Within each entry there is a sub-division between major and minor parties. In both cases basic data is provided on party title, address, leadership, and orientation. In the case of major parties the book also seeks to show their historical evolution and to provide information on electoral performance, internal structure, membership and international affiliation. The book also includes information on defunct parties where they are considered sufficiently important to be of continued relevance to contemporary politics. Entries on major guerrilla organizations are also included.

The dividing line between a political party and a protest movement or pressure group is necessarily imprecise, and varies in accordance with the context in which an organization operates. For the purposes of this volume we have tended to accept self-definition as the starting point for inclusion but, inevitably, editorial judgements have had to be made on a case-by-case basis. This has been true also in deciding whether a party is of sufficient size and importance to warrant inclusion, and whether it should be classed as a major or minor organization. In all cases we have used our regional expertise to adjudicate, attempting to provide the broadest possible range of information while maintaining consistency and accuracy.

A common problem of reference books is that some of the information contained therein may become outdated in the period between going to press and publication. A volume on political parties—which deals with thousands of entities which are, by definition, continually evolving through mergers, schisms and realignments—is particularly prone to this weakness. We have attempted to ensure that the information contained in the volume is correct as of the end of March 1992. By providing details of the evolution and context of parties, however, we hope that the book will remain a valuable reference aid for anyone interested in the politics of the Americas for many years to come.

We wish to thank all of those who made the compilation of this volume possible. This includes the parties themselves, many of which provided invaluable information, but also government departments, High Commissions and Embassies, specialist agencies, libraries, journalists and academics who helped with the information-gathering process. We are also grateful to the resources provided by the editorial offices of CIRCA Research and Reference Information Ltd. (Cambridge). Finally, we wish to acknowledge our debt to the individual contributors to this volume, particularly Giovanna Milia, Joanna E. Peberdy, and Marc Cole-Bailey, for their hard work and diligence.

D. S. Lewis
John Coggins
London, June 1992

Anguilla

Capital: The Valley **Population: 7,500**

Anguilla, a British colony from 1650 to 1967, and then part of the Associated State of St Kitts-Nevis-Anguilla, became a separate British dependency on December 19, 1980.

Constitutional structure

Under the 1982 Constitution executive power is vested in the Governor who represents the British monarch. The Governor is responsible for external affairs, international financial affairs, defence and internal security. In most other matters the Governor acts on the advice of the Executive Council over which he presides. Legislative power is vested in the unicameral House of Assembly which consists of seven elected members, two ex-officio members, two nominated members and a Speaker who is elected by the House. The Executive Council is responsible to the House and consists of a Chief Minister and three other ministers, all four of whom must be elected members of the House of Assembly, and two ex-officio members.

Electoral system

The seven members of the House of Assembly are elected for a maximum term of five years.

Evolution of the suffrage

Anguilla has universal adult suffrage.

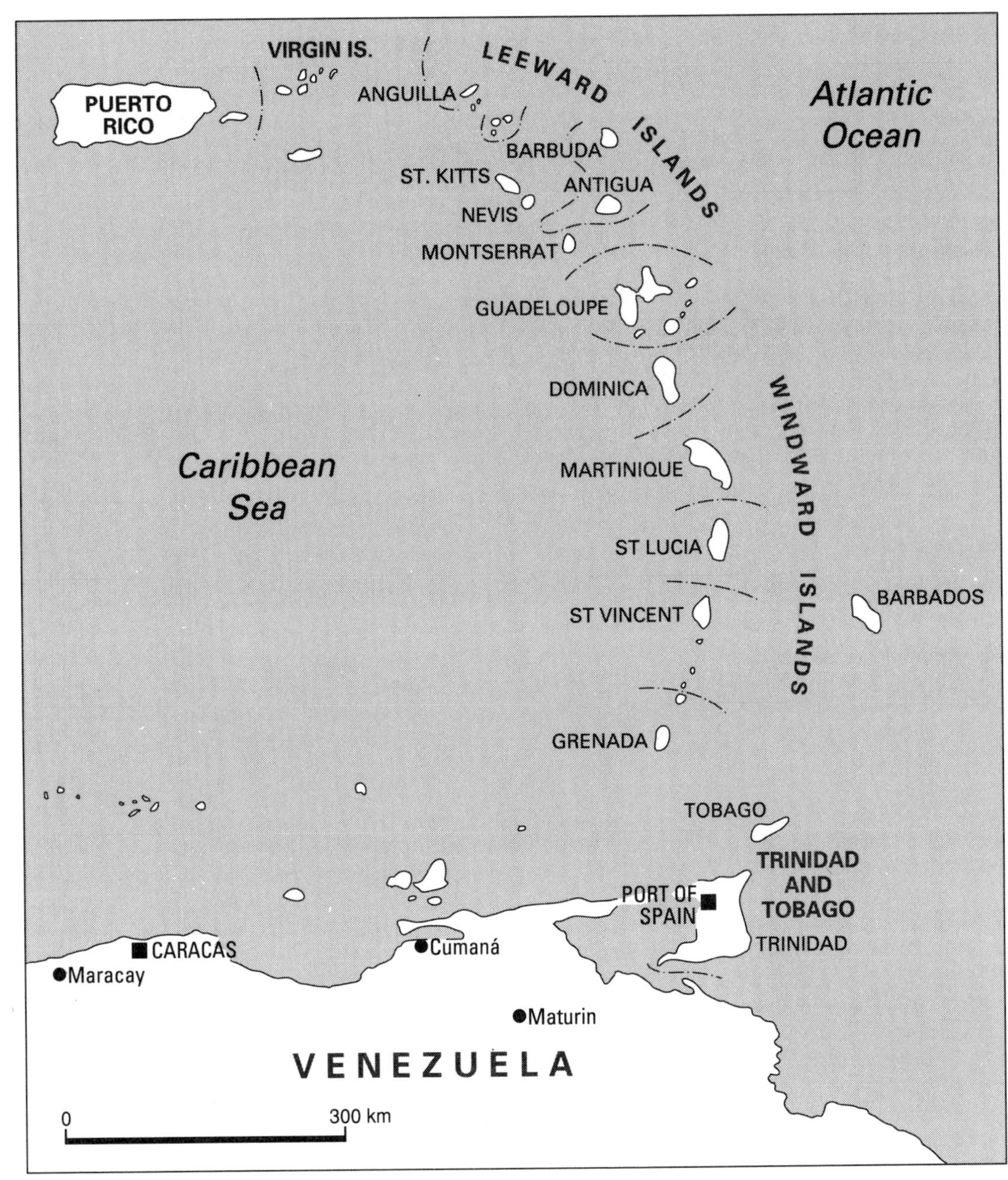
VIRGIN IS.
LEEWARD ISLANDS
Atlantic Ocean
PUERTO RICO
ANGUILLA
BARBUDA
ST. KITTS
ANTIGUA
NEVIS
MONTSERRAT
GUADELOUPE
DOMINICA
WINDWARD ISLANDS
Caribbean Sea
MARTINIQUE
ST LUCIA
ST VINCENT
BARBADOS
GRENADA
TOBAGO
TRINIDAD AND TOBAGO
PORT OF SPAIN
TRINIDAD
CARACAS
Cumaná
Maracay
Maturin
VENEZUELA
0
300 km

Sequence of elections since 1984

Date	*Winning party*
March 9, 1984	Anguilla National Alliance (ANA)
Feb. 27, 1989	Anguilla National Alliance (ANA)

General Election, Feb. 27, 1989

Party	*Seats in House*
Anguilla National Alliance (ANA)	3
Anguilla United Party (AUP)	2
Anguilla Democratic Party (ADP)	1
Independent	1
Total	7

PARTY BY PARTY DATA

Anguilla Democratic Party (ADP)

Address. P. O. Box 20, The Valley, Anguilla.
Leadership. Victor Banks (l.).
Orientation. Centre-right.
Founded. 1981 (as the Anguilla People's Party—APP).
History. After losing the leadership of the ruling People's Progressive Party in 1977 (see ANA), Ronald Webster formed the Anguilla United Party (AUP), which in May 1980 won six of the seven elective seats in the Assembly. Webster returned as Chief Minister but after disagreements within the AUP he was expelled from the party in May 1981 and formed the Anguilla People's Party (APP).

In the early election on June 22, 1981, the APP won five seats and Webster was re-appointed Chief Minister; the AUP lost all of its seats and later dissolved itself. In the 1984 elections, the APP held only two seats and went into opposition. Banks was appointed the new leader following the resignation from the party of Webster, who had lost his seat and went to reactivate the dormant AUP. In 1985, both of the party's elected representatives defected to the ruling ANA.

In the February 1989 general election, the ADP won two seats in the Assembly.

Anguilla National Alliance (ANA)

Address. The Valley, Anguilla.
Leadership. Emile R. Gumbs.
Orientation. Centre-right and believes in a free market but regulation of the off-shore financial sector; holding similar policies with the two other opposition parties, some of whose members it has accommodated in government; although opposed to the island's independence from the United Kingdom, it believes in the enhancement of local powers of administration, although Gumbs has defended the appointment of qualified foreign professionals to train local civil servants.
Founded. 1980.
History. The ANA succeeded the People's Progressive Party (PPP), then the sole party, when its leader Ronald Webster declared the island independent of the associated state of St Kitts-Nevis-Anguilla in 1967. In January 1969 Anguilla was unilaterally declared an independent republic with Webster as the President, but in March, after the arrival of British security forces, he agreed to continued British administration. Following the introduction of the 1976 Constitution, Webster was Chief Minister until February 1977, when he lost a vote of confidence in the Legislative Assembly, in which the PPP held six of the seven elective seats.

A faction led by Gumbs, opposed to Webster's authoritarian grip on the party, deposed him in 1977. Gumbs became Chief Minister and PPP leader and in 1980, when Anguilla formally became a separate dependency of the United Kingdom, the party adopted its present name.

In the Legislative Assembly elections of May 1980, however, the ANA was reduced to a single seat (see Anguilla United Party — AUP), which it increased to two in a fresh election in June the same year.

It was then in opposition until March 1984, when it won four seats in the House of Assembly (as it was restyled in 1982) and Gumbs became Chief Minister. Hubert Hughes, a former AUP member elected to the House as an independent in 1984, later joined the ANA and was given a ministerial post, from which he was dismissed in February 1985. In the same year, the party recruited both Assembly representatives of the opposition Anguilla Democratic Party (ADP).

In the February 1989 general election, the ANA's representation in the House fell from four to three but Gumbs continued in power with the support of an independent MP. In May 1990 Gumbs and the UK government agreed to amend the constitution to allow the Governor to assume greater control of the major offshore financial sector.

A new law passed by the Assembly in December 1991 gave the Governor complete and final authority over the granting of licences to off-shore financial companies.

Anguilla United Party (AUP)

Address. The Valley, Anguilla.
Leadership. Ronald Webster.
Orientation. Centre-right; pro-independence.
Founded. Mid-1980s.
History. Webster, a veteran politician who led an abortive independence campaign against United Kingdom rule in 1969, founded the party following his dismissal as leader of the People's Progressive Party

(PPP — see ANA) in 1977. He simultaneously lost his post as Chief Minister. The AUP comprehensively won the 1980 general election, however, taking six of the seven Assembly seats, and Webster once more became Chief Minister.

Following the collapse of the AUP in 1981, Webster formed the Anguilla People's Party (APP) which won five seats in fresh elections held in the same year. The AUP lost power to the Anguilla National Alliance (ANA) in 1984, retaining only two seats, with Webster losing his seat and then resigning as APP leader.

Webster revived the AUP to contest the 1989 general election. He once again failed to win a seat himself but the party won two seats.

Antigua and Barbuda

Capital: St John's **Population: 79,000**

Antigua and Barbuda has been an independent member of the Commonwealth since November 1981. It has been ruled by the Antigua Labour Party since 1946, with the exception of 1971-76, when the Progressive Labour Movement (PLM) was in power.

Constitutional structure

Under the 1981 Constitution executive power is vested in the British monarch, who is the head of state and is represented by a locally selected Governor-General. The Governor-General appoints the Prime Minister who is the elected member who can best command the support of the majority in the House of Representatives. Legislative power is exercised by a bicameral Parliament. The House of Representatives consists of 17 elected members while the Senate consists of 17 members appointed by the Governor-General—11 (one of whom has to be an inhabitant of Barbuda) on the advice of the Prime Minister, four on the advice of the Leader of the Opposition, one on the advice of the Barbuda Council and one at the Governor-General's own discretion. Barbuda has a separate nine-seat Council which performs the duties of local government.

Electoral system

Election to the House of Representatives is by simple plurality in single-member constituencies for a five-year term. The island of Antigua comprises 16 constituencies with the additional constituency being the island of Barbuda.

Evolution of the suffrage

Universal adult suffrage was introduced by the British colonial administration in 1951. Every citizen of 18 years of age and over is entitled to vote.

Sequence of elections since 1980

Date	*Winnin g party*
April 1980	Antigua Labour Party
April 1984	Antigua Labour Party
March 1989	Antigua Labour Party

General Election March 9, 1989

Party	*Seats*	*% of vote*
Antiguan Labour Party	15	63.8
United National Democratic Party	1	31.0
Barbuda People's Movement	1	3.2
Antigua Caribbean Liberation Movement	-	1.9

PARTY BY PARTY DATA

Antigua Caribbean Liberation Movement (ACLM)

Address. c/o Outlet Publishing Company, St John's, Antigua.
Leadership. Tim Hector (ch.); Adlai Carrott (sec. gen.).
Orientation. Centre-left.
Founded. 1968.
History. The party was founded by Tim Hector as a black power movement. Its change of name from Afro-Caribbean Liberation Movement to its present one in 1979 reflected a gradual move towards a general socialist approach to politics. The party first participated in an election in April 1980, when it won 1.1 per cent of the vote. As the country's main opposition party at the time and with Hector's newspaper the *Outlet* as a powerful vehicle, the ACLM forced an early election in 1984 by publishing allegations of corruption and maladministration by the government. The ACLM, however, did not participate in the election after it failed to reach an electoral agreement with other opposition parties.

In 1985 Hector was convicted for publishing a false statement which was likely to undermine public confidence in the government and had to serve a six-month prison term. The party attempted to form an opposition alliance for the 1989 general election but once again remained unsuccessful.

It ended up standing by itself and with 1.9 per cent of the ballot failed to gain a seat. Due to lack of finance, the ACLM was unable to participate in the by-elections of August 1989 for five disputed seats (see Antigua Labour Party — ALP). In January 1990 the 1985 conviction of Tim Hector was overruled by the Judicial Committee of the Privy Council and the Public Order Act under which he was convicted was ruled illegal. This immediately raised the prestige of the *Outlet*, especially Hector's "Fan the Flame" column, known for its caustic anti-establishment comments.

The ACLM agreed to participate in a National Economic Commission, announced in December 1991 (see ALP), only if the reforms demanded in a March 1991 petition to the Governor-General were implemented by the government. Following allegations of financial impropriety levelled against Prime Minister Vere Bird in January 1992, 200 people staged a demonstration on Feb. 27 outside the parliament on the day of its reconvening. Among those arrested was Hector. ACLM joined the United Opposition Front along with the Progressive Labour movement (PLM) and the United National Democratic Party (UNDP) and mounted pickets outside the PM's office throughout February demanding his resignation.

On March 26, the party amalgamated with the PLM and the UNDP to form the United Progressive Party (UPP—see below).
Affiliation. The ACLM is affiliated to the small National Assembly of Workers (NAW).
Publications. The *Outlet* (weekly).

Antigua Labour Party (ALP)

Address. St Mary's Street, St John's, Antigua.
Leadership. Vere C. Bird Sr (l.); Adolphus Freeland (ch.).
Orientation. Conservative, pro-USA.
Founded. 1938.
History. The party was founded by the present Prime Minister, Vere C. Bird Sr. The ALP, in power since 1946, lost the 1971 election after the affiliated Antigua Trades and Labour Union (ATLU) suffered a split. The party came back to power in 1976 after winning 11 seats in the House of Representatives. Having opposed early independence from Britain in the previous election campaign, the ALP announced that the independence process would proceed and called a general election for 1980.

The ALP increased its seats to 13, and Vere Bird became the country's first Prime Minister after full independence was achieved on Nov. 1, 1981. The party celebrated a landslide victory in the 1984 elections in which it captured all 16 Antiguan seats, partially assisted by divisions among the opposition parties.

A severe split in the ALP emerged in 1986-87 over a scandal involving the Prime Minister's eldest son and senior minister Vere Bird Jr. He was found by an official inquiry to have awarded the building contract of Antigua's international airport to a company of which he was the chairman and legal adviser. A section of the party demanding his resignation was led by his younger brother and Deputy Prime Minister Lester Bird, who had the support of eight ALP Ministers. In

1988, however, Lester Bird was himself involved in a scandal over government corruption. Despite such internal divisions, the ALP went on to win the 1989 general election, and retained 15 seats in the House of Representatives. The opposition, however, alleged that irregularities had taken place in seven constituencies won by ALP candidates, and the High Court, in June, ordered that the result in one of them be nullified.

The ALP members in the other six constituencies resigned in the same month, but as the opposition parties declined to participate in new elections, they were proclaimed the winners of these seats in August.

Divisions in the party re-emerged, however, soon after the elections, centred mainly on the succession to Vere Bird Sr which was contested between his two sons and a faction opposed to the Bird family. Following the report by the government-appointed commission of inquiry, headed by a British QC, Louis Blom-Cooper, on the country's involvement in the 1989 trans-shipment of Israeli arms to Colombian drug barons, Vere Bird Jr was finally forced to resign his post of Communications and Works Minister in November 1990.

However, he refused to give up his parliamentary seat, a decision which prompted Finance Minister John St Luce to resign in February 1991. Bird's brother gave up his ministerial post for the same reason in March and joined in anti-corruption protests of between 8,000 and 12,000 marchers. Both St Luce and Lester Bird returned to the Cabinet in September but the party's credibility was further undermined when in July 1991 all ALP Senators, bar one, blocked the government's Prevention of Corruption Bill after it had been passed unanimously in the House of Representatives the previous month.

In December 1991, the ALP government announced the setting-up of a National Economic Commission to advise on a five-year development plan for the islands, intended to involve a wide sector of the community, which received an unenthusiastic response from opposition parties. In January 1992, allegations against Prime Minister Vere Bird Sr that he had wrongfully obtained US$25,000 from the Treasury sparked off widespread protests.

On the re-opening of Parliament on Feb. 27, 1992, an illegal demonstration of 200 people outside Parliament demanded his resignation and the Prime Minister's office was picketed throughout the month. There followed the firebombing of the ALP's women's group office on March 8 and the opposition pledged further protest marches through the capital until Bird resigned. Lester Bird announced the same month that he would campaign for the ALP leadership if his father chose to step down. On March 31, it was reported that Vere Bird Sr, now 82, had announced that he would not contest the 1994 general election.

Affiliations. The ALP has been affiliated to the Antigua Trades and Labour Union (ATLU) since 1939, of which Vere Bird was a founder member.

Publications. The *Worker's Voice* (twice-weekly) co-published with ATLU. The Bird family own the ZDK radio station.

Barbuda People's Movement (BPM)

Address. Codrington, Barbuda.
Leadership. Thomas Hilbourne Frank (l.).
Orientation. Campaigns for secession from Antigua.
Founded. 1970s.
History. The BPM was founded by Thomas Hilbourne Frank. The party led the Barbuda Council from 1979 to 1985 and unsuccessfully fought against independence as part of a united Antigua and Barbuda and for Barbudan control of land. The party, however, campaigned for greater autonomy for the Barbudan Council, which was granted in November 1981.

In March 1985, it lost control of the Barbuda Council to the more conciliatory Organization for National Reconstruction (ONR), but recaptured control in 1987. In response to the central government's projects for Barbuda, which were implemented without consulting the island's council, the BPM mounted a popular campaign which in March 1989 culminated in the prevention of the unloading of llamas for a wildlife park project.

The party won all nine seats in the Barbuda Council in the local elections of the same month. In the simultaneous general election of March 1989 Frank, who was also chairman of the Council, won the Barbuda seat in the House of Representatives.

Strengthened by the election results, the BPM pressed for an amendment to the constitution to give Barbuda separate status but the government only agreed to exploratory talks on the matter.

Frank brought a case in the same year to restrict the purchase of land on Barbuda to people approved by the local population, a move defeated in the High Court in late November 1989.

Progressive Labour Movement (PLM)

Leadership. Robert Hall (l.).
Orientation. Centrist, in favour of proportional representation and a unicameral legislature.
Founded. 1970.
History. The party was formed as a political wing of the Antigua Workers' Union (AWU) and was in office in 1971-76. The PLM then became the main opposition party before its decline in the mid-1980s after the AWU switched allegiance to United National Democratic Party (UNDP). However, the PLM joined with the UNDP and the Antigua Caribbean Liberation Movement (ACLM) in the three-party United Opposition Front demanding the resignation of Prime Minister Vere Bird following allegations of his embezzlement of treasury funds (see Antigua Labour Party) but the party condemned fire bombings by demonstrators in the capital, St John's, in March 1992.

On March 26, 1992, the party amalgamated with the ACLM and the UNDP to form the United Progressive Party (UPP—see below).

United National Democratic Party (UNDP)

Address. UNDP Headquarters, Nevis Street, St John's, Antigua.
Leadership. Baldwin Spencer (l.).
Orientation. Conservative.
Founded. 1986.
History. The UNDP was created from the merger of the United People's Movement (UPM), founded in 1982, and the National Democratic Party (NDP), founded a year earlier. The UPM's founder and leader George Herbert Walter had been leader of the Progressive Labour Movement (PLM), served as Premier of Antigua in 1971-76 and had to resign from the PLM leadership after allegations of mishandling state finances, a charge of which he was subsequently cleared. On the foundation of the UNDP, Walter declined any major post and the leadership went to the NDP's leader Ivor Heath. The UNDP attracted the support of the Antigua Workers' Union which had previously been affiliated to the PLM, and gradually became identified as the major party of the opposition. In the general election of March 9, 1989, the UNDP obtained 31 per cent of the vote but won only one seat in the House of Representatives. The party challenged this result but when a by-election was called after the resignation of six newly elected members of the Antigua Labour Party (ALP) in June, the UNDP refused to participate unless the electoral system was altered (see ALP). In September 1991 Ivor Heath, who had lost the party leadership to Baldwin Spencer earlier in the year, left the party accusing it of being controlled by the Antigua Workers' Union (AWU). In December 1991, the UNDP declined to join the newly established National Economic Commission (see ALP) and Baldwin Spencer, leader of the opposition in Parliament, refused to participate in the opening of Parliament on Feb. 27, 1992, as opposition supporters demonstrated outside the parliament building. He was among the 30 people subsequently arrested. The party then became the leading member of the three-party United Opposition Front, along with the Antigua Caribbean Liberation Movement (ACLM) and the Progressive Labour Movement (PLM), demanding Vere Bird's resignation after allegations that he had embezzled treasury funds (see ALP). On March 26, 1992, the party amalgamated with the ACLM and the PLM to form the United Progressive Party (UPP).

United Progressive Party (UPP)

Leadership. Baldwin Spencer (see UNDP).
Founded. March 1992.
History. The UPP, an amalgamation of the United National Democratic Party (UNDP), the Antigua Caribbean Liberation Movement (ACLM) and the Progressive Labour Movement (PLM) was announced on March 26, 1992, and officially launched at a public meeting held in St John's, on April 9, 1992. The new party, which reportedly had the support of the Chamber of Commerce and Industry, was judged to pose a potent threat to the ruling Antigua Labour Party (ALP).

Minor parties

Barbuda Independence Movement (BIM); Arthur Nibbsa (l.); a Barbudan party founded in 1983 as the Organisation for National Reconstruction. It won control of the Barbudan Council in the March 1985 election but lost its majority in 1987. The party was reorganized in 1988 when it adopted its present name. Although in the past it favoured co-operation between Barbudans and Antiguans and had been generally supported by the Antigua Labour Party (ALP), it has been campaigning for Barbudan self-government since 1988.

Barbuda National Party; won the Barbuda seat in the House of Representatives in the March 1985 general election but lost it again to the Barbuda People's Movement (BPM) in the March 1989 elections.

Argentina

Capital: Buenos Aires, CF **Population: 32,300,000**

The Federal Republic of Argentina gained independence from Spain in 1816. The country was governed by the Radical Civil Union (UCR) from 1916 to 1930. After several military coups and a series of Conservative governments a new radical era was ushered in with the presidency of the trade union-backed regime of Lt.-Gen. Juan Domingo Perón Sosa (1946-1955). He was overthrown by a disillusioned military in 1955 and was driven into what was to be an 18-year exile. Following a Peronist congressional victory in 1965 the army staged another coup which installed Gen. Juan Carlos Onganía who in 1966 dissolved Congress and banned all political parties. A campaign by Marxist and Peronist guerrillas forced the regime to re-introduce free elections in March 1973, which were won by a Peronist. Perón himself returned from exile for new elections in September and won the presidency in a landslide victory. His widow took over the government after his death in 1974 but was overthrown in 1976 in a military coup. The junta, responsible for a fierce reign of terror, was removed after Argentina's defeat in the Falklands war. The subsequent presidential elections of Oct. 30, 1983, saw a surprise victory by the UCR candidate Raúl Alfonsín Foulkes. His government failed to find solutions to the economic crisis and in May 1989 the Peronists returned to power in the first planned civilian transfer of power for 61 years.

Constitutional structure

According to the 1853 Constitution which was reintroduced in 1983, Argentina has an executive President assisted by a Vice-President and an appointed cabinet. He is "supreme chief of the nation" and Commander-in-Chief of the army. The President is in charge of the general administration of the country and has power to issue instructions for the execution of the country's laws and himself takes part in drawing up and promulgating the laws. Legislative power is vested in a bicameral Congress consisting of the Chamber of Deputies and the Senate. Congress has wide powers including fixing taxation, the budget and social welfare provisions.

Each of the 22 provinces, the Federal District and the national Territory of Tierra del Fuego has its own elected Governor and legislature.

Electoral System

The President and Vice-President are elected for a non-renewable six-year term by a 600-member electoral college chosen by universal adult suffrage. The 254 members of the Chamber of Deputies are elected for four-year terms, with half of the seats renewable every two years. The 46-member Senate is elected by the provincial legislatures (except the Federal District of Buenos Aires) for a nine-year term, with one-third coming up for re-election every three years.

Suffrage

Universal male suffrage was introduced in 1912 and women gained the vote in 1947.

20.76
BOLIVIA
PARAGUAY
BRAZIL
JUJUY
SALTA
FORMOSA
TUCUMAN
CATAMARCA
SANTIAGO DEL ESTERO
CHACO
MISIONES
LA RIOJA
CORRIENTES
SANTA FE
SAN JUAN
CORDOBA
ENTRE RIOS
URUGUAY
SAN LUIS
MEN-DOZA
BUENOS AIRES
LA PAMPA
CHILE
ARGENTINA
NEUQUÉN
RIO NEGRO
Atlantic
CHUBUT
Ocean
SANTA CRUZ
FALKLAND ISLANDS (MALVINAS)
TIERRA DEL FUEGO
0 M 300

Sequence of elections since 1983

Presidential election

Date	*Winning party*
Oct. 20, 1983	Radical Civic Union UCR
Nov. 3, 1985	Radical Civic Union*
Sept. 6, 1987	Justicialist Party - Peronist*
May 14, 1989	Justicialist Party - Peronists/FREJUPO
Aug - Oct 1991	Justicialist Party - Peronists*

*Partial elections for Congress

Election for Electoral College, May 14, 1989

Candidate	*Party*	*Seats*	*% of votes*
Carlos Saúl Menem	PJ-FREJUPO	310	48.5
Eduardo César Angeloz	UCR	211	37.1
lvaro Alsogaray	UCeDé	35	6.4
Others		44	8.0
		600	100.0

Chamber of Deputies after a three round congressional elections for 127 seats Aug. 11-Oct. 27, 1991

Party	*Seats*
Justicialist Party (PJ-Peronists)	119
Radical Civic Union (UCR)	85
Union of Democratic Centre (UCeDé)	10
Group of Eight (G-8)	5
Renovation Party (PR)	4
Republican Force (FR)	4
Neuquén Popular Movement (MPN)	1
Others	26
Total	**254**

Gubernatorial elections, Aug. 11-Dec. 7, 1991

Justicialist Party (PJ-Peronists)	14
Radical Civic Union (UCR)	3
Neuquén Popular Movement (MPN)	1
Renovation Party (PR)	1
Chaco Action (AC)	1
Autonomist Liberal Pact (PAL)	1
Fueguino Popular Movement (Mopof)	1
Civic and Social Front (FSC)	1
Total	**23**

PARTY BY PARTY DATA

Christian Democratic Party

Partido Demócrata Cristiano (PDC)

Address. Cbte. de los Pozos 1055, P.1, 1022 Buenos Aires.

Leadership. Elio Silveira (l.).

Orientation. Centrist.

History. The PDC was one of the five small parties in the *Multipartidaria* democratic movement. The party presidential candidate won 0.3 per cent of the national vote in the Oct. 30, 1983, elections and obtained a seat in the Chamber of Deputies. A rapprochement with the Peronists (PJ) in 1984 led to a conflict in the party which caused a majority of the centre-left Humanism and Liberation faction to split away and join the Intransigent Party (PI). In the congressional elections of September 1987, the party received only 0.2 per cent of the national vote despite greater unity within the party. To improve their electoral chances the PDC joined the FREJUPO electoral alliance supporting the Peronists' presidential candidate Carlos Saúl Menem who won the election on May 14, 1989. The Christian Democrats' support was rewarded on Dec. 15, 1989, with the appointment of Antonio Ermán González as Social Security minister who, on Dec. 15, 1989, was transferred to the important Economy Ministry. González introduced controversial austerity packages in March and September 1990 which included the setting up of a privatization schedule for state companies and the cutting of public sector wages, and from August 1990 he was given total control over central government, federal agency and state company finances. On the request of President Menem he resigned along with all other ministers in January 1991 following allegations of government corruption but was reappointed to the cabinet as Defence Minister. The PDC itself, however, withdrew from the FREJUPO alliance backing the government in October 1990 in protest against González' economic measures.

Membership. 115,000 (1988 figure).

International affiliations. Christian Democrat International; Christian Democrat Organization of America.

Communist Party of Argentina

Partido Comunista de Argentina (PCA)

Address. Av. Entre Ríos 1039, 1080 Buenos Aires.

Leadership. Athos Fava (ch.); Patricio Echegaray (s.-g.).

Orientation. Centrist, but the party's "tactical support" for the military junta in the 1970s (see below) severely dented its credibility.

Founded. 1918.

History. The PCA was formed as the Internationalist Socialist Party by expelled members of the Socialist Party. The party took on its present name in 1920. The party was banned after the 1930 coup but continued to be active in the trades union movement. A year after its reinstatement in 1945 the PCA joined an anti-Perón electoral alliance consisting of Conservatives, Radicals and Socialists. The rise of Peronism meant a falling off of PCA influence in the workers' movement, and its Soviet-influenced opposition to industrial action in meat-packing plants during the Second World War had discredited the party on the left.

The PCA was again banned following Perón's overthrow, and alternated between legality and underground work between 1959 and 1971. In the March 1973 general election the Communist Party supported the centre-left Popular Revolutionary Alliance and succeeded in obtaining two congressional seats. However, against its earlier policies, the party decided to back Perón in the September presidential elections. Banned once again, like all other parties, after the 1976 coup, the PCA was nevertheless tolerated by the 1976-82 military regime because of the Communist Party's "critical support" for the junta (prompted by its grain deals with the Soviet Union), a stand which lost the party a considerable part of its following.

In the congressional elections of 1983 the PCA won only 1.1 per cent of the ballot and supported the Peronist presidential and gubernatorial candidates after fearing that its own candidates would receive few votes. In 1985 the PCA formed the FREPU alliance with the Movement toward Socialism (MAS) and some smaller left-wing groups. After arguments with the MAS over co-operation with left-wing Peronist groups which the PCA favoured, the Communist Party lost its main ally, and formed the new Broad Front for Liberation (FRAL) alliance with other small parties. In October 1988 the MAS agreed to form a new alliance with the PCA and the Popular Democratic

Left (IDP) after protracted negotiations. The United Left Alliance (AIU) attempted to present a left-wing alternative to the ruling Radical Civic Union and the Peronists. However, the PCA's high hopes were dashed when the alliance polled only 2.4 per cent of the vote and obtained no seats in Congress and the alliance's presidential candidate, Néstor Vicente, received only a low vote in the general election of May 14, 1989.

Following the collapse of the Eastern bloc countries, the party has gone through a process of self-examination, but has yet to formally seek re-alignment with another party.

Structure. The National Congress, elected every four years, elects the Central Committee consisting of 92 full and 33 alternate members. The Central Committee elects the general secretary, the eight-member Executive Committee and the party Secretariat.

Membership. 25,000 (1988 estimate).

Publications. Qué Pasa?, weekly; *Aquí y Ahora*, monthly.

Intransigent Party

Partido Intransigente (PI)

Address. Riobamba 482, 1025 Buenos Aires.

Leadership. Oscar Alende (l.); Lisandro Viale (l.); Maria Lorences (s.-g.).

Orientation. Left-wing.

Founded. 1956.

History. The party has its origins in the left-wing Intransigent faction of the Radical Civic Union (UCR) which became the UCR *Intransigente (UCRI)* after the party split in 1956. Its leader Arturo Frondizi, with support from the Peronists, was elected president in 1958 and under him Argentina's industry, particularly the oil industry, was greatly expanded. He was deposed by the military in 1962 because of fears that he would allow the Peronists to be reintegrated into Argentina's political life. After a crisis within the party over the nomination of a presidential candidate, Frondizi left the UCRI to found his own party (see Movement of Integration and Development). Oscar Alende, the UCRI's candidate, came second in the 1963 presidential elections with 16.5 per cent of the vote.

The UCRI changed its name to Intransigent Party in 1972 after the rival People's UCR won the exclusive right to be called Radical Civic Union (UCR). For the presidential elections of 1973 the party joined forces with the Communist Party (PCA) and two other small parties and fielded Oscar Alende as their candidate, who, however, polled only 7.4 per cent of the vote. Following the coup of 1976 the PI was banned and many activists were imprisoned and tortured.

In the first presidential election since Argentina's return to democracy in October 1983 Oscar Alende, with Lisandro Viale as his running mate, came third but won only 2.3 per cent of the valid vote. The party won 1.4 per cent in the simultaneous congressional elections which gave the PI three seats in the Chamber of Deputies. The party gained a further three seats in the partial congressional elections of Nov. 3, 1985, when it won 6 per cent of the vote. After divisions in the party over whether to back the Cafiero section of the Peronist movement (see Justicialist Party) or join forces with the left-wing FREPU coalition, the PI stood separately in the election of September 1987 where it came third but lost one seat.

With its support waning, the PI joined the FREJUPO alliance backing the Peronist candidate Carlos Saúl Menem for the May 14, 1989, elections. Menem won the presidency with a majority in the electoral college (48.5 per cent of the national vote). The PI left FREJUPO in October 1990 over the government's economic policies.

Justicialist Party

Partido Justicialista (PJ-Peronist)

Address. Callao 1134 P.1, 1023 Buenos Aires.

Leadership. Eduardo Menem (pres.); Munir Menem (s.-g.).

Orientation. Peronist, populist in outlook and encompasses groups from the far right to the far left. The dominant pro-government *menemista* faction, promoting a free market economy and wholesale privatization, has taken the party far to the right.

Founded. 1945.

History. The Justicialist Party has its origins in the Peronist movement founded by Col. (later Lt.-Gen.) Juan Domingo Perón Sosa, Secretary for Labour and Social Welfare under the military regime from 1943. As President of Argentina in 1946-55 he pursued co-operatist nationalist policies inspired by Italian fascism and through his wife Evita Duarte de Perón (who died in 1952) advocated social improvement. Perón's populism and strong personal image attracted support from the trade unions, Roman Catholics, dissidents from the Radical Civic Union (UCR) and some conservatives alike. His secularization of the state and legalization of divorce in 1954, however, turned not only the church but also the army against him. Perón's increasingly dogmatic style of government also caused his popularity to decline among the working class. In 1955 he was overthrown by the military and exiled to Spain, from where he continued to lead his now divided movement.

Peronism's star rose again among the Argentinian population as a reaction to a second more intransigent junta, which took control of the unions and imprisoned their leaders. In 1958, the Peronists supported the presidential election campaign of the Intransigent Radical Civic Union's Arturo Frondizi (see Intransigent Party), who, in return, had promised to allow the Peronists to renew political activity. In March 1962 the Peronists were very successful in both the congressional and provincial elections when they won 10 governorships. The army demanded the immediate cancellation of the Peronist seats and overthrew Frondizi when this was only partly achieved. The Peronists, now operating under the name of Popular Union, however, continued to contest congressional and provincial elections both in June 1963 and March 1965. Alarmed at the very real possibility of an impending Peronist victory, the army staged a coup in 1966 and abolished the legislature and all political parties.

The ranks of the already very diverse Peronist factions were swollen during major strikes in 1969 by the left-wing *Montoneros* urban guerrilla group who in 1970 kidnapped and assassinated the former President, Gen. Pedro Eugenio Aramburu. In 1971, while the *Montoneros* were still very active, President Gen. Lanusse granted the Peronists the right to resume political activity and fully participate in elections. As was expected, Héctor J. Cámpora, leader of the Peronist left wing, won the presidential elections of March 1973 with 50 per cent of the vote while the Peronist-led FREJULI coalition (which also included the Christian Democratic Party, the Popular Conservative Party and the Movement for Integration and Development) won the largest bloc of seats in Congress. Perón himself returned to Argentina after nearly 18 years in June of the same year, and a month later, after only two months in office, Cámpora resigned in order to make way for him. Perón was duly elected President in fresh elections in September with 62 per cent of the vote. The Vice-President, Perón's third wife María Estela (Isabelita) Martínez de Perón, was appointed President after his death in July 1974 and took charge of a deteriorating economy. Her austerity programme marked a sharp swing to the right in the Peronists' policies and provoked widespread protests and strikes. In March 1976, with violence and economic chaos at its worst, the armed forces stepped in and arrested Isabelita Perón and other Peronist leaders. She went into exile in Spain and the Peronist movement was driven underground.

Seven years of brutal military repression, however, could not erase the memory of the Peronist government of 1973-76. In the October 1983 elections following the Falklands/Malvinas war and the collapse of the military regime, the Peronists lost to the Radical Civic Union (UCR) in both the presidential and congressional elections but beat the UCR in the provincial governorship elections. The party, with Isabelita Perón restored as its figurehead, obtained 40.5 per cent of the vote which translated into 111 seats in Congress, and its presidential candidate Italo Lúder came second with 40.2 per cent of the vote (compared to Raúl Alfonsín of the UCR's 51.8 per cent). This defeat resulted in a long period of internal turmoil which split the Peronist movement into two main rival factions with parallel leaderships: the right-wing *oficialistas* (official wing) and the *renovadores* (renewalist wing). The Party Congress in July 1985, intended to reunite the party, resulted in an *oficialista* takeover of the party machinery. All *oficialista* candidates were confirmed for the forthcoming congressional elections because of a boycott by the left wing who subsequently put forward their own alternative candidates under the name of the *Frente Renovador* (Renewalist Front), led by Antonio Cafiero. Neither the official PJ, which fought the election as the leading party in the FREJULI alliance, nor the Renovation Front did very well and the overall PJ representation in the congress was reduced by 10 seats.

Despite further splits within the two factions in 1986 which led to four distinct PJ blocs in Congress, the Peronists began to gain in popularity. Benefiting from widespread discontent with the UCR government's austerity measures and its lenient treatment of the army, the PJ won the highest number of votes (41.5 per cent) in the partial congressional elections of Sept. 6, 1987, and narrowed the gap between the PJ and UCR representation in Congress. As well as increasing their congressional seats to 105, the PJ won 16 provincial governorships, including that of the crucial province of Buenos Aires. With the general election of 1989 in view the PJ regrouped. Isabelita Perón was finally replaced as the party's president and a party leadership comprising *oficialistas*, *renovadores* and the "Federalism and Liberation" faction, linked to Carlos Saúl Menem, was elected. Small left-wing and right-wing factions were ignored and Herminio Iglesias' right-wing group, which had contested the elections separately under the name of the October 17 Party, was expelled the following December.

Menem, governor of the rural La Rioja province, was elected presidential candidate of the now renewalist-dominated Justicialist Party in 1988 and in May 14, 1989, won the presidential election with 48.5 per cent of the vote (310 seats in the electoral college). The FREJUPO-PJ alliance also won the congressional elections, gaining 66 seats out of the 125 seats up for election with 44.6 per cent of the vote.

Menem took office on July 8, 1989, five months early and before his official election by the electoral college in August, in order to relieve the Alfonsín government in its struggle with an unstable economy. The Menem government was only moderately successful in dealing with the economic crisis and looming hyperinflation despite various drastic measures such as the devaluation of the austral, the introduction of rationing and an expanded privatization plan for state industries, including the dismissal of a large section of the workforce in the iron and steel sectors in preparation for their sale. Furthermore, on Oct. 31, 1991, President Menem signed a 122-point decree abolishing protectionist economic practices originally introduced by Perón 40 years earlier.

Menem continued Alfonsín's policy of leniency towards the military and in October 1989, despite widespread protests and disapproval from within the party, issued decrees pardoning 217 officers involved in the 1976-83 "dirty war" and those involved in the 1987-88 military uprisings. Even this amnesty, however, did not allay continued discontent within the military over low pay and lack of status and on Dec. 3, 1990, loyal troops put down an army rebellion by disgruntled NCOs in Buenos Aires and the suburbs.

Notwithstanding widespread opposition to the government's strict economic policy and Menem's unpopularity, aggravated by corruption and drug related scandals involving Menem's relatives, the Peronists gained seven seats in the first round of the partial congressional elections of 1991. After the third round in October, the PJ controlled 119 of the 254 seats in Chamber of Deputies and they predicted a clear majority of 143 with the support of small provincial parties. In the simultaneous provincial elections, however, the PJ retained only three governorships.

The election results were generally interpreted as an acknowledgement by the electorate that inflation was down and that therefore Menem's bitter economic pill was working. Success at the ballot box, however, did little to prevent his marginalization within the party where he was accused of rejecting the essence of Peronism. He was particulary criticized, most vociferously by his previous supporters in the left Renewalist faction, for his rapprochement with the US administration and his distancing of the government from the Non-Aligned Movement, from which the country withdrew in September 1991. In particular the *Cruzada Renovadora* group within the Renewalist faction, led by trade union leader Saúl Ubaldini, tried to block Menem's policies and such internal opposition led Menem increasingly to govern by decree.

However, despite his personal unpopularity, Menem in mid-1991 was known to be supporting moves to amend the constitution in order to permit him to stand for a second term.

Structure. By general assent on Sept. 20, 1991, the congress of the PJ granted special powers to a new party directorate, consisting of José Luis Manzano, Interior Minister, Eduardo Duhalde, who was at the time Vice-President, and Carlos Grosso, city mayor of Buenos Aires. Their powers included the right to intervene in provincial committees, designate candidates to elective posts and define the policies of any new political alliance. The party is divided into three major factions: "Renewalists", left-wing, led by Antonio Cafiero; "Menemists", supporters of Carlos Menem, led by Augusto Alasino; and "Officialists", orthodox Peronists, led by José María Vernet.

Justicialist Popular Unity Front

Frente Justicialista de Unidad Popular (FREJUPO)
Address. Callao 1134 P.1, 1023 Buenos Aires.
Leadership. Carlos Saúl Menem (l.).
Orientation. Centrist.
Founded. 1988.

History. FREJUPO, an electoral alliance used by the Peronists to broaden their electoral appeal, supported the successful 1989 presidential campaign of Carlos Saúl Menem (see Justicialist Party—PJ). Founding members of the alliance included the Intransigent Party (PI), the Christian Democratic Party (PDC), the Movement of Integration and Development (MID), the Authentic Socialist Party (PSA), the National Left (IN), and the Patriotic Liberation Movement (MPL). The PI and PDC, the two largest parties in FREJUPO outside of the PJ, strongly opposed the Menem government's economic austerity programme and in October 1990 both parties left the alliance.

Movement of Integration and Development

Movimiento de Integración y Desarrollo (MID)
Address. Ayacucho 49, P.1, 1025 Buenos Aires.
Leadership. Rogelio Frigerio (pres.).
Orientation. The party calls itself "developmentalist".
Founded. 1963.
History. The party was formed by Arturo Frondizi who was overthrown as president of Argentina by the military in 1962. He and his supporters split away from the Radical Civil Union—Intransigent (now the Intransigent Party—PI) after disagreements over policy and the nomination of a presidential candidate for the 1963 presidential elections. The MID supported Gen. Ogania's coup in 1966 against the People's UCR (now UCR) government, which itself had supported the coup against Frondizi in 1962. In 1973 the MID joined the Peronist-led FREJULI alliance backing the successful Peronist presidential candidates Héctor Cámpora in the May elections and Perón in the September elections (see Justicialist Party).

In the October 1983 presidential elections the MID fielded Rogelio Frigerio who won 1.2 per cent of the national vote. Although the party continued to contest elections by itself it continued to support the Peronists in provincial elections. After the party's poor showing in the September 1987 congressional elections (in which it won just 0.9 per cent of the vote) the MID's ranks were reduced by a party split. In 1988 the party became a founder member of the FREJUPO electoral alliance formed to bring the Peronists back to power and assisted with the successful campaign which got the PJ's presidential candidate Carlos Saúl Menem elected in May 1989. The MID continued with its membership of FREJUPO despite heavy criticism of the Menem government.
Structure. The MID holds an annual convention which elects a national committee led by a directorate.

Movement towards Socialism

Movimiento al Socialismo (MAS)
Address. Peru 439, 1067 Buenos Aires.
Leadership. Luis Zamora (l.).
Orientation. Trotskyist; the party gained a high profile on the left mostly due to its campaign for the trial of military officers involved in the "dirty war".
Founded. 1982.
History. The MAS was formed by former members of the Socialist Workers' Party (PST) which like all other parties was banned after the 1976 coup. Luis Zamora contested the presidential elections of 1983 and won 0.3 per cent of the vote. In 1985 the party joined the FREJUPO left-wing alliance and strongly resisted efforts by the Communist Party (PCA) to include left-wing Peronist groups in the alliance. Further disagreements arose when the MAS refused to sign the "Democratic Compromise" (a declaration supporting the government in the aftermath of the Easter 1987 rebellion). In September the MAS refused to join the new Broad Front for Liberation (FRAL) alliance and contested the elections on its own, receiving only 1.4 per cent of the vote.

For the 1989 general election, however, the MAS joined forces with the PCA and the Popular Democratic Left (IDP) in the United Left Alliance (AIU). In the AIU primaries for the candidacy in the forthcoming presidential election Luis Zamora was beaten by the IDP leader Néstor Vicente. The MAS fielded some candidates in the congressional elections under the alliance's banner and the United Left won 2.4 per cent of the congressional vote. The MAS, despite its vociferous opposition to the December 1990 pardoning of military officers involved in human rights abuses during the "dirty war" of the 1970s, has adopted a policy of not opposing the bulk of the government's legislative initiatives.

Progressive Democratic Party

Partido Demócrata Progresista (PDP)
Address. Chile 1934, 1227 Buenos Aires.
Leadership. Rafael Martínez Raymonda.
Orientation. Centrist-liberal, purporting to support neither an overgrown state apparatus nor an entirely

free market economy; the party has regionalist leanings.

History. The PDP participated in the 1980 talks with the military regime negotiating the normalization of political activities and in August of the same year it joined the Union of the Democratic Centre (UCeDé). In the presidential elections of 1983, however, the party's leader, Martínez, stood as candidate for the Democratic Socialist Alliance against the UCeDé's candidate Alvaro Alsogaray and obtained 0.3 per cent of the vote. The PDP contested the partial congressional elections of 1985 as a separate party and gained one seat in the Chamber of Deputies. In the elections of September 1987 the party's share of the national vote was 1.3 per cent and it increased its representation in the Chamber to two seats.

The PDP thereafter joined forces again with the UCeDé and in the presidential elections of May 14, 1989, Alberto Natale of the PDP was running mate to the UCeDé presidential candidate Alvaro Alsogaray who came third with 6.4 per cent of the vote.

Membership. 85,000.

Radical Civic Union

Unión Civica Radical (UCR)

Address. Alsina 1786, 1088 Buenos Aires.

Leadership. Mario Losada (l. and ch. of national committee); César Jaroslavsky (vice-pres.).

Orientation. Centrist.

Founded. 1891.

History. The UCR was set up after the radical faction split away from the mainstream Civic Union and led an unsuccessful revolt against the Conservative government. One of the party's main demands was the enfranchisement of all adult male Argentinians and it did not participate in any elections until 1912 when that demand was met. In 1916, the UCR formed its first government and remained in power until 1930, when President Hipólito Yrigoyen was ousted by a military coup. After losing the elections to the UCR's direct rivals, the Peronists, in both 1945 and 1951, the UCR suffered internal problems which culminated in a dramatic split in 1956, caused by the nomination as the UCR's presidential candidate of Arturo Frondizi of the Intransigent faction who was favourable to some co-operation with the Peronists. Frondizi became the candidate of the newly formed UCR *Intrasigente* (Intransigent UCR, see Movement of Integration and Development and Intransigent Party) and with assistance from the Peronists won the presidency in 1958.

The conservative wing of the party, led by the former UCR presidential candidate Ricardo Balbín, formed the UCR *del Pueblo* (People's UCR—UCRP) in 1956 which was to become the official UCR in 1972, when a court ruling awarded it the sole right to the name. The UCRP supported the military coup against Frondizi in 1962 and in the subsequent elections of 1963 the UCRP's candidate Arturo Umberto Illía was elected President. He was himself overthrown three years later in 1966 in a coup led by Gen. Oganía which was supported by the UCRI. Ricardo Balbín stood again in the 1973 presidential elections for the now renamed UCR and was heavily defeated by Peronists in both the April and September polls.

In 1981 the UCR helped to form a five-party democratic alliance opposed to the military junta which called for the restoration of democracy. When the junta was deposed a year later, the UCR's candidate Raúl Alfonsín Foulkes celebrated a landslide victory in the general election of Oct. 20, 1983. He won 317 of the 600 seats in the electoral college which gave him 51.8 per cent of the electoral college vote. The UCR also won a majority of Chamber of Deputies seats (129 out of 256) but only 16 of the 48 Senate seats and seven of the 24 provincial governorships, including Buenos Aires.

Alfonsín, inaugurated on Dec. 23, 1983, proceeded to make good his election promises of reorganizing the armed forces and putting an end to the cycle of political instability and military intervention. Over half the military high command was forced into retirement and members of the military juntas since 1976 were prosecuted for murder, torture and abduction and were sentenced in December 1985 and May 1986. However, after uprisings in a number of army garrisons in April 1987 and persistent rumours of an impending coup, Alfonsín introduced the law of "Due Obedience", dropping all prosecutions against lower-ranking army and police officers indicted for human rights violations. Further military uprisings by officers demanding greater army spending and an extension of the military amnesty to higher-ranking officers nevertheless followed in January and December 1988, followed in January 1989 by an incident, thought to have been provoked by the armed forces, in which a left-wing group attacked La Tablada barracks in order to suppress a rumoured military coup.

The Alfonsín government also introduced an initially popular "*Plan Austral*" austerity package to cope with an ailing economy and rampant inflation. The electorate's approval for both the military trials and the austerity measures was reflected in the UCR's success in the November 1985 partial congressional elections in which the party won 43.5 per cent of the poll and increased its majority in the Chamber by one seat. The congressional and gubernatorial elections of September 1987, however, proved a defeat for the UCR. This was attributed to widespread discontent over the government's climbdown in respect of the army trials, a new stringent austerity programme and divisions within the UCR over the government's policies. The UCR obtained only 37.9 per cent of the poll, reducing its congressional majority by 13 seats, and lost all but two governorships, including that of Buenos Aires.

As the constitution barred a president from standing for a second term, the UCR party congress elected the governor of the industrial province of Córdoba, Eduardo César Angeloz, as its candidate for the May 14, 1989, presidential elections. Trying to distance himself from the government's failure to halt the economic decline but also emphasizing Alfonsín's preservation of democracy in the face of army hostility, Angeloz promised a total war on inflation and economic growth through privatization, a reduction of state spending and increased exports. He came second with 211 seats in the electoral college, doing somewhat better than the party's congressional candidates who overall won only 28.9 per cent of the vote or 41 of the 127 seats up for election.

Spiralling inflation and a highly unstable economy forced Raúl Alfonsín to relinquish power to Carlos Menem in July 1989, five months before he was due to retire as President on Dec. 10. The UCR remained the main opposition party and the unsuccessful UCR presidential candidate, Angeloz, was invited by President Menem to join his Cabinet in February 1990. He refused the post and instead called for all political parties to sign a pact under which a plan for effective government would be drawn up to preserve and consolidate democracy in an extreme social and economic crisis.

Such proposals and the UCR's criticism of government policies, however, did not improve the party's electoral chances. In the 1991 mid-term elections the UCR lost five seats thus reducing its congressional strength to 85 delegates, and in the gubernatorial elections the UCR managed to retain only three governorships. One of the victims of this poor electoral showing was Alfonsín himself, who following strong criticism from within the UCR resigned the party leadership in mid-November. He then became head of the "Movement for the Defence of the Principles of Social Democracy" faction within the UCR. A further repercussion of the election was the resignation of Eduardo Duhalde as Vice-President of Argentina in order to take up the governorship of Buenos Aires which he won on Sept. 8, 1991. Moves by the UCR to appoint a replacement Vice-President, however, were blocked by President Menem's brother Eduardo who as President of the Senate tried to claim the post for himself.

United Left Alliance

Alianza de Izquierda Unida (AIU)
Leadership. Néstor Vicente (l.).
Orientation. Left-wing electoral alliance.
Founded. October 1988.
History. The successor of the 1987 left-wing Broad Front Alliance *(Frente Amplio de Liberacion*—FRAL), the AIU was set up after months of negotiations between the FRAL's two major forces, the Communist Party of Argentina (PCA) and the Movement towards Socialism (MAS). The Popular Democratic Left (IDP) also joined the alliance and its leader, Néstor Vicente, was selected as the AIU's presidential candidate in the alliance's internal elections in December 1988. The AIU was hoping to become the country's fourth electoral force and put forward a programme of land reform, non-payment of foreign debt and nationalization of all banks. Despite high hopes, the AIU received only a small percentage of the vote in the May 1989 presidential elections, and with 2.4 per cent of the vote failed to obtain a seat in Congress.

Union of the Democratic Centre

Unión del Centro Democrático (UCeDé)
Address. Av. R. S Peña 628, P.1 Of.2, 1008 Buenos Aires.
Leadership. Federico Clerici (l.).
Orientation. Conservative; stands for a free market economy and a reduced public sector.
Founded. 1980.
History. Originally a coalition of eight small centre-right parties, the UCeDé was formed and led by Álvaro Alsogaray, who could count an important position in the 1976 military government among his previous government posts. The party in the October 1983 general elections won only two seats in the Chamber of Deputies, Alsogaray receiving only 0.3

per cent of the presidential vote. In order to improve its chances in the Federal Capital of Buenos Aires in the November 1985 elections, the UCeDé formed the "Popular Centrist Alliance" coalition with the Capital Democratic Party (PDC) and Federalist Centre Party (PFC), both of which are now defunct. The vote for the alliance increased to 3.5 per cent of the national vote (10.3 per cent in Buenos Aires), giving the UCeDé one additional seat in Congress. For the partial congressional election of 1987, the party formed several local alliances with small centrist parties which increased its overall vote to 5.7 per cent (and 18.1 per cent in the Federal Capital) and brought the UCeDé's representation in the Chamber up to seven deputies.

Although Alsogaray was elected as presidential candidate in June 1988, the party leadership at the same time decided to support the Peronist campaign, hoping thereby to raise the UCeDé's profile. This strategy led to the party polling 9.5 per cent of the national vote, giving the UCeDé nine seats out of the 127 up for election in the May 14, 1989, election. Alsogaray came third with 6.4 per cent of the presidential vote. In June 1989 the party leadership was transferred to Federico Clerici, and in July when President Menem (see Justicialist Party) took office Alsogaray was appointed Argentina's foreign debt negotiator. The UCeDé's support for the Peronists also yielded an important post for Alsogaray's daughter and the leader of the "Unity and Opening" faction, María Julia Alsogaray, who became head of the state telephone company which was earmarked for privatization.

The party's representation in the Chamber of Deputies was reduced to only 10 seats after the partial congressional elections of October 1991.

Minor parties

All for the Motherland Movement (*Movimiento Todos por la Patria*—MTP); a left-wing group founded in 1988 which took over the Third Infantry Barracks at *La Tablada* in January 1989 in an armed assault believing that a military coup was under way. In the ensuing fighting, 28 MTP members died and a further 20 died while in custody. A number of members, including one of MTP's leaders Fr Juan Antonio Puigjane, who was not involved in the attack, were sentenced to prison terms of between 10 years and life.

Autonomist-Liberal Pact (*Pacto Autonomista-Liberal*—PAL); a centre-right regionalist party founded in 1983 as an alliance between the Liberal and the Autonomist parties of the far northern border province of Corrientes for the purpose of contesting federal elections. The PAL won both Corrientes Senatorial seats, two seats in the Chamber of Deputies and the governorship of the province. In the November 1985 election it increased its representation in the Chamber to three seats and won a further seat in September 1987. The party retained the governorship in both the 1987 and the October 1991 gubernatorial elections.

Bloquista Civic Union Party (*Unión Cívica Bloquista*—UCB); a conservative regional party mainly based in the San Juan province, control of which it lost to the Peronists in the August 1991 provincial elections.

Chaco Action (*Acción Chaqueña*—AC); a small right-wing party which won the state governorship of the far north Chaco province in October 1991 and whose candidate was José Ruíz Palacios, a retired Colonel who had served as an Under-Secretary in the Ministry of the Interior under the previous military dictatorship.

Christian Popular Party (*Partido Popular Cristiano*—PPC); a progressive social Christian party led by José Antonio Allende.

Civic and Social Front (*Frente Cívico y Social*—FCS); an opposition alliance led by the UCR, and also comprising dissidents of the Justicialist Party (PJ-Peronists) and other minority parties. It won gubernatorial elections on Dec. 1, 1991, in the north-western province of Catamarca with 56 per cent of the vote. Its candidate Arnoldo Castillo defeated the former Peronist governor and MAP candidate as well as the PJ candidate.

Democratic Concentration (*Concentración Demócrata*—CD); Rodriguez Peña 525, 1035 Buenos Aires); a centre-right group led by J. Vicchi, José María Avellaneda and Juan Carlos Cueto Rúa. The party was a member of one of the alliances led by the Union of the Democratic Centre (UCeDé) which contested the 1987 congressional elections.

Democratic Socialist Party (*Partido Socialista Democrático*—PSP); Larrea 1324, 1117 Buenos Aires); Américo Ghioldi (l.); a centre-left party founded in 1958 by a breakaway faction of the now defunct Argentinian Socialist Party. It was a founder member of the UCeDé but in 1983 it supported the PDP's unsuccessful presidential candidate. In an alliance with the PDP and other small parties the PSP won 1 per cent in 1985 and 1.4 per cent of the congressional vote.

Federal Party (*Partido Federal*—PF); Av. de Mayo 962, P. 1, 1084 Buenos Aires).

Fueguino Popular Movement (*Movimiento Popular Fueguino*—Mopof); a right-wing party which won gubernatorial elections in Tierra del Fuego on Dec. 1, 1991, with 43.4 per cent of the vote. Its candidate Juan Estabillo narrowly defeated the PJ candidate in two rounds of voting.

Green Ecologist Pacifist Party (Green Future) (*Partido Verde Ecologista Pacifista (Futuro Verde)*; Sucre 1795, P.1, Of. "F", 1428 Buenos Aires).

Group of Eight (*Grupo de los 8* (G-8)); Luis Brunati (l.); founded 1990, a Justicialist Party (PJ-Peronists) dissident group whose seats in the Chamber of Deputies were reduced from eight to five in the October 1991 congressional elections.

Jujuy Popular Movement (*Movimiento Popular Jujeño*—MPJ); Horacio Guzmána (l.); a regionalist party from the north-western state of Jujuy, the MPJ won a congressional seat in the elections of 1983 and a further seat in 1985. In the 1991 mid-term elections, the party won one seat.

Movement for Dignity and Independence (*Movimiento por la Dignidad y la Independencia*—Modin); formed in 1990 and led by the cashiered Lt.-Col. Aldo Rico, who led military uprisings in Easter 1987 and January 1988. In the 1991 provincial elections the Modin proved to be the third political force in the Buenos Aires province (Argentina's largest electoral district) where it won three seats in the Federal Chamber of Deputies and obtained 10 per cent of the vote.

In September 1991, Aldo Rico announced that he was considering standing as a candidate in the 1995 presidential elections.

Movement of Popular Affirmation (*Movimiento de Afirmación Nacional*—MAP); founded in 1991 by Ramón Saadi, a former Peronist governor who was dismissed by President Menem in April 1991 for corruption and drug trafficking. Saadi, whose family had been effectively running the north-western province of Catamarca for over 40 years, came second in the gubernatorial elections of Dec. 1, 1991, with 34 per cent of the vote.

National Left Party (*Partido de Izquierda National*—PIN); a member of the FREJUPO alliance formed in 1988 to back the successful Peronist presidential campaign of Carlos Menem in May 1989. The party was founded by a former leader of the Patriotic Liberation Movement (also a FREJUPO member) and had supported the Peronists' 1983 presidential campaign.

National Party of the Centre (*Partido Nacional de Centro*—PNC); Raúl Rivanera Carles (l.); a conservative party founded in 1980.

Nationalist Constitutional Party (*Partido Nacionalista Constitucional*—PNC ; Humberto Primo 2087, Buenos Aires).

Nationalist Workers' Party (*Partido Nacionalista de los Trabajadores*—PNT); an anti-Zionist party launched in 1990 and led by former Justicialist Party (PJ-Peronist) member Alejandro Biondini. Biondini was leader of the extreme right-wing group, *Alerta Nacional*, set up within the PJ in 1982. The swastika is the party's official symbol. In order not to infringe the 1988 anti-discrimination law they claim that their party is non-racist but in practice they are openly anti-semitic. The PNT claims a membership of 25,000 but the figure is likely to be closer to the former *Alerta Nacional*'s 350 members.

Neuquén Popular Movement (*Movimiento Popular Neuquino*—MPN); a small regionalist movement which won two seats in each chamber of the federal legislature of the southern province of Neuquén in 1983 and retained them in the 1987 elections. The MPN is led by the brothers Felipe and Elias Sapag who in 1987 became the Governor and Federal Senator of Neuquén respectively. In the 1991 mid-term elections, the MPN retained the governorship and won one seat in the Congress.

Neuquén Unity for Change (*Unidad de los Neuquinos por el Cambio*); unsuccessfully challenged the MPN for the governorship of Neuquén in 1987 and 1991.

Patriotic Liberation Movement (*Movimiento Patriótico de Liberación*—MPL; Av. Rivadavia 1188, 1033 Buenos Aires); a centrist party formed in 1982 as the Popular Left Front. The party suffered a split after the September 1983 presidential elections in which the party's candidate won only 0.1 per cent of the vote. It adopted its current name in 1986 and in

1988 the MPL joined the Peronist FREJUPO alliance which supported Carlos Menem's candidacy in the May 1989 presidential election.

Popular Conservative Party (*Partido Conservador Popular*—PCP; Alberti 950, 1121 Buenos Aires); a right-wing party founded by Vicente Solano Lima. The party, led by J. Amoedo since Solano's death in 1984, has a very small following.

Popular Democracy (*Democracía Popular*—DP; M.T. de Alvear 2387, 1122 Buenos Aires).

Popular Democratic Left (*Izquierda Demócrata Popular*—IDP); a Christian Socialist party founded in 1986 by Néstor Vicente, a member of the Christian Democratic Party (PDC) for 33 years until switching to the Intransigent Party in 1984. The IDP was a founder member of the left-wing Broad Front for Liberation (FRAL) in 1987 and in October 1988 joined the Communist Party (PCA) and the Movement towards Socialism (MAS) in the United Left Alliance (AIU). Néstor Vicente was elected the alliance's presidential candidate in December and in the subsequent elections of May 14, 1989, polled a negligible percentage of the vote.

Popular Socialist Party (*Partido Socialista Popular*—PSP; Entre Ríos 1018, 1080 Buenos Aires); a social democratic party founded in 1982, which has its origins in the 19th century Socialist Party and the 1958 Argentinian Socialist Party. It backed the Peronist presidential candidate Italo Lúder in the 1983 elections. The PSP joined the Socialist Unity coalition in 1985 to contest the 1985 congressional elections in which it won 1 per cent of the vote. The coalition gained one seat with 1.4 per cent of the vote in the 1987 election. Although it is registered, the party's current status is still in doubt.

Popular Union (*Unión Popular*—UP; B. de Irigoyen 558, 1072 Buenos Aires).

Renewalist Party (*Partido Renovador*—PR); a small regionalist and conservative party based in the north-western region of Salta which increased its presence in the Chamber of Deputies from two to four seats in the October 1991 mid-term elections and won the Governorship of Salta. The Governor, Roberto Ulloa, was governor of the province under the military regime from 1977 to 1982.

Republican Federalist Centre Party (*Partido Republicano Federalista de Centro*—PRFC; Av. Córdoba 6237, 1427 Buenos Aires).

Republican Force (*Fuerza Republicana*—FR; Pte. Perón 318, P. 1 Of. 5, 1008, Buenos Aires); Gen. Domingo Bussi (l.); a right-wing party, controlling the north-western Tucumán district, which had loose links with the previous military regime and which increased its seats in the Chamber of Deputies from two to four in the October 1991 mid-term elections.

Revolutionary Workers' Party (*Partido Obrero Revolucionario*—POR); a very small party formed by Homero Cristalli (alias J. Posadas) to establish his own version of Trotskyism. The POR joined the Communist FRAL alliance for the 1985 partial elections.

Rio Negro Party (*Partido Rionegrino*—PR); an active regionalist party based in the province of Rio Negro with minor representation at state level.

Rural Movement (*Movimiento Ruralista*); formed in December 1986 and fronted by the Peronist deputy Raúl Druetta with the aim of bringing together supporters of "farm production at fair prices" who were opposed to speculation.

Social Republican Party (*Partido Social Republicano*—PSR; Uruguay 654, P. 10, Of. 1003, 1015 Buenos Aires).

Socialist Unity (*Unidad Socialista*).

Workers' and People's Party (*Partido del Trabajo y del Pueblo*—PTP; Ecuador 543, 1214 Buenos Aires). A small Maoist party which has supported left-wing Peronist candidates. The PTP publishes a periodical called *Hoy* (Today).

Workers' Party (*Partido Obrero*—PO; Ayacucho 444, 1026 Buenos Aires); a Trotskyist party led by Jorge Altamira, Juan Carlos Capurno and Christian Rath, it was formed in 1982 by ex-members of a 1960s group linked to Silvio Frondizi, a Trotskyist intellectual who was assassinated in 1974.

Workers' Party for Socialism (*Partido de los Trabajadores por el Socialismo*—PTS); founded in the late 1980s by mostly university students and led by Emilio Albamonte, Hugo Manes and Rubén and Pablo Visconti.

Workers' Revolutionary Party (*Partido Revolucionario de los Trabajadores*—PRT); an illegal Trotskyist party created in 1965 and the political wing of the People's Revolutionary Army (*Ejército Revolucionario del Pueblo*-ERP) from its inception in 1969 until the guerrilla group's dissolution in the mid-1980s, which was confirmed by an official declaration by the PRT in 1987.

Aruba

Capital: Oranjestad **Population: 62,365**

Constitutional structure

The Netherlands Antilles (then including Aruba) acquired separate status with full internal self-government within the Kingdom of the Netherlands in 1954, when the Kingdom's Charter came into force. Aruba achieved *status aparte* (self-government) in 1986, pending full independence.

Under the original constitutional arrangements full independence was to be proclaimed in 1996, but this was postponed indefinitely in 1990, primarily over disagreement about the extent of Dutch commitment to the Island's post-independence future. A 10-year transition period was due to operate following independence, during which the Dutch government, represented by the Governor, would continue to be responsible for defence and foreign affairs.

Executive power in internal affairs is vested in a Council of Ministers. Legislative authority is vested in the 21-member unicameral States (*Staten*), established in 1985.

Electoral system

The *Staten* is elected by universal adult suffrage by proportional representation for four years, with the possibility of early dissolution.

Evolution of the suffrage

Before the proclamation of separate status, provisions regarding suffrage passed by the Dutch and the Antilles parliaments also applied to Aruba. The minimum voting age is currently 18.

Sequence of elections since 1985

Staten election, November 1985

	Seats	*% of vote*
People's Electoral Movement (MEP)	8	37.6
Aruban People's Party (PAP-AVP)	7	31.3
Aruban Patriotic Party (PPA-APP)	2	12.3
Aruban Democratic Party (PDA-DAP)	2	10.0
National Democratic Action (ADN-NDA)	2	8.8
Total	**21**	

Staten election, January 1989

	Seats
MEP	10
PAP-AVP	8
ADN-NDA	1
PPA-APP	1
New Patriotic Party (PPN)	1
Total	**21**

PARTY BY PARTY DATA

Aruban Democratic Party

Partido Democrático Arubano (PDA)-Democratishe Arubaanse Partij
Address. Oranjestad.
Leadership. Léonard Berlinski (l.).
Orientation. Anti-independence.
Founded. 1983.
History. The PDA won 4.5 per cent of the vote but no seats in the April 1983 Aruban Council elections. In those of November 1985, establishing Aruba's *Staten*, it secured two seats and 10 per cent of the vote. It joined the ensuing coalition government, in which Berlinski became Economic Minister, but later in 1986 it withdrew its support. In the January 1989 elections, it lost both of its *Staten* seats.

Aruban Patriotic Party

Partido Patriótico Arubano (PPA)-Arubaanse Patriottische Partij (APP)
Address. Oranjestad.
Leadership. Leo Chance (l.).
Orientation. Anti-independence, drawing much of its support from non-Aruban inhabitants of the island.
Founded. 1949.
History. The party held four seats in the *Staten* of the Netherlands Antilles in 1969-73, and it participated in a four-party governing coalition. It was reduced to three seats in 1973, and joined a three-party coalition in 1977. In 1979 it was reduced to a single seat, which it held in 1982.The PPA won 14.9 per cent of the vote and three of the 21 seats in the April 1983 Aruban Council elections.

In the 1985 elections, establishing Aruba's *Staten*, its share of the vote fell to 12.3 per cent and it won two seats, its representatives then joining the ensuing coalition government. In the February 1989 elections, the party won one seat and subsequently joined with the MEP and the ADN in a coalition government, receiving one Cabinet post. The same year, a splinter group from the party formed the New Patriotic Party (PPN).

Aruban People's Party

Arubaanse Volkspartij (AVP)
Address. Oranjestad.
Leadership. J. H. A. (Henny) Eman (l.).
Orientation. Christian democrat; the party has worked for separate status for Aruba while opposing outright independence. However, given the strong possibility of independence, it has worked to ensure that the strongest possible ties are maintained with the Netherlands.
Founded. 1942.
History. The party was formed by Eman, the charismatic leader of the post-war separatist movement (which was fuelled mainly by resentment of the island's status within the Netherlands Antilles, rather than of its membership of the Kingdom of the Netherlands). It held six seats in the *Staten* of the Netherlands Antilles in 1969-73, when it was part of the ruling coalition, but it lost four seats in 1973. It advocated a boycott of the March 1977 referendum, in which there was, however, a 70 per cent turnout with an 83 per cent vote in favour of a proposition favouring eventual independence.

The AVP gained four of the nine seats in the Aruban Council election of 1979, when it also regained representation in the Netherlands Antillean *Staten*. In 1982 it won two seats in the Netherlands Antillean *Staten* and in 1983 increased its Aruban Council representation to five out of 21 seats, securing 22.6 per cent of the vote.

In the November 1985 elections establishing Aruba's *Staten* the party increased its share of the vote to 31.3 per cent and won seven seats. Eman then formed a four-party coalition government and at the beginning of 1986 became the island's first Prime Minister. Four of the seven cabinet posts went to AVP members. The AVP-PDA-APP-ADN coalition government lost the February 1989 *Staten* elections, campaigning principally on its record of economic management; the AVP in particular remained cautious about Aruba's arrangements to proceed to full independence in 1996. The AVP individually won eight seats, becoming the largest opposition party.
International Affiliations. Member party of the Christian Democrat Organization of America, which forms part of the Christian Democrat International.

Democratic Action 86

Acción Democrática 86 (AD-86)
Address. Oranjestad.

Orientation. Centre-left.
Founded. 1986.
History. The AD-86 was formed by a split in the National Democratic Action party (ADN).

National Democratic Action

Akshon Democratico Nashonal-Nationale Democratische Actie-Acción Democratica Nacional (ADN)
Address. Oranjestad.
Leadership. John Booi (l.).
Orientation. Anti-independence.
Founded. 1984.
History. The ADN was founded by Booi and Charro Kelly. It contested the 1985 elections to what was to become the Aruban *Staten*, and secured 8.8 per cent of the vote, giving it two of the 21 seats. It then joined other anti- independence parties, the AVP, PDA and APP, in a coalition administration, with Kelly as Minister of Public Works. In the 1989 *Staten* elections, the party won one seat and joined the MEP and PPA in a coalition government, receiving one post in the Cabinet.

New Patriotic Party

Partido Patriótico Nobo (PPN)
Founded. 1989.
History. The PPN split from the PPA and received one seat in the *Staten* in the 1989 elections.

People's Electoral Movement

Movimento Electoral di Pueblo (MEP)
Address. Cumana 84, Oranjestad.
Leadership. Nelson O Oduber (pres. and l.); J. van de Kuyp (s.-g.).
Orientation. Social democratic and pro-independence. The party has maintained that Aruba is dominated by its neighbouring island, Curaçao, and holds that Aruba has sole rights over any oil deposits off its shores.
Founded. February 1971.
History. The party entered the Netherlands Antillean *Staten* in August 1973 and later joined the ruling coalition. From April 1975 it had a majority on the Aruban Council. In September 1975 the Antillean *Staten* adopted an MEP motion favouring self-determination for Aruba, and in a referendum in 1977 independence received 83 per cent support. The MEP was excluded from the Antilles government after the June 1977 elections, and boycotted the *Staten*, but it joined a new coalition after the elections of July 1979.

Having won 12 of the 21 seats on the Aruban Council in April 1979, the MEP began independence negotiations in 1981. In September 1981 the MEP left the Antilles government because of the latter's view that all six islands had rights over possible oil reserves. In the 1982 Antillean *Staten* elections the MEP won five of the 22 seats. It led the Aruban delegation at a round-table conference in the Netherlands, and in March 1983 it was agreed that Aruba would separate from the Antilles in 1986 and become independent in 1996. Gilberto Francois (Betico) Croes, the founder and leader of the MEP, was shot and wounded at a rally in April 1983, in what an inquiry held to be an accident. The party won the 1983 elections to the Aruban Council, with 13 seats and 58 per cent of the vote.

In September 1984, two MEP members became ministers in a new coalition government of the Antilles. In Aruban elections on Nov. 22, 1985, during an economic crisis arising from a refinery closure, the MEP lost power, securing 37.6 per cent of the vote and eight seats in what became the Aruban *Staten.* Following injuries received in a car crash Betico Croes died in November 1986.

In the February 1989 Aruban *Staten* elections, the MEP succeeded in increasing its share of the seats to 10 and formed a government with the support of the ADN and the PPA, each of which received a seat in the Cabinet.

The Bahamas

Capital: Nassau **Population: 248,000**

The Commonwealth of the Bahamas has been an independent member of the Commonwealth since July 10, 1973. It had gained internal self-government in January 1964.

Constitutional structure

The head of state of the Bahamas is the British sovereign, represented by a Governor-General. Under the terms of the independence Constitution executive power is exercised by the Prime Minister and the Cabinet of which the Prime Minister is a member. The Prime Minister is appointed by the Governor-General as the elected member who can best command the support of a majority of the members of the House of Assembly. Legislative authority is vested in a bicameral Parliament consisting of a popularly elected House of Assembly and an appointed Senate.

Electoral system

The 49 members of the House of Assembly are elected for five years and the 16 members of the Senate are appointed by the Governor-General, with nine chosen on the advice of the Prime Minister, four on that of the Leader of the Opposition and three by the Prime Minister after consultation with the Leader of the Opposition.

Evolution of the suffrage

Adult male suffrage was introduced under British colonial administration in 1959, although members of the electorate satisfying certain property qualifications also received a second vote. Women were granted the vote in 1962 and by 1964 all property qualifications had been abolished.

Sequence of elections since 1982

Date	*Winning party*
June 10, 1982	Progressive Liberal Party (PLP)
June 19, 1987	Progressive Liberal Party (PLP)

PARTY BY PARTY DATA

Free National Movement (FNM)

Address. P.O. Box N-8181, Nassau.
Leadership. Hubert A. Ingraham (l.).
Orientation. Conservative.
Founded. 1970.
History. The FNM was formed by the merger of the old white-dominated United Bahamian Party (UBP) with a dissident PLP faction, the Free PLP, whose leader, Wallace-Whitfield (a former PLP chairman, and a Cabinet minister in 1968-70), led the FNM until 1972. In 1972-75 it held eight seats in the House of Assembly, on a platform of opposition to early independence. In the 1977 elections it was reduced to three seats, and in 1979 two of its elected members joined the Free National Democratic Movement (FNDM) founded by John Henry Bostwick (a former leader of the Bahamian Democratic Party—BDP).

After defections from the BDP and its offshoot, Norman Solomon's Social Democratic Party (SDP), the FNDM was recognized as the official opposition late in 1981, in which year Wallace-Whitfield (who had resumed the leadership in 1975) was replaced by Kendal G. L. Isaacs, a former Attorney-General. The SDP having dissolved itself in April 1982, the FNDM reverted to the name FNM for the June elections, in which it won 42.4 per cent of the vote and 11 out of 43 seats.

Following the party's fifth successive general election defeat, in June 1987, Isaacs resigned and was succeeded by his deputy, Wallace-Whitfield. The FNM did not contest by-elections in December 1991 and January 1992 on the grounds that it was unnecessary in view of the upcoming general election, to be held either in June or December 1992.

Structure. The leading authority in the FNM is the annual convention, which elects a 160-member central committee.

Progressive Liberal Party (PLP)

Address. P.O. Box N-1107, Nassau.
Leadership. Sir Lynden Pindling (l.); Errington Isaacs (ch.).
Orientation. Populist; supported predominantly by Bahamanians of African origin.
Founded. 1953.
History. The PLP was a leading proponent of independence for the Bahamas. It has been in power since the first elections held under universal suffrage, in 1967, when it gained 18 seats in the 38-member House of Assembly with the support of the sole representative of the (since defunct) Labour Party in the House. In elections and a by-election held in 1972 the PLP won 30 seats, and it gained an additional seat in 1977. In 1982 it won 32 seats out of the increased total of 43.

In the June 1987 elections the PLP held 31 of the 49 seats; it vigorously rejected opposition allegations that it had resorted to a "massive fraud" in order to do so. The PLP had survived a crisis in 1983-84 arising from the implication of government ministers in drug smuggling.

At the close of the party's 35th annual convention from Oct. 31 to Nov. 7, 1990, Pindling criticized government ministers, MPs, civil servants and party officials for tolerating "waste, favouritism, and paper-pushing". He claimed "too many people have taken up leadership positions in this party with an eye for prestige rather than a hand for work".

In an attempt to eliminate a US$200,000,000 budget deficit accrued over the previous four years, the government in January 1991 increased taxes and import duties on a large number of products and launched an ambitious investment promotion programme, offering a wide range of tax incentives to attract foreign investors.

However, falling revenues from tourism meant that the government had to introduce a supplementary budget in October and borrow an additional US$86,000,000 in November to cover the deficit in the current financial year.

In December 1991 and January 1992 the PLP won two by-elections not contested by the Free National Movement (FNM). However, the turnout of less than 35 per cent in the first election was the lowest on record. In the second, the PLP took 66 per cent of a reportedly heavy poll.

Minor parties

People's Democratic Force (PDF); Fred Mitchell (l.); a small opposition party founded in 1989.
Social Democratic Party (SDP); an offshoot of the Free National Movement.
Vanguard Socialist Party (VSP); John McCartney (l.).

Barbados

Capital: Bridgetown **Population: 300,000**

Barbados has been a fully independent member of the Commonwealth since November 1966. It had its first elections as an independent state in September 1971.

Constitutional structure

Under the Constitution of 1966, the head of state is the British monarch, represented locally by a Governor-General. Legislative power is vested in the bicameral parliament, consisting of a 28-member House of Assembly (increased from 27 in 1991) and a Senate of 21 appointed members. Executive power is exercised by the Prime Minister and the Cabinet, who are responsible to Parliament. The Prime Minister is appointed by the Governor-General as the elected member of the House best able to command a majority in the House of Assembly, and is a member of the Cabinet. The other Cabinet Ministers are appointed by the Governor-General on the advice of the Prime Minister.

Electoral system

Members of the House of Assembly are elected for a five-year term (subject to dissolution) by simple plurality from single-member constituencies. Members of the Senate are appointed by the Governor-General; 12 are chosen on the advice of the Prime Minister, two on that of the Leader of the Opposition and seven at the Governor-General's own discretion.

Evolution of the suffrage

Universal adult suffrage was introduced by the British colonial administration in 1951. The minimum age for voting was reduced from 21 to 18 years of age in 1962.

Sequence of elections since 1981

Date	*Winning Party*
June 18, 1981	Barbados Labour Party (BLP)
May 28, 1986	Democratic Labour Party (DLP) (
Jan. 22, 1991	Democratic Labour Party (DLP)

General election, January 22, 1991

Party	*% of vote*	*Seats*
Democratic Labour Party (DLP)	49	18
Barbados Labour Party (BLP)	44	10
National Democratic Party (NDP)	7	-
Total	**100**	**28**

PARTY BY PARTY DATA

Barbados Labour Party (BLP)

Address. Grantley Adams House, 11 Roebuck Street, Bridgetown.
Leadership. Henry Deboulay Forde (l.); George W. Payne (s.-g.).
Orientation. Conservative, originally a moderate socialist party modelled on the British Labour Party, but now believes in a free market economy. A supporter of the 1983 US invasion of Grenada, it has long been hostile to the Cuban government.
Founded. 1938, as the Barbados Progressive Party.
History. The BLP, the first modern party to be established in the Anglo-Caribbean, held office in the pre-independence period from 1951 to 1961. Its founder, Sir Grantley Adams (1898-1971), became the first Prime Minister in a British West Indies territory when ministerial government was introduced in Barbados in 1954, and he subsequently became Prime Minister of the West Indies Federation during its brief existence from 1958 to 1962.

In 1961 the BLP lost its majority in the Barbados House of Assembly to the Democratic Labour Party (DLP) and remained in opposition until the elections of 1976. In the elections of that year, standing on a programme attacking government mismanagement, corruption and waste, the party, now under the leadership of J. M. G. "Tom" Adams (Grantley's son) won 17 of the 24 seats. It retained these seats with 52.2 per cent of the vote in 1981 although the lower house had been expanded to 27 members. H. Bernard St John succeeded Adams on his death in 1985 as party leader and Prime Minister and the party suffered an overwhelming defeat in the 1986 general election, winning only three seats out of 24. St John lost his seat and resigned as party leader later in the year to be replaced by Forde who set about the restructuring and decentralization of the party.

The party was replaced as official opposition party by the newly formed National Democratic Party (NDP) in February 1989 but its vigorous opposition to the ruling DLP's economic policies was rewarded in the January 1991 general election when it won 10 of the 28 seats in the enlarged House of Assembly.
Structure. The party has constituency branches and an annual delegate conference which elects a national executive committee of not more than 36 members.
Membership. 10,000 (1988 estimate).
Publications. *The Beacon* (weekly).
International affiliations. Socialist International.

Democratic Labour Party (DLP)

Address. Kennington, George Street, Belleville, St Michael.
Leadership. Lloyd Erskine Sandiford (l.); Reggie Hunt Jnr, (public relations officer).
Orientation. Centre-right, free market.
Founded. May 1955.
History. Formed by dissident members of the Barbados Labour Party (BLP) who claimed it had moved too far to the right, the DLP came to power in 1961, winning 14 of the 24 seats in the House of Assembly. Following its further election victory in 1966, its then leader, Errol Barrows, led the country to independence from the United Kingdom in November of that year. The party adopted left-wing policies in the 1970s, emphasizing economic development and social provision, which enabled it to retain power in 1971. It lost the 1976 general election, however, to the BLP when it won only seven seats and only slightly improved on this in 1981 when it secured 47.1 per cent of the poll and 10 seats in the House. The party returned to power after the elections of May 1986 and Barrows, who died in June 1987, was succeeded as Prime Minister and then as party leader and President by Sandiford.

In December 1988, Sandiford presented a five-year development plan, emphasizing annual growth of 2.5 per cent through the development of tourism as the country's main economic activity. Growth in the economy continued to slow down, however, during 1989 and 1990 in response to the tight fiscal policies introduced by the government to protect the country's foreign exchange reserves and balance of payments. Factional infighting compounded the government's problems and on Oct. 15, 1990, in the run-up to the general election, Senator Gertrude Eastmond resigned from the Senate and the party claiming that the country was "heading for disaster". Despite such predictions, the DLP was re-elected on Jan. 22, 1991, securing half of the vote and winning 18 of the 28 seats in the enlarged House of Assembly.

Sandiford's popularity subsequently plummeted as the economy continued to deteriorate and the government introduced an austerity programme and a consumption tax, policies condemned by the media, trade unions, the church and sections of the business community. Major protest marches by public sector workers took place on Oct. 24 and on Nov. 4, 1991, upwards of 30,000 demonstrators blocked the streets of the capital, Bridgetown, during a 48-hour general strike.

An opposition vote of no confidence in Sandiford was only averted when the government refused to broadcast the parliamentary session on the state-owned CBC television channel. By January 1992 the government had weathered the crisis but had been forced to make concessions to manufacturers on import duties and to the trade unions on severance and unemployment benefits. In an effort to restore its authority the government introduced a controversial company stabilization tax to redress the balance.

Government assurances during the March budget debate that an economic recovery was expected, to be led by the tourism, construction and financial sectors, and that state finances were sound and demonstrated the success of a country living "within its means" were denounced by the opposition. On April 1, Sandiford was forced to reshuffle his Cabinet following the resignation of the Minister of State in the Finance Ministry who accused Sandiford of being more interested in his political survival than the welfare of the country.

Structure. The party has constituency branches, an annual delegate conference, a general council and an executive council.

Membership. 15,000 (1988 estimate).

New Democratic Party (NDP)

Address. Suenos 3, 6th Avenue, Belleville, St Michael.

Leadership. Richie Haynes; George Bispham (s.-g.).

Orientation. Centrist; the party, on its foundation, emphasized the importance of morality and integrity in public life and was opposed to the economic policies of the ruling Democratic Labour Party (DLP) government.

History. The NDP was formed by Richie Haynes following his resignation as Finance Minister in the Democratic Labour Party government on Feb. 1, 1989. Three other DLP backbenchers joined the new party and Haynes was appointed as Leader of the Opposition by the Governor-General Sir Hugh Springer as the NDP's representation in the House exceeded that of the Barbados Labour Party (BLP). Despite its early promise as a viable electoral opponent to the BLP, the party suffered a humiliating defeat in the January 1991 general election, and failed to win a single seat in the House of Assembly.

Belize

Capital: Belmopan **Population: 184,000**

Belize became independent within the British Commonwealth on September 21, 1981. A Legislative Assembly has been in existence since 1935 and was given responsibility for internal self-government under the old Constitution of 1954. The country has since been governed by the People's United Party, with the exception of 1984-89.

Constitutional structure

Under the 1981 Constitution the Belizan head of state is the British monarch, represented by a Governor-General. He acts on the advice of a Cabinet headed by a Prime Minister. The Governor-General appoints the Prime Minister, who is the leader of the party with a parliamentary majority. The Prime Minister is assisted by a Deputy Prime Minister and other Ministers appointed by the Governor-General on the advice of the Prime Minister. The Governor-General is also advised by an appointed Belize Advisory Council. Legislative authority is vested in the bicameral National Assembly, comprising an appointed eight-member Senate, and a House of Representatives with 28 elected members. Legislation may be introduced in either house, except financial legislation which must be introduced in the lower house.

Electoral system

Belize uses the first-past-the-post system with successful candidates securing a simple majority in one of the 28 single-member constituencies. The eight members of the Senate are officially appointed by the Governor-General: five on the advice of the Prime Minister, two on that of the Leader of the Opposition and one after consulting the Belize Advisory Council. The National Assembly sits for a five-year term subject to dissolution.

Evolution of the suffrage

The 1954 Constitution granted universal adult suffrage. All citizens over the age of 18 are entitled to vote.

130.76
Gulf of
Mexico
Tizimín
Mérida
Campeche
Veracruz
Carmen
Coatzacoalcos
Villahermosa
Minatitlán
M E X I C O
Tehuantepec
Gulf of
Tehuantepec
Quezaltenango
Cobán
Mazatenango
GUATEMALA
GUATEMALA
Santa Ana
SAN SALVADOR
EL SALVADOR
Pacific
Ocean
BELIZE
Belize
BELMOPAN
Gulf of
Honduras
Pto. Barrios
Puerto Cortés
La Ceiba
San Pedro Sula
Zacapa
HONDURAS
TEGUCIGALPA
Amapala
NICARAGUA
León
Matagalpa
MANAGUA
Granada
Bluefields
COSTA
RICA
Puntarenas
SAN JOSÉ
Limón
Colón
PANAMA
PANAMÁ
David
Gulf of
Panamá
COLOMBIA
CAYMAN IS.
Camagüey
CUBA
KINGSTON
JAMAICA
Caribbean
Sea
CENTRAL AMERICA
Capital
Pan-American Highway
Railway
0
km
500

Sequence of elections since 1984

Date	*Winning party*
Dec. 14, 1984	United Democratic Party (UDP)
Sept. 4, 1989	People's United Party (PUP)

General Election, September 4, 1989

Party	*% of vote*	*Seats*
People's United Party (PUP)	50.87	15*
United Democratic Party (UDP)	49.02	13
Independent	00.11	—
Total	100.00	28

*An elected member of the UDP crossed the floor to the PUP four days after the election, thus increasing the PUP's representation to 16 seats.

PARTY BY PARTY DATA

People's United Party (PUP)

Address. 3 Queen St, Belize City.
Leadership. George Price (l.).
Orientation. Centrist, it has traditionally drawn more of its support from Catholics, Indians and Spanish-speakers than from the black population.
Founded. 1950.
History. The party was founded as a left-wing reformist party motivated by co-operatist ideas and supported by the General Workers' Union, of which Price was president, and the Roman Catholic Church. In 1951-54 the PUP was thought to have had close relations with the like-minded reformist Arbenz government in Guatemala (deposed by the USA) and campaigned for independence from Britain, a position which helped it win a comprehensive victory in the 1954 general election. Price became PUP leader in 1956 when a faction in the party opposed to independence broke away to form the National Independence Party (NIP). In 1957 the party won all nine assembly seats, and in the elections in 1961 to an enlarged legislature took all 18 seats. Price became the First Minister in 1961 and Premier in 1965. The party then had an unbroken run in office until 1984, during which time the country gained its independence, in September 1961, and Price became Prime Minister.

In the first post-independence election in 1984 the PUP suffered a dramatic defeat, receiving only seven seats in the enlarged 28-member House. As part of the post-electoral shock, former PUP ministers Louise Sylvestre and Fred Hunter left to form the (now defunct) Belize Popular Party (BPP) in July 1985 in protest at a perceived move to the left within the party. To counter-balance this tendency and restore the predominance of the party's centrist faction, the Christian Democratic Party (CDP), led by former United Democratic Party (UDP) leader Theodore Aranda, joined the PUP in 1988. The party returned to power in 1989 when it won 15 seats, narrowly defeating the UDP which gained 13 seats in the general election. Price, once again named as Prime Minister, named a Cabinet balancing the different wings of the party. He promised a mixed economy with a measure of state planning to counteract what he characterized as the UDP government's "savage economic liberalism". The PUP's parliamentary majority was increased when an expelled UDP representative switched political allegiances immediately after the election. The party then consolidated its position by winning all nine seats in the local elections to the Belize city council held on Dec. 7, 1989.

Significantly, during Price's current term of office the country has identified itself more closely with the region, being accepted as a member of the Organization of American States (OAS) in January 1991 and being offered observer status at the inauguration of the Central American Parliament (Parlacén) in October. This process of integration was reinforced in September 1991 by the establishment of diplomatic relations with neighbouring Guatemala, which had long claimed sovereignty over the country.
Publications. The *Belize Sunday Times* (weekly).

United Democratic Party (UDP)

Address. 19 King St, Belize City.
Leadership. Manuel Esquivel.
Orientation. Conservative and free market; its ethnic base is predominantly black (creole) but it claims support among the Mayan and Mestizo sectors.
Founded. September 1973.
History. The UDP emerged from the fusion of the National Independence Party, the Liberal Party and the People's Development Movement as a right-wing opposition to the People's United Party (PUP). In the 1979 general election, it won 46.8 per cent of the vote and five seats on the basis of a campaign alleging that the government was influenced by communism. Opposed to hasty independence from Britain until Guatemala's claims over the country had been neutralized diplomatically, the party unsuccessfully sought a referendum on independence in 1981, subsequently boycotted a parliamentary committee mandated to study the question and refused to participate in the official celebrations, held in September, once independence had been achieved. In July of the same year, radical UDP members had formed the Belize Action Movement (BAM) which co-ordinated sometimes violent anti-government demonstrations.

Esquivel became leader of the party in 1982, deposing Theodore Aranda, who resigned to form the (now defunct) Christian Democrat Party. Esquivel led the party to power in 1984 on a free-market pro-Western platform which also emphasized the country's sovereignty rights and non-alignment. It won a comprehensive victory over the PUP with 21 seats to seven. The party was the unexpected loser of the general election of September 1989, by 15 seats to 13, despite Esquivel's prediction that his free-market economic policies and the promise of increased US investment would receive strong endorsement from the electorate.

Esquivel participated in a bipartisan team which toured the country in October 1991 explaining the implications of the September establishment of diplomatic relations with Guatemala and the significance of a Maritime Areas Bill, establishing conditions for Guatemalan access to the Caribbean Sea.

Membership. 5,000 (1988 estimate).

Publications. Amandala, the *Beacon*, and the *Reporter* are weekly newspapers which support the UDP.

International affiliations. International Democratic Union.

Bermuda

Capital: Hamilton **Population: 56,000**

Bermuda is a Crown Colony of the United Kingdom and was settled by the British from 1609. It was granted internal self-government in 1968.

Constitutional structure

Under the 1968 constitution, amended in 1973 and 1979, Bermuda has a Governor who represents the British monarch. The Governor is responsible for external affairs, defence and internal security. The bicameral legislature consists of an elected 40-member House of Assembly and a Senate of 11 appointed members. Internal executive authority in most matters is exercised by the Premier, who is the House majority leader, and at least six other members of the Cabinet, which is drawn from and is responsible to the Legislature.

Electoral system

The House of Assembly is elected for a maximum term of five years from two member constituencies. The 11-member Senate has five members chosen by the Premier, three by the Leader of the Opposition and three by the Governor.

Evolution of the suffrage

Universal suffrage includes not only Bermudans but also pre-1976 British residents of Bermuda aged 21 or over.

Sequence of elections since 1980

Date	*Winning party*
Dec. 1980	United Bermuda Party (UBP)
Feb. 1983	United Bermuda Party (UBP)
Aug. 1985	United Bermuda Party (UBP)
Feb. 1989	United Bermuda Party (UBP)

General election February 9, 1989

Party	*Seats*
United Bermuda Party (UBP)	23
Progressive Labour Party (PLP)	15
National Liberal Party (NLP)	1
Independent Environmentalist	1
Total	40

PARTY BY PARTY DATA

National Liberal Party

Address. P.O. Box HM 2190, Hamilton HM JX.
Leadership. Cecil Butterfield (ch.); Kath H. Bell (s.-g.).
Orientation. Conservative.
Founded. August 1985.
History. The party was formed following the expulsion from the party of nine right-wing Progressive Labour Party (PLP) members of the House of Assembly in August 1984. They had unsuccessfully sought the resignation of party leader Lois Browne Evans who had resisted pressures to move the party further to the right (see PLP). They then formed an independent bloc under the leadership of Gilbert Darrell and this became the NLP prior to the 1985 elections, in which the party held two seats. In the 1989 election the party won only one seat.
Structure. An annual general meeting determines policy and elects an executive committee and an executive council. The membership is organized in three districts, each of which is made up of three parishes.
Membership. 400 (1988 claim).
Publications. The party has an internal newsletter.

Progressive Labour Party

Address. Court St, P.O. Box HM 1367, Hamilton HM FX.
Leadership. L. Frederick Wade (parl. l.); Elbridge B. Simmons (ch.); Jennifer Smith (dep. ch.); Marie Franklin (s.-g.).
Orientation. Centre-left; initially a socialist party close to the Caribbean "new left", which represented the demands of the underprivileged black majority. In the late 1970s it adopted increasingly moderate policies but continues to draw most of its support from the black population. It had sought early independence from the United Kingdom but no longer prioritizes this in its programme.
Founded. 1963.
History. The PLP was the first party to contest Bermudian elections. Led by Walter Robinson, it campaigned for internal autonomy, winning three of the 36 seats in the House of Assembly in the 1983 elections and on a pro-independence platform won 10 out of 40 seats in the 1968 elections when, under the new Constitution, it became the official opposition. Robinson, however, lost his seat and was replaced as party leader by the more left-wing Lois Browne Evans. The party won 10 seats in the 1972 election, with Robinson again the leader. He relinquished the leadership to Browne Evans in 1976 when the PLP increased its number of seats to 14 (later 15 through a by-election a year later) but still lost to the United Bermuda Party (UBP).

In the 1980 elections, after boundary revisions were introduced in an effort to defuse racial tensions, the PLP's representation in the House rose to 18 members and it narrowly failed to achieve power. However this electoral success was not maintained and in 1983 the PLP fell back to 14 seats. In 1985 this was reduced to five following the defection of nine members in 1984 to found the National Liberal Party (NLP). Browne Evans then resigned and was replaced by her deputy, Frederick Wade. In the 1989 elections, the party restored its political respectability by winning 15 seats.
Structure. The party is led by a 19-member central committee.

United Bermuda Party

Address. John F. Burrows Building, Chancery Lane, P.O. Box HM 715, Hamilton HM CX.
Leadership. John Swann (l.).
Orientation. Conservative, free-marketeer and regards the question of independence as subject to the "will" of Bermudans, but has no plans for a referendum on the issue.
Founded. August 1964.
History. The party was formed by Sir Henry J. Tucker and 23 other pro-government members of the House of Assembly to represent the minority white ruling class which was alarmed at the formation in 1963 of the then socialist Progressive Labour Party (PLP) which sought to represent the poor black majority. The party split in 1966 to give rise to the short-lived Bermuda Democratic Party.

It has held majorities in the Assembly and formed the government since the elections in 1968 in which it won 30 of the 40 seats. Tucker stepped down in 1971 and handed power over to Edward Richards, the country's first black head of government. In the 1972 elections, the party held all of its 30 seats but the next few years saw its popularity wane in the aftermath of great racial unrest, which in 1973 had seen the murder of the Governor-General, Sir Richard Sharples; the racial tension caused intra-party disputes and led to the establishment of a UBP Black Caucus in 1974. Sir John Sharpe took over the premiership from Richards in 1976 and the party's representation in the house was further reduced to 26 seats. The subsequent hanging in 1977 of a black Bermudan for the Sharples murder led to more widespread unrest.

Sharpe resigned in 1977 following a Cabinet revolt and was succeeded as UBP leader and Premier by David Gibbons, the former Finance Minister.

In 1982 the UBP barely clung to power, a mere 150 votes guaranteeing its majority of 22 seats over the PLP's 18 in the Assembly. A new leader, the successful black businessman John Swann, was appointed leader and Premier in place of Gibbons and in 1985 the party restored some of its lost political credibility by winning 31 seats.

Swann set about broadening the party's appeal away from that of the white establishment to other sections of the population, in particular the emerging black middle class.

In the 1989 elections it narrowly defeated the combined opposition by only six seats, returning 26 members to the Assembly.

Structure. The central Council determines party policy, which is implemented by a Central Executive. A youth wing is called Young United Bermuda.

Membership. 5,000 (1987 claim).

Bolivia

Capital: La Paz (administrative); Sucre (legal) **Population: 7,300,000**

Bolivia proclaimed independence from Spain in 1825 and its first Constitution was enforced in November 1826. Since then Bolivia has suffered 189 military coups and several new constitutions. Bolivian politics since the Second World War, despite the continued persistence of military intervention, have been dominated by the Revolutionary Nationalist Movement (MNR) (later the Historic Nationalist Revolutionary Movement—MNRH) under its veteran leader Victor Paz Estenssoro who came to power in the popular revolution of 1952. An inconclusive general election in May 1989 resulted in the formation of a Patriotic Accord (AP) coalition government of the Movement of the Revolutionary Left (MIR) and the right-wing Democratic Action Party (ADN).

Constitutional structure

The present Constitution dates from 1947 and was resurrected after a coup in 1964. Executive power is vested in the President who appoints the Cabinet, as well as the nine department prefects, the country's diplomatic representatives, archbishops and bishops. He is assisted by a Vice-President and a bicameral congress which is made up of a 27-seat Senate and a 130-seat Chamber of Deputies.

Electoral System

The President is elected by direct suffrage for a four-year term and is not eligible to serve two consecutive terms. If no candidate emerges from the elections with an absolute majority the newly elected Congress appoints a President. Senators (three for each of the nine provinces) and Deputies are elected by proportional representation also for a four-year term.

Evolution of the suffrage

There has been universal suffrage in Bolivia since the 1952 popular uprising, when the vote was also given to women and illiterates over the age of 21 and the age of suffrage for married people was reduced to 18. Voting is compulsory, and non-participation in the ballot can lose certain legal rights for up to three months, such as the use of banks.

Sequence of elections since 1989

May 7, 1989, General Election

Presidential Candidates	*votes*	*% of vote*
Gonzalo Sánchez de Lozada (MNRH)	363,113	23.07
Gen.(retd) Hugo Bánzer Suárez (ADN)	357,298	22.70
Jaime Paz Zamora (MIR)	309,033	19.64

In the second round in Congress on August 6, 1989 Jaime Paz Zamora was elected President.

	Chamber of Deputies	*Senate*
Nationalist Revolutionary Movement - Historic (MRNH)	40	9
Democratic Nationalist Action (ADN)	38	8
Movement of the Revolutionary Left (MIR)	33	8
Conscience of the Fatherland (Condepa)	9	2
United Left (IU)	10	-
Total	**130**	**27**

PARTY BY PARTY DATA

Christian Democratic Party

Partido Demócrata Cristiano (PDC)
Address. Casilla 4345, La Paz.
Leadership. Jorge Agreda Valderrama (l.); Antonio Canelas-Galatoire (s.-g.).
Orientation. Centrist.
Founded. February 1954.
History. The PDC had its origins in Roman Catholic socio-political lay study groups and was founded as the Social Christian Party by Remo di Natale. In the 1962 partial elections its leader Benjamín Miguel obtained the party's first congressional seat, and at its November 1964 congress, the party took its present name. Although it boycotted the general election of 1966, called by the military junta, the PDC accepted the Labour portfolio in 1967 in a military government from which it resigned when the President, Gen. Barrientos, sent in the army to fight protesting miners. Thereafter the PDC opposed all subsequent military regimes, which eventually led to the exile of both Miguel and the party's organizing secretary, Félix Vargas, from 1974 until after President Bánzer was overthrown in 1978. In the general election of July 1979 the PDC, in an alliance with the Nationalist Revolutionary Movement-Historic (MNRH) and three minor parties, won nine seats in the Chamber of Deputies and three in the Senate. It was given a Cabinet post after democracy was restored in October 1982. In the general election of 1985 the PDC's presidential candidate Luis Ossio Sanjinés won a mere 1.4 per cent of the vote while the party's representation in Congress dwindled to three seats. In the run-up to the May 1989 elections, the PDC negotiated an alliance with the left-wing MIR, but when the talks broke down in January 1989, the PDC agreed to join forces with the right-wing Democratic Nationalist Action (ADN). Ossio Sanjinés became Bánzer's running mate in the presidential elections on May 7, 1989. On August 6 he was appointed Vice-President of the new Patriotic Accord coalition government as a result of the pact with the ADN. In a major cabinet re-shuffle in August 1991, Ossio Sanjinés retained his post but was unsuccessful in demanding an enlarged "quota of power" for the PDC in government.
Structure. The party membership elects a national consultative council and a national committee, as well as departmental, provincial and regional committees.
International affiliations. Christian Democrat International; Christian Democrat Organization of America.

Communist Party of Bolivia

Partido Comunista de Bolivia (PCB)
Leadership. Humberto Ramírez (s.-g.).
Orientation. Orthodox communist before the collapse of the Soviet Union and the Eastern bloc.
Founded. January 1950.
History. Formed by dissident members of the Party of the Revolutionary Left (PIR) youth section, the PCB attained legal status after the 1952 revolution. The party at first supported the revolutionary MNR government but soon became critical of its one-party rule and stood against it in the general election of 1956, in alliance with the PIR. It won only 1.5 per cent of the vote and in 1960, when the PCB contested an election by itself for the only time in its history, it found support among only 1 per cent of the voters. In 1965 the party split into a pro-Soviet and a pro-Chinese faction and both were banned in 1967 even though their involvement with the guerrillas of Che Guevara's National Liberation Army, then attempting to ignite a domestic revolution, was limited to some pro-Soviet PCB youth section members who were subsequently expelled. Although the ban was later lifted, the PCB was again driven underground during the Bánzer military regime of 1971 to 1978.

The party officially re-emerged as part of the Popular Democratic Union (UDP) coalition which supported the bid of Hernán Siles Zuazo for the presidency (see Nationalist Revolutionary Movement of the Left) in the 1978, 1979 and 1980 elections. When Siles was finally appointed President by Congress in October 1982, he rewarded the PCB with the Labour and Mines Ministries. The two ministers resigned in November 1984 because of their opposition to the government's economic policies and a crisis in the PCB following the ousting of the party from the leadership of the powerful Bolivian Workers' Centre (COB), the major trade union confederation, in September.

The PCB, under new leadership, fought the 1985 general election in the United People's Front alliance with the Revolutionary Party of the National Left (PRIN) and two dissident factions of the MIR, which

won four Congressional seats. In July of that year, it expelled a minority faction which included a large part of the PCB youth wing. In an attempt to improve its appeal to young voters the party joined the left-wing Patriotic Alliance for the 1987 municipal elections and in September 1988 it became a founder member of the United Left (IU). In the general election of May 7, 1989, the IU candidate Antonio Araníbar Quiroga (see Free Bolivia Movement) won a negligible percentage of the valid vote but the alliance gained 10 seats in the Chamber of Deputies.
Structure. The national congress elects the Central Committee, which in turn elects the general secretary and the Political Commission.
Membership. 500 (1989 claim); the PCB has a strong influence in the Bolivian Mine Workers' Union (FSTMB) and the Bolivian Workers' Centre (COB).
Publication. Unidad (Unity).

Conscience of the Fatherland

Conciencia de Patria (Condepa)
Leadership. Carlos Palenque Avilés (l.).
Orientation. Populist.
History. In a general election on May 7, 1989, Condepa won nine seats in the Chamber of Deputies and two in the Senate. During the presidential run-off in the Congress in August, the party threw its support behind Paz Zamora, candidate of the Movement of the Revolutionary Left (MIR), but the party remained in opposition to the subsequent Patriotic Accord (AP) government. The party reaped more success four months later when, in the municipal elections of Dec. 3, 1989, Condepa won in the administrative capital, La Paz, but its candidate Carlos Palenque Avilés failed to attract sufficient votes from other parties in the city council to be named mayor. In July 1991, Condepa joined the MNRH and the MBL in breaking off talks with the AP, claiming that it had violated the impartiality of the new electoral law, approved by Congress in June, by appointing its own preferred choices to the new Electoral Court. In the municipal elections of December 1991, however, Condepa candidate Julio Mantilla Cuéllar was elected mayor of La Paz, with 26.35 per cent of the vote, and the party also won the major neighbouring city of El Alto with 34 per cent of the vote, both results representing the party's most significant achievement to date. Mantilla pledged to use his office to bring justice to the poorest sectors of the population.

Democratic Nationalist Action

Acción Democrática Nacionalista (ADN)
Leadership. Gen. (retd.) Hugo Bánzer Suárez (l.); Guillermo Fortún (s.-g.).
Orientation. Right-wing nationalist, but believes in free market economic policies and the opening up of the country to foreign investment.
Founded. 1979.
History. The ADN was formed as a vehicle for former dictator Gen. (retd.) Hugo Bánzer Suárez (1971-78) for the July 1979 general election in which he came third with 14.9 per cent of the vote. In the 1980 general election his share of the vote increased slightly to 16.9 per cent and the ADN won 30 congressional seats which were finally taken up when Congress was recalled in September 1982. The ADN initially supported the July 1980 coup led by Gen. Luis García Meza but in April 1981 this was withdrawn. A month later Bánzer was arrested on a charge of plotting a counter-coup.

The general election of July 1985 resulted in Bánzer winning the largest volume of votes, 28.6 per cent, and the ADN gained 51 seats in Congress. However, because no presidential candidate had obtained a clear majority, a centre-left alliance in Congress elected Víctor Paz Estenssoro of the Nationalist Revolutionary Movement-Historic (MNRH) as President. Bánzer accepted the election result only under pressure from other Latin American governments. The ADN was nevertheless assured a share of power with the signing of the "Pact for Democracy" with the MNRH on Oct. 16, 1985. The pact was opposed by Bánzer's aide Eudoro Galindo, who was subsequently expelled, causing a small section of the ADN membership and several deputies to defect to his Nationalist Democratic Front (FDN). The Pact remained in place until November 1988, surviving the deep animosity which existed between the ADN and the MNRH, despite their agreement on Estenssoro's controversial economic austerity programme.

For the general election of May 7, 1989, the ADN entered into an alliance with the Christian Democratic Party (PDC). Bánzer, the alliance's joint candidate, won 22.7 per cent of the vote in the presidential election and was narrowly beaten by the MNRH candidate Gonzalo Sánchez de Losada. Personal dislike between the two candidates, however, prevented the ADN-MNRH pact from being renewed and ensured that neither was elected President. On August 5, a day before the scheduled second round of voting in Congress, Bánzer withdrew from the race and switched the votes of the 46 ADN congressional members to the Movement of the Revolutionary Left (MIR) enabling its candidate, Jaime Paz Zamora, to be elected to the presidency.

The subsequent ADN-MIR-led Patriotic Accord (AP) coalition government assumed power on Aug. 8, 1989. In return for the Presidency, Paz Zamora awarded the ADN 10 out of 18 ministerial posts, including the most important portfolios of Finance, Defence and Foreign Affairs. Bánzer personally took the chair of the *Consejo del Gobierno de Unidad y Convergencia* (Political Council of Convergence and National Unity), a post which gave him effective control over government policy, appointments to top public positions and changes in the hierarchy of the armed forces.

The ADN's dominance in the AP coalition was underlined in Cabinet changes in August 1991 and March 1992 when it retained the most influential portfolios. Some prominent ADN ministers were replaced in government to enable them to join Bánzer's campaign staff for the forthcoming 1993 presidential elections. In the same month, MIR leaders had ratified Bánzer as the AP's presidential candidate.

However, over 2,000 local ADN leaders were reported to have resigned from the party in March 1992 in protest at the leadership's increasingly authoritarian style. An anti-MIR faction calling itself ADN-Histórica, based in the eastern city of Santa Cruz, had formed in May 1991 to campaign for an end of the AP coalition.

Free Bolivia Movement

Movimiento Bolivia Libre (MBL)
Address. Calle Batallón, Victoria esq Armentia 807, Casilla 10382, La Paz.
Leadership. Antonio Araníbar Quiroga (l.).
Orientation. Nominally left-wing.
Founded. 1985.
History. The party was formed by the then general secretary of the main Movement of the Revolutionary Left (MIR), Antonio Araníbar Quiroga, after he and a left-wing section of the MIR split away in protest against participation in the Siles Zuazo government. Araníbar fought the 1985 election as the presidential candidate of the left-wing People's United Front alliance and won 2.2 per cent of the vote, while the alliance obtained four seats in Congress.

The municipal elections of 1987 showed an increase in MBL's support—the party won in Bolivia's legal capital Sucre and came second in Cochabamba. In 1988 its electoral success brought the MBL to the leadership of the newly formed United Left (IU). Araníbar fought for the Presidency as candidate for the IU in the May 1989 elections but won a negligible percentage of the vote. In February 1990 the MBL left the alliance.

In 1990 and 1991, the party was prominent in protracted opposition dialogue with the Patriotic Accord (AP) government over such issues as the independence of the Supreme Court and the establishment of a new electoral system presided over by a impartial electoral court. The opposition had withdrawn from the talks, accusing the government of directly manipulating the judicial and electoral systems (see AP). In March 1992, Aranibar led an MBL delegation on visits to China and North Korea, during which he expressed a wish for close relations with the Korean Workers' Party (KWP).

Movement of the Revolutionary Left

Movimiento de la Izquierda Revolucionaria (MIR)
Address. Avenida América 119, 20 Piso, La Paz.
Leadership. Jaime Paz Zamora (l.); Óscar Eid Franco (s.-g.).
Orientation. Left-wing rhetoric but in power the MIR has proved to be conservative. Its power base is mainly the liberal urban middle class.
Founded. September 1971.
History. The MIR arose out of a merger of small left-wing groups and young Christian Democrats and was formed in opposition to the 1971 military coup. It drew considerable support from the radical student movement and was linked to the National Liberation Army (ELN) in the early years of the Bánzer military dictatorship (1971-78).

It gradually moved away from its Marxist roots but nevertheless remained a strong opposition to the regime which continued to persecute and imprison members of the MIR, among them Bánzer's future political ally, Jaime Paz Zamora (see Patriotic Accord).

The party contested the elections of 1978, 1979 and 1980 as part of an alliance led by the Nationalist Revolutionary Movement of the Left (see MNRI) with

Jaime Paz Zamora as running mate to the victorious but ill-fated leader of the Nationalist Revolutionary Movement of the Left (MNRI) Hernán Siles Zuazo, in 1979 and 1980. Zamora was forced into exile under the García Meza military regime which took power following the 1980 election, and eight MIR leaders were tortured and killed during a raid on a party meeting. When in October 1982 Siles finally took office he appointed Zamora Vice-President and gave six Cabinet posts to members of the MIR. Only three months later, in January 1983, the party clashed with Siles over economic reforms proposed by the MIR and resigned from the government.

It rejoined the Siles government in April 1984 despite opposition from the left in the MIR, led by Walter Delgadillo, the general secretary of the Bolivian Workers' Centre (COB), the major trade union confederation. Delgadillo subsequently left the party and formed the MIR-Masses (see Patriotic Alliance—AP). Another faction opposed to the government split away from the MIR in late 1984 and formed the Free Bolivia Movement to which the MIR's general secretary Antonio Araníbar Quiroga defected. In December the MIR ministers again withdrew their support for the Siles government and Zamora gave up his vice-presidential post in order to contest the presidential elections the following year.

Zamora came third with 8.8 per cent of the vote in the July 1985 presidential contest and in the simultaneous congressional elections the depleted MIR won 16 seats. When Congress had to vote in the second round of the presidential elections, the MIR joined with other centre-left parties in electing the presidential runner-up Víctor Paz Estenssoro of the Nationalist Revolutionary Movement-Historic (MNRH) in preference to ex-dictator Bánzer. However, once Paz Estenssoro was in power, the MIR strongly opposed his government's austerity programme to the extent that an MIR ex-minister was among those arrested under the state of emergency imposed following anti-austerity demonstrations in 1986.

It became clear in the December 1987 municipal election results that the MIR's stance against austerity and opposition to the US anti-drugs operations in the country had turned it into one of the two major parties, having especially attracted the votes of disillusioned former ADN supporters. Nevertheless in late 1988 the MIR approached the Christian Democratic Party with a view to forming an alliance but when by January 1989 they had not come any closer to an agreement, the MIR decided to contest the May 1989 general election alone, winning 41 congressional seats, Zamora being placed a close third with 19.64 per cent of the vote in the presidential race. However with no conclusive winner in the presidential election, the runner-up, Gen. Hugo Bánzer, of the right-wing National Democratic Action (ADN), withdrew and switched 46 ADN Congressional members to Jaime Paz Zamora who on Aug. 6 was duly elected by Congress to be President.

The price exacted for this support was the necessity for the MIR to share power with the ADN in a "Patriotic Accord" (AP). In the August 1991 major cabinet reshuffle, three MIR ministerial posts were allocated to members of the MIR-New Majority (MIR-NM) faction, who, due to the domination of the ADN, had previously been circumspect in their support for the party's involvement in the AP coalition (see ADN). However in March 1992, the MIR-NM confirmed its support for Bánzer as AP candidate in the 1993 presidential elections.

Nationalist Revolutionary Movement-Historic

Movimiento Nacionalista Revolucionario Histórico (MNRH)—although the party is now often referred to as the MNR with the demise of previous factions.
Address. Jenaro Sanjines 541, Pasaje Kuljis, La Paz.
Leadership. Gonzalo Sánchez de Lozada (l.); José Luis Harb (s.-g.).
Orientation. Right-wing believing in neo-liberal economic policies.
Founded. June 1941 as the Nationalist Revolutionary Movement (MNR).
History. Founded by among others Víctor Paz Estenssoro, the left-wing Hernán Siles Zuazo and the fascist sympathiser Carlos Montenegro, the party's policies reflected its leader's attempt to combine the nationalist developmentalist ideas of the Peruvian American Popular Revolutionary Alliance Party (APRA) with those of European fascism, especially as extolled by the Italian dictator Benito Mussolini. The MNR first participated in government in 1943-44 under President Villaroel.

When the military overthrew Villaroel in 1946, numerous MNR leaders were killed or exiled. Paz Estenssoro fought the elections of May 1951 from exile as the MNR's presidential candidate and won the highest vote (although not an outright majority). The incumbent President, however, handed over power to a military junta which, less than a year later, was toppled by an MNR-led popular uprising, known thereafter as the 1952 Revolution, assisted by the police and tin miners. Paz Estenssoro was finally allowed to return from Argentina and was appointed President in April 1952.

Paz Estenssoro's coalition government with the Labour Party introduced a number of progressive reforms, including the nationalization of the mines, agrarian reform and the enfranchisement of illiterates. The MNR remained in power for two more terms, with Siles Zuazo taking over the presidency in 1956 and Paz Estenssoro being elected President again in 1960.

In November 1964, following widespread strikes and disorder, Estenssoro was overthrown and forced into exile by his Vice-President, Gen. René Barrientos Ortuño, who took power with the assistance of the army. The MNR was thrown into disarray and only re-emerged on the political scene in 1971 as supporters of the military coup of Gen. Hugo Bánzer (see National Democratic Action).

The MNR participated in Bánzer's government until 1974 when it was expelled for protesting that the promised process of democratization had not begun. By then, the left wing of the party, led by Siles Zuazo, had already broken away and formed the Nationalist Revolutionary Movement of the Left (MNRI), to which Paz Estenssorro's faction, MNRH, came second in the 1979 and 1980 presidential elections; Paz Estenssoro was beaten by Siles in both elections, winning only 35.9 per cent and 20.1 per cent of the vote respectively. The MNRH, however, won 44 seats in the Congress.

Following another period of military government (1980-82) and three years of opposition to the MNRI government, Paz Estenssoro once again made a bid for the presidency. In the general election of June 1985 he obtained 26.4 per cent of the vote, 2.2 per cent less than the ADN's candidate, Bánzer.

However, in a run-off congressional vote in August, the centre-left parties added their votes to those of the 59 MNRH Congressmen and brought Paz to power. His third term in office set a future precedent for the party and the country. He quickly introduced a strict austerity programme to reduce rampant inflation, a policy persisted with despite the collapse of the international tin market in late 1985.

Faced with general labour unrest, repressed under a 90-day state of siege, Paz Estenssoro found greater common ground with the right-wing ADN than with his erstwhile supporters of the centre left. A "Pact for Democracy" between the MNRH and the ADN was duly signed in October 1985. In the municipal elections of December 1987 the MNRH won fewer municipalities than the ADN and MIR, reflecting widespread discontent with the government. This was further fuelled by the USA-assisted anti-drug programme which threatened the livelihood of many peasant coca growers, whose numbers had been swollen by unemployed miners. Nevertheless, in the general election of May 7, 1989, the MNRH presidential candidate Gonzalo Sánchez de Lozada, the former Minister of Planning, won with 23.07 per cent of the vote, not sufficient to give him the presidency. A run-off election in the newly elected Congress, in which the MNRH had 49 seats, did not produce a renewal of the "Pact of Democracy" with the ADN. Personal animosity between de Lozada and ADN leader Bánzer meant the ADN switching its support to Jaime Paz Zamora of the Movement of the Revolutionary Left (MIR) who was elected President.

After the defeat in Congress, the MNRH applied to the National Election Court to declare the elections void because of alleged irregularities in some departments, but without success. In 1990, as the leading opposition party, the MNRH also started impeachment proceedings against Paz Zamora, claiming that by extraditing Col. Luis Arce Gómez to the USA in December 1989 on drug-trafficking charges, he went against the Constitution and the Supreme Court, most of whose judges were linked to the MNRH (see Patriotic Accord—AP). The party participated in national dialogues with the AP government in 1990 and 1991 on the desirability of electoral reform and the need to decentralize the state and ensure the independence of the judiciary. However, the party broke off negotiations, protesting that the AP's impeachment of eight Supreme Court judges in 1990 (see AP) and its manipulation of the appointment of members to a new electoral Court was intended to facilitate an AP victory in the forthcoming (1993) presidential elections. However in the December 1991 departmental and municipal elections, the party won 24.7 per cent of the overall vote, coming a close second to the AP. It won its first departmental victories in two years taking the regions of Cochabamba, Tarija and Santa Cruz and emphatically defeating the AP in the cities of Tarija and Trinidad, and in the country's second most populous city of Santa Cruz de la Sierra.

Patriotic Accord

Acuerdo Patriótico (AP)

Founded. 1989.

History. The AP ruling coalition government, the product of a post-1989 general election agreement, was made up of the unlikely alliance of the left-wing Movement of the Revolutionary Left (MIR) and the right-wing National Democratic Action (ADN), led by the ex-dictator Gen. (retd.) Hugo Bánzer, which assumed power on August 8, 1989, with MIR's Jaime Paz Zamora (who had been tortured and almost died under Bánzer's military regime) installed as President (see MIR). The Christian Democratic Party (PDC) also joined the coalition. Zamora appointed eight MIR members and ten ADN members to his Cabinet, the latter taking the key ministries of Finance, Defence and Foreign Affairs. The MIR were willing partners with the ADN in ensuring that the previous Nationalist Revolutionary Movement-Historic (MNRH) government's economic austerity programme was continued, arguing that such shock therapy would attract increased multilateral and bilateral aid. The AP declared a national state of siege from November 1989 until February 1990, during which strikes were banned. The municipal elections of December 1989 nevertheless showed that the AP still retained support, the MIR-ADN alliance winning six of the nine departments but losing the important and populous municipalities of the (administrative) capital La Paz and the southern (official) capital of Sucre.

Zamora, in the expectation of receiving increased US aid, became a leading advocate of US anti-drugs policies in the region, which emphasized the eradication of coca crops and an all-out war on traffickers. He agreed in December 1990 to the extradition of Col. Luis Arce Gómez (who had served as Interior Minister during the dictatorship of Gen. García Meza in 1981) to the USA for trial on drug-trafficking charges. The extradition brought the government into conflict with the MNRH-dominated Supreme Court which argued that it represented a violation of national sovereignty. Extending its commitment to the anti-drugs war, the AP government in April 1991 approved the training of army anti-drugs units by US advisors. This was an important step towards the full militarization of the fight against drugs, despite widespread evidence of endemic drug-related corruption in the army, a fact which had provoked the US government in February 1991 to threaten to withhold US$100,000,000 in development aid unless remedial measures were enforced. A direct result was the resignation of the head of the Special Force for the Fight against Drug-Trafficking (FELCN), a personal appointment of the Interior Minister Capobianco Ribera, who subsequently resigned when accused of drug trafficking. The militarization of the anti-drugs programme also provoked bitter resentment from peasant growers of coca plants, the raw base for the production of cocaine, in the absence of a planned and well- financed crop substitution programme.

In November 1990 another clash with the Supreme Court over the government's imposition of beer tax led to the impeachment of eight Supreme Court judges, which the opposition claimed was an excuse by the AP to create a compliant judiciary to facilitate its electoral victory in the 1993 presidential elections. In July 1991, the AP continued to alienate further the main opposition parties, the MNR, Conscience of the Fatherland (Condepa) and the Free Bolivia Movement (MBL), when it appointed its own hand-picked members to the new Electoral Court, a move which the opposition argued violated the spirit of the new electoral law, approved by the Congress in June 1991, which had offered the prospect of clean and fair elections in the future.

Equally controversial was the government's privatization law, presented in December 1991, whose chief target was the state mining company (Comibol). This resulted in general strikes being called by the major union confederation, the Bolivian Workers' Centre (COB), in December and January 1992, before it agreed to sign an accord with the AP to negotiate change rather than have it imposed from above. Growing protest was also evident in many towns and cities, especially La Paz, as the government cut back council budgets, with the opposition accusing the AP of favouring the local governments under its control. The AP also announced a plan to reduce the size of the public sector by over 35 per cent in the following five years and one to restructure the Civil Service.

In the December 1991 municipal elections, although winning the largest percentage of the vote, the AP lost political control in three departments and some major cities, most particulary La Paz and its major neighbouring city of El Alto. The result also showed that its support had shifted markedly from urban to rural areas where government development plans and projects had made an impact.

A major Cabinet reshuffle in March 1992 underlined the ADN as the dominant partner in the AP coalition (see ADN) but nationally the government was perceived to be weak. It faced almost constant opposition from within the Congress, with disaffection with the autocratic style of government evident in both ADN and MIR. In early April Paz Zamora stated that "Congress should work properly, so that there should be no need to close it", considered to be a warning that if the legislature persisted in its refusal to pass important government bills, the AP, following the recent example of President Alberto Fujimori in Peru, might use the military to disband it.

Patriotic Alliance

Alianza Patriótica (AP)
Leadership. Walter Delgadillo (l.).
Founded. 1985.
History. The party was formed by Walter Delgadillo, the leader of the radical MIR faction MIR-Masses, and former leader of the Bolivian Workers' Centre (COB) trade union confederation. In September 1988 the AP became a founder member of the United Left (IU) for which Walter Delgadillo fought the elections in May 1989 as the running-mate of Antonio Aranibar Quiroga (see Free Bolivia Movement—MBL).

Revolutionary Front of the Left

Frente Revolucionario de la Izquierda (FRI)
History. In August 1991 the FRI joined the Patriotic Accord government and obtained the Labour portfolio in an August 1991 Cabinet reshuffle.

Socialist Party-One

Partido Socialista-Uno (PS1)
Leadership. Roger Córtez (l.).
Orientation. Left-wing.
Founded. 1971 as the Socialist Party.
History. The PS1 was formed by the merger of three minor parties which had supported the former President, Gen. Alfredo Ovando Candía. In the mid-1970s the party suffered a split: the right wing led by Guillermo Aponte backed the MRNI and the left renamed itself the Socialist Party-One. In the elections of 1978, 1979 (in which the PS1 won five congressional seats) and 1980 (winning 11 congressional seats), the PS1 fielded Marcelo Quiroga Santa Cruz as its presidential candidate. He was assassinated by troops during the 1980 military coup and thereafter the party's popularity declined.

The party contested the 1985 elections with little success, coming sixth with 2.2 per cent of the vote and winning five seats in the Congress. The PS1, which strongly opposed the Paz Estenssoro government's economic and social policies (see Nationalist Revolutionary Movement-Historic), joined the United Left (IU) at its inception in 1988. When the date for the municipal elections for 1991 was announced, the PS1 argued that they should be postponed so that more people would have the chance to register on the electoral roll.

United Left

Izquierda Unida (IU)
Leadership. Germán Gutiérrez (l.).
Founded. September 1988.
History. The IU was the product of an alliance of eight parties formed to contest the May 1989 general election. Led by the Free Bolivia Movement (MBL), the IU fielded MBL leader Antonio Aranîbar Quiroga as its presidential candidate with Walter Delgadillo of the Patriotic Alliance (AP) as his running mate. The IU won 12 congressional seats, a poor result compared with that achieved by its component parties in the 1985 elections, as Aranîbar won a negligible percentage of the total vote. However, in the municipal elections of December 1989 the IU retained the MBL's hold on power in the (official) capital, Sucre. Two months later, however, the MBL left the alliance, leaving it in a state of disarray. In the municipal elections in December, it won 4 per cent of the total vote.
Membership. The leading member parties are the Communist Party of Bolivia (PCB), the **Patriotic Alliance (AP) and the Socialist Party-One (PS1).**

Minor parties

Campesinos Party *(Partido de los Campesinos)*; founded in May 1991 by the Sole Bolivian Farmworkers' Trade Union Confederation (*Confederación Sindical Unica de Trabajadores*

Campesinos de Bolivia—CSUTCB). Its aim is primarily to gain full autonomy for the Indian regions, and the party claims to have established its own army to be used in regaining original Indian territories. During 1991 it organized protests against the Patriotic Accord (AP) government's militarization of the fight against drug-trafficking and the eradication of coca crops without the guarantee of substitute products with viable markets.

Civic Solidarity Union (*Unión Cívica Solidaridad—UCS*); the party won Trinidad, capital of the Beni department, in the December 1989 municipal elections. Its leader and presidential candidate in the May 1989 presidential election, Max Fernández, had his candidacy nullified by the Electoral Court for forging approximately 40,000 of the 60,000 votes he had received. He has nevertheless announced his candidature for the 1993 presidential elections.

Community and Democracy (Communiad y Democracia—CyD); Carlos Calvo Galindo (l.); formed in April 1992 in the eastern city of Cochabamba, following a split from the ADN. Calvo Galindo is ex-President of the Confederation of Private Business of Bolivia.

Nationalist Revolutionary Movement of the Left (*Movimiento Nacionalista Revolucionario de la Izquierda-MNRI*); formed after the left wing of the MNR split away in the early 1970s. It was led by the MNR founding member and former President (1956-60) Hernán Siles Zuazo (see Nationalist Revolutionary Movement—Historic (MNRH). The party was the leading force of the Popular Democratic Unity (UDP) alliance during the 1978 general election. Siles Zuazo won both the 1979 and 1980 presidential elections with 36 and 38.7 per cent but each time was prevented from taking power by a military coup. In October 1982 he was finally allowed to return from his Peruvian exile and take office.

His UDP government, which was increasingly dominated by the MNRI, rapidly lost support from the left, the unions and the peasantry as it tried to placate multilateral lending agencies in the search for international loans, to the neglect of initiating urgent social reforms.

The elections of June 1985 resulted in the massive defeat of the MNRI presidential candidate Roberto Jordán Pando, who received a mere 4.8 per cent of the vote, the party obtaining only eight seats in the Congress. It proved a setback from which the party never recovered.

People's Revolutionary Alternative (*Alternativa Revolucionaria del Pueblo—ARP*); founded in the late 1980s; it opposed a 1988 law reducing the cultivation of coca crops (the raw base of cocaine), the basic livelihood of many Bolivian peasants and redundant workers, especially tin miners, in the absence of any marketable alternatives. The party's candidate in the 1989 presidential elections was the former veteran COB trade union leader Juan Lechín Oquendo who received a negligible percentage of the vote.

Main Guerrilla Groups

Armed Liberation Front Zárate Willka (*Frente Armado de Liberación Zárate Willka—FAL-ZW*); the Armed Liberation Front (FAL) was first heard of in August 1988 when dynamite was thrown at a convoy taking the then US Secretary of State George Shultz from the airport to La Paz. The following year, the group claimed responsibility for the killing of two US Mormon missionaries. Zárate Willka (ZW) emerged at about the same time and is believed to have been formed in imitation of the Peruvian Maoist "Shining Path" (*Sendero Luminoso*) guerrilla group. The ZW claimed responsibility for bombs planted in front of the presidential palace in January 1990 as a protest against the new austerity measures. In 1991 ZW and FAL were believed to have amalgamated.

Néstor Paz Zamora Commission-National Liberation Army (*Comisión Néstor Paz Zamora-Ejército de Liberación Nacional—CNPZ-ELN*); although it claims to wish to revive the Guevara-Teoponte guerrilla spirit of the 1960s, the group does not appear to be strictly left-wing. Its leader, "Comandante Miguel" (Miguel Northtufster, alias Martin Kesner), was an Italian neo-fascist and its activities were directed against US military bases in Bolivia.

In July 1991 the group claimed to be the perpetrators of an attack on a US marines' residence.

Tupaj Katari Guerrilla Army (*Ejército Guerrillero Tupaj Katari—EGTK*); Raúl Pinto (who was arrested on April 12, 1992) is thought to be its chief thinker; a left-wing guerrilla group, taking its name from an 18th-century indigenous rebel leader, which came to prominence following 48 attacks in the cities of La Paz, Cochabamba, Sucre, Potosi and Oruro between

July 4 and March 1992. Its targets included electricity pylons, aqueducts, gas and oil installations, dams and public and private offices. Its members have also undertaken bank and personal robberies, estimated to total US$590,000 by April 1992. The government claimed that the group was claiming to fight for indigenous communities i justify its illegal activities. At least 16 of its leaders had been arrested by April 1992 which the government claimed had "practically dismantled" the group. However, the EGTK claims to have 600 cells with an average of five members in each one. Another group, the **Tomas Katari Comunero Army** *(Ejercito Comunero Tomas Katari—ECTK)*, claimed responsibility for a bomb attack on the AP government headquarters in the southern town of Liallagua on Dec. 1, 1991. The EGTK is also thought to operate under the name "Z Group" *(Groupo Z)* or have contact with a guerrilla group by this name.

Brazil

Capital: Brasília **Population: 150,400,000**

Brazil broke away from Portugal as a separate kingdom in 1822 and became a federal republic in 1889. In 1930 widespread demands for economic and social reform resulted in a coup which installed Getúlio Vargas who ruled Brazil as a benevolent dictator for 15 years. A six-year period of military rule was followed by relative democracy between 1951-64. Brazil came under direct military dictatorship with democratic pretensions from 1964 to 1985. Since that date steps towards full democracy were consolidated by the introduction a new constitution in 1988, leading in November 1990 to Brazil's first fully democratic election since 1960. The government of President Fernando Collor de Mello, inaugurated in March 1990, promised a fresh beginning but its social and economic policies, driven by the belief in the free market and wholesale privatization, increased divisions within the country and caused a prolonged political crisis.

Constitutional structure

Under the 1988 Constitution, executive power lies with the President. He appoints and leads a 13-member Cabinet and has also the power to convene in an emergency a Council of the Republic which consists of the Vice-President of the Republic, the Minister of Justice, the presidents and leaders of the majority and minority in each house, two senators and two deputies elected by their respective legislative house and two people appointed directly by the President of the Republic. An emergency Council of the Republic was convened in September 1991 to advise the President on action to be taken in a deep crisis, including the declaration of a state of siege, especially if mounting unrest in the military became a threat to democracy. Legislative authority is vested in a bicameral National Congress composed of a Chamber of Deputies and a Federal Senate.

Electoral system

The President is elected directly by universal suffrage for a period of five years and is not eligible for a second term. If no absolute majority is won by any one candidate in a presidential election, a second round of voting is contested by the two leading candidates. The first direct presidential elections since 1960 took place on November 15, 1989.

07.90
VENEZUELA
GUYANA
SURINAM
FR. GUYANA
COLOMBIA
Boa Vista
RORAIMA
AMAPÁ
Macapá
Belém
São Luís
FERNANDO DE NORONHA
Fortaleza
Manaus
AMAZONAS
PARÁ
MARANHÃO
CEARÁ
RIO GRANDE DO NORTE
Natal
Teresina
BRAZIL
PARAÍBA
João Pessoa
PIAUÍ
PERNAMBUCO
Recife
TOCANTINS
Miracema do Tocantins
ALAGOAS
Maceió
SERGIPE
Aracaju
ACRE
Rio Branco
Pôrto Velho
RONDÔNIA
MATO GROSSO
BAHIA
Salvador
PERÚ
Brasília
GOIÁS
Goiânia
MINAS GERAIS
Cuiabá
BOLIVIA
MATO GROSSO DO SUL
Belo Horizonte
ESPÍRITO SANTO
Vitória
Campo Grande
SÃO PAULO
PARAGUAY
RIO DE JANEIRO
Rio de Janeiro
PARANÁ
São Paulo
Curitiba
CHILE
SANTA CATARINA
Florianópolis
Pacific Ocean
Atlantic Ocean
RIO GRANDE DO SUL
Pôrto Alegre
ARGENTINA
URUGUAY
0 km 1000

Sequence of elections since 1982

Date	*Type*	*Winning party*
November 1982	Congressional	Social Democratic Party (PDS) but no overall majority
January 1985	Presidential (indirect)	Democratic Alliance (AD) (Tancredo Neves & José Sarney)
November 1986	Congressional	Party of the Brazilian Democratic Movement (PMDB)
December 1989	Presidential (direct)	National Reconstruction Party (PRN) (Fernando Collor)
October 1990	Congressional	No majority

Congressional Elections, Oct. 3, 1990

Party	*Chamber of Deputies seats*
Brazilian Democratic Movement Party (PMDB)	109
Liberal Front Party (PFL)	92
Democratic Labour Party (PDT)	46
National Reconstruction Party (PRN)	41
Social Democratic Party (PDS)	40
Brazilian Social Democratic Party (PSDB)	37
Workers' Party (PT)	34
Brazilian Labour Party (PTB)	33
Christian Democratic Party (PDC)	21
Liberal Party (PL)	15
Brazilian Socialist Party (PSB)	12
Communist Party of Brazil (PCdoB)	5
Christian Socialist Party (PSC)	5
Social Reform Party (PRS)	4
Brazilian Communist Party (PCB)	3
Revolutionary Workers Party (PTR)	2
Socialist Workers Party (PST)	2
National Municipal Party (PMN)	1
Democratic Socialist Party (PSD)	1
	503

The new Deputies took office on February 1, 1991

November 15, 1989 Presidential Election

Candidate	*votes*	*% of votes*
Fernando Collor de Mello (PRN)	20,611,011	30.48
(Lula) da Silva (PT)	11,622,673	17.18
Leonel Brizola (PDT)	11,168,228	16.51
Mário Covas (PSDB)	7,790,392	11.52
Paulo Maluf (PDS)	5,989,575	8.86
Others	10,449,133	15.45

Number of valid votes 67,631,012

Collor de Mello won the second round of the voting on December 17, 1989 with 53.03 per cent of the 66,166,362 valid votes cast.

State Governors Election Oct. 3 and Nov.25, 1990

Party	*No. of Governors*
Liberal Front Party (PFL)	9
Brazilian Democratic Movement Party (PMDB)	7 (incl. Sao Paulo)
Democratic Labour Party (PDT)	3 (incl. Rio de Janeiro)
PTR	2
Brazilian Labour Party (PTB)	2
Social Democratic Party (PDS)	1
PSC	1
Brazilian Social Democratic Party (PSDB)	1
Social Reform Party (PRS)	1
Total	**27**

Members of the Chamber of Deputies are directly elected every four years by proportional representation. The total number of seats in the Chamber of Deputies varies according to the population in each state and federal district, (the three territories elect four deputies each); the current number of deputies is 503. Members of the 72-seat federal Senate serve an eight-year term; two-thirds of them are elected at one time, and the other third four years later. The 23 states, three territories and the federal district of Brasilia each elect three senators by proportional representation.

Each state also directly elects a governor by universal suffrage for a four-year term. A second round of voting takes place in those states where no candidate has obtained 50 per cent or more of the vote, as was the case in the elections of late 1990. The governor of Brasília is nominated by the federal government.

Evolution of the Suffrage

Voting is compulsory for literate people between the ages of 18 and 70. For illiterates and for people aged 16, 17 and over 70 voting is voluntary. Women have had the vote since 1934, when the voting age was reduced to 18. Illiterates were enfranchised in 1977.

PARTY BY PARTY DATA

Brazilian Labour Party

Partido Trabalhista Brasileiro (PTB)
Leadership. Luís Gonzaga de Paiva Muniz (pres.); José Correia Pedroso Filho (s.-g.).
Orientation. Centrist.
Founded. 1980.
History. Like the Democratic Labour Party (PDT), the PTB claims to be the direct successor of the pre-1965 *Partido Trabalhista Brasileiro* founded in the 1940s by President Getulio Vargas. Although made up of a minority faction, the party won a court case shortly after its formation awarding it the use of the old party's name. The PTB generally had a lower profile and gained a lesser share of the popular vote than its direct rival, the PDT. Nevertheless, in the elections of 1982 the party won 14 seats in the Chamber of Deputies and one in the Senate, and in 1983 it joined the powerful Social Democratic Party (PDS) in a short-lived coalition supporting the military-appointed President Figueiredo.

In the congressional elections of October 1986, the party increased its representation in the legislature to 19 deputies who joined the opposition to the Sarney government.

The party's presence in the ranks of the opposition improved its profile (and image) and, following the congressional elections of October 1990, it returned 33 deputies to the Chamber. The party also won two governorships in November 1990.

Brazilian Social Democratic Party

Partido da Social Democracia Brasileira (PSDB)
Leadership. Tasso Jereissati (l.); Mário Covas (pres.).
Orientation. Centre-left.
Founded. June 1988.
History. The PSDB was formed by members of the *históricos* faction of the Party of the Brazilian Democratic Movement (PMDB) opposed to President Sarney's retention of the presidential system and his determination not to shorten his term of office. The catalyst, however, was the unsuccessful challenge by Mario Covas, PMDB leader in the Constituent Assembly, for the PMDB leadership. The new party also attracted defectors from the Liberal Front Party (PFL), the Brazilian Socialist Party (PSB), the Brazilian Labour Party (PTB) and the Social Democratic Party (PDS), and soon after its formation the PSDB became the third largest party in Congress, with eight senators and 60 deputies. The first electoral test for the party came on Nov. 15, 1989 when Covas stood as presidential candidate. He came fourth with 11.52 per cent of the valid vote. In October the following year the party lost 23 seats in the Chamber of Deputies in the congressional elections, leaving it with 37, and won control of one state. The PSDB Senator José Richa proposed a motion for a plebiscite in early 1992 to decide on the adoption of a parliamentary system which would curtail the president's powers. This, however, did not deter the

party from proposing an alliance with the ruling National Reconstruction Party (PRN) in October 1991, which was rejected by President Collor. After a proposal for a parliamentary system was defeated in Congress due to presidential interference, the PSDB declared itself in direct opposition to the government.

Brazilian Socialist Party

Partido Socialista Brasileiro (PSB)
Leadership. Jamil Hadad (pres.); João Herrman Neto (l.).
Orientation. Left-wing.
Founded. 1985.
History. The PSB managed to send only one deputy and two senators to Congress following the elections of November 1986. However, by October 1990 the party had established itself as a left-wing opposition party and increased its representation in the Chamber of Deputies to 12 seats. The PSB formed part of the left-wing bloc openly hostile to the Collor government.

Christian Democratic Party

Partido Demócrata Cristão (PDC)
Leadership. Mauro Borges (pres.); Roberto Balestra (l.).
Orientation. Centre-right; the party aims to continue in the spirit of the old PDC which was banned in 1965, standing for social justice, Christian solidarity but also believing in the market economy and the right to property.
Founded. 1985.
History. The party was formed in time for the 1985-86 electoral campaign and in the elections of November 1986 won three seats in the Chamber and one in the Senate. The party has since gained in strength and following the November 1990 elections it had 21 Deputies in Congress, whose support for the Collor government has fluctuated. The party started a campaign for pay parity between the legislature, executive and judiciary in early 1991.
Structure. The party has directorates at national, state and regional levels.
Publication. *Folhetin* (Broadsheet)

Communist Party of Brazil

Partido Comunista do BrasilM (PCdoB)
Leadership. Harold Lima (l.); Joao Amazonas (s.-g.).
Orientation. The party's continued support for the Albanian Communist party alienated other left-wing parties; this was despite the demise of the Hoxa regime in December 1990 and the mass exodus of Albanians. Never far from controversy, the party in 1990 advocated the exploitation of the Amazonian mineral-rich subsoil.
Founded. 1961.
History. The PCdoB originated in a Maoist faction within the Brazilian Communist Party (PCB — now renamed Popular Socialist Party — PSP). It split away from the PCB and set up as a separate party under the PCB's original name after the Communist Party had abandoned internationalism. Banned as soon as it was founded, the PCdoB worked within the Brazilian Democratic Movement (MDB — see Party of the Brazilian Democratic Movement), the official opposition party. After the death of Mao and the arrest of the "gang of four" in 1976, the PCdoB turned away from China and became pro-Albanian.

In the same year a raid by security forces on a secret meeting in São Paulo resulted in the murder of three central committee members, including the party founder Pedro de Aranjo Pomar, and the arrest of six other members. The 1979 amnesty allowed the party to operate more openly, although it remained officially illegal until June 1985.

In the presidential campaign of 1985 the PCdoB supported the Democratic Alliance (see Liberal Front Party) candidate Tancredo Neves and in November 1986 it participated for the first time in an election under its own name, winning three seats in the Chamber of Deputies. In the hope that the Brazilian voters would choose a left-wing candidate in the first direct presidential election since the 1964 coup, the PCdoB joined the "Popular Front of Brazil" led by the Workers' Party (PT). Following the defeat of the PT's presidential candidate, Lula da Silva, the PCdoB campaigned again by itself in the 1990 congressional elections and won five seats in the Chamber. As part of a large left-of-centre opposition bloc, the PCdoB strongly opposed the policies of President Collor.
Structure. Ten leading members form the party's executive.
Membership. 50,000 (1988 claim; this figure is judged by observers to be wildly exaggerated).
Publication. Tribuna de Luta Operária (Tribune of the Workers' Struggle), weekly.
International affiliation. The PCdoB is officially recognized by the Albanian Party of Labour.

Democratic Labour Party

Partido Democrático Trabalhista (PDT)
Address. Rua 7 de Setembro 141, 3o andar, 20.050 Rio de Janeiro

Leadership. Leonel da Moura Brízola (pres.); Carmen Cynira (s.-g.).
Orientation. Social democratic; claims to stand for redistribution of income, land reform and full employment.
Founded. 1980.
History. Founded by Leonel Brízola, Doutel de Andrade (party vice-president until his death in January 1991) and other exiled members of the old Brazilian Labour Party (PTB) after their return to Brazil under the 1979 amnesty, the party had to adopt its current name after a dissident group won a court case over the old party name in 1980 (see PTB). The PDT had the support of 10 deputies from the start and in the general election of 1982 it increased its representation to 24 deputies and one senator thus forming the largest labour bloc in Congress. In the same elections Brízola was elected governor of Rio state, the party's power base. His school-building and other social programmes, although criticized by the right as a populist gesture to cover up corruption, were highly popular. He retired from the post in March 1987 in order to stand as the party's candidate in the next presidential election. His intended successor in Rio, Darcy Ribeiro, however, lost the 1986 gubernatorial election because of the PDT's criticism of President Sarney's reflationary economic policy when it was still widely supported.

Although the party had thrown its weight behind Tancredo Neves, the victorious Democratic Alliance candidate in the 1985 presidential elections, it was one of the few parties to take an early stand against the economic policies of his running-mate and replacement President Sarney. This unpopular stand, however, was vindicated in 1988, when, following social and industrial tensions, the PDT made major gains in the November municipal elections at the expense of the ruling Party of the Brazilian Democratic Movement (PMDB). The PDT's Progressive Unity Movement, initiated in mid-1987 to campaign for early and direct presidential elections, also drew widespread popular support. However by the time of the elections in November 1989, the majority of voters had turned away from the centre-left and placed their hopes in a newcomer in politics, the conservative Fernando Collor de Mello (see National Reconstruction Party). Leonel Brízola came third with 16.51 percent of the valid votes and was narrowly beaten to second place by the left-wing Workers' Party (PT) candidate "Lula" da Silva, whom he supported in the subsequent run-off.

The PDT recovered in the October 1990 congressional and gubernatorial elections, increasing its representation in the Chamber of Deputies from 24 to 46 seats, and thus becoming the third largest party. Brízola on Oct. 3, 1990, was again elected Governor of Rio de Janeiro. The large bloc of PDT congressional members who took their seats in February 1991 agreed on a truce with Collor to give his policies time to work. However due to the government's refusal to abandon or alter its privatization programme, the PDT declared in October 1991 that the truce was over and began to oppose the government directly.
International affiliations. Socialist International (full member party).

Liberal Front Party

Partido da Frente Liberal (PFL)
Leadership. António Aureliano de Mendonca Chaves (pres.); Ricardo Fuiza (l.).
Orientation. Centre-right.
Founded. 1984.
History. The party was formed by the liberal faction of the right-wing Social Democratic Party (PDS) following disagreements over the appointment of Paulo Salim Maluf as the party's candidate for the 1985 presidential elections. The PFL, with José Sarney (president of the military's official party ARENA 1970-79 and president of the PDS 1979-84) and the Brazilian Vice-President António Aureliano Chaves de Mendonca among its leaders, and 72 deputies and 12 senators having sworn allegiance to the party, became Brazil's third largest party in parliament almost overnight. Although the PFL was not officially a legal political party until June 1985, it nevertheless formed a Democratic Alliance with the Party of the Brazilian Democratic Movement (PMDB) in order to contest the indirect presidential elections of Jan. 15, 1985. Sarney was nominated vice-presidential running mate to the PMDB candidate Tancredo Neves, but had to join the PMDB formally in order to conform with the constitutional requirement that the president and vice-president be of the same party. Neves and Sarney were duly elected, but Neves was taken ill before he could be inaugurated as President in March. After Neves's death Sarney, who had in the interim been acting president, was officially awarded the presidency on April 22, 1985. His coalition

government, appointed by the late president-designate, consisted of members of the PFL, PMDB and some independents.

One of the first reforms under the Sarney government was the passing of a constitutional amendment restoring direct elections by universal suffrage, and, as a further step in the democratization process, Congress acted as a Constitutional Assembly from February 1987. On the other hand President Sarney governed mainly by decree and his refusal to cut short his presidency by more than one year caused great friction within the government alliance. Sarney's early success with the anti-inflationary Cruzado Plan and his agrarian programme to redistribute land, introduced in 1986, proved to be unsuccessful by early 1987.

The PFL grew in membership in 1986 largely through the splits in the Social Democratic Party (PDS) and was very successful in the congressional elections in the same year, obtaining 25 per cent of the national vote, 118 seats in the Chamber of Deputies and 14 in the Senate. In September 1987 the PFL officially withdrew from the Democratic Alliance, claiming that it was too dominated by the PMDB, although some PFL members retained their cabinet and other government posts, including then party leader Marco Antonio de Oliveira Maciel who was Head of the President's Civilian Household until April 1989. Sarney finally acquiesced to the popular demands for early elections, called in November 1989. The PFL's candidate for the presidency was Sarney's Mines and Energy Minister António Aureliano Chames de Mendonca, who obtained only a small percentage of the valid votes. In the elections of the following year, however, his party won the highest number of state governors' posts and again proved to be the second most popular party having gained 92 seats in the Chamber of Deputies. The PFL has used its congressional strength to support Collor's initial package of economic reforms but joined with opposition parties in opposing his increasing use of emergency decrees to impose his will on the Congress.
International affiliations. The party is an observer member of the Liberal International.

Liberal Party

Partido Liberal (PL)
Leadership. Álvaro Valle (pres.); Adolfo Oliveira (l.).
Orientation. Centre-right.
Founded. 1985.
History. The PL secured seven seats in the Chamber of Deputies and one in the Senate in the elections of Nov. 15, 1986. Although the party won no state governorships in the October/November 1990 general election, it more than doubled its representation in the lower house, bringing its number of deputies to 15. The party has been opposed to the Collor government and the new deputies joined the opposition bloc on taking their seats in February 1991.

National Reconstruction Party

Partido de Reconstrucao Nacional (PRN)
Leadership. Fernando Collor de Mello (l.).
Orientation. Conservative; in favour of a free market and privatization.
Founded. May 1989.
History. The PRN was formed as an electoral vehicle for the presidential ambitions of Fernando Collor de Mello, who previous to his candidature was governor of the small north-eastern state of Alagoas. His election promises included social spending, the rooting-out of government corruption and privilege and the streamlining of the civil service and privatizations, policies which appealed to the business community as well as the poor. A lavish campaign on TV Globo, owned by Collor's parents, and other media, together with widespread discontent with the Sarney government, helped Collor win 30.48 per cent of the vote, the highest amount of the valid poll. He drew strong support particularly in the small cities and towns of the south-eastern regions and the city of São Paulo. As he did not win an overall majority as required by the new Constitution, Collor had to contest a second round against the runner-up Lula da Silva of the Workers' Party (PT), whom he defeated on Dec. 17, 1989 with 53.03 per cent of the valid vote.

Collor was inaugurated in March 1990 and with only 24 PRN representatives in the Congress, called for national unity. After offering the defeated PT a share in government, which was refused, he appointed a Cabinet mainly composed of independents. Collor de Mello governed by executive persuasion, criticized by many as an "autocratic" style of government. The congressional elections of Oct. 3, 1990, increased the PRN's seats to 41 in the Chamber of Congress. By 1991 it became clear that the government's heralded anti-inflationary measures introduced in March 1990 were a failure, and Collor replaced them in February 1991 by price freezes. These measures were highly unpopular with businessmen and trade unionists alike, forcing the resignation of their chief architect, the Economy Minister Zélia Cardoso de Mello, in May 1991. The lack of support in Congress for the government became plain when Collor's proposed pay increases for the military and public servants were rejected in July 1991. In early September 1991 Collor formed an emergency Council of Representatives to advise him on action to be taken in a time of deep crisis and when faced with mounting military discontent over pay and conditions.

In an effort to restore his political standing, Collor submitted to Congress two bills to fight official corruption and took visible steps to disband his unofficial inner cabinet of friends and advisors—popularly known as the "Republic of Algoas" after his home state—who were accused of influence-peddling. Collor's wife had been forced to resign as head of a government welfare agency in August accused of the misappropriation of funds. By November 1991, however, Collor was entirely isolated in the Congress after breaking his promise to remain neutral during the passage of a proposal to curtail presidential powers. In an effort to retrieve the situation, he undertook a major re-shuffle of his Cabinet in March 1992 but failed to persuade the Brazilian Social Democratic Party (PSDB) to participate in a "government of national conciliation".

Party of the Brazilian Democratic Movement

Partido do Movimento Democrático Brasileiro (PMDB)

Leadership. Orested Quércia (l.); Ulysses Guimarães (pres.); Tarcísio Delgado (s.-g.).

Orientation. Centrist, Christian democratic in spirit, committed to economic-nationalism and social reform. While it is the largest opposition party in Congress, the PMDB supports President Collor in his opposition to the proposed parliamentary system which would give greater power to Congress.

Founded. 1980.

History. Formed by the moderate elements of the Brazilian Democratic Movement (MDB), disbanded in 1979 and the sole opposition party tolerated under the 14 year military dictatorship, the PMDB inherited a large majority of the old party's branches and 120 members of Congress. Its campaign for democratization attracted support from a wide section of society, ranging from left-wing forces, such as the illegal Communist Party (PCB — now PSP — and PCdoB) and trade unions to moderate conservatives. In late 1981, after a brief period of co-operation, the PMDB merged with the centrist Popular Party (PP), formed in 1980 by Tancredo de Almeida Neves, Prime Minister in 1961-62 and an MDB member under the military regime. The PMDB's first test at the ballot box in 1982 was a resounding success, the party winning 200 seats out of 479 in the Chamber of Deputies and 21 out of 69 seats in the Senate. Nine out of the 23 newly elected governors were also PMDB members. In early 1984 the PMDB took a leading role in the mass campaign for direct presidential elections supported by the church and trade unions. Later that year, faced with an intransigent government, Tancredo Neves agreed to participate in the indirect presidential elections, pledging to introduce a new constitution and direct elections if he won. The PMDB formed a Democratic Alliance with the Liberal Front Party (PFL) to back his candidacy, and on Jan. 15, 1985, Neves won 480 out of 660 votes cast in the electoral college.

Neves fell ill before his presidential inauguration in March 1985 and after his nationally-mourned death in April he was succeeded by his vice-presidential running-mate José Sarney, the first civilian president to take office since 1964. Sarney, who had joined the PMDB from the PFL in order to comply with electoral rules, made no alteration to the coalition Cabinet appointed by Neves and confirmed the government's commitment to democratic and social reforms envisaged by Neves. The anti-inflationary price and wage freeze and introduction of a new currency in February 1986, called the Cruzado Plan, was initially highly successful which was reflected in the government parties' general election results in November 1986. The PMDB became the most powerful party in Brazil, with 22 governorships, 260 out of 487 seats in the Chamber of Deputies and 46 out of 72 seats in the Senate, and thus also dominated the Constituent Assembly which Sarney established in February 1987 to draft the 1988 Constitution. However by September 1987, with the economy in turmoil, an agrarian reform plan held in disrepute and a raging controversy regarding the length of his presidential mandate, the Democratic Alliance was dissolved. The disagreements over the presidential term also threatened to split the PMDB into factions, the centre-right supporting the President and the "historic" faction calling for his retirement after four years.

Sarney agreed to hand over power in March 1990 and in September 1988 endorsed Ulysses Guimaraes' bid to become his successor. In the municipal elections of the same year the PMDB emerged as the principal loser mainly owing to discontent with the austerity programme but also the government's use of the army to break up a strike. The party did poorly in the November 1989 presidential race and although in the congressional and gubernatorial elections of 1990 it gained the largest number of seats in the Chamber of Deputies and won the governorship of São Paulo, it effectively lost 151 seats in the Chamber and 15 gubernatorial posts. The 109 PMDB deputies, to whom Collor had looked for support, increasingly joined the opposition against his attacks on the power of the Congress.

Structure. The Party Congress elects the PMDB's national officers and executive board, and it broadly determines the party's policies.

Popular Socialist Party (PSP)

Leadership. Roberto Freire (l.); Salomão Malina (s.-g.).

Orientation. Independent communist on the Eurocommunist model. The party supports the liberalization of the former Soviet Union. The PSP campaigns for job creation, the abolition of "unproductive landholdings" and autonomy of Amazonia.

Founded. 1922 (renamed to PSP in January 1992).

History. Formed as the Communist Party of Brazil (PCdoB), the party was banned soon after its creation. However, the party remained active in the labour movement and in the late 1920s organized the General Labour Confederation. In November 1935 it took part in an unsuccessful military insurrection against the Vargas government and as a result hundreds of Communists, including the PCdoB's new general secretary Luiz Carlos Prestes (leader of the 1924-26 rebel military forces' Long March) were imprisoned. The PCdoB was legalized in time for the 1945 congressional elections in which it won 10 per cent of the total vote, and returned 14 deputies and one senator to Congress. Because of its continued success, the party was again declared illegal two years later in 1947 and all PCdoB representatives in Congress had to surrender their seats. The party was unofficially allowed to operate from 1956 under the new government of President Kubitschek but legality remained elusive. In 1960 the party adopted its present name and moved away from its previous internationalist outlook in a failed attempt to obtain a share in the electoral process. Instead the new stance led to a split in 1961 when the more orthodox faction sympathetic to China set up as a separate party under the old name (see Communist Party of Brazil).

After the 1964 military coup the PCB once again was forced to go underground. Many party members were imprisoned or killed by the police in the 1960s and 1970s, particularly in 1975-76, but despite the repression the PCB from 1965 onwards campaigned against the junta for civilian rule through the official opposition party, the Brazilian Democratic Movement (see Party of the Brazilian Democratic Movement).

Prestes and other PCB leaders were finally permitted to return to Brazil following the general amnesty of 1979, and in 1980 the party paper *Voz Operaria* resumed regular publication. Officially the PCB was not legalized until June 1985, however, and therefore had to restrict its involvement in the November 1982 Congressional elections to lending its support to the campaigns of both the centrist PMDB and the left-wing Workers' Party (PT). Despite the PCP's increasingly moderate stance the party continued to be the target of intimidation and at its party congress of Dec. 13, the entire central committee was arrested (but released within days). At the party congress of January 1984 the party's Eurocommunist aim of seeking to participate in the parliamentary system and campaign for a nationalist/democratic government was confirmed. Prestes, who had retained his revolutionary ideals, had become isolated among the party leaders and was expelled.

During the 1984-85 presidential campaign the PCB supported the successful PMDB candidate Tancredo Neves who had advocated free elections. Following the party's legalization in 1985 the PCB finally stood under its own name for the first time in 41 years, contesting the 1986 congressional elections in which it won two seats in the Chamber of Deputies. At the party congress of 1987 the PCB supported *glasnost* in the Soviet Union and vowed to adopt it in the party's own policies. In its attitude to the government, the PCB remained loyal to the PMDB, offering critical support for the Sarney government's controversial economic restructuring policies. The PCB remained distanced from other left-wing parties, fielding Roberto Freire as its candidate in the presidential elections of November 1989 (he polled a negligible number of votes) and staying out of the left-wing electoral alliance led by the Workers' Party (PT). In the congressional elections of October 1990 the party was slightly more successful, increasing its representation in the Chamber of Deputies from two to three seats. The PCB deputies subsequently joined the left-wing bloc opposing the Collor government.

Structure. The PCB is a democratic centralist party. Its Central Committee consists of 66 members and 23 alternates elected by the Party Congress. The party's Executive Committee has 16 members and four alternates who are appointed by the CC.

Membership. 150,000 (1989 claim).

Publication. *Voz de Unidade* (Voice of Unity), weekly.

International affiliations. Following the collapse of the Eastern bloc, the party lost the majority of its international political contacts.

Social Democratic Party

Partido Social Democratico (PDS)

Leadership. Antonio Delfim Netto (pres.); Amaral Neto (s.-g.).

Orientation. Right-wing.

Founded. 1980.

History. The PDS was formed as the successor of the official military government party, the National Renewal Alliance (ARENA), which was dissolved in 1979 following President Figueiredo's political reforms. The new party had a majority representation in Congress with 213 deputies and 37 Senators, and having inherited the ARENA party structure, the PDS had over 3,000 branches. In its first test at the ballot box in November 1982 the PDS increased its majority to 235 seats out of 479 in the Chamber of Deputies, 46 out of 69 in the Senate and 12 state governorships. This resounding electoral success, however, was not sufficient to give Figueiredo a working majority in the Chamber of Deputies. In May 1983 the PDS formed a short-lived alliance with the small Brazilian Labour Party (PTB) which allowed a three months' break in Figueiredo's rule by decree. In 1984 the PDS, which opposed the campaign for direct presidential elections, began to lose a considerable number of members. The party leadership further alienated PDS members when in the same year Paulo Salim Maluf, a former governor of São Paulo, was nominated as the party's candidate for the 1985 presidential elections. The liberal faction within the PDS, which included Vice-President Chaves de Mendonca and the former ARENA party-president José Sarney, left the party to form the Liberal Front Party (PFL).

With a reduced representation in Congress, Maluf also lost the indirect presidential elections of Jan. 15, 1985 to the Party of the Brazilian Democratic Movement (PMDB)/PFL candidate Tancredo Neves. The congressional and gubernatorial elections of November 1986 showed how the PDS's popularity had continued to decline. The party failed to win a single governorship and only 36 PDS deputies and five senators were returned to Congress. In the same year the party suffered more membership losses, with many disillusioned members turning to the PFL. Maluf contested the 1989 presidential elections as candidate of the still fragmented PDS and came fifth with 8.86 per cent of the valid vote. The party fared slightly better in the congressional and gubernatorial elections in October 1990, winning 40 seats in the Chamber of Deputies and one state governorship. The PDS largely supported the Collor government, and in October 1990 Col. (retd) Jarbas Passarinho, a PDS leader and former Education and Labour Minister, was appointed Justice Minister. Passarinho became involved in a controversy which further isolated the government. On the request of Collor de Mello he persuaded senators to oppose a proposal for the introduction of a parliamentary system which was making its passage through Congress in November 1991, and which was thus narrowly defeated.

Workers' Party

Partido dos Trabalhadores (PT)

Leadership. Luís Inácio ('Lula') da Silva (pres.); José Luís Fevereiro (s.-g.).

Orientation. The country's first independent labour party; aims for a society without exploiters and exploited and in the last election it called for an end to government corruption and social injustice and advocated subsidies of social services, state control of

the financial system, government consultation of both employers and trade unions and suspension of foreign debt payments until further investigation; the party's power-base traditionally lies in the urban industrial areas, although in state governor elections in October and November 1990, it did poorly in these areas.
Founded. 1980.
History. The party was founded by the leader of the powerful United Confederation of Workers (CUT), Luís Inácio da Silva (known universally as 'Lula'), Jaco Bítar and Airton Soares and emerged from the growing São Paulo *autêntico* independent trade union movement in the late 1970s. Many of the PT's leaders and members had been supporters of the former Brazilian Labour Party (PTB) which had backed the former Presidents Vargas and Kubitschek in the 1950s. Although chiefly supported by urban industrial workers, the party was also active in rural areas. In 1981 Lula da Silva and nine other PT members received sentences from two to three and a half years for incitement to murder, having made speeches at a peasant leader's funeral which was later followed by revenge murders. They were finally acquitted in 1984.

In the first congressional elections the party participated in, it received only six seats in the Chamber of Deputies. The more open elections of 1986 gave the PT 19 seats in the Chamber. However, opposition to President Sarney's austerity measures and support for the strikes and demonstrations called by the CUT greatly broadened the PT's electoral appeal. This became evident in the municipal elections of 1988 when the PT won control of 36 important towns and Luiza Erundina da Souza became mayor of the city of São Paulo, the first woman mayor in Brazil. In the presidential election of Nov. 15, 1989, the PT formed a Popular Front together with the Brazilian Socialist Party (PSB), the Communist Party of Brazil (PCdoB) and other left-wing parties.

As the Front's presidential candidate, "Lula" came second in the first round of the elections with 17.18 per cent of the vote, and despite the backing of the Democratic Labour Party (PDT) and the Brazilian Social Democratic Party (PSDB), did not manage to close the gap sufficiently between himself and the National Reconstruction Party (PRN) candidate Collor de Mello in the second round. Lula won in the large cities of Rio de Janeiro, Belo Horizonte, Brazília and Salvador but nationwide came second to Collor with 46.97 per cent of the vote.

Still smarting from the smearing campaign against "Lula" in the elections, the PT rejected Collor's subsequent offer of some cabinet posts, calling his victory "immoral". In the aftermath of the elections, the bulk of the PT decided to disassociate itself from the PCdoB and expel various "entryist" Trotskyist groups which the leadership blamed for the electoral failure. Socialist Convergence (CS) and other Trotskyist groups, however, remained in the party.
Membership. 150,000 (1988).
Affiliations. Linked to the 15,000,000-member CUT, the Brazilian confederation of independent trade unions.

Minor parties

Christian Socialist Party (*Partido Socialista Cristao — PSC)* centrist, won five seats in the Chamber of Deputies and one governorship in the elections of Oct. 3, 1990.
Democratic Socialist Party (PSD); won one seat in Chamber of Deputies in the October-November 1990 elections.
Green Party (*Partido Verde — PV*); the party was a member of the Worker's Party (PT)-led Brazilian Popular Front in the 1989 presidential election campaign.
National Municipal Party (PMN); won one seat in Chamber of Deputies in the October-November 1990 elections.
Revolutionary Workers Party (PTR); won two seats in Chamber of Deputies and two governorships in the elections of October-November 1990.
Socialist Workers Party (PST); won two seats in the Chamber of Deputies in the October-November 1990 elections.
Social Reform Party (PRS); won one governorship in the October-November 1990 elections.
Socialist Convergence (*Convergenca Socialista — CS*) the main Trotskyist grouping within the Workers'Party (PT) which was threatened with expulsion after the 1989 presidential election. It controls major trade unions, including that of the Rio de Janeiro bank employees.

Canada

Capital: Ottawa **Population: 26,833,000.**

The Dominion of Canada was settled by British and French colonists from the 16th century onwards. In the mid-18th century the country fell solely under British control, although the culture, language and traditions of the French-speaking population in Quebec were recognized by the British authorities. The separate colonies achieved effective self-government in 1848, and the process of their confederation was begun in 1867 with the British North America Act. Under the 1931 Statute of Westminster Canada achieved Dominion status. Newfoundland became part of the Dominion of Canada in 1949. In 1982 Canada was given the right to amend its Constitution without the approval of the British Parliament.

Throughout its history Canada has operated basically as a two-party system as regards the control of federal government. The Liberal Party and the Progressive Conservative Party (PCP), and their various respective antecedents, have sometimes enjoyed lengthy periods in office. The Liberals held power from 1963 to 1984 (apart from a nine-month minority PCP administration in 1979-80), since when the PCP has been in government.

Constitutional structure

Canada is a federalist state with a liberal democratic Constitution. It is a member of the Commonwealth with the British sovereign as head of state represented by a Governor-General. Although the Governor-General is endowed with wide-ranging theoretical powers, real authority is exercised by the country's federal Prime Minister and Cabinet. The federal Parliament comprises a Senate of 104 members appointed by the Governor-General, and a House of Commons of 295 members elected for a maximum of five years. The Governor-General appoints as Prime Minister the person most likely to command a majority in the House of Commons. The Prime Minister governs with the assistance of an appointed Cabinet.

The country's provincial structure reflects that at federal level with a Lieutenant-Governor in each of the 10 provinces who represents the Governor-General, and an elected legislature and executive council, headed by a Premier. (The two territories, Yukon Territory and Northwest Territories, in which the chief executive officer is the federally appointed Commissioner, currently enjoy differing degrees of responsible government.) The precise distribution of power between federal and provincial government constitutes a highly contentious area. Under the 1982 constitution there was a considerable devolution

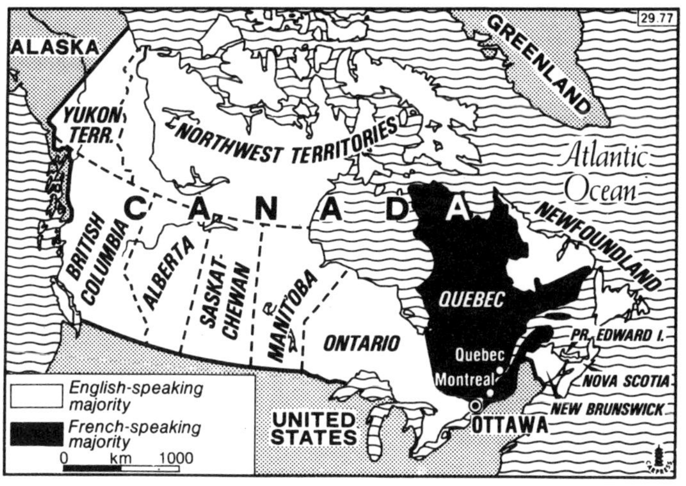
29.77
ALASKA
GREENLAND
YUKON TERR.
NORTHWEST TERRITORIES
Atlantic Ocean
C A N A D A
NEWFOUNDLAND
BRITISH COLUMBIA
ALBERTA
SASKAT-CHEWAN
MANITOBA
ONTARIO
QUEBEC
PR. EDWARD I.
Quebec
Montreal
NOVA SCOTIA
NEW BRUNSWICK
OTTAWA
UNITED STATES
English-speaking majority
French-speaking majority
0 km 1000

Sequence of elections since 1945

Date	*Winning Party*
June 11, 1945	Liberal
June 27, 1949	Liberal
Aug. 10, 1953	Liberal
June 10, 1957	PCP (minority gov.)
March 31, 1958	PCP
June 18, 1962	PCP (minority gov.)
April 8, 1963	Liberal
Nov. 8, 1965	Liberal (minority gov.)
June 25, 1968	Liberal
Oct. 30, 1972	Liberal (minority gov.)
July 8, 1974	Liberal
May 22, 1979	PCP (minority gov.)
Feb. 18, 198?	Liberal
Sept. 4, 1984	PCP
Nov. 21, 1988	PCP

Seats in House of Commons and percentage of vote won in 1980 election

Party	*seats*	*% of votes*
Liberal Party	147	44%
PCP	103	33%
New Democratic Party (NDP)	32	20%
Others	—	3%
Total	**282**	**100%**

Seats in House of Commons and percentage of vote won in 1984 election

Party	*Seats*	*% vote*
PCP	211	49%
Liberals	40	28%
NDP	30	19%
Others	1	3%
Total	**283**	**100%**

Seats in House of Commons and percentage of vote won in 1988 election

Party	*Seats*	*% vote*
PCP	170	43%
Liberals	82	32%
NDP	43	20%
Others	—	5%
Total	**295**	**100%**

of power, but the separatist aspirations of Quebec were such that the province refused to sign the document. Further concessions were made towards recognizing Quebec's unique position within the confederation by the Meech Lake Accord. Although passed by Parliament in 1988, this failed to achieve ratification by all of the provinces within the requisite two-year period. Its collapse in 1990 rekindled widespread demands for Quebec autonomy, and created considerable uncertainty concerning the issue of Canada's future unity.

Electoral system

Both the federal and provincial legislatures are elected by universal adult suffrage under a simple majority system in single-member ridings (constituencies). Candidates who poll 15 per cent or more of the valid votes in their electoral district are eligible for the return of their nomination deposit. Political parties which are registered are eligible to run candidates with the party name designated on the ballot, to receive donations and to be reimbursed by the federal government for certain expenses. To be eligible for registration a party must have had at least 12 representatives in the previous federal Parliament, or must nominate at least 50 candidates at a federal election. A total of 12 registered political parties contested the 1988 general election.

Evolution of suffrage

The secret ballot was introduced in 1874, but the franchise at that time included only males who met property or income requirements (some 15 per cent of the population). Manitoba introduced full male suffrage in 1888, and gradually thereafter property restrictions were relaxed on a province-by-province basis. Women were enfranchised in several provinces in 1916. In 1921 universal adult suffrage was introduced for those over 21 years of age. The age restriction was reduced to 18 in 1970.

PARTY BY PARTY DATA

Liberal Party of Canada

Address. 200 Laurier Avenue West, Suite 200, Ottawa, Ontario, K1P 6M8.

Leadership. Jean Chrétien (l.); Don Johnston (pres.); Sheila Gervais (s.-g.).

Orientation. Centrist. Advocates freedom of the individual, comprehensive social security, equal opportunities.

Founded. 1867.

History. The antecedents of the modern Liberal Party lie in an alliance between the reformist, non-established church elements of Ontario and the anti-business, anti-clerical radicals of Quebec. The beliefs of the former group were strongly influenced by English liberalism, particularly its opposition to government intervention in the economy in the form of tariff protection. Under the leadership of Alexander MacKenzie these elements, known as the "Grits", were successful in ousting the Conservatives (predecessors of the Progressive Conservative Party—PCP)from office in the election of 1874. With the country suffering a severe economic depression, however, the Conservatives were returned in 1878 upon a platform of protectionism. There followed a further three Liberal electoral defeats, but during its years in opposition the party concentrated on building its grass-roots strength. By the time it regained power at federal level, it was already in control of every provincial government except Quebec. Even there, the purging of the more extreme anti-clerical elements meant that it had vastly improved its position.

In 1887 the party elected Sir Wilfrid Laurier as its leader, and he led it to power in the election of 1896 on a platform of provincial rights. Laurier won the next three elections and retained office until 1911, thereby helping to undermine the reputation of the Conservatives as the natural party of government. A pragmatist rather than a liberal ideologue, Laurier sought to expand the role of the federal government and to encourage a consensus between the French and English communities. He built a coherent national Liberal Party through his shrewd use of the Prime Minister's powers of patronage, and by including the party's provincial premiers in his federal government to act as power-brokers for their particular regions. His administration was eventually defeated by the loss of support in Quebec (isolationist elements objected to his plans to build a navy) and by the loss of important support from the Ontario business community which objected to his advocacy of reciprocal free trade with the USA.

During World War I the Liberal Party was almost destroyed by the issue of conscription, with most French-speaking Liberals fiercely opposed to it and English-speaking members of the party largely in favour. The issue was so divisive that some Liberals defected to the Conservatives to form a Unionist government. In 1919 William Lyon Mackenzie King was elected party leader in place of Laurier. He became Prime Minister with a minority government in 1921 and held the office thereafter until 1948, apart from periods in opposition in 1926 and 1930-35. In doing so he became the longest serving prime minister in Canadian history.

Using the party as a mechanism to reconcile the demands of competing groups, King maintained a coalition which included elements as diverse as western free-trade farmers and protectionist manufacturers from Ontario. His success was also due to his maintenance of a high level of support in Quebec, his ability to obscure ideological issues, and his appointment of able cabinet ministers. During his years in power the government undertook extensive redistributive measures, and laid the basis of the country's modern welfare system.

King's programme was continued by his successor as leader, Louis St. Laurent. Although the party retained office until 1957, during these years its national coalition began breaking down as it steadily lost support in the western provinces. The Liberals suffered election defeats in 1957, 1958, and 1962 before returning to power as a minority government following the election of 1963. The party was by now led by Lester B. "Mike" Pearson, an experienced diplomat and a winner of the Nobel Peace Prize, who had been elected leader in 1958.

An indecisive result in the 1965 election condemned Pearson to a second minority term, during which the issue of Quebec separatism became an increasingly urgent problem.

Pearson resigned in April 1968 and was succeeded by Pierre Trudeau, who called an immediate election and won a comprehensive victory. In the election of 1972, however, he lost his overall majority. Another decisive victory in 1974 was followed by the gradual erosion of his personal support, and defeat at the polls in 1979. Weary from a decade in office and beset by personal problems, Trudeau announced his resignation as leader. Unexpectedly, however, the minority PCP government's first budget was defeated in Parliament and, faced with an immediate election, Trudeau agreed to remain as Liberal leader. He led the party to victory in February 1980 and remained as Prime Minister until 1984.

The flamboyant Trudeau was succeeded as party leader and Prime Minister by John Turner, who served as Premier for 79 days—the second shortest tenure in Canadian history—before suffering a crushing electoral defeat at the hands of the PCP. His years as leader of the opposition were marked by bitter internal feuding within the party and frequent criticism of his style of leadership as lacklustre and indecisive.

At the 1988 election, which was dominated by the issue of the free trade agreement, the Liberals increased their representation in the 295-member federal Parliament from 40 to 82, but could not prevent the return of the PCP government. Also, for an organization which had been Canada's natural party of government in the 20th century, the election demonstrated how regionally based it had become, with very little representation in the western provinces.

Following the election defeat Turner announced his intention to resign, describing his departure as "in the best interests of the party". His decision became effective upon the election of Jean Chrétien as his successor at a leadership convention on June 23, 1990. In 1980 Chrétien had led the "no" campaign in the referendum on independence for Quebec, and had been a staunch opponent of the Meech Lake Accord. He stated that he was in favour of Quebec remaining as part of Canada under the principle of "10 equal provinces".

Structure. The party has a national executive consisting of elected office-holders and the presidents of the provincial parties as well as officers of the women's and youth commissions. The Liberal associations in the provinces are member organizations of the national party.

Membership. 4,000,000

New Democratic Party (NDP)

Address. 310 Somerset Street West, Ottawa, Ontario, K2P OJ9.
Leadership. Audrey McLaughlin (l.); Sandra Mitchell (pres.); Dick Proctor (sec.).
Orientation. Social democratic.
Founded. 1961.
History. The NDP, the most successful social democratic party in North America, is Canada's third main party at federal level. The party's predecessor was the Co operative Commonwealth Federation (CCF), a socialist movement founded in 1932. In 1944 it came to power in Saskatchewan, and in 1945 it won 28 seats in the federal Parliament. In the decade which followed, under the impact of post-war prosperity and the Cold War, the party diluted its socialist programme and, with the Winnipeg Declaration of 1956, it committed itself to a "mixed" private and public sector economy.

In 1961 the CCF united with affiliated unions of the Canadian Labour Congress (which had united much of the labour movement in 1956) to form the NDP. The new party attempted to build upon the CCF's traditional rural support but also to extend itself into the industrialized urban areas of Canada. Throughout the 1960s and 1970s, however, under the leadership of Tommy Douglas (1961-71) and David Lewis (1971-75) the party averaged only 23 seats in the federal Parliament. Between 1962 and 1984 it averaged 16.8 per cent of the vote in federal elections but, because of the nature of the Canadian electoral system, it won only an average of 8.7 per cent of the seats in the federal legislature. It did, however, enjoy periods in government in several provinces including Saskatchewan, British Columbia and Manitoba, and in the Yukon Territory.

Ed Broadbent became party leader in 1975 and the NDP won 26 and 32 federal seats respectively in the elections of 1979 and 1980. Prior to the 1988 general election, disillusionment with the two traditional parties meant that the NDP actually moved ahead of them in the opinion polls. In the event, however, old loyalties prevailed and the NDP finished third with only 20 per cent of the vote and 43 seats. Although it was the highest legislative representation ever achieved by the party, its failure to fulfil earlier aspirations was sufficient to cause Broadbent's resignation. Audrey McLaughlin was chosen to replace him by a convention held in Winnipeg on Dec. 2, 1989.

Despite its progress in the 1980s the NDP continued to be identified as a party of the rural western provinces. This situation was altered when the NDP won its most spectacular victory to date in Ontario, Canada's richest province, on Sept. 6, 1990. The NDP defeated the incumbent Liberal administration, increasing its share of the 130 seats in the provincial legislature from 19 to 74. The Liberals won 36 seats, a net loss of 57, whilst the Progressive Conservative Party (PCP) won 20 seats. The victory marked the first occasion that the party had succeeded in winning a provincial election east of Manitoba. The platform upon which the result was achieved included a commitment to raise the minimum wage by 50 per cent, index link pensions, provide better severance pay and retraining opportunities for workers made redundant, increase rent controls, give greater incentives to small businesses and impose stricter anti-pollution measures.

The NDP continued its success at provincial level with election victories in British Columbia and Saskatchewan in October 1991. In the former, on Oct. 17, the party defeated the Social Credit Party government (see below) by winning more than 40 per cent of the vote and securing 51 of the 75 seats in the provincial legislature. In the latter, on Oct. 21, the NDP won 55 of the 66 seats and ousted the PCP government. The victories meant that by early 1992 the NDP was in government in three of the country's 10 provinces which between them contained more than half of the country's population.
Structure. The NDP is a federal organization. The federal party and the party in each of the provinces have separate programmes. The party is based on associations in the individual electoral ridings, which are represented on provincial councils and the federal council. The main policy-making forum is the national convention, which meets at least every two years and which elects party officials. Between conventions the main governing body is the federal council.
Membership. The total membership, including individual members and those who are affiliated to the party through trade unions and co-operatives, is 400,000.
Publications. Ottawa Report (weekly when House of Commons is in session).

International affiliation. Socialist International (full member party).

Progressive Conservative Party (PCP)

Address. National Headquarters, 275 Slater Street (6th Floor), Ottawa, Ontario, K1P 5H9.

Leadership. Brian Mulroney (l.); Jerry St Germain (pres.); Jean-Carol Pelletier (nat. dir.).

Orientation. Conservative. Enshrining an amalgam of British, French and American conservative traditions, the PCP supports laissez faire capitalism, the preservation of the monarchy, multiculturalism and bilingualism and continued Canadian participation in NATO.

Founded. 1854.

History. The PCP was founded as a Liberal-Conservative grouping by Sir John A. MacDonald, and consisted of a coalition between the Anglican establishment of Ontario and the French-Catholic business interests of Quebec. It held power from confederation in 1867 until 1896, apart from a brief Liberal administration between 1874 and 1878. MacDonald, the country's first Prime Minister, died in 1891, and increasingly the coalition began fracturing along ethnic lines. Having lost the 1896 election the party remained out of office until 1911 when its new leader, Sir Robert Borden, used an alliance between anti-free-trade interests in Ontario and nationalists in Quebec to bring down the Liberal government. This alliance disintegrated during the conscription crisis of 1917, and although Borden remained in power—with the support of some Liberals—at the head of a Unionist government, the PCP was defeated at the election of 1921. The party finished in third place behind the Liberals and the Progressive Party, the latter being primarily a protest movement formed by western agrarian interests.

Apart from a brief spell in government in 1926, under Arthur Meighen, the party remained in opposition, and in 1927 Meighen was replaced as leader by Robert Bennet. In 1930 the Conservatives were returned to office and were immediately faced with a severe economic depression. Bennet's initial response was towards greater protectionism combined with attempts to seek imperial preference. Towards the end of his term he advocated social reform and a package of measures based on the US New Deal, but it came too late to avoid a crushing defeat in 1935. In the post-war period the party worked hard to extend the basis of its support. Having changed its name to the Progressive Conservative Party—after consuming right-wing elements of the Progressive Party—in 1942, it was returned to government in 1957-63 under John G. Diefenbaker, a Saskatchewan lawyer, who had become leader in 1956. The PCP formed a minority government after the 1957 election, and Diefenbaker's charismatic leadership won the party an overwhelming victory the following year, securing 54 per cent of the vote and 208 of the 265 seats in the House of Commons. When in office the party displayed little clear vision, however, and it lost its overall majority in the 1962 election. In 1963 it was defeated.

The PCP returned to government (without an overall majority) at the 1979 election, under the leadership of Joe Clark. In December, however, the new government's austerity budget was rejected and, in the ensuing 1980 general election the Liberals were swept back into power. In 1983 the party rejected Clark in favour of Brian Mulroney, a bilingual Quebecois with shrewd organizational skills. The party won an overwhelming victory in 1984 and was returned to power in 1988.

The popularity of Mulroney's government fell steadily in the period following the 1984 victory, as a steady stream of Cabinet ministers was forced to resign by scandals. By 1987 the opinion polls showed that the PCP was badly trailing both the Liberals and the NDP. Mulroney called a premature general election on Nov. 21, 1988, on the issue of the free trade agreement with the USA which he had signed in January 1988. With both the Liberals and the NDP opposing the agreement, Mulroney fought an effective campaign which argued that the accord was essential to Canada's future economic development. Although the number of seats won by the PCP was reduced from 211 in 1984 to 170, and its share of the vote fell from 49 to 43 per cent, the party retained a comfortable overall majority in the House of Commons.

The popularity of Mulroney's government fell even more rapidly in his second term than it had in his first. His government was damaged by the collapse of the Meech Lake Accord and the defection of federal MPs to form the Quebec Bloc (Bloc Québecois), by economic recession (complete with rising unemployment and high interest rates) and by the impact of a seven per cent value-added tax imposed by the government in the face of overwhelming public hostility. Against a background of opinion polls which showed Mulroney recording an unprecedentedly low approval rating of 16 per cent, the Prime Minister addressed a PCP convention in early August 1991. Speaking to an audience of 2,500 party faithful Mulroney declared, "We are going to forge a third victorious Progressive Conservative government. We are going to bounce into the election in 1993 with prosperity all over "

Structure. In addition to its "general meeting" and national executive, the PCP has an executive committee which includes the national leader, president and 12 provincial vice-presidents, which exercises authority between meetings of the national executive.

Membership. 400,000.

Publications. PC Journal.

Quebec Bloc

Bloc Québecois (BQ)

Address. 88 Rue Perras, Hull, Quebec, JBY 6K4.

Leadership. Lucien Bouchard.

Orientation. Separatist. The BQ's definition of the term sovereignty is somewhat imprecise, and it is unclear whether the group demands complete independence or is prepared to settle for greater autonomy within the Canadian confederation.

Founded. 1990.

History. The *Bloc Québecois* was formed as a result of the increase in nationalist sentiment within the predominantly French-speaking province following the defeat in June 1990 of the Meech Lake Accord, the constitutional amendment which had sought to induce Quebec to sign the 1982 federal constitution in return for recognition of the province as a "distinct society". The Bloc was founded by Lucien Bouchard, the federal Environment Minister who resigned from the government in May 1990, and was joined by six other federal legislators who defected from the Progressive Conservative Party (PCP) and the Liberals.

The BQ recorded an impressive by-election win in east-central Montreal on Aug. 13, 1990, in its first test at the hands of the Canadian electorate. The group won some 70 per cent of the vote, compared with 20 per cent for the Liberal Party (which had previously held the seat) and 5 per cent for the PCP. Although the by-election victory of Gilles Duceppe, a union organizer and son of Quebec's best-known actor, increased the group's parliamentary strength to eight, it remained four short of the 12 members needed to be recognized as an official party within the House of Commons.

In 1991 the Parti Québecois (see Quebec Party below) decided to support the BQ in the next federal election. In April of that year, however, the BQ's legislative strength was reduced by the decision of one of its MPs to leave the group and return to the political mainstream.

Structure. The BQ exists essentially as a legislative group.

Membership. The BQ has yet to develop a significant popular base. Although it has a growing amount of support in Quebec, it remains reliant on its group of federal MPs.

Quebec Party

Parti Québecois

Address. 8790 Avenue du Parc, Montreal, Quebec, H2N 1Y6.

Leadership. Jacques Parizeau (pres.); Bernard Landry (ch. of national executive).

Orientation. Separatist. Although primarily social democratic in outlook and programme, like most nationalist movements the PQ contains elements from the left, right and centre of the political spectrum.

Founded. 1968.

History. The *Parti Québecois* was formed as a coalition of separatist elements including members of the *Rassemblement pour l'Indépendence National* (RIN), which had advocated complete independence for Quebec, and the *Ralliement National* (RN) which favoured self-government in association with Canada. Under the dynamic leadership of Rene Levesque the PQ enjoyed meteoric growth, gaining 24 and 30 per cent of the vote respectively in the provincial elections of 1970 and 1973. This rate of progress culminated in the 1976 provincial elections where the party, standing on a platform of independence for Quebec, won 41 per cent of the vote and secured 69 of the 110 seats in the legislature.

In government the PQ proceeded cautiously, recognizing that a majority of Quebec's population did not favour a severance of links with the Canadian federation. The party leadership hoped that by demonstrating its competence in managing the province's affairs, particularly its economic development, many of the remaining doubts over Quebec's ability to survive as an independent entity could be eliminated. The PQ also developed a concept known as "sovereignty association", whereby Quebec would become a sovereign state but would retain close economic ties with English-speaking Canada. A referendum on the issue was eventually held on May 20, 1980, almost four years after the PQ had come to power, in which 60 per cent voted against giving the party a mandate to negotiate sovereignty association with the federal government.

The PQ was thrown into considerable disarray by the referendum result, and by Levesque's announcement in 1984 that he had decided to de-emphasize the sovereignty question in favour of concentrating on economic issues. The move caused a split in the party, with some of those who were committed to outright independence forming the Pro-Independence Party (*Parti Indépendantiste*—PI). The PQ's disarray in turn helped to reinvigorate the Liberal Party within the province. Levesque resigned from the leadership in 1985, and the party lost power in the election at the end of the year, winning only 23 seats compared with the 99 won by the Liberals.

In March 1988 Jacques Parizeau, who had been provincial Finance Minister from 1976 to 1984 and who was identified with the radical separatist wing of the PQ, became leader of the party. In the election of September 1989 the PQ polled 41 per cent of the vote and won 29 seats, compared with the Liberals who polled 50 per cent and won 92 seats.

Under pressure from a resurgent PQ and from the general growth of separatist sentiment following the collapse of the Meech Lake Accord, the Liberal Premier of Quebec, Robert Bourassa, agreed to hold a referendum on secession by October 1992 unless a constitutional formula was adopted which encompassed Quebec's demands for greater autonomy.

Structure. The supreme body of the PQ is its congress. Between congress sessions it is the national council, consisting of local, regional and national representatives. A national executive council, elected by the congress, deals with day-to-day administration.

Membership. 136,000.

Reform Party

Address. 10053 111th Street, Suite 501, Edmonton, Alberta, T5K 2H8.

Leadership. E. Preston Manning (l.); Wesley MacLeod (chief admin.).

Orientation. Right-wing populist movement, advocating fiscal conservatism, greater representation for the western provinces, and opposition to special status for Quebec.

Founded. 1987.

History. The Reform Party emerged from a coalition of interest groups in the western provinces which were concerned to create a broad-based party to give expression to western economic and constitutional concerns. At its founding convention in October 1987 it chose Ernest C. Manning, the son of the former Social Credit Premier of Alberta, as its leader.

In the 1988 general election the party fielded 72 candidates and won some 275,500 votes (2 per cent of the national total). Although in the mould of previous prairie protest movements, since its formation the party has expanded rapidly beyond its original Alberta base. In this it was assisted greatly by the climate of constitutional uncertainty associated with the collapse of the Meech Lake Accord and by the economic recession of the early 1990s. The party's economic message of tough fiscal restraint and unhindered laissez faire capitalism, together with its opposition to bilingualism and to the concession of special status to Quebec, has proved a compelling combination for the early 1990s. The party won its first representation to the federal parliament when, on March 13, 1989, it won a by-election in Alberta. According to a Gallup opinion poll taken in April 1991, the Reform Party had the support of 16 per cent of the total electorate, compared with 14 per cent for the PCP, 26 per cent for the NDP and 32 per cent for the Liberals.

Social Credit Party of Canada

Leadership. Kenneth Campbell.

Orientation. The party was founded to give expression to the underconsumptionist economic analysis of British engineer Maj. C. H. Douglas (1879-1952), who advocated the periodic distribution of money or "social credit" to increase public purchasing power. In practice, when in office, the Social Credit Party has tended to pursue orthodox conservative policies.

Founded. 1933.

History. The simple but coherent economic analysis at the centre of the Social Credit movement was well-received during the severe economic recession of the early 1930s, especially in the western provinces. This was particularly true in Alberta where William Aberhart, a radio evangelist, became a Social Credit convert and led the party to victory in the provincial elections of 1935, capturing 56 of the 63 seats and 54 per cent of the vote. Under Aberhart and his successor Ernest C. Manning, the party won nine successive victories in Alberta, governing the province until 1971, but did little to implement the fundamentals of the Social Credit doctrine.

In 1952 a Social Credit government was elected in British Columbia, but pursued a course of conservative fiscal policy combined with provincial development schemes. The party remained in power until 1972 when it was defeated by the NDP. It returned to government in 1975 under the eccentric William Vander Zalm. Increasingly, however, the government was weakened by scandals and allegations of corruption, one of which forced Zalm's resignation in April 1991. He was succeeded by Rita Johnston, but the change was not sufficient to avoid a crushing defeat by the New Democratic Party (NDP) in the provincial election on Oct. 17. The party won only seven seats (having secured 47 in the 1986 contest, and controlled 43 at the time of dissolution), and finished in third place behind the NDP on 51 and the Liberals on 17.

At federal level the party won 17 seats in the House of Commons in 1935, 15 of which were in Alberta. In the 1950s and 1960s the party held seats in British Columbia. In 1962 the party won 24 federal seats in Quebec, but only four others throughout English-speaking Canada. This imbalance led to tensions within the party and, in 1963, the Quebec branch broke away and formed the *Ralliement des Creditistes du Québec*. It rejoined the party in 1972.

As recently as the general election of 1979 the Social Credit Party won six seats and was the country's fourth largest party. It won no seats in the 1980 election, however, and rapidly disappeared as a viable electoral force. Although it retained power in British Columbia, the provincial government had few links with the rest of the party. In the 1988 general election the party fielded only nine candidates (but retained its registration by virtue of the discretion of the office of the Chief Electoral Officer) but received a minuscule 0.03 per cent of the total national vote.

Structure. The party has a national executive, a national congress, and a national convention which chooses the party leader. There are also provincial congresses and structures. The organization in British Columbia has particularly weak connections with the federal party but close informal ties with the province's conservatives.

Membership. 40,000

Minor Parties

Communist Party of Canada (CPC) (24 Cecil Street, Toronto, Ontario, M5T 1N2); a pro-Soviet party, led by George Hewison (gen. sec.), it has changed its name on several occasions.

It was founded in 1921, legalized in 1924, banned once more between 1931 and 1934 and in the early years of World War II, since when it has been allowed to operate legally.

It has not been represented in the federal Parliament since 1947 (when its only representative was expelled after being convicted of spying for the Soviet Union), nor in any provincial legislature since 1958. In the 1988 general election the party fielded 52 candidates and received 0.05 per cent of the total national vote.

Christian Heritage Party of Canada; in the 1988 general election the party fielded 63 candidates and received 0.8 per cent of the total national vote.

Confederation of Regions Western Party (0732 Oleme Road, Edmonton, Alberta, T6E 5B6); led by Elmer B. Knutson, the party fielded 51 candidates in the 1988 general election, and received 0.3 per cent of the total national vote.

Equality Party (5473 ave Royalmount, Montreal, Quebec, HAP 1J3); founded in 1989 as a vehicle to represent the interests of the English-speaking population of Quebec, the party won four seats in the provincial election of 1989. Richard Holden (l.).

Green Party of Canada (831 Commercial Drive, Vancouver, British Columbia, BC V5L); the party was founded in 1983 and is currently led by Kathryn Cholette. In the 1988 general election the Greens fielded 68 candidates and received 0.36 per cent of the total national vote.

Libertarian Party of Canada (POB 190, Adelaide Station, Toronto, Ontario, M5C 2J1); founded in 1933, in the 1988 general election the party fielded 88 candidates and received 0.25 per cent of the total national vote.

Party for Commonwealth; in the 1988 general election the party fielded 59 candidates and received 0.06 per cent of the total national vote.

Pro-Independence Party (*Parti Indépendantiste*—PI, 5933 rue Waverly, Montreal,

Quebec, H2T 2Y4); founded in 1984 as a breakaway group from the PQ, the PI seeks complete independence for Quebec. The party is currently led by Raymond Villeneuve (dir. gen.).

Rhinoceros Party (*Parti Rhinocéros*, 4534 de Bordeaux, Montreal, Quebec, H2H 2A1); founded in 1963 by Montreal doctor Jacques Ferron in order to provide a satirical commentary on Canadian politics, the party has participated in every general election since its creation. In the 1988 contest the party fielded 74 candidates and received 0.4 per cent of the total national vote, compared with the 0.8 per cent which it had achieved in 1984. Ferron died in 1985 and the party is currently led by Dominique Langevin.

Defunct parties

Progressive Party; established after World War I, the Progressive Party was largely the product of rural discontent, particularly in the western provinces. It constituted the first political force to challenge successfully the Liberal-Conservative duopoly, and emerged from the 1921 federal election as the second largest party.

Despite its electoral breakthrough, its unchecked populism too often manifested itself as a lack of party discipline, however, and by the mid-1920s the party had degenerated into internecine fighting. In the prairie provinces of Alberta and Manitoba the party remained influential into the 1930s and 1940s, before being overtaken by the Social Credit movement and the Co-operative Commonwealth Federation.

Ralliement des Créditistes du Québec (1963-71); see under Social Credit Party.

Major guerrilla groups

Canada does not have any significant guerrilla groups.

Cayman Islands

Capital: George Town (Grand Cayman) **Population: 25,355**

The Cayman Islands, which came under British rule in 1670, were a dependency of Jamaica until 1959, and governed by the Governor of Jamaica until they became a United Kingdom Dependent Territory on Jamaican independence in 1962.

Constitutional structure

Under the 1959 Constitution, as amended in 1973, the Governor, who represents the British monarch, is in charge of defence and external affairs. He chairs the 15-member Legislative Assembly, which serves a four-year term. The Executive Council acts as a Cabinet and has seven members. In February 1992, the post of Chief Secretary, abolished in 1986, was reinstated. The Chief-Secretary is the First Official Member of the Executive Council, the leader of government business in the Legislative Assembly and performs as deputy governor in the absence of the Governor.

Electoral System

In February 1992 it was announced that the number of seats to the Legislative Assembly would be increased from 12 to 15, with the quorum being increased from seven to eight. Assembly members are elected by universal adult suffrage in two-member constituencies for a maximum term of four years. The Executive Council is composed of three appointed officials and four members elected from the Legislative Assembly.

PARTY BY PARTY DATA

There are no formally constituted political parties, and all Assembly members elected on Nov. 14, 1984, were independents favouring economic development and the maintenance of colonial status; there are, however, "teams" of candidates and loose groupings within the Assembly, including one known as **Unity and Teamwork** (led by Truman Bodden) which was the biggest group in the Assembly in 1980-84. A rival "team", known as **Progress with Dignity** (led by Norman Bodden) emerged as the largest grouping after the 1984 elections. At the last election of 1988 Bodden won the island leadership. However, in August 1992, a backbench Assembly member McKeeva Bush launched the **Progressive Democratic Party** (PDP) (the first to be organized since the collapse of party politics in the 1960s) which he claimed would adopt a "progressive political attitude" in support of the islands' status as a dependent territory. He also stated that then proposed constitutional changes (see above) would need a party system to sustain them and forecast that the PDP would begin to operate when they were implemented.

Chile

Capital: Santiago **Population: 13,200,000**

The Republic of Chile won its independence in 1818 and power was monopolised by the Conservative and Liberal parties representing the landed and business elites until a period of military rule from 1927 to 1931. This was followed by a period of popular front politics which was followed by another period of political stability. Growing economic problems in the 1960s and 1970s and denial of popular demands for urgent social reform, brought the left-wing Popular Unity coalition government to power in 1970, ended in September 1973 by the military coup led by Gen. Augusto Pinochet Ugarte which ushered in a period of violent repression. Pinochet, who in 1974 was designated Supreme Chief of State and President of the Republic, sought to replace party and interest group politics with techno-administrative economic and political solutions. Various "constitutional acts" were decreed in 1976 purporting to establish an "authoritarian democracy", with executive and legislative authority vested in the President and the junta, assisted by a Cabinet. All parties were banned in 1977 and human rights were severely restricted.

An ailing economy and the continuing restrictions imposed by the junta led to a growing and visible cross-class opposition movement. In a plebescite held in October 1988, nearly 55 per cent voted against Pinochet remaining in office for a further eight years upon the expiry of his term as president in 1990. In the resulting presidential elections held on Dec. 14, 1989, Patricio Aylwin Azócar of the Christian Democratic Party (PDC), also the representative of the 17-party Coalition for Democracy (CPD), was the clear winner and he took office on March 11, 1990.

Constitutional structure

Under the March 1981 Constitution, amended and approved by referendum in July 1989, executive power lies with the President who is assisted by a 20-member Cabinet. He is directly elected for a four-year term. Legislative power is held by a bicameral National Congress, comprising a 47-member Senate serving an eight-year term and a 120-member Chamber of Deputies elected for a four-year term. The National Security Council consists of the President, the presidents of the Supreme Court and Senate and heads of the armed forces and police.

Electoral System

The President is directly elected for a four-year term and cannot be re-elected for an immediate second term. All 120 members of the Chamber of Deputies are directly elected for a four-year term and 38 of the 47 Senators are also directly elected and nine appointed by the outgoing government and the Supreme Court. The electoral law also provides for army-approved candidates for the Senate who do not necessarily need to win a majority in their constituency to be elected. Non-approved candidates need to obtain twice as many votes to win election.According to a new constitutional reform approved by Congress on Nov. 9, 1991, municipal councils and mayors are elected by direct suffrage and hold their posts for a four-year period.

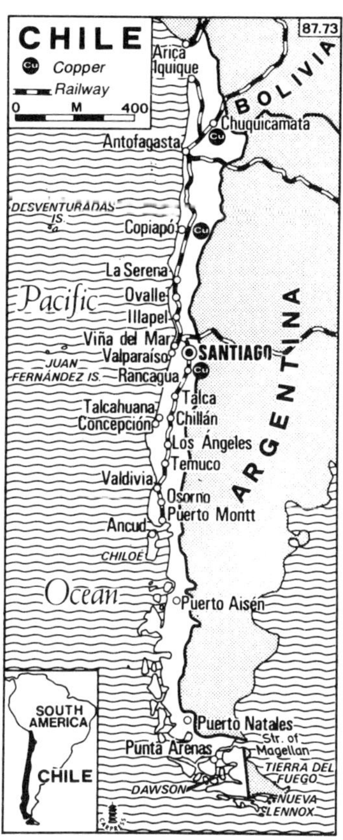
CHILE
Copper
Railway
0 M 400
87.73
Arica
Iquique
BOLIVIA
Chuquicamata
Antofagasta
DESVENTURADAS IS.
Copiapó
La Serena
Pacific
Ovalle
Illapel
Viña del Mar
Valparaíso
SANTIAGO
JUAN FERNÁNDEZ IS.
Rancagua
Talca
Talcahuana
Concepción
Chillán
Los Ángeles
Temuco
ARGENTINA
Valdivia
Osorno
Puerto Montt
Ancud
CHILOE
Ocean
Puerto Aisén
SOUTH AMERICA
CHILE
Puerto Natales
Str. of Magellan
Punta Arenas
TIERRA DEL FUEGO
DAWSON
NUEVA
LENNOX

Evolution of the suffrage

Universal adult suffrage for Chilean citizens of 18 years of age and over was re-introduced in 1989. Women obtained the vote in 1949 and the secret ballot was introduced in 1958.

Elections in 1989

Congressional election, Dec. 14, 1989

Party	*Chamber of Deputies*	*Senate**
Christian Democratic Party (PDC)	38	13
National Renewal (RN)	29	11
Party for Democracy (PPD)	17	4
Independent Democratic Union (UDI)	11	2
Independents of the Centre-Right	8	3
Socialist Party of Chile-Almeyda (now PS)	6	1
Radical Party	5	2
Humanist-Green Alliance Party	1	-
Others	5	2
Total	**120**	**38**

* Right-wing candidates for the Senate approved by the army were given preferential treatment in the elections. Nine further Senators were direct military appointees—see Electoral System

Presidential elections, Dec. 14, 1989

Candidate	*Party*	*% of vote*
Patricio Aylwin Azócar	Christian Democratic Party	55.2
Hernán Buechi	Independent	29.4
Francisco Javier Errázuriz	Independent	15.4

PARTY BY PARTY DATA

Chilean Communist Party

Partido Comunista Chileno (PCCh)
Address. San Pablo 2271, Santiago.
Leadership. Volodia Teitelboim (pres.); Gladis Marín Millie (s.-g.).
Orientation. Centre-left; no longer claims to be Marxist-Leninist following self-examination in the wake of the collapse of the Soviet Union and the Eastern bloc.
Founded. 1912.
History. Formed by Luis Emilio Recabarren as the Socialist Workers' Party, the party adopted its present name in 1922, the year it joined the Third International. The party was outlawed under President Ibañez from 1927 to 1931 and, in accordance with instructions from Moscow, in 1941 joined the Popular Front, whose members included the Socialist Party of Chile (PSCh), the Radical Party (PR), the Democratic Party (PD) and the Radical Socialist Party (PSR). The Popular Front supported the successful presidential campaign of Radical Pedro Aguirre Cerda in 1937. The PCCh continued to support successful Radical presidential candidates after the dissolution of the Popular Front in 1941, and by 1947 the party held three Cabinet posts, five seats in the Senate and 15 seats in the Chamber of Deputies. Fearing the PCCh's increasing strength, President González Videla (1946-52) banned the party under the Law for the Defence of Democracy in 1948.

Nevertheless, the party contested the 1949 general election, obtaining six seats in the Chamber of Deputies under the name of National Democratic Front, which it retained until the PCCh was legalized in 1958. Joining forces with the Socialist Party (PSCh) in 1952, it supported the unsuccessful presidential campaign of Salvador Allende and continued to do so in the elections of 1958, 1964 and 1970. The party's representation in the lower house rose from 15 seats in 1961 to 18 in 1965 and to 22 seats in 1969. By the time it was invited into the Allende government in 1970, the PCCh was one of the largest Communist Parties outside the Eastern bloc. Ironically, it had a moderating influence on the government, opposing factory and land occupations advocated by the Socialists and the Movement of the Revolutionary Left (MIR) and initiating a dialogue with the Christian Democratic Party (PDC) and the army.

The Communist Party was banned following the September 1973 military coup and many of its leaders and activists were imprisoned. Some leaders, including the party's long standing secretary-general Luís Corvalán Lepe, were allowed to go into exile in 1976.

The PCCh, however, continued to operate clandestinely and from 1980 supported mass civil disobedience and armed struggle. Its unofficial links with the Manuel Rodríguez Patriotic Front (FPMR) alienated the party from the Christian Democrats with which the PCCh had tried to form an opposition alliance. In 1983 it created the Popular Democratic Movement together with the MIR, the Christian Left, the United Popular Action Movement (MAPU) and the PS-Almeyda faction of the now split PSCh. The alliance, which organized numerous mass anti-government protest marches, was replaced by the Socialist-dominated United Left (IU) in 1987. The PCCh soon left the alliance following disagreements over the forthcoming plebiscite on whether Pinochet's period as President should be extended. By June 1988, it had joined the other left-wing parties in calling for a "no" vote.

Like other Marxist parties, the PCCh was not permitted to register in 1987 and for the December 1989 elections the party relied on the support of Christian Democrat-led Coalition for Democracy (CPD) and on PCCh-sponsored lists in exchange for the communist support elsewhere.

A month before the December 1989 general elections, the PCCh joined the Broad Party of the Socialist Left (PAIS) which, however, collapsed shortly before the polling day. PCCh candidates won a total of 300,000 votes but due to an electoral law which required non-army candidates to win twice the number of votes to be elected, the party gained no seats in Congress. The party was legalized in October 1990 and during its November 1991 conference, an occasion of intense debate, officially dropped Marxism-Leninism from its new party constitution.
Structure. Leadership is exercised through a politburo of 20, a secretariat of five and a central committee of over 100.
Publication. El Siglo (The Age)

Christian Democratic Party

Partido Demócrata Cristiano (PDC)
Address. Alameda B. O'Higgins 1460, Santiago.

Leadership. Eduardo Frei Ruíz Tagle (pres.); Gutemberg Martínez (vice-pres.); Genaro Arriagada (s.-g.).
Orientation. Christian democratic. The party has close ties with the German CDU but emphasizes its independence.
Founded. July 1957.
History. The PDC was formed as a merger of the National Falange (founded 1934) and the majority faction of the Social Christian Conservative Party. The party's leader, Eduardo Frei Montalva, came third in the presidential elections of 1958. The party built up its support in rural areas, especially through illegal rural unions. In 1961 the PDC became the largest party in Congress (and remained so until the 1973 coup) and in 1964, with the support of the Liberal Party (PL) and the Conservative Party (PC), Frei won the presidency. The recipient of grants from the USA and other sources, the Frei government implemented land and educational reforms but these fell well short of election promises of sweeping reforms. However, moderate social reform policies and increased taxation alienated the right wing of the party, while the left demanded that the PDC join the Popular Unity (UP) front backing the presidential candidacy of the socialist Salvador Allende. The left wing finally broke away from the PDC in 1969 and joined the UP as the United Popular Action Movement (see MAPU).

The Christian Democrats, with help from the USA and funding from the US Central Intelligence Agency (CIA), formed an effective and hostile opposition to the Allende government (1970-73), increasing the pressure on Allende to grant concessions to them and the military.

The Pinochet coup was welcomed by a large majority of the party, including the then party president Patricio Aylwin Azócar. However, its allegiance to the junta diminished as Pinochet developed his own political agenda. In 1977, the PDC was banned, along with all other parties. In August 1983 the party founded the Democratic Alliance (AD), a centre-left alliance which superseded the *Multipartidaria* alliance formed only months earlier. In 1986 the party announced its acceptance of the military's 1980 Constitution but at the same time became the main force in the AD's campaign for free elections and was a signatory to the National Democratic Accord, an opposition document outlining the agenda for a transition to democracy.

The conservative wing gained control of the party in August 1987 when Aylwin was re-elected president of the PDC. Despite strong internal dissent, the PDC registered for the forthcoming elections under the new restrictive party law. Aylwin became the spokesman for the "Command for the No Vote" a 13-party opposition alliance which successfully campaigned against the extension of Pinochet's term as President, an issue submitted to a plebiscite on Oct. 5, 1988. The popular support, energy and enthusiasm generated by the "no" was harnessed to establish the Coalition for Democracy (CPD), a 17-member electoral alliance led by the Christian Democrats. In July 1989 the CPD parties agreed to support Aylwin as the main opposition presidential candidate. His campaign programme included pledges to investigate human rights abuses, improve education and health care and increase the minimum wage within the context of a sound economic programme designed to boost exports and control inflation. In the Dec. 14, 1989, elections, Aylwin was elected President with 55.2 per cent of the valid votes. The PDC, with 38 seats in the Chamber of deputies and 13 seats in the Senate, became the largest party in the Congress.

Aylwin met Pinochet in a private meeting seven days after the elections, and on March 2, 1990, an agreement was reached with the pro-Pinochet Independent Democratic Union (UDI) to appoint the PDC's former president Gabriel Valdés as President of the Senate. (The presidency of the Chamber of Deputies went to another member of a CPD party.) Aylwin, inaugurated on March 11, 1990, set up a CPD coalition government in which the PDC obtained half the cabinet posts, including the important Interior, Finance, National Defence and Justice portfolios. His style of government balanced the need to negotiate with the right while still pursuing the aims spelt out during the election campaign (see CPD). One notable achievement was the establishment of a Truth and Reconciliation Commission (CVR) in April 1990, whose report, released in March 1991, catalogued the cases of thousands of people murdered, tortured and abducted under the Pinochet dictatorship.

In preparation for the presidential elections in 1993, the party elected Eduardo Frei, senator for Santiago and son of the party founder, as its new president on Nov. 23, 1991. Frei, who entered politics only in 1988 as a member of the "Committee for Free Elections" won the leadership with 70 per cent of the votes.

Aylwin came increasingly under pressure from several CPD parties and the right-wing National Renewal (RN) to extend his presidential term, warning that to go ahead with the forthcoming elections would upset the smooth return to democracy, a claim Aylwin flatly rejected. In March 1992 he presented for congressional debate a package of constitutional reforms designed to distance further the government from the military (see CPD).

Structure. In November 1991, for the first time, the party elected its president and national council by the direct votes of individual members.

Publications. La Epoca (The Epoch), daily.

International Affiliations. Member party of the Christian Democrat Organization of America, which forms part of the Christian Democrat International.

Christian Left

Izquierda Cristiana (IC)

Address. Comañía 2404, Santiago.

Leadership. Roberto Celedón (s.-g.).

Orientation. Left-wing Christian.

Founded. 1971.

History. The IC originated in a left-wing faction of the Christian Democratic Party (PDC) which split away in 1971. It joined President Allende's Popular Unity government but joined the opposition in November 1972 when some military officers were invited into the government. Like all left-wing parties, the IC was banned after the 1973 military coup. Although the party remained close to the Communist Party (PCCh), the IC joined the Chilean Socialist bloc in 1983. Although critical of it, the IC was a signatory of the National Democratic Agreement in November 1986. In June 1987 the IC became a founder member of the United Left (IU) which replaced the Communist-led Popular Democratic Movement (MDP). The IU was itself substituted by the short-lived Broad Party of the Socialist Left (PAIS), led by the IC's president Luis Maira, which was dissolved shortly before the December 1989 general election.

Coalition for Democracy

Concertación de los Partidos por la Democracía (CPD)

Leadership. Patricio Aylwin Azócar (l.).

Orientation. Centrist. In his presidential campaign for the December 1989 elections Aylwin campaigned on a platform of social welfare and education reforms, an increase in the minimum wage, an end to human rights abuses (and a full investigation of past abuses), and increased exports and low inflation.

Founded. November 1988.

Member parties. Centre Alliance Party; Christian Democrat Party; Christian Left; Radical Party; Social Democratic Party; Socialist Party; United Popular Action Movement.

History. The CPD arose out of the Democratic Alliance led by the Christian Democratic Party (PDC) and the "Command for the No Vote" opposition alliance which successfully campaigned to prevent Pinochet extending his Presidential term of office beyond 1990, a view subsequently endorsed in a plebiscite held in October 1988. The CPD formed a united front against the right in the December 1989 general election and presented an all-encompassing proposal for constitutional reform in January 1990. Pinochet, under pressure from his own Cabinet and the right-wing National Renewal (PR) party, agreed to discuss the proposals the following March and in May Interior Minister Caceres put forward a 54-point proposal for constitutional amendments. These were cautiously welcomed by the CPD as a step towards an orderly transition to democracy.

In order not to fragment the pro-democracy vote in the Dec. 14, 1989, presidential election, the CPD's 17 member parties officially decided in July 1989 to back Patricio Aylwin, the CPD leader and already the presidential candidate for the PDC (the coalition's largest party). The parties, however, fought the simultaneous congressional elections separately. Aylwin won the Presidency with a clear majority of 55.2 per cent of the valid vote. The CPD parties won an overall majority in Congress, commanding 72 of the 120 seats in the Chamber and 22 in the Senate, although the CPD's dominance in the Senate was erased by the addition of nine military right-wing appointees.

After his inauguration in March 1990, Aylwin formed a CPD coalition government with Cabinet posts allocated to the main alliance parties proportionate to their representation in Congress. After negotiations with the pro-Pinochet Independent Democratic Union (UDI) the presidency of the Chamber and Senate also went to CPD members. Aylwin had the difficult task of implementing the coalition's election promises while adopting a conciliatory approach towards the military and the two main right-wing parties. Thus Aylwin allowed Pinochet to remain Commander-in-Chief of the Armed Forces. However, in December 1990 he vetoed two army promotions put forward by Pinochet. Almost all of the 383 political prisoners were released under Aylwin and in March 1991, responding to popular demands, the Rettig report on human rights was released. This was produced by the Truth and Reconciliation Commission (CVR), set up by Aylwin in April 1990, and catalogued the cases of thousands of people murdered, tortured or kidnapped under the Pinochet dictatorship. In November 1991 the CPD government also passed a new constitutional reform allowing local elections by direct suffrage and in March 1992 further proposed constitutional amendments were announced, operable from 1997 when Pinochet was due to step down as Commander-in-Chief of the Armed Forces, which marked an attempt to distance the government further from the military. Chief among the proposed reforms would be the right of a future President to remove heads of the armed forces, forbidden under the current 1980 military constitution.

Humanist-Green Alliance Party

Partido Alianza Humanista-Verde
Address. Victoria Subercaseaux 181, Of. 43, Santiago.
Leadership. Laura Rodríguez Ricomini (pres.); José Gabriel Pérez Nazarola (s.-g.)
Orientation. An ecological and pacifist alliance which campaigns to legalize divorce, favours social spending programmes and opposes arms spending; over half the party members are women and the average age is 25-28 years.
Founded. 1989.
History. The Humanist Party (*Partido Humanista*—PH) was founded in 1984 by the "Siloista" Human Development Community whose ideas were inspired by Silo Mario Rodríguez Cobo who in the late 1960s called for measures to relieve economic, religious and psychological suffering. The Greens (*Los Verdes*) were founded by Andrés R. Koryzma in 1987. Both parties registered for the forthcoming election under the 1987 electoral law. In order to be more effective the two parties fielded joint candidates under one party name in the December 1989 general election and one of its leaders, Laura Rodríguez, was elected to Congress.

Independent Democratic Union

Unión Demócrata Independiente (UDI)
Address. Suecia 286, Providencia, Santiago.
Leadership. Julio Dittborn Cordúa (pres.); Joaquín Lavín Infante (s.-g.).
Orientation. Right-wing.
Founded. 1980s.
History. The UDI was formed as a right-wing pressure group whose original platform was for the military to authorize the creation of a nominal parliament in order to counteract growing popular demands for a transition to democracy. The UDI merged with two other groups to form the National Renewal (PR) party in 1987 but was expelled in April 1988. It supported Gen. Pinochet's attempt to extend his presidency, voted down in the October 1988 plebiscite. After Pinochet's defeat, the UDI decided against fielding their own presidential candidate. In an attempt to distance itself from the military regime, the party backed the presidential candidacy of Hernán Buechi, the Finance Minister and an independent right-wing technocrat who came second in the December 1989 elections. However, benefiting from the electoral law which favoured army-nominated candidates, the UDI obtained 11 seats in the Chamber and two seats in the Senate. As the fourth largest party in Congress, the UDI was consulted by President Aylwin on such issues as the appointment of the presidents of the Chamber and Senate, the modification of tax laws and the holding of municipal elections in June 1992. The party was dealt a serious blow in April 1991 when its president, Jaime Guzmán, was assassinated. Although two left-wing guerrilla groups claimed responsibility, it was widely believed that he was shot by right-wing *agents provocateurs* in order to destabilize the government and prompt the intervention of the army.

Manuel Rodríguez Patriotic Movement

Movimiento Patriotico Manuel Rodríguez (MPMR)
Leadership. Alfredo Malbrich (l.).
Orientation. Left-wing.
Founded. 1983.
History. The party was originally a guerrilla group set up by Communist Party (PCCh) members to fight the Pinochet regime by kidnapping or shooting members of the junta and the army. In 1987 the Manuel Rodríguez Patriotic Front (FPMR), as it was then called, suspended all guerrilla activities to facilitate the holding of the plebiscite in October 1988 on whether or not Pinochet's term as President should be extended beyond 1990. Despite the recent killing by the security forces of one of its leaders in September,

the FPMR urged its supporters to vote, and following Pinochet's defeat it announced in November that it would abandon the armed struggle in the near future. This decision, however, caused a major rift in the Front and led to the splitting away of the more militant wing (see Autonomous Manuel Rodríguez Patriotic Front). The original FPMR continued its guerrilla existence, marking its fifth anniversary in December 1988 with 20 bomb attacks in Santiago and other cities. In January 1989 it shot down a helicopter, killing three senior army officials. Several of its leaders remained in exile, including Sergio Buschmann, who obtained refugee status in Sweden, and Eduardo Rojas, who returned to Australia, after the USA refused to extradite them to Chile in June 1989. In June 1991 the Front finally laid down its arms and converted itself into a political party, adopting its present name. Although welcoming the move, President Aylwin's Interior Minister warned that he could not guarantee that members would not be prosecuted for past crimes.

Movement of the Revolutionary Left

Movimiento de Izquierda Revolucionario (MIR)
Address. Catedral 1893, Santiago.
Leadership. Patricio Rivas (l.).
Orientation. Left-wing pro-Cuban with some Maoist and Trotskyist influences; the MIR has been suspected of having links with the ETA, the Basque separatist movement.
Founded. 1965.
History. The MIR was formed by a group led by Miguel Enríquez consisting mainly of students at the University of Concepción. Although initially the MIR adopted a policy of guerrilla struggle, by 1970 it lent its guarded support to the Popular Unity (UP) coalition supporting Salvador Allende (see PSU under Socialist Party—PS). The MIR, who were legalized by Allende, participated in the seizure of land and factories and generally campaigned for more radical government policies. Anticipating a renewed attempt by the military to seize power, following the failed coup in June 1973, the MIR prepared for armed resistance, but relied on its own guerrilla campaign rather than linking itself to a spontaneous movement of armed workers who had seized factories and had created no-go areas, especially in the capital, Santiago. MIR attacks continued after the September coup which finally overthrew Allende. A large number of MIR members were killed in gun battles or executed by the Pinochet military regime, including its general secretary Miguel Enríquez. His successor, Andrés Pascal Allende, nephew of the late President, spent several years in exile after seeking asylum in the Costa Rican embassy in 1975.

The MIR continued to be active throughout the Pinochet regime but by the early 1980s concentrated more on the mass protest movement. In 1983 the MIR became a member of the Communist-led Popular Democratic Movement (MPD—see Chilean Communist Party) and in 1987 the majority MIR faction joined the United Left (IU) coalition, although a large proportion of the MIR's leaders were in exile or in prison in Chile. In May 1988 the MIR leadership split into a National Secretariat which opposed registration for the October 1988 plebiscite and supported guerrilla warfare, and the Central Committee, in Chile, which sought to participate in the democratic movement. The latter faction joined the short-lived Broad Party of the Socialist Left (PAIS) in 1989. Following the victory of the Coalition for Democracy (CPD) alliance in the December 1989 general election, the two MIR factions officially rejected any armed action.

National Renewal

Renovación Nacional (RN)
Address. Antonio Varas 454, Providencia, Santiago.
Leadership. Andrés Allamand (pres.); Roberto Ossandón (s.-g.).
Orientation. Right-wing; in the 1989 election campaign the RN promised to protect the 1980 Constitution installed by the Pinochet regime and prevent it being dismantled wholesale.
Founded. 1987.
History. The party was created by a merger of the National Union, the National Labour Front and the Independent Democratic Union (UDI, which was expelled a year later). Although pro-Pinochet, the RN distanced itself from his regime, and following the October 1988 plebiscite rejection of an extension of Pinochet's presidency the party tried to project a moderate image by declaring itself willing to negotiate with the pro-democracy movement. In early 1989 the RN put pressure on Pinochet to consider the constitutional reform proposals put forward by the Coalition for Democracy (CPD). In April 1989, with Pinochet's lukewarm approval, leaders of the RN formed a legal commission with the CPD to agree on

some reforms aimed at re-establishing a workable democracy. These included the re-drafting of Article 8 of the Constitution outlawing Marxist parties, the reduction of the presidential term and the curbing of the powers of the military's National Security Council.

In May 1989 the RN announced the candidacy of Sergio Onofre Jarpa, a former Interior Minister, for the December 1989 presidential elections, but when he withdrew, the party backed the independent right-wing candidate Hernán Buechi, Pinochet's former Finance Minister.

The RN was not so much interested in becoming the dominant party in Congress as in beating its rival, the UDI, in the elections and thus establishing itself as the major right-wing party. Aided by the bias of the current electoral law towards military-approved right-wing candidates, the RN won the second largest representation in the legislature with 29 seats in the Chamber of Deputies and 11 in the Senate.

Furthermore, one of its members, William Thayer, was one of the nine military-appointed senators. The party was accordingly consulted by the CPD government on several occasions and in 1990 was invited to join the government's Truth and Reconciliation Commission (CVR), investigating human rights abuses under the military (see CPD), an offer it refused. In late 1991 Jarpa, together with some CPD parties, tried to persuade President Aylwin to extend his mandate, claiming that presidential elections in 1993 would be disruptive of the smooth return to democracy.

Party for Democracy

Partido por la Democracia (PPD)
Address. Padre Luis Valdivia 327, Santiago.
Leadership. Erick Schnake Silva (pres.); Sergio Bitar Chacra (s.-g.).
Orientation. Centre-left.
Founded. December 1987.
History. The party was founded by Ricardo Lagos as a political vehicle for the illegal Socialist Party (PS), of which all PPD members and leaders retained their membership. The PPD supported the "no" campaign leading up to the October 1988 plebiscite and was a member of the Coalition for Democracy (CPD) from its inception in November 1988. After the CPD victory in the December 1989 general election, the PPD became the third largest party in Congress with 17 seats in the Chamber and four seats in the Senate despite the anti-left bias in the electoral law. Lagos was appointed Education Minister in the CPD government. The post of Secretary General of the Government went to another member of the PPD. Following the unification of the various socialist factions into one party and legalization of the PS, the PPD's automatic membership of the PS was officially withdrawn in December 1990.

Radical Party

Partido Radical (PR)
Address. Londres 57, Santiago.
Leadership. Carlos González Marquez (pres.); Mario Astorga Gutiérrez (s.-g.).
Orientation. Social democratic.
Founded. 1861.
History. The PR was formed by a group which split away from the Liberal Party (PL). It was Chile's main progressive party in the decades around the turn of the century and was in government from 1938 to 1952.

The party lost power following bitter faction fights which led to the breakaway of two groups. The party held some ministerial posts in the National Party government of Jorge Alessandri (1958-64) but in 1969, after the defection of its right-wing faction to Alessandri's camp, it joined the broad Popular Unity (PU) alliance backing the presidential candidacy of the socialist Salvador Allende (see Socialist Party).

The PR won over 13 per cent of the vote in the 1970 election and held several cabinet posts in the PU administration. Driven underground after the 1973 military coup and divided over a new party constitution, the party split into three factions. The left-wing and centrist factions went into exile in Mexico while the moderate faction, led by Enrique Silva Cimma, continued to operate within Chile and retained the larger domestic following.

This faction was a founder member of the Democratic Alliance led by the Christian Democratic Party (PDC) and formed in August 1983, and in 1988 it joined the Coalition for Democracy (CPD). The factions in exile supported the Popular Democratic Movement (MDP) led by the Communist Party (PCCh) and in 1987 became a founder member of the MDP's successor, the United Left (IU). The different factions were re-united in the CPD after the dissolution of the IU coalition. The Radical Party became an influential force in the CPD and after the election of the CPD candidate Patricio Aylwin to the presidency in December 1989, the PR obtained the Agriculture and Foreign Affairs portfolios in the CPD government. *International affiliations.* Member of the Socialist International.

Socialist Party

Partido Socialista (PS)
Address. Concha y Toro 36, Santiago.
Leadership. Ricardo Nuñez Muñoz (pres.); Manuel Almeyda (s.-g.); Jorge Arrate (vice-pres.).
Founded. 1933.
Orientation. Centre-left.
History. The Socialist Party was formed by a merger of six parties which had supported the Socialist Republic proclaimed by Col. Marmaduke Grove which lasted 13 days. It had a strong trade union base and committed itself to Marxism-Leninism. Its ranks swelled by the merger with the Trotskyist Communist Left party, the PS won 19 seats in the Chamber of Deputies in the 1937 elections as part of a left-wing Popular Front alliance. After several conflicts with the Communist Party of Chile (PCCh) the Socialist Party suffered a major split in 1948, dividing into the Socialist Party of Chile (PSCh), which supported three deputies expelled from the PS for voting for the banning of the Communist Party (PCCh), and the Popular Socialist Party (PSP) which was led by Salvador Allende. In 1952 Allende contested the presidential elections for the PSCh after losing the election for nomination as PSP candidate. Both parties (together with the Communist Party) became allies in the Popular Action Front (FRAP) in the early 1950s and merged in 1957 as the Socialist Party (PSCh). Allende again stood unsuccessfully for the presidency in 1958 and 1964. The reunited Socialist Party (PS) joined the Popular Unity alliance (UP) in 1969 and with Allende as its candidate won the 1970 presidential elections, the PS receiving 22.8 per cent of the overall UP vote.

Allende's reforms included the full nationalization of the copper industry, a price freeze and an increase in wages. The Socialists, who held four ministerial posts in the Allende coalition government, proved to be the most radical force, initially supporting land and factory seizures but then increasingly calling for moderation and refusing to arm the working class when a coup seemed imminent. The Allende government, dogged by spiralling inflation, a US embargo, economic sabotage by the business sector and pressure from the army, made increasing concessions to the right and in late 1972 included members of the military in the cabinet.

After the 1973 coup, in which Allende lost his life, many of the PS leaders were either killed, imprisoned, tortured or exiled. The party fragmented as a result of disagreements over Allende's failure, and continued to split throughout the 1970s and 1980s. In 1983 the establishment of the Chilean Socialist bloc failed to reunite the various Socialist groups. Instead the PS left-wing faction, led by Clodomiro Almeyda Medina (Foreign Minister under Allende), joined the Popular Democratic Movement (MDP) led by the Communist Party (PCCh). The other main faction, led by Ricardo Núñez, along with other minor PS factions, became a member of the moderate Democratic Alliance until 1987. In 1987 the PS-Almeyda faction combined with two other minor PS factions and dominated the United Left (IU), set up in the same year, which the Núñez PS wing refused to join. The PS-Almeyda campaigned for the "no" vote in the 1988 plebiscite (see CPD), a position which alienated it from other IU members—the PS "Historic" faction, together with the PCCh and part of the MIR—who boycotted the plebiscite. In 1989, both the PS "Historic" and "Almeyda" factions participated with the Communist party (PCCh) in the short-lived Broad Party of the Socialist Left (PAIS). The PS-Almeyda and left-wing Radicals subsequently made a pact with the Coalition for Democracy (CPD) supporting the victorious presidential campaign of Patricio Aylwin in December 1989. In the simultaneous congressional elections, the PS-Almeyda won six seats in the Chamber of Deputies and one in the Senate.

After the elections, the Socialists reunited in the Unified Socialist Party (PSU), which attracted members of the United Popular Action Movement (MAPU) and the Christian Left (IC) and was supported by the socialist wing of the Party for Democracy (PPD). The PSU was given four cabinet posts in the new coalition government.

The merger of the main PS factions—the PS-Almeyda, the moderate Núñez PS "renewalists" and the left-wing Unitary Socialists (PS-Unitario)—occurred in early 1990. At the PS party congress in December 1990 Nuñez and Jorge Arrate, both members of the renewalist faction, agreed to share the leadership by switching the posts of president and vice-president each year. At the same

Congress, it was also decided to abolish the automatic membership of the PS by members of the PPD.

Minor parties

Centre Alliance Party (*Partido Alianza de Centro*—PAC, Marín 0550, Santiago); led by Pedro Esquivel Santander (pres.), Patricio Rosende (s.-g.); a centrist party, the PAC is a member party of the Coalition for Democracy (CDP) and after the December 1989 elections was awarded the Public Works portfolio in the Aylwin government.

Communist Renewal Assembly (Asamblea de Renovación Comunista—ARCO).

Left Democratic Participation (*Participación Democrática de Izquierda*—PDI, Pasaje República 15, Depto. 11, Santiago); Fanny Pollarolo pres., Antonio Leal s.-g.; formed in late May 1991 by a Communist group which split away from the left-wing Communist Renewal Assembly (ARCO).

Liberal Party (*Partido Liberal*—PL, San Antonio 418, Of. 803, Santiago); Hugo Cepeda Barrios (pres.) Eduardo Díaz Herrera (s.-g.); the result of the merger in May 1990 of the Liberal Party (PL), led by Cepeda, and the Party of the South (PdeS), led by Díaz.

National Advance (*Avanzada Nacional*—AN); Col. (retd.) Alvaro Corbalán pres., Patricio Hidalgo vice-pres; an ultra right-wing party supporting Pinochet.

National Centrist Party (*Partido Nacional de Centro*—PNC, Compañía 1263, Santiago); a centre-right party founded in May 1990 through a merger of the National Party, the National Vanguard Party, the Free Democratic Centre and the Social Democratic Faction. The party claims a membership of 137,000.

Social Democratic Party (Partido Social Demócrata—PSD); Arturo Venegas (pres.); formed in the early 1980s, the PSD became a member of the Democratic Alliance in 1983 (see Christian Democratic Party). In 1986 the party supported the National Democratic Accord demanding free elections but in August 1988 the PSD defected from the "Command for the No Vote", which it rejected because of the involvement of left-wing parties, and supported Pinochet in the October 1988 plebiscite (see Coalition for Democracy).

United Popular Action Movement (Movimiento de Acción Popular Unitaria—MAPU); founded in 1969; by a left-wing group which broke away from the Christian Democratic Party (PDC). Soon after, MAPU joined the Popular Unity (UP) coalition backing the successful presidential candidacy of Salvador Allende. The party split into two main factions after going underground following the 1973 coup. Both factions joined an alliance affiliated to the Communist-led Popular Democratic Movement (MDP—see Communist Party) in 1983 and became founder members of the MDP's successor, the United Left, in 1987. MAPU joined the Coalition for Democracy (CPD) when the United Left broke up.

Guerrilla Groups

Autonomous Manuel Rodríguez Patriotic Front (Frente-Patriótico-Manuel Rodríguez-Autónomo FPMR-A); formed following a split in the Manuel Rodríguez Patriotic Front (FPMR) in 1988 as a result of the denunciation of violence by the Communist Party (PCCh). While the main FPMR followed the PCCh party line and laid down its arms after the restoration of democracy in 1990, the FPMR-A continued with the armed struggle. In March 1990 the group made an assassination attempt on the former air force chief and participant in the 1973 military coup, General Gustavo Leigh. The FPMR-A threatened to carry out other acts of "popular justice" if police and military personnel involved in the Pinochet regime were not tried. A sub-group, the Manuel Rodriguez Patriotic Front Militias (Milicias Rodriguistas), bombed the office of the National Renewal Party (RN) and business and residential areas in the capital, Santiago, in September 1991 to mark the anniversary of Pinochet's accession.

Lautaro Popular Rebel Forces (*Fuerzas Rebeldes Populares Lautaro*—FRPL); a nominally left-wing urban terrorist group which killed two policemen in July 1989 during a clash with people trying to occupy housing. A spin-off, the Lautauro Youth Movement Militias, claimed responsibility for a bomb attack on the University of Santiago in September 1991 to mark the anniversary of Pinochet's accession.

People's Fatherland Subversive Co-ordinating Board; believed to be a right-wing terrorist organization and reported to have claimed responsibility for several bomb explosions in Santiago on March 30, 1992.

Colombia

Capital: Bogotá **Population: 33,000,000**

The Republic of Colombia gained independence from Spain in 1819 after liberation by the forces of Simón Bolivar and, after several boundary changes, became a Republic in 1886. Until recently Colombian parliamentary politics was dominated by the Liberal Party (CPL) and the Conservative Party (now Social Conservative Party—PSC), which were both founded in the 1840s. Colombia's only military government this century was overthrown in 1958, when the two rival parties joined forces and formed a National Front coalition government which lasted from 1958 until 1974. The PL and PSC continued to dominate the political system until the general election of May 27, 1990, when other parties came to the fore.

Constitutional structure

Approved by 90 per cent of the votes cast (26 per cent of registered voters) in a referendum which took place simultaneously with the general election of May 27, 1990, a National Constitutional Assembly was established to revise the Constitution of 1886. In December 1990, 70 members were directly elected and three seats were allocated by the government to former guerrilla groups. The Assembly opened on Feb. 5, 1991, and the new Constitution came into force at midnight on July 5, 1991.

Executive authority is vested in the President. Under the new Constitution new posts of Vice-President, Fiscal General, and Defender of the People were created to assist the President in policy-making. The President is also assisted by a 14-member Cabinet which he appoints. Legislative power is vested in a bicameral Congress which was reduced to 102 seats in the Senate and 161 in the House of Representatives. Members of Congress cannot hold any other public post. The President was given temporary special legislative powers until a new Congress was installed on Dec. 1, 1991. The indigenous population was given judicial autonomy in minor internal disputes within certain recognized territories.

Electoral system

The President is elected directly for a four-year term by direct universal suffrage and may not serve a second consecutive term. A system of proportional representation operates for the election of members of both houses, who are also elected for a four-year period. The Senate has 99 nationally elected members; indigenous people in specific regions have two appointed Senators selected in special elections and one elected Senator. Each of

84.78
Caribbean
Sea
Santa Marta
Barranquilla
Cartagena
Valledupar
Coveñas
Montería
PANAMA
Petrólea
Cúcuta
Magdalena
VENEZUELA
Bucaramanga
Pacific
Ocean
Medellín
Paz del Río
La Dorada
Pto. Carreño
Orinoco
Manizales
Pereira
BOGOTÁ
Meta
Ibagué
Villavicencio
Pto. Inírida
Buenaventura
Cali
Neiva
COLOMBIA
Popayán
Pasto
Florencia
Mitú
Mocoa
Caquetá
BRAZIL
ECUADOR
Putumayo
PERU
Amazon
Railway
0 km 400
Leticia
COLOMBIA
SOUTH AMERICA
CARPRESS

Sequence of elections since 1980

Congressional elections took place on March 11, 1990. The Liberal-dominated Congress was again dissolved by the Constitutional Assembly on July 2, 1991, to hold fresh legislative elections.

	Winning Party	
Date	*Congress*	*President*
1982	Liberal Party	Conservative Party
1986	Liberal Party	Liberal Party
1990	Liberal Party	Liberal Party
1991	Liberal Party	Liberal Party

Presidential election of May 27, 1990

Presidential candidate	*Party*	*% Votes*
César Gaviria Trujillo	Partido Liberal (PL)	47.4
lvaro Gómez	National Salvation Movement (MSN)	23.8
Antonio Navarro Wolff	Alianza Democrática M-19 (ADM-19)	12.6
Rodrigo Lloreda	Partido Social Conservador (PSC)	12.2
Other eight candidates		4.0

Congressional and Gubernatorial elections, October 27, 1991

Party	*Senate*	*House of Represent-atives*	*Governors*
Liberal Party (PL)	58	86	18
Social Conservative Party (PSC)	10	15	3
Democratic Alliance (ADM-19)	9	15	-
New Democratic Force (NFD)	9	12*	-
National Salvation Movement (MSN)	5	12	1
Christian National Party (PNC)	1	-	-
Patriotic Union (UP)	1	2	-
National Conservative Movement (MNC)	1	-	-
National Progressive Movement (MNP)	1	-	-
United Movement for Colombia (MUPC)	1	-	-
Christian Party	1	-	-
Unitary Metapolitico (UM)	1	-	-
Independent	1	-	-
Indigenous elected	1	-	-
Indigenous appointed	2	-	-
Coalition	-	-	2
MC	-	-	1
Antioquian Untd. Movement (MAU)	-	-	1
Popular Movement of the Caribbean (MPC)	-	-	1
Totals	**102**	**160**	**27**

*estimated

the 23 departments, four intendencies and five commissaries (32 states) elects two members of the House of Representatives and further seats are allotted to each state on the basis of population. Governors, under the new constitution, are elected directly in the 27 departments and intendencies.

Evolution of the suffrage

All Colombian citizens aged 18 or over are eligible to vote, except members of the armed forces on active service, the national police and people who have been deprived of their political rights. Women obtained the vote in 1957.

PARTY BY PARTY DATA

April 19 Movement

Movimiento 19 de Abril (M-19)
Leadership. Otty Patiño (l.).
Orientation. Left-wing, former guerrilla group; the party stands for national independence and "Bolivarism", economic and political democracy, and social justice.
Founded. 1973.
History. The M-19 was formed by National Popular Alliance (ANAPO) supporters as the party's armed wing in reaction to the disputed April 19, 1970, election results. The group's ideology was originally an amalgam of Marxism-Leninism and the radical liberal ideas of Jorge Eliécer Gaitán (assassinated 1948), which attracted dissident members of the FARC guerrilla group to M-19. As its first public act, M-19 seized Simón Bolívar's sword and spurs in January 1974. ANAPO, which had shifted to the right, disassociated itself from M-19 soon after.

M-19 started its guerrilla activity, involving mainly kidnappings and sabotage of multinational companies, in 1976, with the abduction and killing of a trade union leader whom M-19 suspected of having links with the CIA. In early 1982 the guerrillas suffered heavy losses in counterinsurgency operations and clashes with the new right-wing paramilitary group Death to Kidnappers (MAS). In August 1984, M-19, by now Colombia's most prominent guerrilla group, announced its intention to become a political party and agreed to a one-year ceasefire with the Betancur government. In June 1985, however, M-19 resumed its guerrilla warfare against the government in response to army and MAS attacks on its camps in which several of its leaders, including its founder Carlos Toledo Plata, were killed. On November 6-7, 1985, M-19 occupied the Palace of Justice in Bogotá and in the ensuing storming of the building by the army all 41 guerrillas and over 60 other people, including 12 members of the Supreme Court, were killed. In the same year the M-19 group set up the Simón Bolívar National Guerrilla Co-ordinating Board (CNGSB) to co-ordinate Colombia's guerrilla movements.

In May 1988 M-19, in an attempt to force the government to hold peace talks, kidnapped the former PSC presidential candidate Alvaro Gómez Hurtado. The Barco government put forward a peace plan the following September as a result. The M-19 called a unilateral ceasefire, and negotiations began in January 1989. An agreement with the government on reintegration of the M-19 into civilian life was signed on March 17, 1989. The CNGSB subsequently announced that the M-19, having disregarded the agreed guidelines on negotiations, was no longer a member. In October 1989 the M-19 was constituted as a political party and on March 9, 1990, the guerrillas signed a final peace treaty with the government and surrendered their arms. In exchange the government guaranteed the M-19 a general amnesty, full political participation in elections and the holding of a referendum on the question of a new constitution.

In April 1990 the M-19 leader and popular presidential candidate for the newly-formed Democratic Alliance M-19 (ADM19) Carlos Pizarro Leongómez was gunned down, it was thought, at the instigation of the Medellín drugs cartel. He was replaced as candidate in the May presidential elections by Antonio Navarro Wolff who came third with 12.6 per cent of the vote. The new President, César Gaviria Trujillo, appointed Navarro Wolff, to his Cabinet, for which he had to relinquish his post as leader of the M-19. Navarro Wolff was Health Minister until he resigned in November to stand in the Constitutional Assembly elections of December 1990, and his Cabinet post was taken up by Camilo González Pozo, also of the M-19. The M-19 won the majority of the 19 ADM-19 seats and as leaders of the Constitutional Assembly's largest opposition block made an important contribution to the drawing-up of the Constitution which came into effect in July 1991. In the congressional and gubernatorial elections of October 27, 1991, the M-19 suffered a drop in support although the ADM-19 won the third-largest number of votes and gained 9 seats in the Senate and 15 in the House of Representatives. Navarro Wolff was largely blamed for this by a group within the ADM-19 which believed that the M-19 had excessively compromised principles it should have defended more vigorously in the Constitutional Assembly. In the municipal elections of March 1992 the party suffered further losses, especially in the capital, Bogotá.

Colombian Communist Party

Partido Comunista de Colombia (PCC)

Address. Carrera 34, 9-28 Apartado Aéreo, 8886 Bogotá.

Leadership. Gilberto Vieira (l.); Francisco Caraballo (sec.-gen.).

Orientation. Communist in name only, chiefly reformist; campaigns for free social services, agrarian reform and nationalisation of the oil and coal industries.

Founded. 1930.

History. The party originates in the Communist Group, later called the Socialist Revolutionary Party, which disbanded in 1930. The PCC became very active in peasants' land seizures and in dockers' and plantation workers' unions, and PCC candidates held seats in Congress under the Liberal (PL) governments of 1934-38 and 1942-45. The PCC's support for the Liberal Party's traditionalist faction against the populist leader Gaitán in the 1940s caused the Communist Party to split into three factions. The party was forced underground in the late 1940s and was banned under the Rojas dictatorship of 1956. In 1958, having been restored to semi-legality the previous year, the PCC gave its support to the first PL/Social Conservative Party (PSC) "National Front" government. Some PCC members were elected to Congress on PL lists, while the party won some local elections in alliance with the Revolutionary Liberal Movement (MRL) which lasted until 1974. At the same time the PCC became involved in the armed struggle and in 1966 the Revolutionary Armed Forces of Colombia (FARC), whose leader Manuel Marulanda had been a member of the PCC's Central Committee since 1960, was adopted as the Communist Party's armed wing. From 1974 the PCC fought national elections in alliance with other small parties. Although around 20 per cent of Colombia's organized labour was represented by PCC-controlled trade unions, its electoral coalitions performed badly at the polls: the presidential candidate for the United Front (UNO) won 3 per cent of the vote in 1974 and 2 per cent in 1978; the new Democratic Unity of the Left (UDI) alliance gained two Congressional seats in 1982. In 1985 the PCC became the main force behind the formation of the Patriotic Union (UP) which was set up in response to President Betancur's peace proposals to Colombia's guerrilla groups. The PCC has since operated with the UP as one, and following the UP's electoral successes, PCC members suffered increased repression. By 1987 the PCC claimed that some 500 of its members had been killed. Two Central Committee members (and UP leaders) were assassinated in early 1989: Téofilio Forero on Jan. 27 and José Antequera on March 3. The latter killing was claimed by the right-wing Death to Kidnappers (MAS) group and was suspected to be a retaliation for the killing a few days earlier of drug trafficker and "emerald king" Gilberto Molina.

Following the UP's disappointing election results in October 1991 it was announced by the PCC spokesman that a new alliance comprising the PCC, the "A Luchar" movement and splinter groups of the PL and PC would be formed after the UP congress in mid-December 1991.

Membership. 16,000 (1989 estimate).

Structure. The 80-member central committee is elected by a national congress every four years. The central committee in turn appoints an executive committee (14 members) and secretariat.

Publication. Voz Proletaria (Proletarian Voice), weekly.

Democratic Alliance M-19

Alianza Democrática M-19 (ADM-19)

Leadership. Antonio Navarro Wolff (l.).

Orientation. A left-wing coalition; in the 1990 presidential election campaign, the ADM-19 called for a new constitution and opposed the extradition of suspected drug traffickers to stand trial in the USA.

Founded. April 1990.

History. The alliance, led by the former guerrilla group April 19 Movement (M-19), was set up in conjunction with former Director of the anti-guerrilla Department for the Administration of Security (DAS) Gen. José Joaquín Matallana, the Christian Democrats (DC) and the small United Colombia organization. It was primarily formed to contest congressional and municipal elections of March 11, 1990, in Bogotá and the surrounding province and to back the presidential candidacy of the M-19 leader Carlos Pizarro Léongómez in May. Léongómez, however, was assassinated on April 26, days before the ADM-19's founding congress. One of the alliance's main demands was the introduction of a new constitution, and Pizarro's successor in the M-19 and AD leadership, Antonio Navarro Wolff, staged a hunger strike on May 24 to highlight this cause. In the presidential elections three days later Navarro Wolff won 12.6 per cent of the vote and came third.

In August 1990 Navarro Wolff, was awarded a Cabinet post in the Gaviria government, which he held until November. He resigned as Health Minister after only four months in the post in order to stand in the December Constitutional Assembly elections, and his ministry was taken over by another leader of the M-19, Camilo González Pozo. The ADM-19 coalition won 19 seats, only five seats less than the ruling Liberal Party (PL), and thus helped to break the long-standing political duopoly of the PL and PSC. As the second largest block in the Assembly, which opened on Feb. 5, 1991, the ADM-19 formed a majority bloc with the conservative National Salvation Movement (MSN) and some indigenous and ex-guerrilla delegates. The ADM-19 therefore had a considerable say in the drafting of the new Constitution, which came into force on July 5, 1991. The alliance's success at the ballot box was repeated in the general election of Oct. 27, when the Democratic Alliance M-19, won nine seats in the Senate and 15 seats in the House of Representatives and became the second-largest opposition block in Congress. However, the number of votes it attracted fell dramatically, from an estimated 900,000 in the Constitutional Assembly elections the previous December to 400,000 in the October general election. The drop was attributed to Navarro Wolff's "abandonment of revolutionary principles" and the resulting assimilation to government and big business of the ADM-19. The criticisms of the dissident group within ADM-19, led by Carlos Alonso Lucio, were countered by a pro-Navarro block but continued disagreements threatened to split the alliance. The Alliance suffered serious reversals in the March 1992 municipal elections, when on a very low turnout, M-19 city councillors were among the bulk of members failing to be re-elected in the capital Bogotá.

Member organizations. The main parties of the 13-member ADM-19 coalition are: April 19 Movement (M-19); *Aperturista* faction of the Patriotic Union (UP); Social Democrats (SD); Popular Front (FP); United Colombia (CU).

Hope, Peace and Freedom

Esperanza, Paz y Libertad (EPL)

Leadership. Francisco Caraballo, Bernardo Gutiérrez (ls.), Jairo Morales (Constitutional Assembly leader).

Orientation. Left-wing.

Founded. March 1991.

History. The EPL was formerly the guerrilla Popular Liberation Army (also EPL), founded in 1968 by the Communist Party of Colombia—Marxist-Leninist to conduct a "people's war". In August 1984, the EPL was one of the guerrilla groups to sign an initial one-year ceasefire agreement with the government, although some factions continued to clash with the army. The EPL did not join other guerrilla groups in the formation of the Simón Bolívar National Guerrilla Co-ordinating Board (CNGSB) after the peace plan broke down in 1985, but officially maintained the truce until November 1985, when a right-wing paramilitary group killed the EPL leader Oscar William Calvo.

In March 1989 the EPL, following the example of the M-19, agreed to hold peace talks with the government, and in the months of exploratory talks which followed, the guerrillas kept a unilateral ceasefire. The truce came to an end in mid-November after an army raid on the EPL's main camp in which EPL commander Arnulfo Jiménez and 30 other guerrillas were killed. In February 1990, with elections due in March and May, the EPL announced a unilateral ceasefire. As a first step in demobilization the EPL congregated in the "neutral zone" of the northern coastal locality of Necoclí in mid-June. The group finally disbanded and reformed as a political party in March 1991 after signing a peace pact with the government in late January. In return for laying down arms, the guerrillas obtained a general amnesty, special access to land, credit, education and health care and maintenance payments for six months to help them adapt to civilian life. The government promised the new party two seats in the Constitutional Assembly where the EPL was due to join the Democratic Alliance (AD). In the general election that followed the adoption of the new Constitution, however, the party obtained no seats in Congress. However there was ambiguity surrounding its political status and whether or not it had really joined the political mainstream, with several units still referring to themselves as the Popular Liberation Army (but possibly renegades) still mobilized and undertaking guerrilla attacks during 1991 and early 1992 in several departments spread across the country.

Liberal Party

Partido Liberal (PL)

Address. Avenida Jiménez 8-56, Bogotá.

Leadership. Alfonso López Michelsen (l.).

Orientation. Centrist; for free enterprise and privatization of state companies; in his 1990 inauguration speech President Gaviria also gave a commitment to raising standards of living, maintaining public services and fighting international drug trafficking.

Founded. 1840s.

History. The Liberal Party emerged from the rise of the American-born Spanish middle-classes influenced by European republican and radical utopian ideas. Although its major founding forces were the political discussion clubs which opposed Simón Bolivar, the PL's classic liberal reforms, such as the abolition of slavery, reduction of church power, decentralization of government, an end to state monopolies and the introduction of freedom of the press, were inspired by the earlier independence movement. After a period of civil war the PL returned to power in 1861 and governed the country for 25 years dogged by persistent localized armed conflicts. The party went into opposition in 1886 after the Liberal President Rafael Núñez had turned to the Conservative Party (PC), for support against the radical wing of the PL.

The Liberals were instrumental in the 1895 revolt and the uprising of 1899 which plunged the country into the "War of a Thousand Days" but by and large the PL's challenge to Conservative rule remained unsuccessful until 1930. In that year a split in the Conservative Party, caused by the international economic crisis, assured the moderate Liberal Enrique Olaya Herrera the presidency in the first peaceful change of power in Colombia. He was succeeded after the elections of 1934, which were boycotted by the Conservatives, by Alfonso López Pumarejo. His governments of 1934-38 and 1942-45, influenced by "new liberal" ideas emphasizing the reformist role of the state, implemented educational, social welfare, fiscal, land tenure and labour law reforms. The party's moderate faction, opposed to the reforms, succeeded in having their candidate Eduardo Santos elected in 1938. López's second term was marred by a deterioration in the security situation which eventually forced him to resign as President in 1945. His successor, who remained in power for only a year, was Alberto Lleras Camargo.

The ten years of *la violencia* ("the violence", 1946-56) which followed, saw in 1948 the assassination of the radical Liberal leader Jorge Eliécer Gaitán which led to an escalation of the fighting. The PL supported the successful coup by Col. Rojas Pinilla in 1953 against the Conservative government but thereafter made peace with its rival. The Liberals and Conservatives agreed on a power-sharing arrangement whereby the presidency would be held by each party in rotation and the Cabinet posts would be divided equally between the two parties. This National Front agreement was approved by a referendum on December 1957 and in the subsequent general election the Liberal candidate, former President Lleras Camargo, became the first National Front President. Even though the parity agreement between the PL and PC officially expired in 1974, the Liberals, who won the elections of 1974 and 1978, continued to award half the Cabinet portfolios to Conservatives. Both elections also gave the PL a clear majority in both Houses of Congress and this success was followed in the congressional elections of March 1982, when the PL won 114 out of 199 seats in the House of Representatives and 62 out of 114 seats in the Senate. In the May presidential election, however, the divisions between traditionalists (*legitimistas*) and "new liberals" (*Nuevo Liberalismo—NL*) within the PL caused two Liberal candidates to stand against each other. The combined votes of the former President Lopez Michelsen and Senator Luis Carlos Galan Sarmiento (NL) totalled 51.9 per cent, but the presidency went to the individual candidate with the highest vote, Belisario Betancur Cuartas of the PC. The official PL fared well again in the congressional elections of March 1986, winning 60 seats in the Senate and 100 in the House of Representatives. The New Liberalism faction candidates won only 7 per cent of the votes and subsequently withdrew their presidential candidate. This helped the official candidate Virgilio Barco Vargas win a landslide victory in the presidential election the following May with 58.3 per cent of the vote.

Even though the Liberals had a majority in both Houses, Barco offered the Conservatives a share of power as junior coalition partners. The offer was declined and in August 1986 a Liberal government took charge. At his inauguration, Barco announced his intention to put an end to political violence, and fight poverty, drug trafficking and the cultivation of coca (from which cocaine is processed). Barco was committed to extraditing major drug traffickers to the USA for trial, but was opposed by the Colombian Supreme Court which in December 1986 and June 1987 declared an extradition treaty with the USA unconstitutional. His efforts were also undermined by the Colombian authorities who in December 1987 refused to extradite a leading international cocaine trafficker and later freed him. The Liberal government also proved largely ineffective against the illegal drugs trade and the escalating violence which in 1988 alone saw an estimated 18,000 political and drug-cartel-related killings. In the political turmoil of 1989 leading PL members were among victims of the growing spate of assassinations of politicians: on March 3, 1989, the PL leader Ernesto Samper Pizano was seriously injured in an attack by right-wing paramilitaries (in which the Patriotic Union (UP) leader Antequera was killed, and in mid-August the popular leader of the PL's New Liberalism faction, Luis Carlos Galán Sarmiento, who was favoured as the PL's next presidential candidate, was murdered by killers hired by the Medellín or Cali drug barons.

After initial problems Barco had some considerable success in the peace process with Colombia's guerrilla groups. Possible talks were nearly jeopardised when Barco abolished the independent mediating commission in 1987. However, in September 1988 after the kidnapping of Alvaro Gómez Hurtado of the Social Conservative Party (PSC—hitherto the Conservative Party) by the M-19 guerrillas which forced his whole Cabinet to resign, Barco declared his commitment to peace negotiations with guerrillas who were willing to give up the armed struggle and resume civilian life. This resulted in the peace treaty with the M-19 signed on March 9, 1990 and preliminary agreements with other guerrilla groups.

The PL's relatively poor performance in the March 1988 municipal elections, caused by divisions in the party and the government's impotence against drug traffickers and the mounting violence, boded ill for the 1990 congressional elections. Nevertheless, on March 11, 1990, the PL increased their seats in the Senate to 72 and in the House of Representatives to 120. The PL also regained the important mayorships of Medellín and Bogotá which it had lost in 1988. The Liberal victory was crowned in the presidential election of May 27, 1990, when the PL candidate César Gaviria Trujillo won 47 per cent of the vote. Gaviria appointed four PSC members and one M-19 ex-guerrilla to his "national unity" Cabinet before taking office on August 7. His inauguration pledge to continue his predecessor's campaign against "narco terrorism" but not his policy of extraditing drug traffickers came to fruition on October 8, when Gaviria issued a decree offering drug barons, who called themselves the "Extraditables", a guarantee that they would not be extradited to the USA if they surrendered to the authorities. Although this was generally seen as a concession to the Medellín cartel, the deal was followed by the surrender of several major drug traffickers and an end to all-out war between the government and the drug cartels. This in turn had the desired effect of stabilizing the country for economic growth. At the end of 1991 Gaviria announced a major investment in infrastructure to assist this trend. The Liberal government also continued the peace initiatives with the country's remaining guerrilla groups and by the time of the opening of the Constitutional Assembly in February 1991, peace agreements with the National Liberation Army (EPL), the Quintín Lame group and the Workers' Revolutionary Party (PRT) had been signed.

In the Constitutional Assembly elections, which Gaviria had set for December 1990, the PL won 24 out of the then 70 seats (the number was extended later to accommodate disarmed guerrillas), insufficient to command a majority in the Constitutional Assembly even with the support of the PSC. However, the new Constitution, which came into force at midnight on July 5, 1991, was seen as a major achievement of the Gaviria administration. To coincide with its launch, Gaviria lifted a seven-year state of siege. The

Liberal-led Congress had been dissolved by the Constitutional Assembly three days earlier and Gaviria was now given special powers until new congressional and gubernatorial elections were held in October.

In these, the PL was confirmed as the dominant party, gaining 58 seats in the Senate, 86 in the House of Representatives and 18 governorships. However, on a low turnout, the PL suffered a loss of support in municipal elections in March 1992, with some of its most public critics among former PL cabinet ministers especially critical of the governments extradition policy, who topped the poll in the elections of councillors in the capital, Bogotá.

National Salvation Movement

Movimiento de Salvación Nacional (MSN)
Leadership. Alvaro Gómez Hurtado (l.).
Orientation. Conservative; opposed the extradition of the drug cartel bosses and proposed the international legalization of cocaine to undermine the drug cartels' power and increased involvement in the UN's narcotics commission in a peace proposal to the drug barons.
Founded. 1990.
History. The MSN was founded by Álvaro Gómez Hurtado and a splinter group from the Social Conservative Party (PSC) just before the presidential elections of May 27, 1990. Hurtado had been a PSC presidential candidate in 1974 and 1986 and was abducted by the M-19 guerrillas on May 29, 1988, and held for nearly two months as a bargaining tool to bring about peace talks. His split from the PSC to form the MSN seriously weakened his former party, as the presidential election results made clear. Gómez came second with 23.8 per cent of the valid vote, almost twice the vote for the PSC candidate.

In the December 1990 Constitutional Assembly elections the MSN won 11 seats (two more than the PSC) out of the 70 allocated by direct vote. As the third largest party in the Constitutional Assembly, the MSN joined forces with the Democratic AllianceM-19 (ADM-19) against the ruling Liberal Party (PL) and the . In its first legislative election on Oct. 27, 1991, the party again proved to be a major political force, winning five seats in the Senate, 12 in the House of Representative and one governorship. The MSN subsequently obtained the Mines and Energy portfolio in President Gaviria's Cabinet.
Publications. Gómez Hurtado is the publisher of *El Siglo*.

New Democratic Force

Nueva Fuerza Democrática (NFD)
History. In the Oct. 27, 1991, congressional elections, the NFD won nine seats in the Senate and in November President Gaviria gave Jorge Ospina Sardi the Economic Development portfolio in his "national unity" Cabinet.

Patriotic Union

Unión Patriotica (UP)
Address. Calle 23, 17-51 Bogotá.
Leadership. Diego Montaña Cuellar (pres.); Ovidio Salinas (exec. sec.).
Orientation. Left-wing; the UP has exposed international drug traffickers and therefore more than 1,000 of its members have been killed since 1985; the party campaigns for political and trade union liberties, agrarian reform, administrative decentralization and opposition to US interference.
Founded. 1985.
History. The Patriotic Union was established by the Communist Party of Colombia (PCC) and other left-wing groups and trade unions in order to integrate the Revolutionary Armed Forces of Colombia (FARC) guerrilla group into Colombia's political system following President Betancur's peace initiative.

The UP first participated in a legislative election on March 9, 1986, and won one seat in the Senate and 10 in the House of Representatives. The party candidate in the presidential election of May 25 was Jaime Pardo Leal, who came third but obtained only a disappointing 4.5 per cent of the valid vote, ascribed to a low turnout at the polls. However, enemies of the UP, drug traffickers in particular, did not stop at intimidation of the electorate. UP leaders, congressmen and members became targets of right-wing hit squads which in November 1986 led to the UP's temporary withdrawal from Congress in protest at the government's ineffective intervention. In October 11, 1987, the former presidential candidate Pardo Leal was gunned down by right-wing paramilitaries and in early 1989 the UP leader José Antequera became the 928th member to be assassinated since the UP's foundation. The following February Bernardo Jaramillo Ossa, leader of the *Aperturista* faction (which wanted to distance itself from the FARC's armed struggle), was forced to travel to Europe for his personal safety. He returned for the legislative elections in March 11, 1990, in which he won the only UP seat in senate. He was murdered eleven days later at Bogotá airport by a hired gunman suspected to have been in the pay of the Medellín cartel, although the cartel denied involvement.

Jaramillo had brought together the PCC and *Aperturista* faction but soon after his death the *Aperturistas* clashed with the PCC and broke away from the UP to join the Democratic Alliance M-19 (ADM-19). No UP candidate stood in the May 1990 presidential election and in the December elections no UP candidate was elected to the Constitutional Assembly. The party played little part in the discussions leading up to the disbanding of Congress in July 1991 and in the October 1991 congressional elections it won only one seat in the Senate and two in the House of Representatives. The poor result provoked the creation in November of an anti-Communist faction within the UP, led by former PCC central committee member Carlos Romero, which announced that it would pursue the aims of the late UP leaders Jaramillo and Pardo, in order to pose a serious opposition to the government, and especially its economic and social policies. In response to this challenge, the PCC decided to form a new alliance after the UP congress in December. 1991 (see PCC), leading to expectations that the UP would cease to function.

Social Conservative Party

Partido Social Conservador (PSC)

Address. Instituto de Estudios Políticos, Cra 5, No 25c-50P3, Bogotá.

Leadership. Misael Pastrana Borrero (l.); Hernando Barjuch Martínez (s.-g.).

Orientation. Conservative; the PSC has recently advocated talks with the Medellín drug cartel, opposing extradition to the USA of the drug barons.

Founded. 1849 (as the *Partido Conservador*).

History. The PSC was founded as the Conservative Party (PC) by Mariano Ospina Rodríguez, a leading member of the conservative Popular Societies, and supporters of President José Ignacio Márquez (1837-42). The party drew its members and leaders chiefly from the landed classes and monopoly capitalists. The party originally stood for protectionism and a centralised state controlled by the traditional élite, their power being legitimized by the Roman Catholic Church which was given an important role in society. Opposed to Liberal reforms, the Conservatives launched an unsuccessful revolt in 1951. Mariano Ospina Rodríguez was elected President in 1857 and after a period of civil war the party again lost power to the Liberals and remained in opposition from 1861 until 1886. The Conservatives resumed power when the Liberal President Rafael Núñez turned to them for support against the radical wing of the PL in the early 1880s. In 1886 the conservative government introduced a centralist Constitution which was to last for 105 years. The Conservatives remained in power until 1930, despite frequent social protests and outbursts of civil war over unfulfilled promises of economic advancement, leading to the "War of a Thousand Days" in 1899-1901.

The Conservative Party was weakened at the end of the 1920s by internal divisions, and widespread opposition to the government's repressive policies ensured that the 1930 election was lost to the Liberal Party. Control of the party subsequently went to the right-wing faction led by the falangist Laureano Gómez. In the presidential elections of 1946 victory went to the conservative Mariano Ospina Pérez, a supporter of Gómez. A decade of violent struggle between liberals and conservatives, known as *la violencia*, flared up under his presidency and brutal government repression followed the 1948 popular uprising in Bogotá (the *bogotazo*). Nevertheless Ospina's successor, elected in 1950, was again a Conservative—the right-wing Laureano Gómez.

Gómez was overthrown in 1953 by a military coup supported by all parties and the Roman Catholic Church. However, under the dictatorship of Rojas Pínilla the Conservatives and Liberals made an agreement to work together for the restoration of democracy. The co-operation between the two parties was continued after the overthrow of Pínilla in 1957, and in December of that year a popular referendum ratified the National Front power-sharing agreement between the two parties. Under this, the two parties alternated in the presidency and had equal representation in the Cabinet and the national and provincial legislatures from 1958 to 1974. Thereafter the National Front continued to operate on an informal basis until 1978, when the Liberals won the presidency and a majority in Congress. The Conservative Party had been divided between the Alvarista faction supporting Alvaro Gómez Hurtado (the unsuccessful presidential candidate in the 1974 election and later founder of the National Salvation Movement—MSN) and the Ospina-Pastranistas, supporters of former President Pastrana Borrero (1970-74). With the factions reconciled again in 1981 the Conservatives increased their vote in the March 1982 congressional elections, gaining 51 seats in the Senate and 84 in the House of Representatives. The conservative candidate Belisario Betancur Cuartas, benefited from a divided Liberal Party and with the support of a centre-right alliance of parties won the presidential election with 46.8 per cent of the vote the following May.

President Betancur was inaugurated in August 1982 and his administration, hampered by a Liberal-dominated Congress, still managed to pass a variety of social and economic reforms. In November 1982, in an attempt to bring about peace, Betancur announced an amnesty for the country's guerrilla groups and in mid-1984 secured agreement for a year-long ceasefire with three groups, the Revolutionary Armed Forces of Columbia, the National Liberation Army and the April 19 Movement (M19—see Democratic Alliance-M19).

However this first step towards reconciliation with the country's guerrilla groups was quickly overshadowed by an escalating war with the powerful drug cartels. After the murder of Justice Minister Rodrigo Lara Bonilla in May 1984, Betancur imposed a state of siege and in November of the following year, with the internal situation rapidly deteriorating, he declared a state of economic and social emergency. In the subsequent congressional elections of March 9, 1986, and the presidential elections on May 25, the PC was defeated by its old rival, the PL, its seats in the Senate reduced to 45 and in the House of Representatives to 82; the party's presidential candidate Alvaro Gómez Hurtado came second with 35.9 per cent of the vote in the presidential race. Although the victorious PL President Virgilio Barco made an offer to the PC to join the government as a junior partner, the party's leadership opted to go into opposition.

In 1987 the PC changed its name to the current Social Conservative Party. The new PSC won 415 municipalities, only 12 fewer than the PL, in the March 1988 municipal elections, and defeated the PL in the important cities of Bogotá and Medellín. In late May 1988 the former presidential candidate Alvaro Gómez Hurtado, was abducted by the M-19 group for two months, which caused widespread protests against the government and demands for his release.

Gómez subsequently broke with the PSC in 1990 to form the National Salvation Movement (MSN), a move which greatly damaged the party. In the general election of March 11, 1990, the PSC came second with 41 seats in the Senate, and in the presidential elections of May 27 Rodrigo Lloreda Caicedo, the party's presidential candidate, came only fourth with 12.2 per cent of the vote.

In August President Gaviria appointed three PSC members to his new "national unity" Cabinet. In the elections for seats in the Constitutional Assembly the following December, the PSC came fourth with nine seats. When the Assembly opened in February 1991 the PSC delegates joined the PL bloc against the MSN and ADM-19, final proof that it had lost its place as one of the two dominant Colombian parties. In the legislative and gubernatorial elections of Oct. 27, 1991, however, the PSC staged a recovery, placed second overall with 10 seats in the Senate, 15 in the House of Representatives and three governorships. The party therefore was again given cabinet posts in the Gaviria government, namely the important Foreign Affairs Ministry and Labour and Social Security.

Membership. 2,900,000.

International Affiliations. International Democrat Union (full member).

Minor parties

Christian Democrats (*Democracia Cristiana*—DC); a centrist party led by Juan A. Polo Figueroa (pres.) and Diego Arango Osorio (s.g.). It was founded in 1964 and was, until 1965, a member of the "United Front", led by the radical priest Fr Camilo Torres, before Torres chose to join the guerrilla struggle. Although electorally the party has been insignificant, the DC has been ideologically influential in Colombian politics.

The DC backed Belisario Betancur Cuartas of the then Conservative Party (see Social Conservative Party) in the presidential elections of 1970, 1978 and 1982 and its own presidential candidate in the 1974 elections came fifth. The party helped to found the Democratic Alliance April 19 Movement (see ADM19) in April 1990.

National Conservative Movement (*Movimiento Nacional Conservadora*—MNC); won one Senate seat in the 1991 congressional elections.

Christian National Party (*Partido Cristiano Nacional*—PCN); won one seat in the Senate in the October 1991 congressional elections.

National Progressive Movement (*Movimiento de Desarrollo Nacional*—MDN); won one Senate seat in the October 1991 congressional elections.

Quíntin Lame; Carlos Andrade (l.); an indigenist ex-guerrilla group founded in 1979 which operated mainly in the Cauca department. A former member of the Simón Bolivar National Guerrilla Co-ordinating Board (CNGSB) the Quíntin Lame group reportedly laid down arms on May 21, 1991, after signing a peace agreement on March 6. It was allocated a seat in the Constitutional Assembly.

United Colombia (*Colombia Unida*—CU) was founded in September 1989 by 43 politicians and intellectuals with the aim of campaigning for a genuinely pluralist Colombian democracy. The CU was a founding group of the Democratic Alliance M-19 (see ADM19) set up by M-19's Carlos Pizarro Leongómez in April 1990.

Unitary Metapolitico (*Unidad Metapolitico*—UM), won one senate seat in the October 1991 congressional elections.

United Movement for Colombia (*Movimiento Unido por Colombia*—MUPC), won one senate seat in the 1991 October congressional elections.

Workers' Revolutionary Party (*Partido de los Trabajadores*—PRT), founded in 1984 as a Marxist guerrilla group, the PRT was one of the original member group of the Simón Bolívar National Guerrilla Co-ordinating Board (CNGSB). The PRT signed a peace pact with the government on Dec. 28, 1990, and disarmed in Sucre Province on Jan. 26, 1991. The newly constituted party was allocated one seat in the Constitutional Assembly which was opened on Feb. 5, 1991.

Guerrilla organizations

Death to Kidnappers (*Muerte a Secuestradores*—MAS); this ultra right-wing paramilitary death squad, founded in 1981, started off as a counter-insurgency group fighting guerrillas such as M-19. By the mid-1980s, however, human right activists, trade unionists and left-wing academics became their main victims. Possibly under one of the drug cartels' orders, the MAS killed Communist Party and Patriotic Union leader José Antequera and seriously wounded PL leader Ernesto Samper Pizano on March 3, 1989.

Movement of National Restoration (*Movimiento de Restauración Nacional—MORENA*); an extreme right-wing group founded in July 1989 with the assistance of the Association of Peasants and Ranchers (ACDEGAM) of the Middle Magdalena valley drug region which had been promoting paramilitary attacks on left-wing politicians, trade unionists and peasant organizers since 1983. MORENA is said also to have links with the Medellín cartel.

National Liberation Army

Ejército de Liberación Nacional—ELN).

Leadership. Manuel Pérez alias "Poliarco" (l.); Francisco Galán (negotiator in peace talks).

Orientation. Pro-Cuban; demands the nationalization of the multinational oil companies and specializes in attacking oil installations, particularly the strategic Caño Limón- Puerto Coveñas oil pipeline.

Founded. 1964.

History. The guerrilla group was formed by Fabio Vásquez Castaño and was officially named the *Unión Camilista*-ELN after the radical priest, Camilo Torres who was killed in action a month after joining the ELN in 1966.

In the 1970s the group was seriously weakened by the military counter-insurgency in 1973 and the resignation of Vásquez three years later. When he returned in 1985, the ELN suffered from defections as several fronts accepted the government's ceasefire proposal first put forward in 1984 which the ELN had officially rejected. In October 1987 the ELN joined the Símon Bolívar National Guerrilla Co-ordinating Board (CNGSB). Together with the Revolutionary Armed Forces of Columbia (FARC), the ELN rejected President Barco's peace proposals in September 1988, and in 1989 was the last group in the CNGSB to agree to peace talks.

Since the integration of the former guerrilla groups, the M-19, Quintín Lame and the PRT, into mainstream politics, the ELN has mainly worked in conjunction with the FARC in both CNGSB operations and peace negotiations. In September 1991 a group split away from the ELN to form the Socialist Renewal

Movement, in an attempt to negotiate a return to civilian life.
Membership. 950 over 15 fronts (1988 estimate).
Radio station. Radio Patria Libre (Free Homeland Radio) set up in 1988.
Peasant Self-Defence Groups (*Autodefensas Campesinas*—AC); an umbrella group for illegal right-wing paramilitaries. The groups were originally intended as self-defence organizations for peasants in the Middle Magdalena valley against the encroachment of the drug cartels and anti-drugs operations by the army and state police. Infiltrated by right-wing paramilitaries they have since mainly functioned as death squads for the drug cartels who have targeted Patriotic Front and other left-wing group members. Several of the Peasant Self-Defence Groups' leaders were assassinated in 1991, including AC founder Gonzalo Pérez and his son Henry de Jesús Pérez (killed July 1991). Their successor Luis Meneses, alias "Ariel Otero", was murdered in January 1992 by the Medellín cartel who claimed he was a hired killer for the Cali cartel.

Revolutionary Armed Forces of Colombia

Fuerzas Armadas Revolucionarias de Colombia (FARC)
Leadership. Manuel Marulanda Vélez (l.); Alfonso Cano (second-in-command).
Orientation. Left-wing; it is estimated to be fighting on 50 fronts.
Founded. 1949.
History. The FARC is the oldest Latin American guerrilla group. It was founded by the peasant leader and member of the Communist Party of Colombia (PCC) central committee Fermin Charry Rincón, as the defence force of the Republic of Gaitania (an occupied area of approximately 2,000 square miles in the high Andes south of Bogotá).

After the invasion of the territory by the Colombian army in 1964, the independent republic's armed forces re-formed as a guerrilla force. The group, led by the PCC central committee member Manuel Marulanda, alias *Tirofijo* ("Sharpshooter"), since Charry's death in 1960, was officially recognized and given its present name by the PCC at its 1966 party congress.

As Colombia's largest guerrilla force, the FARC gained considerable negotiating power through its successful operations. It was first approached for peace talks which the army quashed by President López Michelsen (1974-78). A proposed amnesty, in exchange for the FARC laying down arms, put forward by President Turbay Ayala (1978-82) was rejected. In March 1984, after intensified attacks against government forces, the FARC finally signed a one-year ceasefire agreement which came into effect at the end of May 1984.

The government Peace Commission promised the FARC integration into civilian politics and the demilitarization of rural areas and, apart from a splinter group the FARC strictly complied with the terms of the truce. Although right-wing terrorists, against which the government seemed to be reluctant to act, inflicted heavy losses on the FARC, the guerrillas nevertheless signed extensions to the ceasefire treaty in November 1985 and March 1986.

A political party, the Patriotic Union (UP), was founded in 1985 by the PCC and other groups as a vehicle for the FARC's integration into the mainstream politics. The peace effort, however, was undermined by continuing army operations against the FARC and escalating assassinations of UP leaders by right-wing death squads which in October 1987 led to the FARC's joining the Simón Bolívar Guerrilla Co-ordinating Board (CNGSB).

In December 1988 the FARC declared a unilateral ceasefire (which they were accused of using to rearm) and in March 1989, together with other CNGSB groups, announced its willingness to hold peace talks. Violent skirmishes with the army (including the bombing of the FARC "Casa Verde" headquarters in the la Uribe region in the Meta Department) and major attacks by the FARC on oil installations and the Colombian electricity network have continued to punctuate CNGSB talks with the government, the latest round breaking down temporarily in March 1992.
Membership. 8,000 (1991 estimate).
Ricardo Franco Commando (*Comando Ricardo Franco*); a dissident wing of the Revolutionary Armed Forces of Colombia (FARC) which split away in May 1984 after the latter signed a one-year ceasefire with the Betancur government. The group was a founder member of the Simón Bolívar National Guerrilla Co-ordinating Board (CNGSB) but was expelled within months for killing 166 guerrillas accused of "infiltration". In November 1988 Ricardo

Franco attempted to murder the Defence Minister Gen. Guerrero Paz.

Simón Bolívar National Guerrilla Co-ordinating Board

Coordinadora Nacional Guerrillera Simón Bolívar (CNGSB)

Leadership. Timoleón Gómez (FARC); Nicolás Rodríguez (ELN).

Orientation. Left-wing alliance of guerrilla groups; their demands include the dismantling of right-wing paramilitary groups, the democratization of economic policy and management of national resources, more regard for human rights, freedom of movement for all CNGSB members and international and regional supervision of a possible ceasefire.

Founded. 1985.

History. The guerrilla alliance was formed by the M-19, Quintín Lame, and the Ricardo Franco Commando (which was expelled soon after) as the Guerrilla Co-ordinating Board (CNG). The aim behind the formation of the CNG was not only to co-ordinate Colombia's left-wing guerrilla groups, but also to co-operate in a united front with other Latin American guerrillas. In 1986 the CNG formed links with groups from Panama and Venezuela and participated in operations with the Ecuadorian "Alfaro Vive, Carajo!" and the Tupac Amaru Revolutionary Movement (MRTA) under the name *Batallón América* (American Battalion). In October 1987, following the Betancur government's infringement of its ceasefire with the Revolutionary Armed Forces of Columbia (FARC) and mounting violence, the National Liberation Army, the Popular Liberation Army, FARC, the Workers' Revolutionary Party and the EPL splinter-group *Patria Libre* joined the M-19 and Quintín Lame in the re-named Simón Bolívar Co-ordinating Board. Several member groups, however, acted independently when it came to peace talks. While President Barco's three-phase peace plan in September 1988 was officially rejected by the CNGSB, both the FARC and M-19 gave a positive response. In January 1990, the M-19 surrendered arms and entered civilian politics as a political party, followed by Quintin Lame and PRT in May and December of the same year.

To coincide with the opening of the Constitutional Assembly in early February 1991, the CNGSB launched a major country-wide offensive with attacks on infrastructure and direct clashes with the army. By Feb. 20 the government had agreed to exploratory peace talks with the CNGSB, with a view to encouraging the guerrillas to give up arms and enter civilian life without losing face. An anti-terrorist law passed in September 1991 jeopardized peace talks in Venezuela in the same month, but these were resumed in October and November. The latest round temporarily collapsed in March 1992.

Socialist Renewal Movement (*Corriente Revolucionario Socialista*—CRS); a group of National Liberation Army (ELN) dissidents which was formed in September 1991 because of "changes in the old socialist world" who expressed a need for "political readjustment". It did not, however, rule out future co-operation with the ELN.

Defunct parties

National Popular Alliance (*Alianza Nacional Popular*—ANAPO); a nationalist, moderately reformist party with a radical slant, founded in 1960 as a political vehicle for the former dictator Gen. Gustavo Rojas Pinilla (1953-57). It was not constituted officially as a political party until 1971, and until 1970 its candidates stood on either Liberal (PL) or Conservative (PC) party lists. In the elections of April 19, 1970, ANAPO emerged as the main opposition group with 72 out of 210 seats in Congress. Pinilla came second in the simultaneous presidential elections with 38 per cent of the votes cast, a figure which was much disputed by ANAPO supporters, who alleged that the counting of the votes had been fraudulent.

The party's military wing, formed in 1974, adopted the date of the election in its name—April 19 Movement (M-19—see Democratic Alliance-M19). In the presidential and legislative elections of April 1974 ANAPO's congressional seats were reduced to 15, and the presidential candidate, Rojas's daughter María Eugenia Rojas de Moreno Díaz, won 10 per cent of the vote. The loss of popularity was partly due to the victorious PL's reform programme, which resembled ANAPO's earlier "Colombian socialist" programme, and its swing to the right following Rojas de Moreno Díaz's take-over of the party's leadership. The party's ideological change increased after the death of Gen. Rojas in January 1975 and caused the severing of links with M-19. An alliance in the general election of 1978 with the insignificant National Opposition Union (UNO) and the Independent Liberal Movement (MLI) produced only four seats in the House of Representatives for ANAPO. These were all lost in the subsequent elections of 1982.

Costa Rica

Capital: San José **Population: 2,550,000**

Costa Rica gained independence from Spain in 1821 and was a member of the United Provinces of Central America until 1838. Following a bloody civil war in 1948 a new constitution was promulgated disbanding the army, an important factor behind the country's claim to be the longest lasting democracy in Latin America. The social democratic political tradition, represented by the National Liberation Party (PLN), barring brief periods, dominated national politics until 1990. The more conservative tradition, represented in a coalition in 1978, finally triumphed in February 1990 when the Social Christian Unity Party (PUSC) assumed power.

Constitutional structure

Under the 1949 Constitution, a unicameral Legislative Assembly is made up of 57 members. Executive power rests with the President who appoints a Cabinet. The President may not be a member of the clergy, related to an incumbent President or have served as either a cabinet minister, as a director of an autonomous state agency, or as a member of the Electoral Tribunal or the Supreme Court in the period immediately preceding the electoral campaign. The President may not stand for re-election for a period of eight years after the completion of one term of office.

Electoral system

The President is elected directly by universal adult suffrage for a four-year term. Members of the Legislative Assembly are elected by proportional representation for the same period to coincide with the presidential term.

Evolution of the suffrage

Voting is compulsory for all men and women over 18 and under 70 years of age.

Elections since 1982

Date	*Winning party*
1982 (presidential and legislative)	National Liberation Party (PLN)
February 1986 (presidential and legislative)	PLN
February 1990 (presidential and legislative)	Social Christian Unity Party (PUSC)

Presidential elections, 1990

	% of vote
Rafael Angel Calderon Fournier (PUSC)	51.4
Carlos Manuel Castillo (PLN)	47.3
Daniel Camaco (United People—PU)	*
Fernando Ramírez (National Alliance -AN)	*
Isaac Azofeifa (Progressive Party -PP)	*
Edwin Badilla (Revolutionary Workers Party - PRTL)	*
Rodrigo Cordero (indep.)	*

** all approx. 1% of vote*

Congressional elections, 1990

Party	*Number of seats*
PUSC	29
PLN	25
Accion Agricola Cartaginesa	1
Partido Union Generalena	1
Partido Alianza Popular	1

PARTY BY PARTY DATA

Cartago Agricultural Action

Acción Agrícola Cartaginesa

Address. Frente Iglesis Cervantes, Alvarado Cartago.

Leadership. Juan Guillermo Brenes Castillo (pres.); Rodrigo Fallas Bonilla (s.-g.).

Orientation. Regionalist.

History. The party, formerly known as the *Unión Agrícola Cartaginesa*, has always operated as a lobbyist at national level for the interests of the state of Cartago, the country's fourth largest. In the 1978 elections it won one seat in the Legislative Assembly which it lost in 1982, regained in 1986 and held on to in the presidential and legislative elections of February 1990.

General Union Party

Partido Unión Generalena

History. A regional party which won one seat in the Legislative Assembly in the February 1990 presidential and legislative elections.

National Liberation Party

Partido de Liberación Nacional (PLN)

Address. Calle 28, Avenidas Central y 2, Apartado 2919, San José.

Leadership. Carlos Manuel Castillo (pres.); Walter Coto (s.-g.).

Orientation. Nominally social democratic but the party pursued conservative policies in office.

Founded. October 1951.

History. The successor to the Social Democratic Party (PSD) (founded in 1948), the PLN was formed by supporters around José "Pepe" Figueres Ferrer who promised social and economic reforms, the restructuring of the government and the better management of the State-owned sector. The party lost the presidential elections in 1958 but regained the presidency in 1962 and held it for the periods 1970-1974, 1974-78, 1982-1986 and 1986-1990. The PLN also had near continuous control of the National Assembly during the same period except for the period 1978-1982 when it lost control to an opposition Unity (*Unidad*—PUSC) coalition see Social Christian Unity Party). The nomination of Oscar Arias Sánchez as presidential candidate in 1986 marked a rupture with the old guard in the party who had a conservative pro-USA foreign policy and were hostile to the Sandinistas in Nicaragua. Arias gained international status for his peace plan for Central America and as a consequence received the Nobel Prize for Peace in 1987. However, domestically, the effects of the foreign debt burden, and pressure from the conservative wing of the party for economic restructuring, including the privatization of the state sector and banking reform, led to the defeat of the more moderate social democratic wing. Drug-related scandals involving prominent party figures, including Daniel Odúber Quirós, party president from 1974-79, damaged the party's image and the shift in policy failed to restore it. The party's conservative candidate for the 1990 presidential elections, Carlos Manuel Castillo was subsequently defeated.

Structure. A 70-delegate National Assembly is the party's supreme body and this elects a three-member national executive committee and a seven-member national political committee. In addition, there are seven provincial, 80 cantonal and 410 municipal committees, appointed by assemblies at the respective levels.

Membership. 367,000 (1984 claim).

Publications. Combate, monthly (est. 15,000).

International Affiliation. Socialist International (full member party) since the early 1960s.

Social Christian Unity Party

Partido Unidad Social Cristiana (PUSC)

Address. Apartado 725-1007, Centro Colón, San José (HQ); Apartado 1080-1000 San José (international secretariat).

Leadership. Mario Quitana (pres.); Danilo Chaverri (s.-g.).

Orientation. Right-wing Christian Democrat.

Founded. December 1983.

History. The PUSC was the product of four parties—the Christian Democratic Party (PDC, founded 1962), the Calderónist Republican Party (PRC, founded 1970), the Popular Union (UP, founded 1974), and the Democratic renewal Party (PRD, founded 1971)—which in 1978 formed a Unity (*Unidad*) coalition whose candidate Rodrigo Carazo Odio won the 1978 presidential elections and which took 28 seats in the National Assembly, one short of a majority. The coalition combined the right-wing republican tradition of ex-president Rafael Angel

Calerón Guarda (1942-1944) and the conservatism of the coffee barons with the guiding principles of Christian democracy. Carazo's government clashed with the trade unions and cooled relations with Cuba and with the Sandinistas in Nicaragua. The Unity candidate Rafael Angel Calderón Fournier lost the 1982 presidential elections and the party's strength in the assembly was reduced to 18 seats.

The first electoral test for the new PUSC was in 1986 when Calderón standing on a platform that advocated opposition to agrarian reform, cuts in public spending and the privatization of state assets came second in the presidential race to the PLN candidate but the party increased its number of seats in the assembly. In opposition, it pressed for the breaking of diplomatic relations with Nicaragua, tax reforms and increased law and order. Calderón finally gained the presidency in February 1990, and the party a majority in the Assembly, promising more moderate economic measures and new social packages for the majority of the population. Instead the government implemented drastic IMF-approved economic shock measures in June 1990 which provoked widespread opposition, particularly from public sector trade unions. Government attempts to form a social pact with the trade unions and business sector failed as did its attempt to gain public acceptance for a plan it proposed to deal with poverty.

As Calderón's popularity plummeted, many PUSC officials and delegates in the Assembly publicly characterized the government's emphasis on economic re-adjustment as "excessive" and argued that more pressing social problems were being neglected. However the conditions for a third phase of the government's economic structural re-adjustment policies were being finalized with the IMF in January and February 1992.

International Affiliation. Member party of the Christian Democrat Organization of America, which forms part of the Christian Democrat International.

Popular Alliance Party

Partido Alianza Popular (PAP)

Address. A/c Asamblea Legislativa, Apartado 1013, San José.

Founded. 1985.

History. The PAP was originally known as the Popular Democratic Union (UDP), an electoral alliance then made up of the Popular Vanguard Party (PVP), the Broad Democratic Front (FAD) and the New Republic Movement (MNR). In 1986 the PAP won a single seat in the Legislative Assembly but its FAD presidential candidate Rodrigo Gutiérrez Sáenz secured less than one per cent of the vote. In the February 1990 elections, the PAP retained its Assembly seat.

Minor parties

There are over 30 minor parties which do not have political status because they have failed to receive at least 1.5 per cent of the national vote. Chief amongst these are the following:

United People (*Pueblo Unido*—PU), founded in 1978, in the 1978 and 1982 general elections won three and four seats respectively in the Legislative Assembly. Its presidential candidate Roberto Gutiérrez Sáenz (see PAP) won 3.2 per cent of the vote in 1982.

The 1984 split in the Vanguard Popular Party (PVP) and the consequent establishment of the Popular Alliance Party (PAP) reduced the PU's representation in the assembly to one seat. Its candidate Alvaro Montero of the Costa Rican Socialist Party (PSC) won less that one per cent of the vote in the 1986 presidential election, a performance repeated by Daniel Camacho of the People's Party, who received 0.6 per cent of the vote as PU candidate in the February 1990 presidential elections.

Vanguard Popular Party (*Partido Vanguardia Popular*—PVP), founded in 1931 as the Communist Party (PC) but constitutionally banned until 1975, and joined forces with the Costa Rican People's Party (PPC) (most of whose members were expelled from the "pro-Soviet" PVP in 1984 for being "Castroists") to support the PU candidate in the February 1990 presidential elections.

Guerrilla groups

Costa Rican People's Army (*Ejército del Pueblo Costarricense*—EPC); founded 1984, left wing.

Santamaria Patriotic Organization (*Organización Patriótica Santamaria*—OPS); left-wing, linked to grenade explosions outside the US Embassy in 1986 and 1988. Police claim that their purpose is to de-stabilize the government and that they have received training in Libya to attack US, French and Israeli targets in the country.

In addition there are 15 private right-wing para-military and police organizations, allegedly trained by the Israeli secret service, the US FBI, the US DEA and the armies of Guatemala and El Salvador, which are known to parallel the government's security forces and which operate in secrecy. These are: the **Organization for National Emergencies**; the **Costa Rica Free Movement** (founded in 1961 to combat "Cuban expansionism" and integrated by other groups such as the Blue Berets and the Tridents); the **Patriotic Union**; the **Fortín Group**; **Democratic Actions from the Northern Front**; **Coyotepe 55**; **Comando Tomás Guardia**; the **Vigilance Commandos**; the **Mau Mau commandos**; the **Simón Bolivar Brigade**; the **Black Berets**; the **Patria y Libertad** founded 1985; the **ABC Group**; the **Babies**; and in addition, reservists from the National Liberation Party (PLN).

Cuba

Capital: Havana **Population: 10,495,000**

Cuban politics were dominated from 1933 to 1958 by Sgt. (later Gen.) Fulgencio Batista, who served as President from 1940-1944 (pursuing a liberal policy) and seized power in 1952, when he established a dictatorship widely regarded as brutal and corrupt. The situation was changed dramatically by the revolution of 1958 when Batista was overthrown and Fidel Castro Ruz assumed the premiership, a position he has maintained to date. Since then, the government withstood a 30-year US economic embargo and a US-sponsored coup attempt in 1961 at the price of making Castro, originally a non-communist, heavily dependent on the Soviet Union. The collapse of the Eastern bloc in 1991, however, left the country in an extremely isolated position, economically and politically.

Constitutional structure

The 1976 Constitution describes Cuba as "a socialist state of working people and other manual and intellectual workers", and recognizes the leading role of the Communist Party. Other political parties are currently prohibited. Legislative power is invested in Cuba's unicameral parliament, the National Assembly of People's Power (*Asamblea Nacional del Poder Popular*).

Electoral system

A 499-member National Assembly is elected indirectly for a five-year term by the municipal assemblies, which in turn are elected by direct universal suffrage, in either a first or second ballot, for a two-and-a-half-year term in office. The National Assembly elects the 30-member Council of State, the president of which is head of state and government.

Evolution of the suffrage

The first post-independence constitution (1901) provided for universal male suffrage with a voting age of 21, and this was extended to include women in 1934. Under the present Constitution (1976) the voting age was reduced to 16.

Sequence of elections since 1974

The first popular post-revolution election to the municipal Assemblies took place in October 1976 following an experimental election in the Matanzas province in 1974, subsequent elections being held in October 1981 and October 1986. Although voting is not obligatory, as it had been under the Batista era, the first-round turnouts proved to be extremely high at all three elections, never falling below 95.2 per cent.

HAVANA
Marianao
Matanzas
Güines
Pinar del Río
C
U
B
A
Colón
S.Clara
Cienfuegos
I. of Pines
Trinidad
Caibarien
S.Spíritus
Ciego de Avila
Camagüey
Atlantic
Ocean
Holguín
Banes
Caribbean
Sea
Manzanillo
Bayamo
Palma Soriano
Guantánamo
Santiago de Cuba
0 M 200
UNITED STATES
MEXICO
CUBA
SOUTH AMERICA
5769

PARTY BY PARTY DATA

Communist Party of Cuba

Partido Comunista de Cuba (PCC)

Address. Havana, Cuba.

Leadership. Fidel Castro Ruz (1st sec.); Raúl Castro Ruz (2nd sec.).

'Orientation. Until 1988 pro-Soviet, it reacted negatively to *perestroika*. The need to reduce the country's economic dependence on sugar, for which the Soviet Union was a major market, had led to an emphasis on the diversification of agriculture and the development of industry and tourism. This inevitably made the country more Western-orientated. Emphasis is laid on the development of education and the health service and on the mobilization of the entire population for national defence against the threat of US intervention. The PCC, in the past, prided itself on its revolutionary nationalism but the severe economic crisis has encouraged a more pragmatic approach to ensure national survival.

Founded. 1961.

History. The PCC was formed by the merger of three distinct organizations, the urban based Popular Socialist Party (PSP-the former Communist Party), Fidel Castro's July 26 Movement and the student based Revolutionary Directorate. The Communist Party, founded as an underground organization in 1925, was legalized in 1938, and changed its name to the PSP in 1944. It returned 10 deputies in the 1940 elections, and was represented in Batista's government of 1940-44 by Juan Marinello, the first communist in Latin America to hold ministerial office. Its influence declined after 1944, however, and in 1953 Batista banned it.

On July 26, 1953, Castro led an armed revolt against the Batista regime, which was easily crushed. Released under an amnesty in 1955, he went to Mexico, where he organized the July 26 Movement. In December 1956 he returned in the yacht *Granma* with 81 followers, 70 of whom were killed by government troops on landing.

The survivors, including Castro and the Argentinian Ernesto "Che" Guevara, launched a guerrilla campaign in the eastern rural Sierra Maestra territory, which gradually spread and gained the support of the urban based anti-Batista student movement, the Revolutionary Directorate. The government's resistance collapsed in December 1958, with troops deserting to the guerrillas and in the following month the *Fidelistas* took power.

The July 26 Movement was democratic, socialist and nationalist rather than Marxist, and was hostile to the PSP, which had given no support to the revolt until the summer of 1958. US hostility, however, compelled Castro to ally himself with the PSP, then the best organized party in the country. Early in 1961, the July 26 Movement, the PSP and the Revolutionary Directorate formed an alliance, the Integrated Revolutionary Organizations (ORI), and in December Castro formally announced his commitment to Marxist-Leninism and the dictatorship of the proletariat. The United Party of the Socialist Revolution (PURS) was established in the following year as the sole legal party, and was renamed the Communist Party of Cuba (PCC) in 1965.

After attempting to remain neutral in the Sino-Soviet controversy, the PCC adopted a pro-Soviet attitude in 1963. Relations between the two soured during 1964-68, however, as Castro insisted on the PCC's independence, declaring that "we are not and never will be anybody's satellite", and criticized both the Soviet and Chinese communists for attempting to seek supporters within the PCC. During this period, the PCC pursued a policy of active assistance to guerrilla movements in Latin America, such as "Che" Guevara's unsuccessful attempt to organize a revolt in Bolivia in 1966-67. Castro attacked the Bolivian and Venezuelan Communist Parties for refusing to support such movements and denounced the Soviet Union's policy of extending diplomatic and economic relations to Latin American governments irrespective of their political complexion, as well as its internal problems which he described as "capitalist". The leading "old communists" (former PSP members) were purged from the government in 1964-65 and replaced by *Fidelistas* from the July 26 Movement, and 37 of them were expelled from the PCC in 1968 and imprisoned for forming a pro-Soviet "anti-party group".

The failure of Guevara's revolt and Cuba's economic difficulties forced Castro to modify his policies. Relations with the Soviet Union improved after he supported the Soviet invasion of Czechoslovakia in 1968, and in 1972 Cuba entered the Council for Mutual Economic Assistance (Comecon).

At the first PCC congress, held in 1975, Castro admitted that the Cuban leaders had been guilty of "utopian attitudes" and "disregard for the experience of other processes", and the PCC subsequently supported the Soviet intervention in Afghanistan and the imposition of martial law in Poland.

In 1984-85 the party moved towards a more independent policy. More "old communists", including a member of the PCC's secretariat, were removed from their posts and replaced by younger officials who favoured limited encouragement of the private sector; home ownership was transferred from the state to the tenant; official attitudes to the Roman Catholic Church were softened; and attempts were made to improve relations with the USA and to expand trade with Western countries. At the third PCC congress, held in February 1986, 10 of the 24 members of the party's Political Bureau and about a third of the 225 Central Committee members were replaced in order to bring more women, blacks and youth into the leadership; a new party programme received provisional approval.

The experimentation with economic liberalism was suspended in 1986 when peasant markets were shut down and a new period of "rectification of errors and negative tendencies" was announced, prompted by fears that social inequalities and tensions were reappearing. The new line gradually brought Cuba into open disagreement with the policy of perestroika promoted by the Soviet Leader Mikhail Gorbachev. Castro marked the 30th anniversary of the revolution by re-affirming Cuba's commitment to Marxist-Leninism and during 1989 he expressed his dismay over the developments in Eastern Europe. A purge of senior military and party officials in June and July was interpreted by many observers as a move intended to eliminate supporters of *perestroika*, although the main reason officially given for this was the accused's involvement in the Medellín cartel's export of cocaine from Colombia to the USA.

During 1990 and 1991, the impact of the Eastern European developments had a devastating effect on the country at a time when the domestic economy was rapidly contracting. Imports of essential products were sharply reduced and the replacement of Comecon meant the loss of established markets and suppliers. In particular, the new Russian Federation confirmed that all oil supplies would now have be paid for at international market prices and would no longer be exchanged for Cuban sugar at preferential rates. In response, the country was put on a near war footing. Rationing of food and basic goods was dramatically increased, bureaucracy was cut back and a drive began to stamp out corruption. Armed vigilance brigades were also formed in an effort to stem the rising crime rate and to protect food and other supplies. In the process opposition groups campaigning against growing human rights violations were increasingly repressed and their leaders imprisoned.

In the 4th PCC party Congress, held on Oct. 10-14, 1991, Castro called for sacrifices to preserve the basic social achievements of the revolution and rejected the mixed economy and Western style multiparty systems. However, some reforms were approved, and these were interpreted as signs that the party leadership had made tactical concessions or recognized the need for gradual change. From now on, small scale enterprises were to be allowed to operate for a profit, which effectively gave official sanction to the thriving black economy. Other changes allowed Christians to join the party and in future all delegates to the National Assembly of People's Powers were to be directly elected. However, while the PCC's secretariat was abolished the membership of the party's central committee was increased from 146 (plus 76 alternates) to 225 and granted extraordinary powers to take policy decisions during the current crisis period.

Membership. 600,000 (1989 claim).

Publications. Granma, daily; *Juventud Rebelde* (Rebel Youth), daily newspaper of the Union of Communist Youth.

Illegal parties

Alternative Criterion (*Criterio Alternativo*); a dissident group, one of whose prominent members, Maria Elena Campos Cruz Varela, was arrested by the Cuban authorities for illegal political activities in December 1991 and sentenced to two years' imprisonment. In 1989 she was awarded the officially sponsored Casas de Las Americas poetry award.

Cuban Commission on Human Rights and National Reconciliation (*Comisión Cubano por*

Derechos Humanos y de Conciliación Nacional); Elizardo Sánchez Santa Cruz (l.); a human rights organization which incorporated other human rights groups, including the Party for Human Rights (PDH), in February and March 1989 and which operates as an arena of popular political protest and discontent. Sánchez Santa Cruz, a veteran human rights campaigner frequently imprisoned, was again detained by the authorities in December 1991.

Opposition parties in exile

Cuban-American National Foundation (CANF); Jorge Mas Canosa (l.); the main hardline anti-Castro party based in Miami and receiving the tacit support of the US administration. In December 1991 it opened an office in Moscow and was lobbying the new Russian government to halt all economic aid to Cuba.

Christian Democratic Party (*Partido Democratico Cristiano*—PDC); José Ignacio Rasco (l.); the party is a member of the Cuban Democratic Platform and held its first congress in Miami in May 1991. It is a member party of the Christian Democrat Organization of America, which forms part of the Christian Democrat International.

Cuban Democratic Platform (*Plataforma Democrática Cubana*); a more moderate anti-Castro coalition (in exile) of the Cuban Social Democratic Party, the Christian Democratic Party, and the Liberal Party, led by Enrique Baloyra and Carlos Alberto Montaner (who is based in Madrid). The alliance's aim is achieve unity with hardline Miami-based anti-Castro groups in order to negotiate with the Castro regime a peaceful transition to a multiparty political system. It participated in a conference, held in Moscow in April 1992 on the future of Russian-Cuban relations, and asked the Russian government to increase its political and economic pressure on Castro in order to effect democratic change. The conference was attended by Ricardo Bofill, president of the Human Rights Committee of Cuba and the dissident writer and veteran of the Cuban revolution Carlos Franqui.

Cuban Liberal Union (*Unión Liberal Cubana*); Carlos Alberto Montaner l; a member of the moderate Cuban Democratic Platform based in Madrid. In March 1992, Cuba officially protested following the first meeting between the Spanish government and Montaner.

Cuban Social Democratic Party (*Partido Social Democratico Cubano*—PSDC); Enrique Baloyra (l.); a member party of the Cuban Democratic Platform of which Baloyra is a leader.

Liberal Party (*Partido Liberal*—PL), a member party of the Cuban Democratic Platform.

Patriotic Committee "José Joaquín Palma" (*Comité Patriótico José Joaquín Palma"*) an anti-Castro party founded in 1991 in Guatemala by Cuban Guatemalans.

Dominica

Capital: Roseau **Population: 82,000**

The Commonwealth of Dominica became a fully independent republic within the British Commonwealth in November 1978. Since the introduction of universal suffrage in 1951 politics has been dominated by the Dominica Labour Party (DLP) and since 1980 by the conservative Dominica Freedom party (DFP). Two abortive coup attempts took place in 1981.

Constitutional structure

Legislative power is vested in a 31-member unicameral House of Assembly composed of 21 elected members, the Speaker and nine senators who may be elected or appointed (five on the advice of the Prime Minister and four on that of the Leader of the Opposition). A nominally executive President is the head of state but effective executive power is exercised by the Prime Minister, who is the elected member judged to be best able to command a majority of the elected members of the House. The Prime Minister and the Cabinet are responsible to the House of Assembly.

Electoral system

The President is nominated for a five-year term jointly by the Prime Minister and the Leader of the Opposition, although if there is a disagreement the President is elected by the members of the House of Assembly. The elected members of the House of Assembly (known as representatives) are elected for a five-year term (subject to dissolution) by simple plurality from single member constituencies by universal suffrage. For electoral purposes, the island is divided into 21 constituencies of roughly equal size in terms of population.

Evolution of the suffrage

Universal adult suffrage was introduced by the British colonial administration in 1951. The minimum age for voting was reduced from 21 to 18 in 1975.

Sequence of elections since 1980

Date	*Winning party*
July 1980 (general)	Dominica Freedom Party (DFP)
July, 1985 (general)	Dominica Freedom Party (DFP)

General election, May 28, 1990

Party	*Seats*
Dominica Freedom Party (DFP)	11
Dominica United Workers' Party (DUWP)	6
Labour Party of Dominica (LPD)	4
Total	**21**

PARTY BY PARTY DATA

Dominica Freedom Party (DFP)

Address. Cross Street, Roseau.
Leadership Dame Mary Eugenia Charles (l.); Alvin Knight (s.-g.).
Orientation. Right-wing and pro-Western, promotes neo-liberal economic policies.
History. In the 1970 elections, the DFP won five out of the 14 seats in the legislature, but in 1975 its representation in the 21-member House of Assembly was reduced to three. A leading DFP member was appointed to the Cabinet, formed in June 1979, of the ruling Democratic Labour Party (DLP—see Labour Party of Dominica) but was dismissed in January 1980 after he had called for an early general election. The DFP had meanwhile remained in opposition to the government.

For the elections of July 21, 1980, the DFP nominated 19 candidates, of whom 17 were elected, giving the party an overwhelming majority in the House of Assembly and enabling it to form a government with Charles as the Caribbean's first woman Prime Minister.

The Charles government pursued policies perceived as pro-Western, while retaining a nominal commitment to non-alignment. It was an enthusiastic proponent of the US military invasion of Grenada in 1983. In the 1985 elections, the party was returned to power with a reduced majority and its 11 seats in the general election in May 1990 belied Charles' pre-poll prediction that the party could win all 21 seats. In April 1991 the government narrowly defeated an opposition motion of no confidence vote by 11 votes to 10. The Charles government was accused of discriminating against its opponents and victimizing farmers, the police and especially civil servants who were to be deprived of union recognition and the right to air political views.

Dominica United Workers Party (DUWP)

Address. House of Assembly, Roseau.
Leadership. Edison James (l.).
Orientation. Centre-left.
Founded July 1988.
History. The new party was launched to provide a more effective opposition to the DFP. James, a former general manager of the Dominica Banana Marketing Corporation, was elected leader at the party's first convention in October 1988. Proof that the party had emerged as the chief opposition party came in the May 1990 general election, when the DUWP finished second with six seats. James moved an opposition vote of no confidence in the government in April 1991 which it narrowly survived (see Dominica Freedom Party).

Labour Party of Dominica (LPD)

*Address.*House of Assembly, Roseau.
Leadership. (Michael A. Douglas died April 30, 1992.).
Orientation. Centrist; the party advocates a "new socialism" based on a mixed economy, with the island's resources being locally owned and controlled. It has a non-aligned foreign policy.
Founded. January 1985.
History. The LPD's antecedents date back to the Dominica Labour Party (DLP), founded in 1955 from the People's National Movement and other groups, which under Edward Le Blanc first came to power in the 1961 elections to the Legislative council. At the time of the October 1970 elections (the first since Dominica had become an Associated State of Great Britain in 1967), the DLP was divided into two factions—the Le Blanc Labour Party, which obtained eight seats in the legislative assembly, and the DLP which gained only one seat. The party was re-united in 1974, when Le Blanc retired as leader and Premier, and continued in power until June 1979, when Patrick R. John, then leader of the DLP, was forced to resign with his government, following a general strike and unrest caused by disclosures of government negotiations with South African concerns.

In June 1979, a group comprising about half the 16-strong DLP bloc in the House of Assembly, under the leadership of Oliver J. Seraphine, broke away to form a Dominica Democratic Labour Party (DDLP or Demlab) and a broadly based government. However, in elections held in July 1980, the DDLP retained only two seats in the House of Assembly, not including that of Seraphine, and the DLP none. Both parties thereupon went into opposition, and in mid-1983 the DDLP was re-united with the DLP, with Seraphine as leader and John as his deputy of a reunified party which retained the name of the DLP. A further split, this time more minor, led to the creation of the short-lived, left-wing, Dominica Progressive Force under Lennard Baptiste.

A United Dominica Labour Party (UDLP) had meanwhile been formed by a dissident DDLP member of the House, Michael Douglas, along with his brother Rosie, after the former failed to win the leadership of the DDLP from Seraphine in 1981.

The UDLP was represented in the house until January, when lengthy negotiations culminated in the merger of the UDLP with the DLP to form the Labour Party of Dominica (LPD).

Michael Douglas, who had served as a minister in the Seraphine government, became leader of the combined party, with Seraphine as his first deputy and Henry Dyer—a dismissed Dominica Freedom Party minister who defected to the opposition in 1983—as second deputy.

In the 1985 elections, five official LPD candidates were returned, as was Rosie Douglas, who was refused LPD endorsement on account of his left-wing sympathies but who indicated his intention of voting with the LPD bloc. Of the LPD's victorious candidates, two were sympathizers of the Dominica Liberation Movement Alliance (which merged with the LPD in 1985) and one was former Prime Minister John, who was at the time awaiting trial on charges of conspiring with members of the dissolved Dominica Defence Force to overthrow the Charles government in 1981. He was convicted in October 1985 and sentenced to 12 years imprisonment.

The LPD lost its position as the main opposition party following the general election of May 1990, when it could only retain four seats (see Dominica United Workers Party).

Dominican Republic

Capital: Santo Domingo **Population: 6,700,000**

The Dominican Republic gained its independence from Spain in 1844 but was occupied by the USA in 1916-24. The country was subjected to the dictatorship of Gen. Rafael Trujillo from 1930 to 1961, when, after his assassination, a modicum of democratic rule was restored. A civil war broke out in 1965 as a result of the overthrow of the moderate socialist government of Juan Bosch Gaviño by the military, which the US Government had inspired and used as a pretext to intervene militarily. Joaquín Balaguer, a former Trujillo supporter, was elected President in tightly controlled elections in 1966. The rivalry between Bosch and Balaguer, now octogenarians, has been a feature of the country's political life ever since, with Balaguer narrowly defeating Bosch in the May 1990 presidential elections.

Constitutional structure

Under the 1966 Constitution the Republic has an executive President and a legislative body, the National Congress, consisting of a 120-member Chamber of Deputies (increased from 91 members in 1982) and a 27-member Senate (composed of one Senator for each of the country's 26 provinces and one for the national district). The President, who takes office on August 16 following the election, is assisted by a Vice-President and a Cabinet, which he appoints and presides over. Among his duties are also the nominating of secretaries and assistant secretaries of state and other public officials and the promulgating and publishing of laws and resolutions of Congress. All legislative proposals need an absolute majority of the members of each house of the National Congress; a two-thirds majority is required for urgent matters.

Electoral system

The President, the Vice-President and members of both houses of the National Congress are directly elected for a four-year term. The President and Vice-President are elected by simple majority, as is the Senate. Elections for the Chamber of Deputies are held under a party list proportional representation system.

Evolution of the suffrage

Voting is compulsory for all citizens aged 18 and over and all married citizens below that age. Women obtained equal voting rights to men in 1942.

PARTY BY PARTY DATA

Dominican Liberation Party

Partido de la Liberación Dominicana (PLD)
Address. Avenida Independencia 69, Santo Domingo, DN.
Leadership. Juan Bosch Gaviño (l.); Max Puig (s.-g.). Bosch announced that he had resigned in March 1991 but withdrew his resignation a month later.
Orientation. Centre-left; Bosch has described himself as a Marxist but the PLD is generally regarded as a social democratic party.
Founded. 1973.
History. The PLD was formed by Bosch after the opposition Dominican Revolutionary Party (PRD), which he had founded during his exile in 1930-62 and in which he had served as President of the Republic in 1963, voted to participate in the 1974 elections. The PLD won slow but consistently increasing support in subsequent elections, winning 1 per cent of the vote in 1978, 10 per cent in 1982, 18 per cent in 1986 and 34 per cent in 1990. Its congressional representation increased from seven seats in 1978 to 18 in 1986, when it held the balance of power, to 12 seats in the Senate and 44 in the chamber of Deputies after the May 1990 congressional elections, thus depriving the ruling Social Christian Reformist Party (PRSC) of its overall majority. Bosch, then aged 81, and his supporters hotly disputed the result of the May 1990 presidential election, which went to a recount, claiming that long-time rival Joaquin Balaguer, 83, of the PRSC had won by fraud. Balaguer obtained 678,268 votes to the Bosch's 653,123 votes. However, a call for civil disobedience in protest at the result soon petered out.

In April 1992 the party entered into a serious crisis when 47 of its highest ranking members, mostly on the left, announced their collective resignation in protest at the expulsion of Nélsida Marmolejos, the well respected congressional deputy for the district of Santo Domingo and a well known trade unionist. He had criticized the government's proposals for a new labour code.

Dominican Revolutionary Party

Partido Revolucionario Dominicano (PRD)
Address. 27 de Febrero 265, Oficina 210, Santo Domingo, DN.
Leadership. José Francisco Peña Gómez (pres.); Hatuey de Camps Jiménez (s.-g.); Emilio Ludovino Fernández (international secretary).
Orientation. Social democratic although the PRD government of Jorge Salvador Blanco (1982-86) was conservative in its economic policy and was hostile to Cuba, Nicaragua and other socialist states.
Founded. 1939.
History. Formed in Cuba as a moderate left-wing party by refugees from the Trujillo dictatorship, the PRD was finally established in the Dominican Republic in July 1961, after Trujillo's assassination. In December 1962, Juan Bosch, its founder and leader, won the presidential election and took office in February 1963. However, with US encouragement, he was overthrown by the military in September. In April 1965, the PRD, supported by leftist army officers, led an insurrection against the military regime, to which the US administration (under President Johnson) immediately responded, landing 42,000 marines with the stated intention of restoring order and preventing a communist take-over, an invasion retrospectively supported by the Organization of American States (OAS). In the 1966 elections carefully controlled by a provisional (conservative military) government, Bosch was defeated and the US-backed Joaquín Balaguer of the Social Christian Reformist Party (PRSC) installed in power. For the next 12 years, the PRD was in opposition; a split in 1973 led to the formation by Bosch of the Dominican Liberation Party (PLD).

The party returned to power following an overwhelming victory in the May 1978 elections by presidential candidate Silvestre Antonio Guzmán, only made possible, however, by the intervention of the US administration (under President Carter) which intervened to prevent another military coup. Guzmán, who committed suicide in July 1982 on evidence of gross corruption among his close aides had already been succeeded by Jorge Salvador Blanco who won the May presidential elections with 46.6 per cent of the vote. The PRD also secured an absolute majority in the Congress and Peña Gómez, the current leader, was elected mayor of Santo Domingo. The party then proceeded to tear itself apart with a right-wing Structure (*La Estructura*) faction, led by businessman Jacobo Majluta (interim President until Blanco took office in August) fighting both a left-wing faction led by Peña Gómez and a pro-Blanco bloc for control of policy and the 1986 presidential nomination. This was won after a gun battle during the party convention, by Majluta, who subsequently lost the presidential elections by a narrow margin, officially obtaining 39.5 per cent of the vote, with Peña Gómez as his reluctant and lacklustre vice-presidential running mate. The PRD also saw its strength in the Chamber reduced to 48 seats and to four in the Senate. Peña Gómez supporters, in a gesture of protest, had shifted their support to the PLD, vastly increasing its vote (see PLD). The PRD's fortunes were further damaged by the indictment in 1987 of Blanco, who fled abroad to avoid imprisonment on charges of corruption while in office.

In 1989, Majluta formed the Independent Revolutionary Party (PRI) to contest the 1990 presidential elections, despite the efforts of Peña Gómez to reunite the party. The status of the PRI as a separate party or faction of the PRD remained ambiguous. A group of minor left-wing parties, as well as the Venezuelan President Carlos Andrés Pérez, then urged Peña Gómez to seek an alliance with the PLD. This failed to materialize and Peña Gómez, named official PRD candidate, came third in the election, with 25 per cent of the poll.
Structure. The national executive committee exercises power between national congresses.
Membership. 750,000 (1987 claim).
International Affiliation. Socialist International (full member party) of which Peña Gómez is a vice-president.

Independent Revolutionary Party

Partido Revolucionario Independiente (PRI)
Leadership. Jacobo Majluta Azar (l.).
Founded. 1989.
Orientation. Right-wing.
History. The PRI, whose status as either a separate party or a faction of the Dominican Revolutionary Party (PRD) remained ambiguous, was founded as a personal vehicle for the 1990 presidential candidacy of Majluta, who came a poor fourth with 6.9 per cent of the vote. In the concurrent congressional elections, the PRI won two seats in the Chamber. Majluta had formed the right-wing Structure *La Estructura* faction in the PRD in 1985, which also operated as a separate party. It clashed with the left-wing faction led by José Francisco Peña Gómez for control of party policy and the 1986 presidential nomination. Majluta, as the PRD presidential candidate, narrowly lost the election and was expelled by Peña Gómez from the PRD in 1987, although the expulsion was later annulled by the national electoral council.

Social Christian Reformist Party

Partido Reformista Social Cristiano (PRSC)
Address. Lab. Licar C. x A., Autopista Duarte Km 6 1/2, Edificio Brigitte 5, Santo Domingo, DN.
Leadership. Joaquín Balaguer Ricardo (l.), Joaquín A. Ricardo (s.-g.), Juan Luis Seliman (international secretary). Balaguer announced his intention to retire as party leader in March 1991, but with no specified date when this would take place.
Orientation. Right-wing; once a nationalist, land based party advocating land reform and economic development to increase the size and power of the middle class but now promoting a free-market liberal economic policy.
Founded. 1985.
History. Balaguer served as Education and Foreign Minister and Vice-President of the Republic under the Trujillo dictatorship (1930-61). He was titular President in 1960-62, surviving Trujillo's assassination only to be ousted by the military and forced to flee to the USA. Here he founded the conservative Reformist Party (PR) and unceremoniously returned to the office of the presidency in 1966, the US military invasion the previous year (see Dominican Revolutionary Party—PRD), and served three consecutive terms until 1978. In what were called the fairest elections in two decades, Balaguer, with 36.5 per cent of the vote, lost the 1982 presidential elections to the PRD, a result he then reversed by a narrow two-point margin in the 1986 poll, widely described as fraudulent. Balaguer, despite strong PRD protests, was duly recognized as President, having stood as the candidate of the Social Christian Reform Party (also PRSC) which was the product of the 1985 merger of the PR and the Social Christian Revolutionary Party (PRSC) led by Fernando Alvarez Bogaert. Balaguer took office for the fifth time in August, then aged 79. In the simultaneous congressional elections, the PRSC won 56 seats in the Chamber and 21 in the Senate, forcing it to seek alliances with the Quisqueyoist Democratic Party (PQD).

Balaguer again was adjudged to have won the barest of victories in the May 1990 presidential elections and the main opposition party, the Dominican Liberation Party (PLD), accused the government of widespread and systematic fraud despite the presence of international observers. In a June recount Balaguer was given 678,268 votes to 653,123 votes for the PLD's Juan Bosch. In the simultaneous May congressional elections, the PRSC maintained control of the senate, winning 16 seats, but lost control in the Chamber, with 42 to the PLD's 44 seats. Undeterred by the opposition claims that he had no mandate to govern, Balaguer introduced stringent austerity measures in August which generated intense local resentment and a succession of general strikes called by the nine union federations. Rather than bring him down as expected, the policy, endorsed by the International Monetary Fund (IMF) won Balaguer grudging support as inflation was dramatically reduced in 1991. The equally controversial Colón lighthouse, a pet project of Balaguer's and which over the previous decade of construction had drained the economy, was used to boost the country's image in the region in preparation for the 500th anniversary in October 1992 of Columbus's arrival in the Americas.

Minor Parties

Democratic Integration Movement (*Movimiento de Integración Democrática*—MID); Francisco Augusto Lora (l.); a centre right party which fought the 1970 and 1978 elections, the latter in alliance with the National Conciliation Movement and Quisqueyoist Democratic Party.

Dominican Communist Party (*Partido Comunista Dominicano*—PCD); Narcisco Isa Conde (l.); orthodox communist before the collapse of the Eastern bloc, the party was founded clandestinely by students in 1944 as the Dominican Revolutionary Democratic Party (PDRD), legalized in 1946 as the Popular Socialist Party (PPS) but banned the following year. After Trujillo's death in 1961, it resumed its activities, being banned again in 1963, and took part in the 1965 civil war. It resumed the name PCD the same year. Legalized again by President Balaguer in 1977, in an attempt to split the opposition in the coming elections, it contested the 1982 elections, with Isa Conde as presidential candidate, in the Socialist Unity alliance with the Movement for Socialism. During the late 1980s, the PCD strongly criticized the increasingly pragmatic Juan Bosch of the Dominican Liberation Party (PLD) for having "sold out" as he became a strong contender for the presidency in 1990 (see PLD; Social Christian Reformist Party).

The PCD became less hostile to the Roman Catholic Church in response to the advance of liberation theology.

Dominican Popular Movement (*Partido Popular Dominicano*—MPD); Julio de Pena Valdés (l.); founded by exiles in Cuba in 1956, the MPD began activities in the Dominican Republic after Trujillo's death in 1961 and adopted a pro-Chinese orientation. It was banned in 1963, but continued to operate underground. It contested the 1982 elections as part of the United Left Alliance. Several MPD militants were arrested together with Costa Rican separatists in November 1985, accused of plotting to assassinate prominent conservatives.

Dominican Workers' Party (*Partido de los Trabajadores Dominicanos*—PTD); Rafael Chaljub Mejía, José González Espinoza (ls.); founded in 1979, the PTD contested the 1982 elections as part of the United Left Alliance.

It later merged with the then (pro-Albanian) Labour Communist Party of the Dominican Republic (POCRD) led by Chajub Mejía. The united party, which retained the name of the PTD, held its first congress in 1985. The PTD fought the 1990 congressional election jointly with the Dominican Revolutionary Party (PRD) and the small Socialist Block, gaining one seat in the Chamber.

National Conciliation Movement (*Movimiento de Conciliación Nacional*—MCN); Jaime M. Fernández (pres.); Víctor Mena (s.-g.); a right wing party founded in 1969 by Héctor García Godoy the former provisional President (1965-66) which backed the Balaguer administration in 1970-77 and in 1978 allied itself with the Quisqueyoist Democratic Party, the Democratic Integration Movement and other opposition groups. During the 1980s it continued to claim a membership of over 650,000 members, but failed to gain a single seat in the Congress.

Quisqueyoist Democratic Party (*Partido Quisqueyano Democrática*—PQD); Gen. Wessin y Wessin; a right-wing party founded in 1968. In the 1982 and 1986 elections, the PQD allied itself with President Balaguer.

Socialist Block (*Bloque Socialista*); an ally of the Dominican Revolutionary Party (PRD) which won one seat in the Chamber of Deputies in the 1990 congressional elections.

Ecuador

Capital: Quito **Population: 10,781,000**

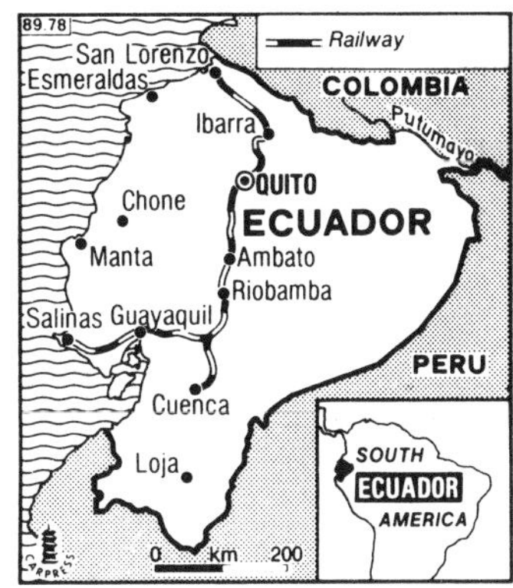

The Republic of Ecuador achieved independence from Spain in 1822 as part of Gran Colombia and became a separate republic in 1830. Its first 120 years were marked by frequent changes of government, particularly the period from 1925 to 1948, during which 22 heads of state held office. In 1963 the Liberal government of President Velasco was toppled by a military coup. Velasco was reinstalled in 1968 for a fifth term and from 1970 assumed dictatorial powers. He was ousted by the military in 1972 and a civilian democratic government was not restored until 1979. During the mid-1980s the conservative government of President León Febres Cordero was openly challenged by military nationalists led by Gen. Frank Vargas Pazzos. The election of 1988, however was won by the centre-left Democratic Left (ID) candidate Rodrigo Borja Cevallos. The ID government prided itself in being the only country in South America not to opt for the wholesale privatization of state enterprises. However, lower international oil prices in the aftermath of the Gulf war in early 1991 led to a slowing of economy, and an austerity policy failed to halt spiralling inflation, high unemployment and widespread poverty. In the May 1992 presidential and congressional elections, the ID was heavily defeated by right-wing parties.

Constitutional structure

Under the 1979 Constitution the Republic has an executive President who is assisted by a Vice-President and a Cabinet. He appoints the ministers and governors of Ecuador's 20 provinces, including the Galapagos Islands. Legislative power is exercised by the National Congress which sits for a 60-day period from Aug. 10 of every year. Special sessions of the National Congress may be called. Congress is required by the Constitution to set up four full-time Legislative Commissions to consider draft laws when the House is in recess.

Electoral system

The President is directly elected together with a Vice-President for a four-year term and is precluded from seeking re-election. If no candidate wins an absolute majority, there follows a run-off election between the two best-placed candidates. The National Congress has 65 members elected on a provincial basis every two years, and 12 members elected for a four-year term on a national basis.

Sequence of elections since 1984

Date	*Winning Party*
May 6, 1984 (presidential)	Social Christian Party (PSC)
Jan. 29, 1984 (legislative)	Democratic Left (ID)
June 1986 (legislative)	Social Christian Party (PSC)
May 8, 1988 (presidential)	Democratic Left (ID)
Jan. 31, 1988 (legislative)	Democratic Left (ID)
June 17, 1990 (legislative)	Social Christian Party (PSC)
May 17, 1992 (legislative)	Social Christian Party (PSC)

Presidential election 1988

First round Jan. 31, 1988

Candidate	*Party*	*% of votes*
Rodrigo Borja Cevallos	Democratic Left (IU)	20
Abdalà Bucaram Ortiz	Ecuadorean Rodolsista Party (PRE)	15
Sixto Duràn Ballën	Social Christian Party (PSC)	13
Others		52
Total		**100**

Second round May 8, 1988

Rodrigo Borga Cevallos	Democratic Left (ID)	47.4
Abdalà Bucaram Ortiz	Ecuadorean Rodolsista Party (PRE)	40.3
Spoilt votes		12.3
Total		**100.0**

Legislative election, June 17, 1990

Party	*Seats*
Social Christian Party (PSC)	16
Democratic Left (ID)	14
Ecuadorean Roldosista Party (PRE)	13
Ecuadorean Socialist Party (PSE)	8
Popular Democracy-Democratic Christian Union (DP-UDC)	7
Concentration of Popular Forces (CFP)	3
Liberal Radical Party (PLR)	3
Ecuadorean Conservative Party (PCE)	3
Alfaroist Radical Front (FRA)	2
Broad Left Front (FADI)	2
Popular Democratic Movement (MPD	1
Total	**72**

Presidential election, May 17, 1992

First round

	S of vote
Sixto Duràn Ballën Republican Unity Party (PUR)	36.1
Jaime Nebot Saadi (PSC)	26.2
Abdalà Bucaram Ortíz (PRE)	20.7
Raül Baca (ID)	8.4
Others	8.6

Durán and Nebot were to dispute a second round on July 5, 1992.

Congressional elections, May 17, 1992

	Seats
PSC	21
PRE	13
PUR	12
Popular Democratic Movement (MPD)	4
ID	7
Ecuadorian Conservative Party (PCE)	6
People Democracy - Democratic Christian Union — DP-UDC	5
Ecuadorian Socialist Party (PSE)	2
Liberal Radical Party (PLR)	2
Alfaroist Radical Front (FRA)	1
Concentration of Popular Forces (CFP)	1
Ecuadorian Popular Revolutionary Action (APRE)	1
National Liberation Party (PLN)	1

Evolution of the suffrage

Voting is compulsory for literate men and women over the age of 18. Voting is optional for those over 65 and illiterates, who were only enfranchised in 1978.

PARTY BY PARTY DATA

Alfaroist Radical Front

Frente Radical Alfarista (FRA)
Address. G. Moreno y Gómez Rendón (esquina), Guayaquil.
Leadership. Cecilia Calderón de Castro (national director).
Orientation. Centre-left.
Founded. 1972.
History. The party, named after the leader of the 1895 Liberal Revolution, Eloy Alfaro, was formed by Abdón Calderón Muñoz and a dissident faction from the Radical Liberal Party (PLR). The former Liberal Party (PL) faction leader won nine per cent of the national vote in the 1978 presidential election and in December of the same year he was assassinated by political opponents. The FRA's legal status was cancelled the following January because it could not muster sufficient provincial candidates and thus was barred from participating in the elections of April 29, 1979 (although the FRA went on to support the Concentration of Popular Forces presidential candidate in the second round). Under the leadership of Calderón's daughter, the economist Cecilia Calderón, the party won 20 per cent of the vote in the 1980 local elections and in the congressional elections of January 1984 gained one national and five provincial seats.

The FRA initially went into opposition but in mid-1985 joined the conservative government of León Febres Cordero, whereupon Iván Castro Patiño of the FRA was elected Vice-President. However, in the June 1986 mid-term congressional elections, the party held on to only two provincial seats and became the election's most prominent casualty. Its fortune did not improve in the January 1988 general election, when the FRA presidential candidate Carlos Julio Emanuel Morán came eighth and the party's representation in Congress remained at two deputies, one provincial and one national. In the presidential second round in May the FRA supported Rodrigo Borja of the Democratic Left (ID) but on his inauguration, the party went into opposition. The FRA won one seat in the May 17, 1992, congressional elections.

Broad Left Front

Frente Amplio de la Izquierda (FADI)
Address. Huancavilca 416 y Chimborazo, Guayaquil.
Leadership. Xavier Garaycoa O. (pres.).
Orientation. Left-wing.
Founded. 1977.
History. The alliance was a successor to the left-wing Popular Democratic Union (UDP) founded in 1966 and included a large proportion of the old alliance's member parties, such as the Ecuadorean Communist Party (PCE), the Ecuadorean Revolutionary Socialist Party (PSRE) and the Revolutionary Movement of the Christian Left (MRIC). The FADI, under the UDP name, fielded the PCE leader René Maugé Mosquera in the presidential elections of 1978; he came sixth with five per cent of the national vote. In the congressional elections in 1979 the alliance won one seat only and in 1980 FADI's ranks were greatly depleted when the PSRE and smaller left-wing parties left to found the Ecuadorean Popular Revolutionary Union (URPE, now defunct). Maugé fought the elections of January 1984 as the alliance's presidential candidate under its real name FADI, having been officially registered in 1983. He won few votes and in the second round of the presidential election the FADI supported Rodrigo Borja of the Democratic Left (ID).

The alliance increased its congressional representation to two seats in the legislative elections of the same year and joined the opposition Progressive Parliamentarian Block. FADI's seats in Congress increased by one when Maugé was elected in the mid-term elections of 1986. The alliance suffered a split the following year when the "Rebel FADI" faction left to form the National Liberation Party (PLN). A further group supporting the presidential candidacy of Lt.-Gen. Vargas Pazzos left to join the People's Patriotic Union (UPP). In August 1987 FADI had formed the United Front of the Left electoral alliance with the Popular Democratic Movement (MPD) and the Ecuadorean Socialist Party (PSE) which unsuccessfully fielded the MPD leader Jaime Hurtado in the presidential elections of January 1988. The simultaneous congressional election resulted in one provincial and one national seat for FADI. The alliance again backed Rodrigo Borja (ID) in the presidential run-off and after his victory FADI struck a parliamentary agreement with the ID and the People's Democracy (DP).

In the congressional elections of June 17, 1990, FADI could not increase its parliamentary representation and retained its two seats. Its presidential candidate in the May 17, 1992, elections was Gustavo Iturralde who received a negligible percentage of the vote.

Concentration of Popular Forces

Concentración de Fuerzas Populares (CFP)
Address. Boyacá entre Sucre y Colón, Guayaquil.
Leadership. Rafael Santelices Pintado (supreme director).
Orientation. Centre-right populist.
Founded. 1946.
History. The party was formed as the Popular Republican Union and changed to its current name two years later. Carlos Guevara Moreno, the party's leader until 1961, was elected mayor of Guayaquil in 1951. Although the party won the highest percentage of votes in the 1956 elections of any single party, it was defeated by a Conservative coalition. The party's fortunes nevertheless did not improve when in 1960 it formed an electoral alliance with the Socialist Party (PS) and the Ecuadorean Communist Party (PCE). In 1962 the mayorship of Guayaquil, by then the CFP's stronghold, went to the party's new leader Asaad Bucaram.

Bucaram dominated the party with his own personality but did not put himself forward as its presidential candidate until his return in 1972 from a two-year exile in Panama imposed on him by the Velasquez government. However, his political ambitions were cut short by the 1972 military coup and when free elections were called in 1978 Bucaram was excluded from running, on the pretext that his Syrian father was foreign-born.

His substitute in the elections of 1978-79 was his niece's husband Jaime Roldós Aguilera, who with the additional backing of the Christian Democrats won both rounds and was sworn in as President in August 1979. The CFP also won a congressional majority but became seriously divided when Roldós tried to move the party away from Bucaram's dominance and towards social democracy. Roldós' supporters, including half of the CFP's 24 deputies, then left to found People, Change and Democracy (PCD) in 1980.

After the deaths of Asaad Bucaram and Roldós in 1981, the CFP moved to the right under the leadership of Averroes Bucaram Záccida, the former leader's son. It supported the government of the Christian Democrat Osvaldo Hurtado until 1984, when its representation in Congress was reduced to eight seats.

The CFP signed a political accord with the conservative Febres government (see Socialcon Christian Party—PSC) and in June 1985 Bucaram was elected President of Congress. In order to distance itself from the increasingly unpopular government, the CFP withdrew from the coalition shortly before the 1986 mid-term elections.

The party's representation in the Chamber nevertheless decreased to four seats. Despite faction fights between a group supporting Averroes Bucaram and one led by Avicenas Bucaram, which had weakened the party since May 1987, the CFP managed to increase its congressional seats to six. The party's presidential candidate Angel Duarte Valverde, who was widely thought to be the right's favoured candidate, came only fifth and the CFP advised its supporters to spoil their ballot papers in the presidential run-off. Although the party's seats were halved in the June 1990 elections, Averroes Bucaram was elected president of Congress the following August and almost immediately tried to stage a constitutional coup against the Borja government by impeaching several ministers who were subsequently dismissed by Congress.

His impeachment of President Borja, however, failed to be ratified by Congress and Bucaram subsequently lost his post. In 1991 Bucaram was selected as the CFP's presidential candidate in the May 17, 1992, elections and received a negligible percentage of the vote. The party won one seat in the congress.

Democratic Left

Izquierda Democrática (ID)
Address. Juan León Mera 268 y Jorge Washington, Quito.
Leadership. Andrés Vallejo Arcos (dir. nat. exec.).

Orientation. Social democratic, but once in office implemented conservative neo-liberal economic policies.
Founded. 1970.
History. The party was formed by a faction of the Radical Liberal Party (PLR) led by Rodrigo Borja Cevallos opposed to President Velasquez, together with some independents and dissident members of the Ecuadorean Socialist Party (PSE). In 1978 the ID obtained its first opportunity to contestb presidential elections but Borja came only fourth with 11 per cent of the vote. However, the ID became the second largest party in Congress after winning 15 seats in the 1979 legislative election and threw its support behind the newly elected President Jaime Roldós who had problems with some deputies of his own party, the Concentration of Popular Forces (CFP). In 1982, with its ranks reduced to 12 after the mid-term elections of that year, the ID gave its support to Roldós' successor, Osvaldo Hurtado of the People's Democracy (DP-UDC).

The elections of 1984 were fought jointly with the late President Roldós' People, Change and Democracy Party (PCD). The ID won 24 seats, by far the largest number obtained by any single party, and Borja won the first round of the presidential election on Jan. 29 but failed to gain an absolute majority. He obtained 47.8 per cent of the vote in the second round and was narrowly beaten by the Social Christian León Febres. Raúl Baca Carbo, who had been Borja's running-mate in 1978-79, was elected President of Congress and the ID, together with some other parties, used its large congressional representation to form an effective opposition to the conservative Febres government. The Progressive Parliamentarian Block, however, lost its majority when the ID managed to hold on to only 17 congressional seats in the 1986 legislative elections. The Presidency of the National Congress went to an ID member, Andrés Vallejo, who was followed in 1987 by Jorge Zavala Baquerizo. The 1988 general election brought the ID to power, Borja having won the first round of the presidential elections with 20 per cent and the second round on May 8 with 47.4 per cent.

Rodrigo Borja was inaugurated as President of Ecuador on Aug. 10, his government based on a pro-government alliance consisting of 30 ID Congressmen and 13 from the People's Democracy (DP-UDC) and other parties. His first task was to deal with Ecuador's economic problems which he did by implementing highly unpopular austerity measures, which, although modest in comparison to other shock measures in other Latin American countries, lost the ID the 1990 mid-term legislative elections and 13 seats in the Congress. The party's congressional majority had already been twice threatened in 1989 when the DP-UDC withdrew from the alliance. In addition, six cabinet ministers were impeached and removed by the legislature after the elections, and Borja himself narrowly escaped impeachment, in proceedings started against him by the president of Congress, Averroes Bucaram, in October 1990. Borja retained his office only with the support of three opposition deputies who voted with the pro-government block.

Success in negotiating the surrender and disbandment of the Alfaro Vive Carajo! (AVC) guerrillas in October 1991, whose members subsequently joined the ID, restored some confidence in the government's claim that its overall aim was to promote national conciliation. In an attempt to boost the ID's elections prospects in the forthcoming May 1992 general election, Borja submitted a letter of intent to the IMF in January proposing higher levels of public spending and the increased availability of credit to the private sector. The ID's candidate in the May 17, 1992, was Raúl Baca Carbo, the former president of Congress, thought to be too closely linked to the Borja government to have a chance of winning. He came a poor fourth with 8.4 per cent of the vote and the party won seven seats in the Congress.
International Affiliation. Socialist International (full member party).

Ecuadorean Conservative Party

Partido Conservador Ecuatoriano (PCE)
Address. Leonidas Plaza 1067 entre Baquerizo y Lizardo García, Quito.
Leadership. Alberto Dahik Garzozi (general director).
Orientation. Right-wing traditionalists.
Founded. 1855.
History. The PCE was founded by Gabriel García Moreno who was assassinated in 1875 after ruling the country as a dictator for 15 years. Traditionally the party represented the country's oligarchy, the church and the army, and its ideology has remained unchanged despite major reorganizations of the party in 1925 and 1989. In 1940 it supported the Arroyo del Rio Liberal government but four years later switched

sides and joined the Ecuadorian Democratic Alliance which brought José María Velasco Ibarra to power. The PCE came to dominate the Constituent Assembly in 1946 and the conservative Vice-President Mariano Suárez Veintimilla was installed as President following the military coup in 1947 which overthrew Velasco. The Conservatives, however, failed to gain the presidency in the elections the following year. In 1956-60 the PCE participated in government as part of a Popular Alliance backing Camilo Ponce of the Social Christian Party (PSC).

In the June 1962 congressional elections, standing alone, it won 22 seats but once again, in 1968, it joined other right-wing organizations to support the unsuccessful candidacy of Ponce for the presidency. The party suffered internal disputes throughout the military dictatorship of 1972-78 and in 1978 a progressive faction merged with the Christian Democratic Party to form the Popular Democracy (DP-UDC). After backing the unsuccessful candidacy of the PSC Sixto Durán Ballén in 1979, the PCE formed a majority congressional block together with the ruling Concentration of Popular Forces (CFP). In the 1984 general election the PCE joined the National Reconstruction Front coalition supporting the victorious presidential candidate León Febres Cordero of the PSC and was given a cabinet post in his government. In the 1986 congressional elections the PCE's two seats were reduced to one which it retained in the general elections two years later.

Despite internal upheavals resulting in the reorganization of the party, the PCE managed to increase its parliamentary representation to three seats in the 1990 mid-term elections. In the May 17, 1992, congressional elections, the party won six seats.

Ecuadorean Roldosist Party

Partido Roldosista Ecuatoriano (PRE)

Address. Urdaneta Y Escobedo, Guayaquil.

Leadership. Rosa Pulley de Bucarám (supreme director).

Orientation. Right-wing, populist.

Founded. 1982.

History. The party was founded by Abdalá Bucaram Ortíz and was named after his brother-in-law, President Jaime Roldós Aguilera (see Concentration of Popular Forces and People, Change and Democracy—PCD). It started as a movement within the PCD and registered as a party in its own right after Roldós' death in 1981. Abdalá Bucaram was elected mayor of Guayaquil in 1984 but had to flee the country a year later when he was charged with offences against state security for questioning the share of the budget allocated to the armedforces.

The party won three seats in the 1984 elections and retained them in the 1986 mid-term elections. Bucaram was granted an amnesty by the opposition-dominated Congress in the same year but was then arrested in exile in Panama and detained by the Panamanian authorities until January 1987. He returned to Ecuador in August to campaign for the January 1988 presidential elections in which he came second with 15 per cent of the vote in the first round, increased to 40.3 per cent in the run-off election, insufficient to defeat his rival Rodrigo Borja (see Democratic Left). The PRE won six seats in the Congress.

Bucaram fled into exile in Panama once more when faced with charges of embezzlement when mayor of Guayaquil, but led the party from there. Elsa Bucaram of the PRE was elected mayor of Guayaquil in the same year. The party's strong opposition to the Borja government paid dividends in the 1990 congressional elections when the PRE increased its representation to 13 seats. The party joined forces with the Social Christian Party (PSC) and, as the dominant congressional block, caused the Borja government serious problems. Abdalá Bucaram was selected again as PRE candidate for the May 1992 presidential election. However, it was feared, in view of his past adverse comments about the army, that if he were elected there might be a military coup. He came third with 20.7 per cent of the vote and the party won 13 seats in the congress (see PSC).

Ecuadorean Socialist Party

Partido Socialista Ecuatoriano (PSE)

Address. Pasaje San Luis No. 340, Quito.

Leadership. Víctor Granda Aguilar (secretary general).

Orientation. Socialist.

Founded. 1926.

History. The party was formed by Ricardo Paredes who together with other pro-Moscow members split away from the PSE a year later and in 1931 formed the Ecuadorean Communist Party (PCE). The Socialist

Party underwent a complete re-organization and re-orientation in 1933, and in 1937-38 the party took part in the government of Gen. Alberto Enríquez Gallo under whose presidency major social reforms were implemented. Although the PSE was part of the Ecuadorean Democratic Alliance which overthrew Arroyo del Río and installed José María Velasco Ibarra in 1944, the PSE withdrew its support when Velasco took on dictatorial powers, and was subsequently persecuted by his regime. The PSE supported the Galo Plaza government of 1948-52 after initial reservations.

The majority decision to back Galo Plaza's presidential candidacy in the 1960 election caused the breakaway of a pro-Cuban faction which founded the Ecuadorean Revolutionary Socialist Party (PSRE) a year later. The PSE's support base decreased throughout the 1960s and 1970s and consistently failed to obtain congressional representation. However, in the elections of 1984 the party won one seat and became a member of the Progressive Front opposition block.

The mid-term elections of 1986 increased the Socialist seats to six and the PSE's Enrique Ayala Mora won the congressional vice-presidency. In September 1987 the PSE entered into a coalition with the National Liberation Party (PLN) and the Ecuadorean Popular Revolutionary Action (APRE).

The alliance's presidential candidate and leader of an unsuccessful military rebellion against the Febrero government in 1987, Gen. Frank Vargas Pazzos (see People's Patriotic Union—UPP) fought the 1988 presidential elections with Enríque Ayala Mora of the PSE as his running-mate and came fourth. The PSE declared that it wanted nothing to do with the Democratic Left (ID) government before President Borja was sworn in, and in 1989 went into outright opposition.

This reflected well on the party who in the 1990 legislative elections increased its number of deputies from three to eight. The PSE stood alone again in the May 17, 1992, elections and fielded León Roldós Aguilera as its presidential candidate, who received a negligible percentage of the vote.

Roldós, the brother of the charismatic late President Jaime Roldós Aguilera (1979-81, see Concentration of Popular Forces and People, Change and Democracy), served as vice-president to his brother's successor. The party won two seats in the concurrent congressional elections.

People's Democracy-Democratic Christian Union

Democracia Popular-Unión Demócrata Cristiana (DP-UDC)

Address. Luis Saa 153 y Pazmiño, Quito.

Leadership. Vladimiro Alvarez Grau (nat. pres.).

Orientation. Centre-left; its stated principles are humanism, communal socialism, democracy and Latin American nationalism.

Founded. 1978.

History. The DP-UDC had its origins in the Christian Democratic Party (PDC), formed in 1964, which merged with the progressive faction of the Ecuadorian Conservative Party (PCE) led by Julio César Trujillo in 1978. In 1979 Osvaldo Hurtado Larrea, (formerly PDC leader), was elected Vice-President to President Jaime Roldós of the Concentration of Popular Forces (CFP) and after his death in 1981 assumed the presidency.

Hurtado's DP-UDC government became unpopular with the left for his policy of reducing state spending and the austerity measures which were introduced in 1983, but also with the right who opposed any state intervention in the running of the economy. The DP-UDC formed an alliance with the Democratic Left (ID) and the CFP after People, Change and Democracy (PCD, a party formed by Roldós during his presidency) went into opposition in January 1982. In the 1984 elections the DP-UDC fielded Julio César Trujillo, who won only a small percentage of votes, and the party was reduced to three seats in the Congress.

The party recovered ground in the 1988 election when its congressional representation increased from four to seven seats. After fielding the then party leader Jamil Mahuad as their own presidential candidate in the first round, the DP-UDC supported the successful ID candidate Rodrigo Borja in the run-off. The party was invited to take part in Borja's coalition government and was given a cabinet post. The presidency of the National Congress also went to a member of the DP-UDC, Wilfrido Lucero Bolaños. However, in 1989, the DP-UDC announced that it wished to retain only a congressional alliance with the ID but remain independent from the government so that it could present its own candidate in the 1992 presidential elections. In November of the same year, the DP-UDC withdrew completely from the alliance,

following disagreements over the government's vegetable oil price rises. This distancing from the government saved the DP-UDC from suffering the fate of the ID (whose seats were nearly halved), and the party managed to retain its seven seats. The party leader Vladimiro Alvarez Grau was the DP-UDC's presidential candidate in the May 17, 1992, elections and received a fraction of the overall vote. The party won five seats in the congress.
International Affiliation. Member party of the Christian Democrat Organization of America, which forms part of the Christian Democrat International.

Popular Democratic Movement

Movimiento Popular Democrático (MPD)
Address. 10 de Agosto y Riofrío, Quito.
Leadership. Jorge Moreno Ordóñez (nat. dir.).
Orientation. Left-wing said to be pro-Chinese; the party 's central objective is a patriotic, democratic and revolutionary government of the people based on a well-grounded socialist programme.
Founded. 1978.
History. The MPD was formed by the pro-Chinese Ecuadorean Communist Party, Marxist-Leninist (PCE-ML) as an electoral vehicle. The party's then leader Jaime Hurtado González became a deputy in 1979 and stood as the MPD's presidential candidate in the elections of 1984 in which he won 6.1 per cent of the poll. In the simultaneous general election the MPD increased their congressional representation to three deputies who joined the opposition Progressive Parliamentary Bloc. Hurtado was again selected as the party's presidential candidate in the 1988 elections and was also backed by the Broad Left Front (FADI) and the Ecuadorean Socialist Party (PSE) with which the MPD had formed an electoral alliance. The party held on to the four seats it had won in the 1986 mid-term elections but although the MPD opposed the Borja government, it lost three seats in the 1990 congressional elections. Fausto Moreno Ordóñez was the candidate in the presidential elections of May 17, 1992, and received a negligible percentage of the vote. In the concurrent congressional elections, the party won four seats.

Radical Liberal Party

Partido Liberal Radical (PLR)
Address. Pasaje Andrade Coello 108 y 12 de Octubre, Quito.
Leadership. Carlos Luis Plaza A. (nat. dir.).
Orientation. Liberal; the party's claimed aims are to realize an authentic democracy based on equality and freedom of all Ecuadorean citizens, and the creation of the necessary economic and social conditions to make this possible.
Founded. 1947.
History. The PLR is a direct descendant of the Liberal Party which had held continuous office from its foundation in 1895 to 1944. The PLR emerged after the Liberal Party fragmented into different groups in 1944 and was registered under its present name three years later. The party itself has suffered several splits. In 1970 a dissident group which disagreed with the party's support of the Velasco government left to found the Democratic Left (ID). In 1972 a further faction, led by Abdón Calderón Muñoz, broke away to form the Alfaroist Radical Front (FRA).

The PLR presidential candidate in the 1978 election, Raúl Clemente Huerta Rendón, came third with 21 per cent, and the party won the mayoralty of Quito. In 1979 the PLR won four congressional seats which it held in the 1984 general election when it formed part of the National Reconstruction Front supporting the conservative candidate León Febres Cordero (see Social Christian Party). The PLR's Blasco Peñaherrera Padilla won the Vice-Presidency and the party was given a cabinet post in the Febres administration. The June 1986 congressional election reduced the PLR's seats to three and in October of the same year the party went into opposition which caused internal dissent. The party's candidate in the 1988 elections, Miguel Albornoz, won only a small percentage of the ballot and the party retained only two seats in Congress. Further arguments within the party ensued. The party's congressional representation increased to three seats in the June 1990 election. Bolívar Chiriboga was the candidate of the PLR in the presidential election of May 17, 1992. He won a negligible percentage of the vote and in the simultaneous congressional elections, the party won two seats.

Republican Unity Party

Partido Unidad Republicana (PUR)
Address. Rábida 417 y La Niña, Quito.
Leadership. Mauricio Gándara Gallegos (nat. dir.).
Orientation. Centre-right.
Founded. Oct. 10, 1991.

History. The party was formed by dissidents from the Social Christian Party (PSC) led by Sixto Durán Ballén Cordovez. As the PSC's presidential candidate Ballén came third with 13 per cent of the poll in the January 1988 election. Public opinion polls before the May 17, 1992 elections suggested that he would be elected President and he duly won in the first round of voting with 36.1 per cent of the vote, gaining most votes in the highlands and significant support in the western coastal regions. He faced Jaime Nebot Saadi in a run-off on July 5 and was expected to pick up the votes of the dispersed left-wing. In the simultaneous congressional elections, the party won 12 seats.

Social Christian Party

Partido Social Cristiano (PSC)
Address. Carrión 548 y R. Victoria, Quito.
Leadership. Marco Lara Guzmán (nat. pres.).
Orientation. Conservative and aggressively free-market.
Founded. 1951.
History. The PSC was formed as the Social Christian Movement to support Camilo Ponce Enríquez who was until 1952 Minister of Government in the third Velasco government and served as President of Ecuador in 1956-60. The party adopted its present name in 1967 and the following year Ponce's presidential candidacy attracted the support of the Conservative Party (PC) but he failed to be elected. The party continued to operate during the 1972-79 military dictatorship, but after Ponce's death in 1976 the party went through a temporary crisis. The PSC fielded Sixto Durán Ballén (see PUR) in the 1978-79 presidential elections and won second place in both rounds. In 1983 the PSC formed the National Reconstruction Front, an alliance with the Radical Liberal Party (PLR), the Ecuadorean Conservative Party (PCE) and the Nationalist Revolutionary Party (PNR), to support the presidential candidacy of León Febres Cordero Rivadeneira in 1984. He came second in the first round but won the run-off with 52.2 per cent of the vote.

The National Reconstruction Front (FRN) government led by President Febres at first had a minority in Congress. In June, however, a narrow majority was established by forming an alliance with the Concentration of Popular Forces (CFP) and the Alfaroist Radical Front (FRA). In September 1984 the Febres government came into conflict with thelegislatureovertheappointmentsprocedureforthe Supreme Court which degenerated into violent exchanges in Congress in the following months. The President at the same time introduced austere economic policies which provoked strikes and public disorder. The measures nevertheless were believed to be working and in the mid-term elections of June 1986, the PSC's seats increased from nine to 15. Other FRN parties, however, did not fare as well and the government was again reduced to a congressional minority. The opposition block proposed a resolution demanding his resignation, a challenge Febres barely defeated. In January 1987 he was kidnapped by air force units who released him in return for an amnesty for the progressive Lt.-Gen. Vargas Pazzos (see People's Patriotic Union) who had led two military rebellions less than a year earlier, forcing the dismissal of the Minister of Defence and an army commander.

The election campaign for the January 1988 election was adversely affected by the track record of the Febres administration, which was criticized for human rights violations in relation to its counter-insurgency campaign and for its failure in turning the economy round despite the high level of social sacrifice it had exacted from the population.

The PSC's presidential candidate Sixto Durán Ballén (see Republican Unity Party), came third with 15.6 per cent of the vote and the party was reduced to only six deputies in Congress. The PSC did not support either of the two finalists in the second round of the presidential elections and went into opposition to the Democratic Left (ID) government. Febres was subsequently involved in a financial scandal in which he was charged with embezzling $150,000 (US) from state funds. He was also rumoured to have been the head of a plot by right-wing groups to launch a coup against the Borja government.

This, however, did not diminish the PSC's success in the June 1990 mid-term elections in which the party won 16 seats, making it the largest party in Congress. The PSC entered into a parliamentary alliance with the Ecuadorean Roldósist Party (PRE) and together they controlled Congress. Jaime Nebot Saadi was the presidential candidate in the May 17, 1992, presidential elections, and came second to the PUR's Sixto Dúran Ballén with 26.2 per cent of the vote, forcing a second round run-off scheduled for July 5. Nebot appealed for support from the third place candidate Abdalá Bucaram Ortíz but such a right-wing populist alliance was considered unlikely.

In the simultaneous congressional elections the PSC won 21 seats, making it the largest party bloc.

Minor parties

Assad Bucaram Party (*Partido Assad Bucaram*—PAB; Ayacucho 4317 y Quinceava, Guayaquil); this populist party, named after the late leader of the Concentration of Popular Forces (CFP), was founded on July 31, 1991, and fielded Bolívar González in the May 17, 1992, presidential elections; he received a small fraction of the vote. The party's national director is Avicena Bucaram.

Ecuadorean Communist Party (*Partido Comunista Ecuatoriano*—PCE); founded in 1926, was an orthodox party before the changes in Eastern Europe. It was a member of the left-wing Popular Democratic Union (UDP) alliance founded in 1966 and became a leading member of the Broad Left Front (FADI). The PCE's secretary-general René Maugé Mosquera was FADI's presidential candidate in the 1978 election and came sixth with 5 per cent of the ballot. In the 1988 election the PCE's Efraín Alvarez was selected by FADI as the running mate to Jaime Hurtado, leader of the Popular Democratic Movement (MPD). The party, like all members of FADI, opposed the Democratic Left government for its austerity programme and joined in various protests and strike actions. The PCE controls the Ecuadorean Workers' Confederation (CTE) which contains about 20 per cent of the country's trade unionists.

Ecuadorean Communist Party, Marxist-Leninist (*Partido Comunista Ecuatoriano, Marxista-Leninista*—PCE-ML), a Maoist splinter group of the Communist Party founded in 1963. The PCE-ML formed the Popular Democratic Movement (MPD) in 1978 in order to participate in the 1979 congressional elections in which the PCE-ML leader Jaime Hurtado González became a deputy. He contested the presidential elections in 1984 when he won 6.1 per cent of the vote, and again in 1988. The party's membership was estimated in 1989 as being 600.

Ecuadorean Popular Revolutionary Action (*Acción Popular Revolucionaria Ecuatoriana*—APRE, 18 de Septiembre 554 y Páez, Quito); APRE was formed in the 1970s. In the 1984 presidential elections it backed the Social Christian (PSC) candidate in the first round but supported the Democratic Left (ID) candidate in the second round. It has since opposed both the PSC and the ID governments. This centrist party is headed by Lt.-Gen. (retd.) Frank Vargas Pazzos, a progressive self-styled leftist and former armed forces chief-of-staff, who led two failed military rebellions in March 1986 forcing the resignation of the Minister of Defence and an army commander who had accused him of embezzlement. Lt.-Gen. Vargas was amnestied in January 1987 in return for the release of the kidnapped President Febres Cordero (see PSC). Vargas was a member of the People's Patriotic Union (UPP) until 1989 and stood as the UPP's presidential candidate in the 1988 election, with the backing of APRE and the Socialist Party. He came fourth and APRE elected him party director in 1989. APRE failed to win any representation in Congress. Vargas was chosen as the party's presidential candidate in the May 1992 presidential election and received a negligible percentage of the vote. The party won one seat in the simultaneous congressional elections.

National Confederation of the Indigenous Population of Ecuador (*Confederación Nacional de Indígenos del Ecuador*—CONIAE); this indigenist organization campaigns for the return of traditional community-held lands, the payment by petrol companies of compensation to tribes for environmental damage and for the recognition of Quechua as an official Ecuadorean language. CONIAE co-ordinated a march on Quito in May 1990 of about 1,000 people to submit a petition for the recognition of their land rights. In June of the same year CONIAE organized an uprising by indigenous people spanning seven provinces in which members of the army were held hostage in order to force President Borja to negotiate. The organization is supported by the major trade union confederation United Workers' Front (FUT) with whom it launched a joint campaign in January 1991, after which Borja accused CONIAE of wanting to set up a state within a state. CONIAE called on its members to boycott the May 17, 1992, presidential and congressional elections.

National Liberation Party (*Partido Liberación Nacional*—PLN; 10 de Agosto 1731 y San Gregorio, Quito), led by Alfredo Castillo (s.-g.) the party was formed in 1987 by a breakaway group from the Broad Front of the Left (FADI), calling itself "Rebel FADI" but adopted its current name in the same year. In the 1988 presidential elections the PLN supported the campaign of Lt. Gen. Frank Vargas Pazzos of the People's Patriotic Union (UPP). The party was officially registered with the Supreme Electoral Tribunal in 1989 and won one seat in the May 17, 1992, congressional elections.

People, Change and Democracy (*Pueblo, Cambio y Democracia*—PCD, 9 de Octubre 416 y Chile, Ed. City Bank, 8vo. piso, Guayaquil); the PCD was founded in 1980 by supporters of President Roldós within the Concentration of Popular Forces (CFP) and was joined by 12 CFP deputies. After his death in May 1981 the party had disagreements with his successor President Hurtado of the People's Democracy—Democratic Christian Union and went into opposition. The party lost all its seats in the 1984 election and apart from one seat gained in 1986 it has not since been represented in Congress. Although Aquiles Rigail of the PCD obtained the Social Health portfolio in the right-wing Social Christian Party (PSC) Febres Cordero Cabinet in 1987, the PCD discussed a possible merger with the Democratic Left (ID). In the 1988 presidential elections the PCD advocated a vote against the PSC candidate but stated no preference between the ID or Ecuadorean Roldosist Party candidate. Since 1988 the party has been led by Julián Palacios Cevallos.

People's Party (*Partido del Pueblo*—PP, 9 de Octubre 1904 entre Los Ríos y Esmeraldas, Guayaquil); a centre-left party formed in 1984 by its current leader Alejandro Román Armendáriz, a former member of the Democratic Left (ID) and Administrative Secretary General in the Roldós government (1979-81—see Concentration of Popular Forces and People, Change and Democracy. Originally called the Socialist Democratic Movement, the party registered as the PP in 1986. It supported the ID in the 1988 elections but later opposed the Borja government. The PP has so far failed to win any congressional representation.

People's Patriotic Union (*Unión del Pueblo Patriótico*—UPP). The party was founded in 1987 and attracted a section of the Broad Left Front (FADI) after it decided to field Lt.-Gen. Frank Vargas Pazzos in the presidential election of January 1988. His candidacy was also supported by an alliance of several other parties which included the National Liberation Party (PLN), the Socialist Party (PSE) and the Ecuadorean Popular Revolutionary Action (APRE). Vargas had been forced to retire as chief of staff of the armed forces in 1986 and shortly after led two military rebellions in March 1986 forcing the resignation of the Minister of Defence and an army commander. Lt.-Gen. Vargas was amnestied in January 1987 in return for the release of President Febres Cordero who was kidnapped by rebel air force officers (see PSC). Lt.-Gen. Vargas joined APRE in 1989 after having won a significant share of the presidential vote in the 1988 elections, coming fourth. The UPP did not win any congressional seats.

Guerrilla groups

Montoneros Free Fatherland (*Montoneros Patria Libre*—MPL) are the only guerrilla group remaining in Ecuador after the disbanding of the "Alfaro Lives, Dammit!" (*Alfaro Vive, Carajo!*—AVC) in 1991 (see Democratic Left). The MPL was formed by a small splinter group of the above guerrillas. Its first action, in January 1986, was to capture a military museum in Quito. Soon after, several MPL members were captured and given prison sentences for kidnapping a magistrate. The MPL subsequently held President Febres'representative on the Constitutional Guarantees Tribunal in an unsuccessful attempt to force Febres to stand trial for failing to implement his election promises. In 1988, in order to denounce the newly elected ID government's economic policy as a continuation of Febres', the MPL seized and held four media employees. Although the MPL were the initiators of a dialogue between the Borja government, the AVC and themselves in October 1988, the group later announced that it wanted no part in the ensuing peace agreement between the government and the AVC. The MPL has since turned to violent action and bank robberies, whose proceeds are believed to be used for arms purchases.

El Salvador

Capital: San Salvador **Population: 4,860,000**

The Republic of El Salvador was ruled by Spain until 1821 and only finally gained full independence in 1839. Throughout its history, military dictatorships have either ruled directly or dominated the civilian administrations nominally in power, frequently intervening in the electoral process to choose a president suitable to the requirements of ther current dictatorship and of the country's rich and powerful oligarchy. The elections since 1982 relied on substantial political, financial and practical support from the United States in an effort to combine stability with a degree of respectability. Against current trends, this secured the victory of the US-favoured Christian Democratic Party in the 1984 presidential elections, a victory which the oligarchy, though still dependent on US military aid, reversed with the victory of the Republican Nationalist Alliance (Arena) in the 1989 presidential elections.

Constitutional structure

Under the 1983 Constitution, legislative power is vested in a unicameral Legislative Assembly (which replaced the National Constituent Assembly in 1985), enlarged to 84 seats in 1991. Executive power rests with the President who appoints a Council of Ministers and is assisted by a Vice-President. Every two years, the legislature appoints three substitute Vice-Presidents to assume the presidency in the case of the Vice-President being unable to do so.

Electoral system

The President and Vice-President are elected nationally by universal adult suffrage for a five-year term and may not stand for immediate re-election. The members of the Legislative Assembly are elected for three-year terms.

Evolution of the suffrage

Suffrage is universal for nationals over 18 years of age, except for members of the armed forces who are not permitted to vote. Elections are regulated by the electoral law of 1961 which established the electoral council as a supervisory body for all elections.

Sequence of elections since 1982

Date	*Winning party*
March 1982 (legislative)	Christian Democratic Party (PDC)
May 1984 (presidential)	(PDC)
March 1985 (legislative)	(PDC)
March 1988 (legislative)	(Arena)

The legislative election of 1982, in real terms, was a victory for five right-wing parties over the PDC, which secured only 26 seats out of the 60 seats in the then Constituent Assembly, subsequently replaced in 1985 by the current Legislative Assembly. In the 1991 elections, Arena lost its working majority in the Assembly.

Presidential elections, March, 1989

	% of vote
Alfredo Cristiani Burkard (Arena)	53.8
Fidel Chavez Mena (PDC)	36.0
Rafael Moran National Conciliation Party (PCN)	4.1
Guillermo Ungo Democratic Convergence (CD)	3.9
Other	2.2
Total	**100.0**

Legislative elections, March, 1991

Party	*seats*
Arena	39
PDC	26
PCN	9
CD	8
Nationalist Democratic Union (UDN)	1
Authentic Democratic Christian Movement (MADC)	1

PARTY BY PARTY DATA

Christian Democrat Party

Partido Demócrata Cristiano (PDC)
Address. La Calle Poniente 924, San Salvador, El Salvador.
Leadership. Fidel Chávez Mena (l.).
Orientation. Originally claimed to be seeking a "third way" between capitalism and communism but years of co-habitation with the military during the 1980s shifted the party to the right, especially in the late 1980s when it called for the "reprivatization" of the economy.
Founded. 1960.
History. The PDC was founded by José Napoleón Duarte who was elected mayor of El Salvador in 1964. Although it contested National Assembly and presidential elections in 1964 and 1967 respectively, it was not until the 1970s that it made a significant political impact. In 1972 and 1977 the PDC led an opposition electoral alliance, the National Opposition Union (UNO) backing Duarte's candidacy for the presidency. Duarte was elected President in 1972 but was forced to flee the country following a military coup. He returned from exile in 1979 to join the "government junta" formed after the overthrow of the Romero military regime and in December was appointed President, the first civilian to hold the post in almost 50 years.

The PDC remained in two more national junta governments until 1982, relying on a tacit pact with the military following the departure of former allies like the MDN and UNO and at the price of a split within its own ranks. A left-wing faction led by Rubén Zamora broke away to form the Popular Social Christian Movement (MPSC). Right-wing parties controlled the National Assembly following the 1982 elections but the PDC's 24 seats legitimized its participation in a Government of National Unity. Duarte's victory in the presidential elections of March 1984 was widely believed to have been reliant on US assistance.

The outcome, however, ensured that the existing "unity Cabinet" was replaced by a PDC one. The party consolidated its hold on power in the March 1985 elections in which it won 33 Assembly seats and gained control of the majority of local councils. PDC members were elected as president and vice-president of the Legislative Assembly.

The Duarte government was involved in intermittent efforts to negotiate a peace settlement with the Farabundo Martí National Liberation Front (FMLN) but was constrained by the aggressive hardliners in the military high command opposed to any major concessions. It retained the support of the US administration under President Reagan whose financial aid permitted the quadrupling of the army and the intensification of the civil war against the guerrillas. The PDC's political support also drained away, especially among the poor affected by 60 per cent unemployment, and among the rich after they were threatened with special taxes, which were subsequently ruled unconstitutional. A serious political split over the PDC presidential nomination for the 1989 elections also debilitated the party and led to the PDC's loss of control of the Legislative Assembly in 1988 when it won only 25 seats. Fidel Chávez Mena, known to be favoured by the private sector and the US administration, won the nomination forcing Julio Adolfo Rey Prendes, a proponent of Duarte's centre-right line, to break away to form, with the small right-wing Stable Centrist Republican Movement (MERECEN), the Authentic Christian Democratic Movement (MADC).

Chávez Mena shifted the party appreciably to the right and promoted liberal economic policies but was comfortably defeated in the first round of the 1989 presidential elections by Alfredo Cristiani Burkard of the Republican Nationalist Alliance (Arena).

In elections to an enlarged 84-seat Legislative Assembly in March 1991, the PDC won 26 seats, coming second to Arena which failed to win an overall majority. In the ensuing battle for power in the legislature, the PDC refused to take up three seats reserved for it on a congressional executive board until all the internal procedures governing the legislature were changed. Chávez Mena accused the Democratic Convergence (CD), who had taken up its allocation of seats on the board, of betraying the interests of the people. However, other Assembly delegates accused Chávez Mena of political brokering to further his own political ambitions. In an attempt to broaden its electoral base, the PDC made an alliance with two labour organizations, the National Union of Peasant Workers (UNOC) and the Center of Salvadorean Workers (CST).

International Affiliations. Member party of the Christian Democrat Organization of America, which forms part of the Christian Democrat International.

Democratic Convergence

Convergencia Democrática (CD)
Leadership. Jorge Villacorta (dir.); Ruben Zamora (l.).
Orientation. Social democratic.
Founded. November 1987.
History The CD emerged from the experience of the Democratic Revolutionary Front (*Frente Democratico Revolucionario*—FDR), itself an umbrella organization representing upwards of 30 professional and labour organizations and formally structured around an alliance of five Marxist parties and the National Revolutionary Movement (MNR) and Popular Social Christian Movement (MPSC), the latter two providing the focus and direction. The FDR, formed in April 1980, became the spearhead of civilian opposition to the military-backed regimes and allied itself to the recently formed Farabundo Martí National Liberation Front (FMLN). In January 1981, the FDR established a diplomatic political commission, in exile, in Mexico City which was recognized by the Mexican, French and Dutch governments as a representative political force.

Negotiations between President José Napoleon Duarte (see Christian Democratic Party) and the FDR leaders took place in 1984 and 1986, without success.

In the mid-1980s the FDR's future was placed in doubt by FMLN plans to create a single vanguard party and by moves by the MNR and the MPSC to re-enter the political arena.

The subsequent alliance of the MNR and MPSC with the Social Democrat Party (*Partido Social Demócrata*—PSD), founded 1987, gave birth to the CD, which campaigned for an end to US military intervention, a ceasefire in the civil war and free elections.

In addition, it called for social and economic reforms, respect for human rights and political non-alignment internationally to free the country from the grip of cold war ideology. The then MNR leader Guillermo Ungo and the PSD's Mario Reni Roldán were the CD's candidates for the presidency and vice-presidency in the presidential elections held on March 19, 1989. They received only 3.9 per cent of the vote, a cause of much resentment in the alliance and directly attributed to the FMLN's call for an election boycott.

Undaunted, the CD decided to participate for the first time in the legislative elections held in March 1991 because, in the words of Ungo, the social situation was desperate due to the civil war, extreme poverty was apparent everywhere and the majority realized that the present democracy structures had failed. Rúbem Zamora, leader of the MPSC, stated that it was the duty of the CD to win a majority in the enlarged Legislative Assembly in order to "propel the peace process". This time, the FMLN did not disrupt the elections and the CD took 12.2 per cent of the vote and won eight Assembly seats.

The CD's subsequent promotion of the UN-sponsored peace process meant that with the formal signing of a peace treaty in January 1992, it was well placed to play a leading role in a re-alignment of the opposition in preparation for the 1994 general election.

National Revolutionary Movement

Movimiento Nacional Revolucionario (MNR)
Orientation. Social democratic, advocating radical social reforms and a modernized mixed economy.
Founded. 1968.
History The MNR emerged from the fusion of the Radical Democratic Party and other groups. It was led initially from exile in the early 1970s by the writer Italo López Vallecillos whose successor Guillermo Ungo saw fit to join the civilian-military junta set up after the overthrow of the Romero regime in 1979 (see Christian Democrat Party). Ungo resigned in 1980, however, in protest at the government's "swing to the right", one consequence of which was the escalation in the activities of right-wing death squads who killed many MNR activists. The entire party leadership was forced into exile, where it remained until the end of 1987.

In April 1980, the MNR had joined with the MPSC to form the Salvadorean Democratic Front (FDS) which later in 1980 allied itself with five Marxist parties to form the Democratic Revolutionary Front (FD—see Democratic Convergence), the effective political wing of the FMLN guerrillas. Ungo was elected FDR president in January 1981 and from exile in Panama achieved international status as the main spokesman and negotiator for the extraparliamentary opposition and the various rebel groups. He returned to the country in 1984 and in late 1987 to test the political climate and concluded that the MNR could not operate in safety. This was enough to convince the MNR leadership to join with the Popular Social Christian Movement (MPSC) and the Social Democrat Party (PSD, see CD) in the formation of the Democratic Convergence (CD) in a bid to create a new national initiative for peace and free elections. Ungo died in Mexico city in February 1991.

National Conciliation Party

Partido de Conciliación Nacional (PCN)
Address. Calle Arce No. 1128, San Salvador, El Salvador.
Leadership. Hugo Carillo (l.); Raúl Molina Martínez (s.-g.).
Orientation. Right-wing.
Founded. September 1961.
History. The PCN, the direct successor of the now defunct Revolutionary Party of Democratic Unification, was the ruling party from 1961 to 1979 until a coup overthrew President Carlos Humberto Romero in October 1979. The party was a vehicle for a succession of fraudulently elected military presidents, supported by the elite families, and which also used patronage to maintain the loyalty of civilian officials.

In the 1982 elections the PCN obtained 14 seats in the 60-seat Constituent Assembly and received four Cabinet posts in a Government of National Unity, despite the party's strong anti-reformist bias and remaining close ties with the military. The party, however, split in the same year, with the right-wing, including nine Assembly delegates, forming the Authentic Institutional Party (PAISA). In 1985, the PCN, as a junior partner in a alliance with the Republican Nationalist Alliance (Arena) party, won 12 seats in the 1985 elections, a short-lived partnership ending when the party expelled three leaders who had colluded with the Arena to get the elections declared void. In 1987, in an attempt at political rehabilitation, the party claimed to have rediscovered its "social democratic" roots and opposed the Christian Democrat Party (PDC) government's austerity package, including a war tax. The manoeuvre produced scant reward, the party winning only seven seats in the March 1988 legislative elections and its candidate in the 1989 presidential election received a modest 4.9 per cent of the vote. In July 1989 the party temporarily joined an alliance with the PDC and the Democratic Convergence (DC), claiming to be interested in promoting dialogues with the Farabundo Martí National Liberation Front (FMLN). In the lead up to the March 1991 legislative elections, the party had clear problems deciding where to locate itself on the political spectrum, one leader claiming that the party was "to the left of Arena and to the right of the PDC". It chose not to ally itself with Arena and came third after the PDC, winning nine per cent of the vote and nine seats.

Popular Social Christian Movement

Movimiento Popular Social Cristiano (MPSC)
Leadership. Rubén Zamora, Roberto Lara Velado, Jorge Villacorta (ls.) .
Orientation. The party believes in respect for human rights, social justice and a more equitable distribution of wealth within the context of a mixed economy and its christian democratic background leads it to seek political consensus to achieve these aims.
Founded. 1980.
History. The MPSC was formed by members of the Christian Democrat Party (PDC) who opposed the participation of the PDC leader, José Napoleón Duarte, in the junta which took power in 1979 (see PDC). Hounded by the army and death squads, the party sought to merge itself in broad opposition alliances while retaining its identity. It first allied itself with the National Revolutionary Movement (MNR) to establish the Salvadorean Democratic Front (FDS) in April 1980 and then, with five Marxist parties, the Democratic Revolutionary Front (FDR, see CD) in the same year. Operating in exile, Zamora became a leading international figure arguing for a peaceful solution to the civil war. Along with MNR leader Guillermo Ungo, he returned to the country at the end of 1987 to examine the possibilities of working politically inside the country and helped set up the Democratic Convergence (CD) along with the Social Democratic Party (PSD).

Republican Nationalist Alliance

Alianza Republicana Nacionalista (Arena)
Address. Calle el Progreso 3210, San Salvador, El Salvador.
Leadership. Armando Calderon Sol (pres.); Roberto Angula (l.).
Orientation. Ultra-right. The party is split between hard-liners standing for nationalism, law and order and against any accommodation with left-wing guerrillas

and modernizers who, however reluctantly, supported the peace process ending the 11-year civil war in return for political and economic stability.

Founded. 1981.

History. Arena was founded by Roberto D'Aubuisson Arrieta, a former major and once head of the intelligence section of the notoriously brutal National Guard. This complemented his involvement during the 1970s in the National Democratic Organization (ORDEN), a mass-based paramilitary organization linked to the security forces and the White Warriors Union, one of several right-wing death squads. Trained in the art of political warfare in police academies in Washington and Taiwan, D'Aubuisson modelled Arena on the Chinese nationalist Kuomintang which had its own military wing. Arena quickly became a leading political force, winning 19 seats in the 1982 elections to the National Assembly, of which D'Aubuisson was elected president, while retaining its close associations with the death squads. D'Aubuisson was accused of personally organizing political killings from an office in the Assembly, the most notorious of which was the assassination in March 1980 of Monsignor Oscar Arnulfo Romero, Archbishop of San Salvador and a fierce critic of state violence.

Long associated with right-wing Republican politicians in the USA, D'Aubuisson had been shunned by the Carter administration but was rehabilitated by President Ronald Reagan as part of his administration's anti-communist cold war stance towards Central America. However, D'Aubuisson's continued association with the death squads meant that the USA did not endorse his candidacy for President in 1984 but instead supported, and some said "engineered", the victory of José Napoleon Duarte of the Christian Democrats. The defeat provoked the first split in Arena, D'Aubuisson's vice-presidential running mate Hugo Barrera breaking away in May 1985 to form the Liberation Party (PL).

Eager for increased influence and respectability, Arena's September 1985 national general assembly accepted D'Aubuisson's resignation as secretary-general and elected him as honorary life president. Under Alfredo Cristiani Burkard, Arena presented a more moderate image, especially to the USA, and won the 1988 presidential elections on a programme that offered the prospect of national reconciliation. To retain the support of the landed ruling class and to increase Arena's middle class support, Cristiani promised to reverse the Christian Democrat's land reforms and to liberalize the economy by removing state control over trade and banking. In an effort to placate the opposition he promised to increase state welfare provision, reform the administration of justice and open a dialogue with the guerrillas to end the 11-year civil war.

In the March 1991 legislative elections, the party lost its overall majority in the Legislative Assembly, and although it remained the country's largest party, the result encouraged moderate elements to pursue a course of political consensus.

Tentative peace negotiations with the Farabundo Martí National Liberaton Front (FMLN), which hardline elements in both the army and Arena tried to sabotage, began in April 1990 under UN auspices; a peace treaty was formally signed in January 1992 and a ceasefire established in February 1992. D'Aubuisson, who died of throat cancer in February 1992, adopted an increasingly "pragmatic" approach to the peace process and was judged to have played a crucial role behind the scenes in keeping Arena's most fundamentalist anti-communist factions behind Cristiani.

Structure. Arena's supreme body is the national general assembly, which elects the party officers and an executive council.

Minor parties

Authentic Democratic Christian Movement (*Movimiento Auténtico Democrático Cristiano*—MADC); founded by Julio Adolfo Rey Prendes, a centre-right party which in the March 1991 Legislative Assembly elections won one seat.

Authentic Institutional Party (*Partido Auténtico Institucional*—PAISA); Roberto Escobar García (s.-g.); founded October 1982, a right-wing split-off from the National Conciliation Party (PCN).

Democratic Action (*Acción Democrática*); founded 1981, Ricardo González Camacho (l.); liberal and in favour of a mixed economy, the party achieved modest representation in the National Assembly in 1982 and 1985, a faction led by González supporting the Christian Democrat Party (PDC) government until December 1987. Since then its fortunes have declined markedly and in the March 1991 legislative elections it failed to win a single seat, and its future legal status as a party was in doubt.

Democratic Unionist Party (Partido Unionista Democrático—PUD); centre-right.
Liberation Party (Partido Liberación—PL, also known as the Free Homeland *(Patria Libre)*; founded 1985, Hugo Barrera (s.-g.); a party without representation in the Assembly which had former associations with the Arena party.
Nationalist Democrat Union (Unión Democrata Nacional—UDN); a left-wing party, once allied with the clandestine Communist Party of El Salvador (PSCE—see Farabundo Martí National Liberation Front) leadership, in exile from 1980-1989. The party had not participated in an election for 14 years until the March 1991 Legislative Assembly elections when it won one seat.

Major guerrilla groups

Farabundo Martí National Liberation Front (Frente Farabundo Martí para la Liberación Nacional—FMLN).
Orientation. Left-wing, but the leadership, especially during the peace process, has increasingly distanced itself from a Marxist-Leninist perspective, seeing the FMLN, on a return to the political mainstream, to be a party attractive not only to the bulk of the "dispossessed" in town and country (since they believe the working class to be in a minority) but also to liberal elements in the middle class and the Catholic church.
Founded. October 1980.
History. Four guerrilla organizations (the FPL, ERP, FARN and the PCS—see below), formed the Unified Revolutionary Directorate (Directorio Revolucionario Unificado—DRU) in June 1980. It was replaced in October by the FMLN, which took its name from a Communist Party leader of the 1932 peasant revolt. The FARN, which had temporarily broken away, rejoined along with the PRTC (see below).

Under the FMLN, the 15-strong DRU co-ordinated the work of the five component groups whose individual leaders formed an executive commission charged with overall command. The FMLN maintained direct links with its political arm, the Democratic Revolutionary Front (FDR, see Democratic Convergence) via a political and diplomatic commission on which both were represented.

The FMLN launched a general offensive in January 1981, during which it secured strongholds in most of the northern departments of Morazán and Chalatenango, as well as launching penetrating attacks elsewhere.

By February 1982, it was estimated to control one-quarter of the country and by the end of 1983 large stretches of the Pacific coast. Then, in 1984, the army, the recipient of large supplies of US military aid, secured the military initiative, forcing the guerrillas to reduce their activities in rural areas and to disperse into smaller units. The bulk of the membership were transferred to the towns to build up civilian support.

From the mid-1980s onwards, the FMLN was almost as active on the diplomatic front as it was militarily, proposing various power sharing solutions to end the civil war and it appeared ready to accept an electoral solution. Sustained violence from the right, however, blocked this path but the guerrillas claimed that the 53 per cent abstention rate in the 1989 general election justified its struggle for radical political reforms.

Subsequently, the FMLN saw its task as making the country ungovernable so long as the ruling Arena party resisted a negotiated settlement. It launched large scale military offensives in May and November 1990, both of which penetrated into the capital, San Salvador, to strengthen its position in UN-sponsored peace talks with the government. Key short-term FMLN demands were a purge of human rights violators from the army, the reduction of the armed forces and a new public security force "to guarantee public order and avoid anarchy and crime".

A breakthrough occurred in September 1991 but the resultant peace agreement, formally signed in January 1992, was already under strain by March 1992. The FMLN, itself required under the peace agreement to retire to designated areas prior to eventual demobilization, accused the government of compromising the effectiveness of a future National Civilian Police Force (PNC) by not dismantling the National Guard and Treasury Police, the repressive security apparatus, which was to be relocated into the army.

In May 1992, without prior discussion with the Cristiani government who did not welcome the decision, the FMLN announced that it intended to form itself into a political party.
Structure. The FMLN is an umbrella grouping of the People's Revolutionary Army (*Ejército Revolucionario del Pueblo*—ERP), Joaquín

Villalobos (l.); the Popular Liberation Forces (*Fuerzas Populares de Liberación*—FPL) Leonel González (l.); the National Resistance Armed Forces (*Fuerzas Armadas de Resistencia Nacional*—FARN—Fermán Cienfuegos l.); the Armed Forces of Liberation (*Fuerzas Armadas de Liberacion—FAL*—the military wing of the Communist Party of El Salvador—*Partido Comunista Salvadoreño*) Jorge Schafik Handal (l.); and the Central America Workers' RevolutionaryParty (*Partido Revolucionariode de Trabajadores Centroamericanos*—PRTC) Roberto Roca (l.).

Falkland Islands

Capital: Stanley **Population: 1,915**

Constitutional structure

Under the 1985 Constitution the Falkland Islands (*Islas Malvinas*) and their former dependencies, South Georgia and the South Sandwich Islands, are administered by a Governor representing the British monarch. The Governor presides over an Executive Council with two other (non-voting) ex officio members and three elected by and from the Legislative Council. The latter body has two non-voting ex officio members and eight elected by universal adult suffrage. Decisions of the Executive Council are subject to veto by the Governor and the British Foreign Secretary.

Electoral system

In the elections of Oct. 11, 1989, all eight seats on the Legislative Council went to independent candidates standing on a predominantly "no links with Argentina" platform and supportive of continued British jurisdiction. All the candidates of the **Desire for the Right**, formed in the latter part of 1988 and the island's only political party, failed to be elected.

French Guiana

Capital: Cayenne **Population: 114,678**

French Guiana became a French overseas department in 1946 and was granted regional status in 1974, which increased its economic autonomy.

Constitutional structure

French Guiana has a 19-member General Council and a 31-member Regional Council, both serving a six-year term subject to dissolution. It has two directly-elected members in the French National Assembly and one in the French Senate. The French government is represented locally by a Government Commissioner. French Guiana is also represented at the European Parliament in Strasbourg.

Electoral system

Members of the General Council and Regional Council are elected by universal adult suffrage for a six-year term, the General Council by majority voting in two rounds and the Regional Assembly by proportional representation of party lists.

ST. LUCIA
BARBADOS
ST. VINCENT
GRENADA
Cumaná
TRINIDAD
& TOBAGO
Atlantic
Ocean
Area of
insert
SOUTH
AMERICA
VENEZUELA
GEORGETOWN
GUYANA
PARAMARIBO
CAYENNE
SURINAM
FRENCH
GUIANA
Macapá
BRAZIL
Belém
0
500 km

Sequence of elections since 1983

Date	*Winning party*
Feb. 1983 (Reg. Council.)	Workers' List of Guiana (indep. list)
March 16, 1986 (Reg. Council.)	Guianese Democratic Action (ADG)

Regional Council election, March 16, 1986

Party	*% of votes*	*seats*
Guianese Socialist Party (PSG)	43.00	15
Rally for the Republic (RPR)	27.68	9
Guianese Democratic Action (ADG)	12.22	4
Union for French Democracy (UDF)	8.91	3
National Front (FN)	3.65	-
Guianese Popular National Party (PNPG)	1.41	-
Others	3.13	-
Total	**100.00**	**31**

Regional Council election, March 22, 1992

Guyanese Socialist Party (PSG)	16
Guianese Démocratique Front (FDG)	10
Other	5
Total	31

PARTY BY PARTY DATA

Guianese Democratic Action

Action Démocratique Guyanaise (ADG)
Address. Ave. d'Estrées, Cayenne.
Leadership. André Lecante (l.).
Orientation. Left-wing; pro independence and has been opposed to metropolitan governments, either conservative or socialist.
Founded. Early 1980s.
History. Formed as the Pro-Independence Party of Guianese Unity (*Parti Indépendaniste de l'Unité Guyanaise*—PIUG). In January 1983, the PIUG had supported public sector strikes and called on the French government to recognize "the right of the Guianese people to self-determination". As the ADG, it contested the March 1986 Regional Council elections winning 12.2 per cent of the vote and four seats.

Guianese Democratic Front

Front Démocratique Guyanais (FDG)
Leadership. Georges Othily (l.).
History. The party was founded by Othily, President of the Regional Council and a veteran politician expelled by the Guianese Socialist Party (PSG) in 1989 (see PSG). In the March 1992 Regional Council elections, the party won 10 seats, to make it a potent political force. Othily however was defeated in the election to the presidency of the Council by the PSG's Antoine Karam.

Guianese Popular National Party

Parti National Populaire Guyanaise (PNPG)
Address. Ave. d'Estrées, BP, 265, Cayenne.
Leadership. Alain Michel (l.).
Orientation. A separatist left-wing party seeking greater autonomy for France as a prelude to full independence.
Founded. 1985.
History. Originally formed as the Union of Guianese Workers (UGT), it supported an independent list *(Liste des Travailleurs de Guyane)* which in the 1983 Regional Council elections secured 1,141 votes (8.9 per cent) and three seats, which subsequently gave it the balance of power. Its successful candidates, then led by Guy Lamaze, afterwards joined the socialist-led coalition administration. The party adopted its current name in November 1985 and in the March 1986 Regional Council elections took 1.4 per cent of the vote but won no seats.

Guianese Socialist Party

Parti Socialiste Guyanais (PSG)
Address. Cité Césaire, B. P. 46, Cayenne.
Leadership. Elie Castor (l.); Antoine Karam (s.-g.).
Orientation. Centrist, in line with those of the French Socialist Party of which it is the local branch.
Founded. 1956.
History. The strongest party, the PSG has continually held the presidency of the General Council. In 1981, Castor was elected as the country's sole deputy to the French National Assembly, to which he was re-elected, with 48.1 per cent of the vote, in March 1986 along with another deputy from the Rally for the Republic (RPR).

The PSG-backed *Liste pour une Décentralisation Vrai et Démocratique en Guyane* won 14 of the 31 seats in the Regional Council in February 1983, whereupon it joined with other left-wing forces to form an administration. It won an additional seat in 1986 when it had 42.1 per cent of the total vote and the PSG's Georges Othily was elected the Council's president. In September and October 1988, the left, led by the PSG, strengthened their control of the General Council by winning 14 of the 19 seats, thus increasing their majority over the right-wing and centre parties. Castor was re-elected as president of the General Council. In the municipal elections held in March 1989 this trend was maintained with 13 left-wing mayors being elected compared with six for right-wing parties.

Othily, who had been expelled from the PSG in June 1989 for allegedly collaborating with the opposition, successfully contested the September election for the country's sole seat in the French Senate. He defeated the PSG incumbent Raymond Tarcy by attracting the support of those opposed to the PSG's domination of national politics.

In March 1992, the party won 16 seats in the Regional Council election and its secretary-general Antoine Kram defeated Othily by 19 votes to 10 to be elected as the Council's president. In cantonal elections in March 1992, Castor was returned as president of the General Council.
Structure. The biennial congress, always held in November, elects a secretary-general, a general

treasurer and a 23 other members of the central committee which, in turn elects nine members who, with the secretary-general and treasurer, form an executive committee. The membership is organized in sections by *commune* with larger sections being divided into *toulouris* (branches).
International affiliations. As part of the French Socialist Party, the PSG has relations with parties in the Socialist International.

National Front

Front National (FN)
Address. B.P.478, 97384, Kourou.
Leadership. Guy Malon.
Orientation. Extreme right wing and promotes authoritarian and white supremacist ideas.
Founded. 1985.
History. The FN is an affiliate of the metropolitan National Front led by Jean Marie Le Pen. In the March 1986 Regional Council elections it won 571 votes and no seats.

Rally for the Republic

Rassemblement pour la République (RPR)
Address. 84 ave. Léopold Héder, Cayenne.
Leadership. Paulin Bruné (pres.); Paul Rullier (s.-g.).
Orientation. Right-wing, the party is the local branch of the metropolitan Gaullist party of the same name. It supports the retention of the country's departmental status.
History. The party, which has been consistently well represented in the General Council, provided the country's sole deputy in the French National Assembly until 1981 (see Guianese Socialist Party) and Bruné won one of two seats in 1986.

It contested the February 1983 Regional Council elections as party of the *Guyane d'Abord, Union d'Accord* (Guiana First, Yes to Unity) alliance with the Union for French Democracy (UDF) and other centre right groups, jointly winning 40.1 per cent of the vote and 13 of the 31 seats. Standing alone in 1986, the RPR won nine seats in the Regional Council with 27.7 per cent of the vote.

In 1988 it retained its seat in the French National Assembly.

In the September and October 1988 General Council elections, the RPR-UDF-led right wing alliance performed poorly, taking only five of the 19 seats being contested. Equally, in the March 1989 municipal elections, the right wing won control of only seven out of the 20 municipalities.
Publications. Objectifs.

Union for French Democracy

Union pour la Démocratie Francaise (UDF)
Address. 11 bis rue Christophe Colomb, B. P. 472, 97331 Cayenne.
Leadership. Claude Ho A Chuck (l.).
Orientation. Centre-right; the party supports the country's current status but seeks greater decentralization of control from France.
Founded. 1979.
History. Established as the local branch of the metropolitan party of the same name, the UDF absorbed two earlier groups, the *Rassemblement pour la Défense de Guyane* and the *Mouvement pour le Progrés Guyanais* (MPG).

Then led by Serge Patient, the party contested the 1983 Regional Council elections in an opposition alliance (see RPR) which won 13 seats.

On its own, it won 1,390 votes and three seats in the 1986 Regional Council elections. Since then, in alliance with the Rally for the Republic (RPR), it fared badly in the 1988 General Council elections and the 1989 municipal elections.

Minor Parties

Front of the Ant-Colonialist Struggle (*Front de la Lutte Anti-Colonialiste*—FULAC); Michel Kapel (l.).

Grenada

Capital: St George's **Population: 96,000**

Grenada became an independent state within the British Commonwealth in 1974, with the British monarch, represented by a Governor-General, as head of state. The Grenada United Labour Party (GULP) government, headed by Sir Eric Gairy, was overthrown by a coup in 1979, when a People's Revolutionary Government headed by Maurice Bishop took power. Bishop was overthrown and murdered in 1983, whereupon US forces occupied the island. Elections held in 1984 resulted in a victory for a conservative New National Party coalition, which formed a government headed by Herbert Blaize, who led the country until his death in December 1989. An inconclusive general election in March 1990 was followed by the appointment of Nicholas Brathwaite as Prime Minister by the Governor-General. Braithwaite's centrist National Democratic Congress, one of the parties to develop from within the 1984 NNP coalition, had won seven of the 15 seats in the House of Representatives.

Constitutional structure

Under the terms of the 1974 independence Constitution, legislative power is vested in a bicameral Parliament, composed of a 13-member Senate and a 15-member House of Representatives. Executive power is exercised by the Prime Minister who appoints the Cabinet. The Prime Minister and the Cabinet are both answerable to Parliament.

Electoral system

Members of the House of Representatives are elected for a five-year term (subject to dissolution) by simple majority in single-member constituencies, by universal adult suffrage. The Prime Minister, who is the majority leader in the House of Representatives, directly appoints seven members of the Senate; three others are chosen on the advice of the Leader of the Opposition and the remaining three by the Prime Minister, but this time after consulting various interests.

Evolution of the suffrage

Universal adult suffrage was first introduced by the British colonial administration in 1951. The age of voting was reduced from 21 to 18 years of age in 1974.

Sequence of elections since 1984

Date	*Winning party*
December 1984 (legislative)	New National Party (NNP)

Legislative elections Dec. 3, 1984

	Distribution of seats	*% of vote*
New National Party (NNP)	14	58.6
Grenada United Labour Party (GULP)	1 (see GDLP)	35.9
New Jewel Movement (NJM)	-	-
Maurice Bishop Patriotic Movement (MBPM)	-	4.9
Grenada National Party (GNP)	-	-

Legislative elections March 13, 1990

Winning party	*seats*
National Democratic Congress (NDC)	7
Grenada United Labour Party (GULP)	4
The National Party (TNP)	2
New National Party (NNP)	2
Total	**15**

PARTY BY PARTY DATA

Grenada United Labour Party (GULP)

Leadership. Sir Eric Gairy (l.).
Orientation. Right-wing.
Founded. 1950.
History. The GULP, formerly the Grenada People's Party (GPP), was formed with trade union support and held a majority of the elected seats in the then colony's Legislative Council from 1951-57. In 1961, it won eight of the 10 seats, and its leader, George Clyne, became Chief Minister, but was soon afterwards succeeded in both posts by Gairy. After corruption allegations, the GULP was reduced to four seats in fresh elections in 1962, but it regained power in 1967, when Gairy became Chief Minister. The party was returned to office in 1972 and 1976, with Grenada becoming independent, and Gairy Prime Minister, in 1974. Knighted in 1977, Gairy was regarded by the opposition as corrupt, eccentric and authoritarian, and he was overthrown by the New Jewel Movement (NJM) (see Maurice Bishop Patriotic Movement—MBPM) in a bloodless coup in March 1979. At the time, Gairy was in New York advising the UN on unidentified flying objects.

Gairy went into exile, but returned in January 1984 in the aftermath of the US invasion (see MBPM). Efforts to re-establish the GULP as the major party proved fruitless, however, and in the December 1984 general election (in which Gairy was not a candidate) it won 35.9 per cent of the vote but under the election system was accorded only one seat in the House. Gairy decided to boycott Parliament claiming electoral fraud and expelled from the party the GULP's lone MP Marcel Peters who decided to take up the seat. Peters, along with others, subsequently formed a new party. In the 1990 general election, the GULP was awarded four seats having won 28 per cent of the vote but Gairy failed to be elected and one party member crossed the floor to give the National Democratic Congress (NDC) government an absolute majority. The GULP still remained the largest opposition party, led in the parliament by Winifred Strachan. The defection of one more MP to the government in 1990, and the resignation from the party of another in May 1991 to sit as an independent, was severely damaging to the party's credibility. In June, political observers said the party was "crumbling".
Publications. The *Grenada Guardian*, weekly.

Maurice Bishop Patriotic Movement (MBPM)

Leadership. Terrence Marryshow (l.).
Orientation. Nominally s2rocialist.
Founded. March 1984 (as the Maurice Bishop foundation).
History. The MBPM was the successor to the Movement for the Assemblies of the People, founded by Maurice Bishop and Kendrick Radix in 1972, and the Jewel (Joint Endeavour for Welfare, Education and Liberation) movement, founded in the same year by Unison Whiteman and Selwyn Strachan, which merged in 1973 to form the New Jewel Movement (NJM). The NJM contested the 1976 elections in alliance with two other parties, winning three of the 15 seats in the House of Representatives. In 1979, it overthrew the repressive GULP government of Eric Gairy in an almost bloodless coup, and established a People's Revolutionary Government with Bishop as Prime Minister.

The new government pursued socialist and non-aligned policies, carrying out a number of useful reforms in the fields of health, education, housing and employment. Its close ties with Cuba, however, alienated it from the USA and the more conservative Caribbean states, while inside the NJM Bishop's moderate policies aroused strong opposition from a pro-Soviet faction led by Bernard Coard, the deputy premier.

On Oct. 13, 1983, Bishop was overthrown by this faction and placed under arrest, and six days later he was shot, together with Whiteman and two other members of the government.

The US administration (under President Reagan), supported by military contingents from six Caribbean states, seized the opportunity and on Oct. 25 ordered marines into Grenada who, despite strong resistance, quickly established control and overthrew the Revolutionary Military Council (RMC) headed by Coard and Gen. Hudson Austin. Coard, Strachan and a number of their supporters were subsequently arrested and charged with Bishop's murder. Thirteen of them received death sentence in 1986 (subsequently appealed and commuted to life imprisonment in 1991).

Only one member of the Coard faction, Ian St Bernard, remained at liberty in Grenada, occasionally issuing declarations in the name of the NJM. However, the latter was effectively defunct and public opinion and the MBPM openly supported the death sentences.

The MBPM was founded in May 1984 and was led initially by the former Ministers Kendrick Radix and George Louison. Largely due to the violent way the NJM regime ended, the new movement attracted very little electoral support, winning 5 per cent of the vote and no seats in the 1984 elections. Its development was occasionally hampered by official acts, such as the arrest of various leaders early in 1986 for questioning about alleged armed subversive activities. However, after four unspectacular years, the MBPM improved its public image in 1988 when its convention adopted a much more charismatic young leader Terrence Marryshow. The grandson of a national hero, Marryshow was described by some observers as a "new Maurice Bishop". Marryshow's charismatic qualities did not impress the electorate, however, and the party in the March 1990 general election failed to win any seats and attracted less than two per cent of the popular vote.

Publications. The *Indies Times*, weekly; the *Democrat*, biweekly.

International affiliations. The MBPM has the support of groups in Britain, the United States, Canada and Sweden, and maintains close relations with Cuba.

National Democratic Congress (NDC)

Address. c/o Houses of Parliament, Church St, St George's.

Leadership. Nicholas Brathwaite (l.).

Orientation. Centrist.

Founded. June 1987.

History. The NDC was formed by a dissident breakaway group from the ruling New National Party (NNP) led by George Brizan, who in April 1987 had resigned from the government over its economic and labour policies after accusing Prime Minister Herbert Blaize of being autocratic. The new party, a minor partner of which was the Democratic Labour Congress (DLC) formed in August 1986 by former NNP junior minister Kenny Lalsingh, immediately attracted the support of five other opposition members to command six of the 15 seats in the House. It was to some extent a reconstruction of Brizan's (now defunct) National Democratic Party (NDP), which he had merged into the NNP in August 1984. The NDP itself had previously absorbed the Grenada Democratic Movement led by Francis Alexis. Brizan, who in late 1987 was recognized as the Leader of the Opposition, gave way as party leader in 1989 to Nicholas Brathwaite, a former head of the post 1984 invasion Advisory Council interim government. In the March 1990 general election, the NDC won seven seats, and Brathwaite was appointed Prime Minister by the Governor-General, Sir Paul Scoon, and formed a government with the support of two MPs of the right-wing minority group, The National Party (TNP). A GULP MP defected to the party later and, even with the subsequent withdrawal of the resignation of Jones, the party by mid-1991 counted on the support of 10 out 15 members of the House (see GULP).

New National Party (NNP)

Address. Lucas St, St Geogre's.

Leadership. Keith Mitchell (l.).

Orientation. Conservative.

Founded. August 1984.

History. The party was the product of the merger of two conservative parties, the Grenada National Party (GNP), led by Herbert Blaize and the Grenada Democratic Movement (GDM) of Francis Alexis who joined up with the centrist National Democratic Party (NDP) formed in 1984 by George Brizan and Robert Grant.

The GNP, founded in 1956, had held a majority of the elective seats on the colonial Legislative Council from 1957-61, and six of the 10 seats from 1962-67, when Blaize was Chief Minister, before being in opposition from 1969-79. The GNP, like the GDM and NDP, was largely inactive during the New Jewel (NJM) regime which came to power in 1979 (see Maurice Bishop Patriotic Movement—MBPM). All three resumed activity in the aftermath of the October 1983 US military invasion which overthrew the NJM government. In April 1984, they formed a "Team for National Togetherness" coalition (TNT). The TNT broke up in May but under pressure from the USA and the governments of Barbados, St Vincent, and St Lucia the three merged in August to form the NNP in order to prevent the electoral victory of Sir Eric Gairy of the Grenada United Labour Party (GULP). In the December general election, the NNP achieved an emphatic victory, winning 14 of the 15 seats in the house and Blaize became Prime Minister.

The NNP government quickly succumbed to serious internal strains, largely caused by Blaize's autocratic hold on power. The election in 1986 of his close ally,

Ben Jones, as deputy leader, triggered the April 1987 resignation of Brizen who led an anti-Blaize breakaway with two other cabinet members to form the National Democratic Congress (NDC). Increasingly isolated by the departure of more party officials, Blaize was eventually voted down as party leader and replaced by Keith Mitchell, the NNP secretary-general, in 1989. In retaliation, Blaize dismissed Mitchell and Larry Joseph, the party's chairman from the government, provoking the resignations of two more ministers which, in turn, led to the loss of Blaize's parliamentary majority. In a vain effort to rejuvenate his political fortunes, Blaize formed The National Party (TNP), which on his death in December 1989 was led by Jones and gained two seats in the March 1990 general election. The NNP, now led by Mitchell, also won two seats.

International Affiliation. International Democrat Union (full member).

Minor parties

Christian Democratic Labour Party (CDLP); a centrist party formed in April 1984 by Winston Whyte, whose United People's Party (UPP) had been an electoral ally of the New Jewel Movement (NJM) in 1976 (see Maurice Bishop Patriotic Movement). Whyte was subsequently arrested in 1979 (when leader of the People's Action Group) for conspiring against the NJM government. The CDLP, after a brief alliance with the National Democratic Party (NDP—see National Democratic Congress) continued its journey along the political spectrum, joining the right-wing New National Party (NNP) on its formation in August 1984. It left in September and failed to win a single seat in the December general election.

The National Party (TNP); Ben Jones (l.); formed in 1989 by the beleaguered government of Prime Minister Herbert Blaize (see NNP), won two seats in the March 1990 general election. Jones then offered his support to Nicolas Brathwaite of the National Democratic Congress (NDC) enabling a "national unity government" to be formed, with Jones as Agriculture, Forestry, Lands and Fisheries Minister.

The party withdrew its support during the January 1991 budget debate and Jones resigned from the government. However, TNP Parliamentary Secretary for Health and Community Development Alleyne Walker did not follow him to the opposition benches.

Guadeloupe

Capital: Basse-Terre **Population: 340,000**

Guadeloupe is an overseas department of France which obtained its status of a region in 1974.

Constitutional structure

France is represented by a Government Commissioner, who exercises the powers not devolved to the 43-member General Council or the 41-member Regional Council. The island group also elects four deputies to the French National Assembly in Paris and has two indirectly-elected senators. Guadeloupe is also represented at the European Parliament in Strasbourg.

Electoral system

Members of the General Council and Regional Council are elected by universal adult suffrage for a maximum term of six years. General Council members are elected by majority voting in two rounds and the Regional Assembly members by proportional representation.

Sequence of elections since 1983

Date	*Winning party*
February 1983	Rally for the Republic-Union for French Democracy (RPR-UDF)
March 16, 1986	Rally for the Republic (RPR)

Regional Council Elections, March 16, 1986

Party	*% of votes*	*seats*
Rally for the Republic (RPR)	33.09	15
Socialist Party (PS)	28.65	12
Guadeloupe Communist Party (PCG)	23.77	10
Union for French Democracy (UDF)	10.71	4
Others	3.78	-
Total	**100.00**	**41**

Regional Council Elections, March 22, 1992

Party	*seats*
Martinique Objective (see RPR)	15
Socialist Party (PS)	9
Socialist Party (Larifla faction)	7
Guadeloupean Progressive Democratic Party (PPDG)	5
Guadeloupe Communist Party (PCG)	3

PARTY BY PARTY DATA

Guadeloupe Communist Party

Parti Communiste Guadeloupéen (PCG)
Address. 119 rue Vatable, B.P.329, 97169 Pointe-á-Pitre.
Leadership. Christian Céleste (s.-g.).
Orientation. Independent communist; supports the autonomy of the department but in 1981 condemned political violence and stated that it was opposed to "independence at any price". It was in favour of the Gorbachev reforms in the former Soviet Union. It plays a leading role in the General Confederation of Labour of Guadeloupe, the island's largest trade union federation.
Founded. 1944.
History. Founded in 1944 as a federation of the French Communist Party, the PCG became an independent party in 1958. It won a seat in the French National Assembly in 1981, and 11 seats in the Regional Council in 1983. The ninth congress of the party in March 1988 saw the resignation of Guy Daninthe, who had been secretary-general for 18 years. It was decided that in future the post of secretary-general would be chosen by secret ballot of the central committee, rather than by the congress. During the same year, the party was active in left-wing campaigns to protect the French overseas departments from the effects of European integration. It refused to support the French Communist Party's list of candidates in the 1979 and 1984 European elections and advocated abstention, on the grounds that EC policies operated against the island's interests.

In the French general election in 1988, the party's candidate won only 4,198 votes in Guadeloupe. In the French National Assembly elections of the same year, it contested all four of the island's seats, winning one for Ernest Moutoussamy, a deputy since 1981. In partial General Council elections in 1988, the party won four seats, giving it a total of 10 out of 43, although some of its councillors were allies rather than PCG members. A PCG member became second vice-president of the Council. Early in 1992, a dissident faction, led by Moutoussamy, broke away to form the Guadeloupean Progressive Democratic Party (PPDG).

In the Regional Council elections in March 1992, the party won three seats. Afterwards, it joined with the Popular Union for the Liberation of Guadeloupe (UPLG) in seeking an political alliance with the Jalton wing of the Socialist Party (PS) to counteract the intended alliance between the dissident Larifla PS faction and the Rally for the Republic (RPR) (see PS, RPR).
Membership. 1,500 (1988 claim, but reduced following the split by members leaving to join the PPDG).
Publications. *L'Etincelle* (The Spark), weekly. The PCG also has a radio station.
International affiliations. The party has close ties with the French Communist Party, but does not automatically follow its lead.

Guadeloupean Federation of the Rally for the Republic

Fédération Guadeloupéenne du Rassemblement pour la République (RPR)
Address. 1 rue Baudot, Basse-Terre.
Leadership. Daniel Beaubrun (pres.).
Orientation. The RPR is a conservative Gaullist party.
History. The party held all three seats representing Guadeloupe in the French National assembly until 1981, when it lost one each to the Socialist Party (PS), the Communist Party (PCG) and the Union for French Democracy (UDF). In the 1983 Regional Council elections, an alliance between the party and the UDF, known as the Union for Development and Progress and led by the then President of the General Council Lucette Michaux-Chevry, won 44.8 per cent of the vote and 21 of the 41 seats, and RPR leader José Moustache was elected as President of the Council. Michaux-Chevry founded in 1984 the conservative Guadeloupe Party (LPG) (now defunct) which forged strong links with the RPR. However in the March 1985 elections to the General Council, the RPR and UDF alliance was defeated by the combined force of the PS and PCG.

Moustache resigned from the RPR in February 1986 and joined the UDF. In March, the RPR and UDF presented separate lists for the general election to the French National Assembly, with the RPR winning two seats (Michaux-Chevry and Henri Beaujean) but the UDF failed to have its deputy re-elected. In the simultaneous elections to the Regional Council, the RPR-UDF alliance came second, losing control to the left. Post-election acrimony between the RPR and the

UDF led to the resignation of Moustache as President of the regional Council. The alliance's credibility was further damaged in September following the publication of details of RPR-UDF financial irregularities when it controlled the Regional Council. In June 1988, Beaujean lost his seat in the French National Assembly to PS's Dominique Larifla and the alliance was again defeated by the left in the General Council elections. In March 1989 the left also won a clear victory in municipal elections.

The RPR, running under the name Guadeloupe Objective (*Objectif Guadeloupe*), however staged a political comeback in the March 1992 Regional Council elections when it emerged as the largest party, with 15 seats, and was given the strong prospect of a working majority following serious divisions on the left (see PS). Michaux-Chevry was subsequently elected as President of the Regional Council.

Guadeloupean Federation of the Socialist Party

Fédération Guadeloupéenne du Parti Socialiste (PS)
Address. Ave. de Général de Gaulle, Cité Jardin du Raizet, 97110 Abymes.
Leadership. Dominique Larifla (1st sec.).
Orientation. Its policies are broadly in line with those of the French Socialist Party.
Founded. Became autonomous from the French Socialist Party in March 1987.
History. In 1981 the party won one of three Guadeloupean seats in the French National Assembly and in 1983 won 20.4 per cent of the vote and nine seats in the Regional Council. This made it, after the Communist Party (PCG), the island's second largest opposition party. In March 1985, the PS, together with the PCG won a majority on the General Council, of which PS member Dominique Larifla was elected President.

In March 1986, the party won 10 seats on the Regional Council and the PS's Felix Proto was elected its President (see Guadeloupean Federation of the Rally for the Republic). Also in 1986, the PS representatives in the French National Assembly and the Senate, Frédéric Jalton (also a member of the Regional Council) and Francois Louisey were re-elected. In the September 1988 elections to the General Council, the PS and PCG took 26 of the 42 seats and in the municipal elections in March 1989, won control of 20 of the 33 municipalities. In March 1988, Larifla had defeated the RPR incumbent to take one of four Guadeloupean seats in the French National Assembly.

Prior to the Regional Council elections in March 1992, the PS became seriously divided, a dissident faction, headed by Larifla, clashing with the PS's "orthodox" wing led by Jalton, known as the PS "patriarch". In the elections, Larifla's faction ran as a separate PS bloc, taking seven seats to nine for Jalton. Despite talks between Jalton, the PCG and the Popular Union for the Liberation of Guadeloupe (UPLG), no new alliance resulted to threaten the largest party, the right-wing Rally for the Republic (RPR). The newly formed Guadeloupean Progressive Democratic Party (PPDG) also failed to reach an agreement with Jalton. The split in the PS ranks and Larifla's tacit support for the RPF enabled the RPR's Michaux-Chevry to be sworn in as Regional Council President with the expectation of a working majority. Jalton referred to the Larifla dissidents as "renegades" who "represented a menace for Guadeloupe and Democracy". It was rumoured that he was contemplating an alliance with Michaux-Chevry to bring Larifla down. In the March 1992 cantonal elections, Larifla was returned as President of the General Council.

Guadeloupean Federation of the Union for French Democracy

Fédération Guadeloupéenne de l'Union pour la Démocratie Française (UDF)
Address. Point-á-Pitre.
Leadership. Marcel Esdras (pres.).
Orientation. Conservative.
History. In the 1981 general election the UDF's Marcel Esdras won one of Guadeloupe's three French National Assembly seats. It was a junior partner in a successful coalition with the Rally for the Republic (RPR) in the 1983 Regional Council elections. In February 1986, José Moustache, the RPR president of the Regional Council, defected to the UDF, causing a breach in the two parties' alliance. Esdras lost his National Assembly seat to an RPR candidate in March and at the same time the left won control of the regional council and ousted Moustache (see RPR). Since then, the party has been of minor political importance.

The Guadeloupe Party

Le Parti de la Guadeloupe (LPG)
Address. Pointe-a-Pitre.

Leadership. Lucette Michaux-Chevry (l.).
Orientation. Centrist.
Founded. January 1984.

Guadeloupean Progressive Democratic Party

Parti Progressiste Démocratique Guadeloupéen (PPDG)
Leadership. Ernest Moutoussamy (l.).
Orientation. Centrist.
Founded. 1992.
History. The party was established by dissidents, led by the French National Assembly deputy, Moutoussamy, who had broken with the Guadeloupe Communist Party (PCG). In the March 1992 Regional Council elections, the PPDG won five seats but failed to reach a formal alliance with any other party, in particular the Socialist Party, although it was thought likely that it might join up with the Larifla PS dissident wing in the Regional Council.

Popular Union for the Liberation of Guadeloupe

Union Populaire pour la Libération de la Guadeloupe (UPLG)
Address. Basse-Terre.
Leadership. Claude Makouke (pres.); Roland Thésauros (l.).
Orientation. Centre-left; was for complete independence from France but in recent years has modified this arguing for associated statehood as part of a transition to independence.
Founded. 1978.
History. The UPLG boycotted the electoral process during the 1980s, instead chanelling its efforts towards the active pro-independence movement. Despite its opposition to violence, it helped to organize protest rallies in April 1989 to demand the release of political prisoners, which resulted in serious clashes with police. In May, it also participated in the broad based Guadeloupean Committee for the Support of Political Prisoners (COGUASEP) which campaigned for the release of pro-independence activists held in France and against increased integration with the metropolis and Europe via the creation of a single European Community (EC) market by 1992. In the aftermath of a French National Assembly amnesty conferred in June 1989 for crimes committed prior to July 1988, the UPLG decided to participate in elections, and won two seats in the Regional Council in March 1992. It has close ties with the Communist Party.

Guatemala

Capital: Guatemala City **Population 9,200,000**

Guatemala's modern political history has been very unstable. Three separate constitutions have been promulgated since 1955 and there have been four successful military coups (1957, 1963, 1982 and 1983) and two failed coups (in May and December 1988). Left-wing political parties are illegal and a 30-year civil war by left-wing guerrillas has yet to break the monopoly on power held by a small ruling class and the military. Peace talks aimed at national reconciliation, the expansion of democracy, the ending of gross human rights abuses and the demilitarization of the country, are currently proceeding between the government, moderate sections of the army and the guerrillas.

Constitutional structure

Under its 1985 Constitution, which came into effect in January 1986, the Republic of Guatemala has a unicameral National Congress of 116 members, 87 of whom are directly elected and 29 are elected on the basis of proportional representation. Both President and congressional deputies are elected for a five-year term. The President may not be re-elected. If in the presidential elections none of the candidates secures an absolute majority, a second round between the two leading candidates takes place. The President is assisted by a Vice-President and an appointed Cabinet.

Evolution of the suffrage

Voting is compulsory for those 18 years of age and older who can read and write but is optional for illiterates from the same age group. Non-voting is punishable by a small fine. The police and active duty military personnel are not allowed to vote.

Sequence of elections since 1990

Date	*Type*	*Winning Party*
March 1982	Presidential	Coalition involving Democratic Institutional Party and Revolutionary Party
July 1984	Constituent Assembly	No majority
November 1985	Presidential	Christian Democratic Party (Mario Vinicio Cerezo)
November 1985	Congressional	PDCG
November 1990 & January 1991	Presidential	Solidarity Action Movement (Jorge Serrano Elias)
November 1990	Congressional	Union of the National Centre (UCN) with no overall majority

Presidential elections

First round, November 1990

	% of votes
Jorge Carpio Nicolle (UCN)	25.7

Run-off, January 1991

*Jorge Serrano Elías (MAS)	68.1
Jorge Carpio Nicolle (UCN)	

**Took office on Jan. 14 1991.*

Congressional elections November 1990

	seats
Union of National Centre (UCN)	41
Christian Democracy of Guatemala (DCG)	27
Solidarity Action Movement (MAS)	18
"No Sell-Out" Platform (PNV)	12
National Advancement Party (PAN)	12
National Liberation Movement-National Advancement Front coalition (MLN/FAN)	4
Revolutionary Party (PR)	1
Democratic Socialist Party/Popular Alliance 5 (PSD/AP5)	1

Turnout: 57%

PARTY BY PARTY DATA

Democratic Institutional Party

Partido Institucional Democrático (PID)
Address. 2a Calle 10-73, Zona 1, Guatemala City, Guatemala.
Leadership. Oscar Humberto Rivas García (s.g.).
Orientation. Right-wing, believes in free enterprise.
Founded. 1965.
History. The party was formed by the leader of the 1963 coup and then dictator Col. Enrique Peralta Azurdia together with businessmen, leading propertied families and members of the army. It met with defeat in the 1966 presidential election despite being the "official" party. Thereafter the PID mostly fought elections in alliance with other parties (1970 and 1974 with the extreme right-wing National Liberation Movement (MLN); 1978 with the centre-right Revolutionary Party (PR); and 1982 within the centrist Popular Democratic Front (PDF), made up of the PID, PR and the Front for National Unity (FUN)) and enjoyed twelve years in government. The PID's fourth term in government was cut short by a military coup in March 1982, soon after Gen. Aníbal Guevara became President. Modest results were achieved in the two elections following the counter-coup of 1983. In 1984 the PID won five seats in the Constituent Assembly and in 1985, in coalition with the MLN, one seat in the Congress. In the 1990 elections, the party joined the FUN and the Guatemalan Republican Front (FRG) in the No Sell-Out Platform (PNV) supporting the former dictator Gen. (retd) Efraín Ríos Montt who was generally thought to be the most likely victor in the presidential race before he was barred from standing. The coalition nevertheless won 12 seats in the Constitutional Assembly.

Democratic Socialist Party

Partido Socialista Democrático (PSD)
Address. 12 Calle 10-37 Zona 1, 01001, POB 1279, Guatemala City. Tel. (2) 53-3219; Fax (2) 20819
Leadership. Mario Solórzano Martínez (s.-g.).
Orientation. Nominally centre-left but its determination to secure an expanding role in the political mainstream led Solórzano to accept the post of Labour Minister in 1990, despite the government's strict austerity programme.
Founded. 1978.
History. The PSD went underground and its leaders into exile in 1980 following the shooting of some of its leading members by right-wing death squads. From their Costa Rican exile the PSD leaders joined other opposition groups in the Guatemalan Committee of Patriotic Unity (founded February 1982) in denouncing the 1982 elections, marred by violence and fraud, and endorsing the Guatemalan National Revolutionary Unity guerrilla coalition's "popular revolutionary war" as the only way forward. The PSD boycotted the 1984 elections, but in early 1985, with the prospect of relatively free and fair elections, its leaders returned to Guatemala and re-registered the party. The United Revolutionary Front centre-left coalition, of which the PSD was a leading member, gained two seats in Congress. For the November 1990 elections the PSD joined forces with the Popular Alliance 5 (AP5) and went ahead with their election campaign despite threats by right-wing paramilitaries to their candidates and the killing of a regional party secretary. The PSD-AP5 won one seat in the Congress and the PSD secretary-general, Mario Solórzano was made Labour Minister in the new government.
Structure. The annual party congress elects a political bureau and party officers.
International Affiliation. Socialist International (full member party).

Guatemalan Christian Democracy Party

Partido Democracia Cristiana Guatemalteca (DCG)
Address. 8a Avda 14-53, Zona 1, Guatemala City.
Leadership. Alfonso Cabrera Hidalgo (s.-g.).
Orientation. Centre-right. Despite its reformist rhetoric, once in power the party has been conservative.
Founded. 24 August 1955.
History. The DCG came out of an anti-Communist tradition and was founded with the help of the Roman Catholic Church in the belief that a Christian approach to politics would prevent reformist governments that held power in 1944-54, which they classified as left-wing. The DCG's policy was to oppose violence and promote social justice through direct church assistance while at the same time closing ranks with the extreme right-wing National Liberation Movement (MLN) in 1958. The contradictions within the DCG came to a head during the Peralta regime

(1963-1966), when an anti-Communist faction accepted 10 seats in Congress while the majority of the party campaigned in opposition for basic social welfare and reforms of the army. After the expulsion of the right-wing faction, the party gained considerable support from students, trade unionists and rural communities during the unrest and repression of the 1960s. By default, the DCG was banned under the 1965 Constitution which prevented it from participating in the March 1966 elections.

In 1968, the DCG was finally legalized and in 1970 it fielded a army officer as candidate (like all subsequent DCG candidates until 1985) in the presidential elections. He came third, but because of his campaign for agrarian reform, did particularly well in the rural highland regions. In 1974 the party led the National Opposition Front (*Frente Nacional Opositor*—FNO) which entered Gen. Efraín Ríos Montt (see No Sell-Out Platform) in the presidential race. Despite having been Chief-of-Staff during the worst periods of repression, Montt was regarded by many as honest. He was thought to have won the popular vote, but in order to avoid confrontation with the army, accepted second place. Four years later the presidential candidate for the National Unity Front (made up of the DCG and the now disbanded Authentic Revolutionary Party—PRA and Popular Participation Front—FPP) gained third place with 36.5 per cent of the vote.

Following attacks by right-wing paramilitaries and the murder of several of its leaders, the DCG went underground in June 1980 but re-emerged for the 1982 election campaign as a partner of the National Renewal Party in the National Opposition Union (UNO). The alliance won three seats in Congress and the PNR presidential candidate came third with 15.6 per cent. The DCG initially supported the 1982 coup led by Ríos Montt who promised to put an end to violence and corruption but distanced itself from the regime when it became an open dictatorship. The DCG gained the reputation of being the party least involved in repression and corruption and the one most likely to promote social reforms. In the 1984 Constituent elections it won the most seats (20 out of 88). This paved the way for the resounding victory in the November 1985 general election when the DCG, with the support of sections of the business community and approval of the United States government, won an absolute majority in Congress (51 seats out of 100) and 73 per cent of municipal councils. Its presidential candidate Mario Vinicio Cerezo Arévalo, with 68 per cent of the second-round vote (38.6 per cent in the first round), became the first civilian President elected in 16 years.

The Cerezo government, which took office on 14 January 1986, proved to be a conservative one. It reassured the business community of its privileges in order to stimulate investment and introduced and enforced deflationary policies which stabilized the economy at the expense of the poorest sectors. It also refused official approval for a popular campaign for agrarian reform supported by DCG activists. Cerezo played an instrumental role in promoting the Central American peace proposals put forward by Costa Rica's President Arias, but at home he failed to challenge the military's power. The government nevertheless suffered three coup attempts and a number of coup plots by the extreme right wing and sections of the army between 1987 and 1989. Danilo Barillas, a prospective presidential candidate to unite left and right-wing factions of the party was assassinated by right-wing death squads. His substitute, the party's secretary-general Alfonso Cabrera Hidalgo, caused René de León Schlotter, the leader of the party's left wing, and his supporters to split away from the party, de León Schlotter becoming the presidential candidate for the Democratic Socialist Party. The DCG attempted to recreate its progressive image by forging an alliance with the Democratic Convergence (DC), but this could not counteract the worsening effects of the economy, the allegations of corruption levelled against the party's leadership and the general disillusionment with the DCG.

The party managed to muster only 27 seats in the November 1990 congressional elections, and Alfonso Cabrera, unable to campaign through illness, came third with 17.3 per cent of the votes. In the second round of the presidential elections the DCG supported the runner-up, Jorge Carpio Nicolle of the UCN. When Congress actually opened in January 1991, however, the DCG joined a congressional bloc made up of the ruling Solidarity Action Movement party and the FRG and National Advancement Party to keep the Union of National Centre (UCN) out of power. The DCG's Catalina Soberanis (Labour Minister 1986-87) won the ensuing contest for President of Congress. After President Serrano alleged that DCG leaders had misused government funds and had been involved in

fraud, the DCG joined the UCN in the Senate to block the government's emergency financial measures.
Membership. 130,000
International affiliations. Christian Democrat International; Christian Democrat Organization of America.

Guatemalan Labour Party

Partido Guatemalteco del Trabajo (PGT)
Leadership. Carlos González Orellana (s.g. of the *camarilla* faction).
Orientation. Was pro-Soviet before the political upheavals in the Eastern bloc countries and the Soviet Union. A formal abandonment of guerrilla warfare in the mid-1970s led to serious splits in the party but by the late 1980s two major factions came together to support the efforts of the Guatemalan National Revolutionary Unity (URNG) guerrillas to achieve national reconciliation.
Founded. Formally named in 1952.
History. The PGT has its roots in the Socialist Labour Unification which was founded in 1921, reorganized as the Communist Party of Guatemala in 1924, and severely repressed after a peasant revolt in neighbouring El Salvador in 1932. Revived in 1947 as the Democratic Vanguard, it was renamed the Communist Party of Guatemala in 1949 and finally as the Guatemalan Labour Party in 1952. Under the reformist Arbenz government (1951-54) it dominated the trade union movement and exercised considerable political influence, although holding only four seats in the Congress. After the 1954 military coup, it was banned and most of its leaders were murdered or driven into exile, since when it has been forced to work underground. In 1961 it came out openly in favour of armed struggle, at first conducting guerrilla operations alone and later with the November 13 Revolutionary Movement (MR-13), the two joining forces in 1962 to form the Rebel Armed Forces (FAR). The PGT provided the FAR's political leadership but gradually abandoned practical support for the armed struggle in 1968-71. It suffered severely from right-wing para-militaries with close connections with the army and police. Two of its general secretaries, 19 Central Committee members and the leader of its youth wing, the Patriotic Labour Youth, were murdered between 1972-83.

In 1978, the PGT suffered a major split over the armed struggle question and other organizational issues which left the party divided into three weak organizations. Out of the strongest faction (the consecuentes) emerged the PGT National Leadership Nucleus, which became independent, as did the PGT Military Commission. Both groups were critical of the *camarilla* faction led by Carlos González, general secretary of the PGT since 1975. The *camarillistas* were the last to become committed to the armed struggle, which they finally endorsed in May 1981, before declaring a readiness to join the URNG guerrilla alliance in December 1982. However, they also continued to engage in mass work via their own militants working in the trade unions. In 1985 the PGT had further subdivided into at least five factions but by 1988 the *camarilla* and the Leadership Nucleus were effectively reconciled and issued a joint document in support of the URNG's campaign for a national dialogue for peace.
Publications. Verdad (irregular).

National Advancement Party

Partido de Avanzada Nacional (PAN)
Leadership. Alvaro Arzú Irigoyen (l.).
Orientation. Centre-right.
Founded. 1989.
History. The party's founder, Alvaro Arzú Irigoyen, gained his reputation as an efficient administrator during his years as mayor of the capital, Guatemala City (1985-1990). He resigned from his mayoral post and formed the PAN to contest the 1990 general election. His candidature was regarded favourably by the business community and the US government. Arzú came fourth in the first round of the presidential elections with 17.3 per cent of the vote, and the PAN obtained 12 seats in the Congress. A PAN member, Oscar Berger, with 34 per cent of the vote was elected mayor of Guatemala City. In return for supporting the victorious presidential candidate Jorge Serrano of the Solidarity Action Movement—MAS, Arzú was named as Foreign Minister in the new government and the PAN was also given the Communications, Transport and Public Works portfolio. However, it became clear during the Mexico peace talks with the Guatemalan National Revolutionary Unity (URNG) guerrillas in May 1991, to which Arzú was not invited, that Serrano would not allow him a major role in government. Arzú resigned as Foreign Minster in September 1991 in protest at Serrano's decision to establish diplomatic relations with Belize, sovereignty over which had long been claimed by Guatemala.

National Liberation Movement

Movimiento de Liberación Nacional (MLN)

Address. 5a Calle 1-20, Zona 1, Guatemala City.
Leadership. Mario Sandóval Alarcón (l.).
Orientation. Extreme right-wing; strongly opposed to negotiations with guerrilla groups; traditionally has represented agrarian and industrial élites, especially coffee growers, and has close links with the army.
Founded. 1960.
History. The self-proclaimed "party of organized violence" was founded by Mario Sandóval Alarcón as the successor of Col. Castillo Armas' National Democratic Movement (MDN) which, with US backing, overthrew the reformist Arbenz government in 1954. The MLN staged the 1963 coup led by Col. Peralta Azurdia (see Democratic Institutional Party—PID) and formed a government with the Revolutionary Party (PR) until it was itself overthrown in 1964. The MLN's presidential candidate came third in the 1966 elections, but from 1970 the party was in government for eight years, its leader Col. Carlos Araña Osorio was President from 1970-1974, and in 1974-1978 Gen. Kjell Laugerud presided over an MLN-PID government, with Sandóval as acting Vice-President. The 1970s also saw the height of the activity of MLN-linked death squads. In the following two elections MLN presidential candidates (1978: Peralta; 1982: Sandóval) were unsuccessful and came second. The MLN enthusiastically supported the 1982 military coup, although within months it joined other parties in their demand for free and democratic elections. An MLN split led to Leonel Sisniega Otero, a leading party member, leaving the country with his own MLN faction to found the Anti-Communist Unification Party (PUA—now disbanded). For the July 1984 constituent elections the MLN entered into a coalition with the Authentic Nationalist Central (CAN) and won most of the coalition's 23 seats which made it the largest block in the Constituent Assembly. It entered into another coalition with the PID before the November 1985 general election, but by then the party's ruling class supporters had shifted their loyalties to the newly formed National Democratic Co-operation Party (PDCN). In the presidential race, Sandóval came fourth with 12.6 per cent of the vote, and both MLN and PID won six seats each in the Congress. The MLN secretary-general, Héctor Aragón Quiñonez, and his supporters, subsequently left the party. The MLN strongly opposed the policies of the new DCG government and in particular its position of support for the Central American peace process, accusing it of being Marxist. In December 1986 the MLN claimed it was training 8,000 volunteers to fight with the right-wing Contras in Nicaragua but only a few hundred at most were thought to have been so organized. The MLN had also strongly condemned the government's efforts to end the 30-year war with left-wing guerrillas but, by early 1990, their attitude to the peace process had mellowed. In response to the opening of peace talks with the Guatemalan National Unity Movement (URNG) guerrillas in the Norwegian capital Oslo, the MLN supported the eventual incorporation of the URNG into the political mainstream. In the November 1990 general election, the MLN, in coalition with the National Advancement Front (FAN), won a mere four seats in the Congress and their presidential candidate Col. Luis Ernesto Sosa came fifth in the first round of the presidential contest, receiving 17.3 per cent of the vote.

No Sell-Out Platform

Plataforma No Venta (PNV)
Leadership. Gen. (retd.) José Efraín Ríos Montt (l.).
Orientation. Extreme right-wing and populist, standing for strict law and order
Founded. 1989.
History. The coalition was formed to support the candidature of Gen. (retd) Ríos Montt in the 1990 presidential elections. The coalition parties were the Institutional Democratic Party (PID), the National Unity Front and the Guatemalan Republican Front.

Ríos Montt, a member of the California-based evangelical "Church of the World" since 1978, previously stood for President in the 1978 elections as the candidate for the National Opposition Front formed around the Christian Democrats, but is thought to have been denied victory by rivals in the army high-command. He seized power in a military coup led by young officers in March 1982 and promised to put an end to violence and corruption and to install true democracy. However, when his authoritarianism developed into a dictatorship he was overthrown by the army in August 1983. During the 1990 general election campaign, Ríos Montt was the pre-poll favourite for the presidency. Despite his bad track record on human rights and his outspoken evangelism, he drew support chiefly among Roman Catholics, and in particular from Indian communities who had suffered the most from his regime's anti-guerrilla scorched earth policy, which saw thousands of Indians murdered. Riós Montt, however, was remembered by them as having been an improvement on his military predecessors.

In an atmosphere of escalating national violence Ríos Montt's electoral promise of a law and order clampdown drew strong public support, and the fact that he was strongly disliked by all major parties created the impression that *No Venta* was free from political corruption. The sustained hostility of other parties to *No Venta*, however, helped quash Ríos Montt's presidential ambitions. In October 1990, the Constitutional Court ruled that his candidature was in breach of Article 186 of the 1986 Constitution which debarred from elections anybody who had benefited from a military coup. The Supreme Court upheld the ruling even though the article had been specifically inserted with Ríos Montt in mind; he advised his supporters to spoil their votes in protest but still to vote for *No Venta* candidates in the congressional and municipal elections. It became clear, however, that the majority of them transferred their allegiance to the evangelical businessman Jorge Serrano Elías (see Solidarity Action Movement—MAS). The *No Venta* coalition captured 12 congressional seats and 18 municipalities. When Congress opened in January 1991, *No Venta* sided with the government bloc against the Union of the National Centre.

National Unity Front (*Frente de Unidad Nacional*—FUN); founded 1977, extreme right wing. It was joined by the former dictator Col. Enrique Peralta (see National Liberation Movement) in 1978. The FUN fought the 1985 election with the now disbanded Anti-Communist Party (PUA) without success. It joined the No Sell-Out Platform formed in 1989 to support Gen. Ríos Montt's presidential campaign. Guatemalan Republican Front (*Frente Republicano Guatemalteco—FRG)*; founded in 1989 to back Gen. Ríos Montt's candidacy, it was part of the No Sell-Out Platform formed in the same year to support his campaign.

Revolutionary Party

Partido Revolucionario (PR)

Leadership. Jorge García Granados (l.); Carlos Enrique Chavarría Pérez (s.-g.).

Orientation. Reformist, wavers between centre-right and right-wing positions.

Founded. 1957.

History. The PR started life as a left-wing party, formed by veteran supporters of the 1944 progressive government of President Juan José Arevalo Bermejo. At the 1959 party convention, however, most of the radical wing was expelled. In 1966 general election, Julio César Méndez Montenegro was elected President and the party captured 30 out of 55 seats in the Congress. The victory was attributed partly to a secret pact with the army, which then constantly hampered Méndez Montenegro's reformist plans. In the 1970 elections the PR lost power to the right-wing National Liberation Movement (MLN), and the party plunged into a protracted turmoil which caused two splits. In 1974 the left of the party split away to found the United Front of the Revolution (FUR) with the remainder in the PR going to the right by forming an alliance with the Institutional Democratic Party (PID). In 1978 a reformist faction in the PR left to form the Authentic Revolutionary Party (PRA) (now defunct). The PR's alliance with the right proved successful. In 1978, the PR-PID candidate, Gen. Romeo Lucas won the presidency as did Gen. Aníbal Guevara, candidate for the Popular Democratic Front (consisting of PR, PID and National Unity Front, see No Sell-Out Platform) in 1982, although Guevara was prevented from taking office by a military coup. In 1984 the PR won 10 seats in the Constitutional Assembly (out of 88) and later that year joined forces with the newly formed UCN and the smaller National Renewal Party (PNR). For the 1985 general election, however, the PR began to swing to the left and entered into a coalition with the Democratic Party of National Co-operation (PDCN) on a programme promising agricultural and administrative reforms. The PR-PDCN presidential candidate, Jorge Serrano Elías (see Solidarity Action Movement and PDCN), came third and the coalition together won 11 congressional seats. Following four years in opposition, the PR's presidential candidate José Angel Lee obtained a mere 2.15 per cent of the vote in the November 1990 general election, ending up in seventh place, and the party won two seats in the Congress. In the second round of the presidential elections, the PR supported the victor, Serrano.

Solidarity Action Movement

Movimiento de Acción Solidaria (MAS)

Leadership. Jorge Serrano Elías (s.g.); Miguel Angel Montepeque (assist. s.g.); Manuel Conde (sec. of political affairs).

Orientation. Right-wing, represents mainly business interests and believes in the de-regulation of the economy.
Founded. 1986.
History. The party was formed by Jorge Serrano Elías, a businessman, evangelical Christian, veteran anti-Communist and former president of the Council of State created under Gen. Ríos Montt's military junta in 1982. He stood as the presidential candidate for the Revolutionary Party—Democratic Party of National Co-operation (PR-PNDC) coalition in the 1985 general election and after coming third with 13.8 per cent of the vote, left the PDCN. In the November 1990 elections, Serrano campaigned on a platform of law and order, respect for human rights and "total peace" with the guerrillas (he had been a member of the National Reconciliation Commission in peace negotiations with the Guatemalan National Revolutionary Unity (URNG) guerrillas. Serrano attracted votes from supporters of the disqualified fellow evangelical Gen. (retd.) Ríos Montt (see No Sell-Out Platform—PNV). Serrano came a surprise second in the first round with 24.3 per cent of the vote and the MAS obtained 13 seats in the Congress. In the second round, backed by the Emergent Movement of Harmony (MEC), National Liberation Movement (MLN), PNV and especially the National Advancement Party (PAN), Serrano was swept to power with 68.1 percent of the vote. He rewarded the PAN for its support as soon as he was sworn in on 6 January 1991 by forming a MAS-PAN alliance and appointing two leading PAN members to his Cabinet. Five further cabinet posts went to non-party businessmen and technocrats, which alienated the trade unions, who viewed the government's offer of "social pact" as a device to avert social protest over an economic austerity programme. Serrano agreed a four-point framework peace agreement with the URNG guerrillas in July 1991. The latest round of peace talks, held in Mexico in February 1992, ended without agreement, although mediators of the National Reconciliation Commission stated that "important progress" had been made towards an agreement on human rights. In mid-February, Serrano modified his defensive and aggressive stand towards perceived international "meddling" in the country's internal affairs. In an effort to improve its international image and to revive its diminishing foreign aid income, the government passed a seven-point plan to safeguard human rights and revive the peace talks, while Guatemalan diplomats visited Latin American countries and Europe. In the same month, the European Parliament had approved a resolution calling for an end to the "deplorable situation of human rights abuses" in the country, a view endorsed by the US State Department which blamed the military, the right-wing para-military Civil Self Defence Patrols and the police for the worst excesses. However the prospects for peace receded in April, when it was reported that the government, as a matter of urgency, was arming upwards of 2,000 campesinos (peasants) to confront the URNG in the southern coastal region. The army also announced that it was escalating its military action against the guerrillas (see URNG).

Union of the National Centre

Unión del Centro Nacional (UCN)
Address. 14a Avenida 4-33, Zona 1, Guatemala City.
Leadership. Jorge Carpio Nicolle (l.); Juan José Rodil Peralta (party sec.).
Orientation. Claims to be a "stabilizing centrist" party, although Carpio surrounded himself with conservative economists during the 1990 election campaign and his running-mate came from the extreme right. Election promises included greater efficiency in agriculture and in the collection of taxes, but offered no promise of social reforms.
Founded. 14 July 1983.
History. The UCN was formed by Carpio, a newspaper publisher, as a vehicle for his presidential aspirations. At first the party adopted an anti-Communist stance, but at times it attempted to project a left-wing image. It fought the 1984 Constituent Assembly elections with a lavish media campaign never seen in Guatemala and reaped instant success, winning 21 seats and became the biggest single party bloc in the Constituent Assembly. In the 1985 general elections, Carpio was favoured by sections of the army, and like his direct opponent, the Guatemalan Christian Democracy Party's (DCG) Vinicio Cerezo, was also supported by the US administration. He came second with 31.6 per cent in the second round of voting and his party gained 22 congressional seats. The UCN acted as leader of the parliamentary opposition between 1986-1990, generally supporting the government's foreign policy but criticizing its excessive spending and, at times, condemning its domestic policies as being right wing. In the November 1990 general election, the UCN won a convincing victory, winning 41 of the 116 congressional seats and a clear majority of mayoral representations. Carpio, standing as the UCN presidential candidate, came first with 25.7% of the vote, but because he did not get an overall majority he had to contest a second round. He managed to win the backing of the DCG, but nevertheless came only second to the surprise winner, Jorge Serrano of the Solidarity Action

Movement. The new government, along with the DCG, National Advancement Party and Guatemalan Republican Front ensured that the UCN was completely excluded from cabinet posts and congressional commissions.

Publications. *El Informador* (monthly); *El Gráfico*, a major Guatemalan daily owned by Carpio (circulation 60,000).

International affiliations. Liberal International.

Minor parties

Six further parties participated in the 1990 congressional elections but because each of them received less than 4 per cent of the vote, they lost their political status:

Democratic Party (*Partido Democrático*—PD).

Democratic Party of National Co-operation (*Partido Democrático de Cooperación Nacional*—PDCN); Rolando Baquiaux Gómez (s. g.). A centre-right party founded in 1983 by Acisclo Valladares Molina and, after failing to win a seat in the 1984 Constitutional Assembly elections, re-organized by Jorge Serrano Elías (see Solidarity Action Movement—MAS). The PDCN fought the 1985 general election in alliance with the Revolutionary Party (PR) and together they won 11 seats. Serrano left the party soon after coming third in the presidential race. Between 1986 and 1990 the PDCN supported the ruling Guatemalan Christian Democracy Party (DCG), but for the November 1990 general election campaign it entered into a coalition with the PR. However, this coalition was dissolved when the candidate, Fernando Andrade Díaz Durán, withdrew and the PR entered its own candidate.

Emergent Movement of Harmony (*Movimiento Emergente de Concordia*—MEC); a right-wing party founded in 1983 by Col. Francisco Luis Gordillo Martínez, who was a member of Ríos Montt's junta in 1982. The MEC unsuccessfully fought the 1984 Constituent Assembly election and the 1985 and 1990 general elections.

National Opposition Union (*Unión Nacional Opositora*—UNO).

Nationalist Renewal Party (*Partido Nacionalista Renovador*—PNR); a right-of-centre party founded in August 1979. Its leader and former National Liberation Movement (MLN) member Alejandro Maldonado Aguirre stood for President for the National Opposition Union (UNO) coalition in 1982 and came third. In the July 1984 the PNR won five seats in the Constituent Assembly elections but in the 1985 general election won only one seat in the Congress.

United Front of the Revolution (*Frente Unido de la Revolución*—FUR); a left-wing party founded by Marco Tulio Collado and Humberto González Gamarra. Both left the FUR to found the Democratic Revolutionary Unity (URD) in mid-1990 and were murdered by right-wing death squads, Collado in January 1990 and Gamarra in October 1990.

Other Parties

Authentic Nationalist Centre (*Central Auténtica Nacionalista*—CAN); a right-wing party founded in 1980 as the successor of the *Central Arañista Organzado* (itself founded in 1979 by supporters of Gen. (retd) Carlos Manuel Araña Osorio, President 1970-1974). The CAN was in favour of a military coup following the March 1982 elections but by September called for free elections. The party reached its peak in 1984, as the junior partner in the alliance with the National Liberation Movement (MLN) which, with 23 seats, became the largest bloc in the Constitutional Assembly. Since the dissolution of the coalition in 1985 the CAN only managed to win a single seat in Congress in the 1985 elections. It did not participate in the 1990 elections.

Civic Action Committee (*Comité de Acción Civil*—CAC); a group based in the capital, Guatemala city, whose leader Rafael Escobar Donis, president of the National Housing Bank (BANVI) came second in the Guatemala City mayoral elections in November 1990.

Democratic Convergence (*Convergencia Democrática*—CD); the party was founded 1988 by leading left-wing members of the PSD and has close links with FUNDAGUA, a private foundation which finances human rights and similar organizations. The CD was a target of right-wing death squads and did not participate in the November 1990 elections. However, it did support the electoral campaign of the Christian Democrat Party (DCG) and fielded some congressional and municipal candidates under DCG auspices. One such successful congressional candidate, Dinora Gosseth Pérez Valdez, was killed by extreme right-wing gunmen in May 1991 and another party leader, Luis Zurita Tablada, fled to Canada on May 13, 1991, after, receiving death threats.

Democratic Revolutionary Unity (*Unión Revolucionaria Democrática*—URD); founded in mid-1990 by the militant left-wing journalist Humberto González Gamarra and Marco Tulio Collado, the left-wing mayor of the municipality of Escuintla. The URD immediately became a target for right-wing death squads and on Oct. 15, 1990, Gamarra was assassinated.

Popular Democratic Force (*Fuerza Demócrata Popular*—FDP); a populist party founded in 1983 by Francisco Reyes Ixeamey. It unsuccessfully contested the 1984 constituent elections and in 1990 the FDP supported Ríos Montt's *No Sell-Out* campaign until he was banned from the presidential elections.

Indigenist Organizations

Committee of Campesino Unity (*Comité de Unidad Campesina*—CUC); a peasant group opposed to the celebrations of the 500th anniversary of Colombus' discovery of Latin America.

Communities of the Population in Resistance of the Mountains (*Comunidades de Población en Resistencia de las Montañas*—CPR); a non-combatant group of peasants (campesinos) of three different ethnic and linguistic origins who were displaced in 1981-1983 when the army destroyed 440 villages in the departments of Alta Verapaz, Huehuetenango and El Quiché. The CPR claim to represent 15,000 displaced campesinos and they continue peacefully to resist the army in the mountain region north of Chajul, in the department of El Quiché. Their demands include demilitarization, liberty, peace, security, true democracy and respect for human rights.

Council of Ethnic Communities "Runujel Junam" (*Consejo de Comunidades Étnicos Runujel Junam*—CERJ); Amílcar Méndez (party president), founded in 1988. The CERJ is an indigenist group, based in the department of EL Quiché, whose aims are to advance democracy, justice and dignity for the Mayan people.

Guerrilla Groups

Guatemalan Labour Party-National Leadership Nucleus (*Partido Guatemalteco del Trabajo (PGT)-Nucleo de Dirección Nacional*); founded after a split in the Guatemalan Labour Party in 1978.

Guatemalan National Revolutionary Unity

Unidad Revolucionaria Nacional Guatemalteca (URNG).

Leadership. Commanders Gaspar Illom (Rolando Asturias Amado), Rolando Morán, Pablo Monsanto, Luis Becker Guzmán, Miguel Angel Sandoval, Francisco Villagrán and Luz Mendez.

Orientation. Nominally Marxist but its programme calls for social reforms, increased democracy and the demilitarization of the country. It relies mainly on spectacular actions damaging to the economic infrastructure.

Founded. 1979.

History. The URNG is an umbrella organization consisting of the following guerrilla groups:

Armed People's Organization (*Organización del Pueblo en Armas*—ORPA); founded in 1972 by a group of ex-Rebel Armed Forces (FAR) members. ORPA started armed activities in 1979 and recruited mainly among the rural Indian population. Strategic base: Santiago Atitlan. Leader: Rodrigo Asturias Amado (Com. Gaspar Illom).

Guerrilla Army of the Poor (*Ejército Guerrillero de los Pobres*—EGP); founded in the late 1960s by ex-FAR members in exile; follows the ideas of Che Guevara; Leader: Rolando Morán.

Rebel Armed Forces (*Fuerzas Armadas Rebeldes*—FAR) founded in 1962 as an alliance of the Guatemalan Labour Party (PGT), the November 13 Revolutionary Movement of Radical Officers (MR13) and students. Both PGT and MR13 broke away in the mid-1960s. The FAR has mainly been influenced by the Vietnam war and is the largest group in the URNG.

Urban Revolutionary Command (*Comando Urbano Revolucionario*—CUR); a small Guatemala City-based group which joined the URNG in 1989.

The URNG was formed by the EGP, FAR and PGT (ORPA joined a year later) in order to present a unified front against the army offensives. The framework for a central military command was set up in early 1982, but until the late 1980s the individual member groups continued to operate separately. The new period of civilian rule which began in 1986 encouraged the guerrillas to seek an agreement with the government and army that would allow the URNG to enter the political mainstream. Guerrilla activities were scaled down until October 1987, when peace talks with the Guatemalan Christian Democrat Party (DCG) government proved unproductive and the army went on a renewed offensive. While the government, intimidated by a series of army coup plots, continued to postpone further talks, the URNG stepped up their activities again in 1989. Semi-official peace talks with the National Reconciliation Commission (CNR) (made up of representatives from Guatemalan political parties and "notable citizens") started in Norway in March 1990 and resulted in the Oslo Accords, which set a rough timetable for peace negotiations. In June peace talks in the Spanish capital Madrid the URNG agreed not to disrupt the forthcoming November general election. Meetings between the URNG, the CNR and representatives of the Guatemalan business community followed in August in Ottawa, Canada, and in November in Metepec, Mexico. A major breakthrough in the peace process came in the Mexico City talks of April 1991 when, for the first time, representatives of the Guatemalan armed forces agreed to attend. In July 1991, a framework peace was agreed upon as a basis for future negotiations. The latest rounds of peace talks with the Solidarity Action Movement (MAS) government ended without agreement in February 1992, although the key URNG demand for a formal agreement on human rights remained in reach (see MAS). However the possibility of a peace accord was receding in April 1992 as the government, as a matter of urgency, was arming and mobilizing upwards of 2,000 campesinos (peasants) to confront the URNG in the southern coastal region. It was felt that this would be achieved by using the right-wing para-military Civil Self Defence Patrols (*La Patrullas de Autodefensa Civil*), which claim to have 100,000 armed campesino supporters nationally, and have been a major impediment to the successful conclusion of the peace process and are among the chief violators of human rights. The army also announced that it would escalate its military action against the guerrillas.

Membership. 3,500 guerrillas (1988 claim).

Political Wing. United Representation of the Guatemalan Opposition (*Representación Unitaria de la Oposición Guatemalteca*—RUOG) led by Raúl Molina Mejía

Publications. Noticias de Guatemala (irregular).

Secret Anti-Communist Army (*Ejercito Secreto Anti-comunista*—ESA); founded in 1989. A right-wing death squad which tried to destabilize the Cerezo government and threatened the Spanish ambassador and his staff during the May 1990 Madrid talks between the Guatemalan government and the URNG.

New Guatemalan Revolutionary Movement (Nuevo Movimiento Revolucionario Guatemalteco—NMRG); emerged in early 1991 and claimed to be Marxist. Local analysts, however, believe they are an ultra right-wing group trying to disrupt the peace negotiations between the URNG and the government.

Guyana

Capital: Georgetown **Population:800,000**

Guyana, formerly a colony of the United Kingdom, achieved independence in 1966. Since the inauguration of elections under the British in 1953, the Progressive People's Party (PPP) was the dominant political force until 1964 when its offspring, the People's National Congress (PNC), began its long tenure of office up to the present, a feat widely judged to have been dependent on the systematic repression of the opposition and the manipulation of elections. The general election due by March 1991 was repeatedly postponed, and the current parliamentary session extended to September 1992.

Constitutional structure

Under the 1980 Constitution, a unicameral National Assembly is made up of 65 members. Executive power is exercised by the President who appoints a first Vice-President and the Prime Minister, both of whom must be members of the legislature, and a Cabinet, which may have up to four members from outside the legislature. The President also appoints as leader of the opposition the member of the legislature considered as the most able to command the support of other opposition members.

Electoral system

The President is directly elected by universal adult suffrage for a five-year term, as are 53 of the 65 members of the National Assembly, using a national party list system of proportional representation whereby voters cast their ballot for a party's list of candidates, and seats are then allocated to parties on the basis of proportional representation. Of the remaining 12 National Assembly members, 10 are elected by the 10 regional democratic councils and two are elected by the national congress of local democratic organs, a nominally consultative body whose members are elected by the members of the regional councils from among themselves.

Evolution of the suffrage

Universal adult suffrage was introduced in 1953. In 1963, due to British pressure, proportional representation was introduced, and in 1966 Guyana became a self-governing dominion within the British Commonwealth. In 1968, overseas Guyanese were enfranchised. All Guyanese citizens 18 years of age and older are entitled to vote.

Sequence of elections since 1980

National Assembly Elections Dec. 15, 1980

	Distribution of directly elected seats
People's National Congress (PNC)	41
People's Progressive Party (PPP)	10
The United Force (TUF)	2
Working People's Alliance (WPA)	-
Total	**53**

National Assembly Elections Dec. 9, 1985

PNC	42
PPP	8
TUF	2
WPA	1
Total	**53**

PARTY BY PARTY DATA

Guyanese Action for Reform and Democracy (Guard)

Address. c/o Naccie, High St, Kingston, Georgetown.
Leadership. N. K. Gopaul co-ordinator (see Guyana Labour Party). A steering committee of members consists of representatives of the business community, trade unions and the church.
Orientation. A non-partisan centrist pressure group campaigning for free and clean elections.
Founded. 1990.
History. The Guard was formed as a reform movement to compile a "civic list" of candidates to contest upcoming elections. It insisted that it would not constitute itself as a formal political party but wished to see the establishment of a two-year interim government which would revise the constitution, promote democratic reform and oversee basic economic recovery. In this vein, it supported the demand of the Working People's Alliance (WPA) in July 1991 for a caretaker government (see WPA). The Guard's programme also includes the restoration of public institutions, the elimination of excessive executive powers and the return of real power to the legislature. Gopaul formed the separate Guyana Labour Party (GLP) in January 1992 and his future relationship with the Guard remained unclear.

Patriotic Coalition for Democracy (PCD)

Orientation. A centrist grouping, campaigning for free and clean elections.
Founded. January 1986.
History. The PCD was formed by the Working People's Alliance (WPA), the People's Progressive Party (PPP), the Democratic Labour Movement (DLM), the National Democratic Front (NDF—see National Democratic Party) and the People's Democratic Movement (PDM), along with trade union and community groups. The coalition called for an early and fair general election and boycotted the municipal elections in December 1986. In 1990 the PCD's relevance and effectiveness was increasingly questioned with the formation of the broader based Guyanese Action for Reform and Democracy (Guard), the expulsion of the PDM in May 1991 for non-attendance of meetings and the increasingly independent positions being adopted by the WPA and PPP.

People's National Congress (PNC)

Address. Congress Place, Sophia, Georgetown.
Leadership. Hugh Desmond Hoyte; Seeram Prashad (s.-g.).
Orientation. Under the former leadership of Burnham, the PNC declared itself to be in favour of "socialist co-operatism", a sufficiently vague concept at odds with his autocratic style of government. The current Hoyte regime, which has promoted conservative economic policies, has been accused of retaining power through electoral fraud. The PNC draws most of its support from the African-descended population.
Founded. 1957.
History. The party was founded by Forbes Burnham, the former leader of the People's Progressive Party (PPP). In the 1957 and 1961 elections, it was the main opposition party but in 1964, after a change in the electoral system, it joined the Unified Force (UF) in a coalition government, which led the country to independence in May 1966. The party went on to dominate government, winning the 1968, 1973 and 1980 elections and gaining in each case clear majorities in the National Assembly. However each election was considered by independent observers to have been seriously flawed.

On Burnham's death, Hoyte, the Vice-President and leader of the centrist wing of the party favourable to an accommodation with the PPP, assumed the presidency in August 1985. He was confirmed in office by the general election of December 1985, similarly denounced as fraudulent, when the party was adjudged to have won 78.5 per cent of the vote and 42 seats.

Ineligible for IMF aid since 1985 due to non-payment of debt requirements, the government rejected "socialist co-operatism" and introduced severe austerity measures to prepare the ground for a stringent Economic Recovery Programme (ERP), formally introduced in April 1989, which subsequently attracted support from multilateral lending agencies. The degree of popular resentment towards the government, expressed in rolling strikes in both the private and public sectors, was augmented by demands for electoral reform, the establishment of an independent electoral commission, and the guarantee of free and clean elections.

A general election, constitutionally due by March 31, 1991, was repeatedly postponed by the government who claimed that a new electoral register was incomplete while denying opposition claims that it was involved in a delaying procedure designed to get Hoyte re-elected. An indefinite state of emergency was declared in November. Due to the delay, the current parliamentary session was repeatedly extended, provoking the opposition to boycott the Assembly in protest.

New checks on the voters' list began in December and three opposition parties, the PPP, the Workers' People's Alliance (WPA) and the United Force (UF) agreed to take up their seats in the Assembly, the PPP subsequently objecting to the PNC decision in February to prolong the parliamentary session until September 1992, unless a general election was called in the meantime.

Publications. The state-owned daily, the *Guyana Chronicle* supports the party, whose official organ is the *New Nation.*

People's Progressive Party (PPP)

Address. Freedom House, 41 Robb St., Lacytown, Georgetown.

Leadership. Cheddi Jagan (l.); Janet Jagan (exec. sec.).

Orientation. Before the collapse of the Eastern bloc, the party was pro-Soviet, but under Cheddi Jagan has always adopted a pragmatic approach and promises consensus government if returned to power. It has traditionally drawn its support from the Asian (Indian) community.

Founded. January 1950.

History. The PPP was founded in 1950 as the successor to the Political Affairs Committee, formed in 1946. In the first elections held under universal suffrage, the party won 18 of the 24 seats in the House of Assembly in April 1953 on a manifesto calling for independence from the United Kingdom. Cheddi Jagan, the PPP leader formed a government, but in October theUnited Kingdom Conservative government suspended the constitution and dismissed the ministers, claiming that the PPP was engaged in "communist subversion".

The party split in 1955 and Forbes Burnham, a member of Jagan's government, was expelled and subsequently formed the People's National Congress (PNC).

New elections in 1957, under a revised constitution, resulted in a victory for the PPP, which formed a government with an absolute majority in the Assembly, and Jagan became the first Chief Minister. In 1961, by which time internal autonomy had been conceded by the British, the party won 20 of the 35 seats in the Assembly and Jagan became Prime Minister.

Riots, strikes and disturbances in 1964—allegedly fomented by the US Central Intelligence Agency (CIA)—were followed by elections in December 1964 under the British-imposed proportional representation system. Despite receiving the largest vote, the PPP won only 24 seats out of 53, and the other two parties, the PNC and the United Force (now defunct) formed a coalition government. In protest, the PPP boycotted the Assembly for six months. The PPP also denounced the results of the 1968 elections as fraudulent. The PNC obtained a majority (30 seats to 19 for the PPP and four for the United Force), since when it has ruled alone.

The PPP openly identified with the world communist movement for the first time in 1969, when it participated in the Moscow conference of Communist parties. The PPP also claimed widespread fraud in the 1973 elections. It won 14 seats and boycotted the Assembly until 1976, during which time a rapprochement took place between the PNC and PPP, which offered to give critical support to the government. Negotiations broke down in 1977, however, when Burnham rejected the PPP's proposal for the formulation of a "national patriotic front government", and the PPP thereupon reached an alliance with the opposition Working People's Alliance (WPA).

The party boycotted the 1978 constitutional referendum and denounced the elections of 1980 and 1985, in which it obtained 10 and eight seats respectively in the Assembly, again amidst widespread allegations of ballot-rigging by the government.

During the 1980s, the PPP's line was inconsistent. In January 1986, the PPP joined the WPA, the Democratic Labour Party (DLM), the People's Democratic Movement (PDM) and the National Democratic Front (NDF) in forming the Patriotic Coalition for Democracy (PCD), which campaigned for free elections and representative democracy.

However , on other occasions it called for the establishment of a national government of the PNC, itself and the WPA, and held bilateral negotiations with the PNC.

As part of the PCD, the party continued to press for electoral reform but boycotted the November 1990 municipal elections. The PPP resigned its seats in the Assembly in April 1991 in protest at the government's decision to extend the life of the current parliamentary session, its failure to call elections and draw up a legitimate voters' list.

However, later the same month, in return for a government promise to consider the reform of the election commission, following persistent claims that it was an arm of the PNP, the PPP promised to respect electoral procedures.

The PPP, emerging as the favourite to win the elections, parted company with the WPA in October, who called for a caretaker government, including the PNC and the opposition parties. The PPP then also opposed a PDC decision to call for a boycott of the poll, set for Dec. 16, but subsequently postponed by the government.

In the aborted election campaign, Jagan, the PPP's presidential candidate, had stated that he was committed to the formation of a "broad based multiparty, multi-ethnic, multi-ideological government". Far from capitalizing on public opposition to the government's Economic Reform Programme (ERP), he also stated that a new government headed by him would not break off relations with the IMF but would seek modified terms. He also promised not take a "dogmatic" position on the privatization of state enterprises and to review taxes, with a view to lowering them in order to "mobilize capital to finance investment".

The PPP once more participated in the Assembly but objected to the PNC's decision to re-extend the parliamentary session, pending an election, to September 1992. Instead, it proposed a cut-off date for the session of May 31.

Structure. A triennial congress (representing local groups and district and regional committees) elects a central committee, which in turn elects the general secretary, executive committee and secretariat.

Publications. Mirror (pro-PPP weekly); *Thunder* (official theoretical quarterly); *Guyana Information Bulletin* (international monthly).

International affiliations. Prior to the collapse of the Soviet Union and the Eastern bloc countries, the party was recognized by Soviet-bloc countries and has contact with other communist and workers' parties.

The United Force (TUF)

Address. Unity House, 96 Robb and New Garden Streets, Bourda, Georgetown.

Leadership. Manzoor Nadir (l.).

Orientation. Right-wing, favouring industrialization and a mixed economy. The party has drawn its much of its support from the whites, Amerindians and other minority communities.

Founded. 1961.

History. The TUF is the main conservative party which in elections before independence from the United kingdom in 1966 and since then, only managed to win minor representation in the National Assembly. In 1964, following its best ever electoral performance of seven seats, it joined a coalition government with the People's National Congress (PNC) but ended this arrangement in 1968 when it opposed the enfranchisement of many emigrant Guyanese. It failed to contest the 1973 elections but later took up two seats awarded to its ally, the (now defunct) Liberator Party, a conservative opposition movement which had declined the seats because of alleged ballot-rigging.

In the 1980 and 1985 elections, the TUF won respectively 2.8 per cent and 3.4 per cent of the vote and each time won two seats. Like opposition parties to the left of it, it boycotted the National Assembly in 1991 in protest at the PNC's decision to extend its sessions and thus delay the general election.

Working People's Alliance (WPA)

Address. Walter Rodney House, 45 Croal St, Stabroek, Georgetown.

Leadership. Eusi Kwayana, Rupert Roopnaraine (co-leaders).

Orientation. An independent party with Marxist roots which advocates the restoration of democracy, free elections, the redistribution of income, land reform and the renegotiation of the foreign debt as steps towards "the building of genuine socialism on the basis of popular consent and the subsequent creation of a classless society". Unlike the PNC and PPP which draw their support mainly from the Afro-Caribbean and Indian communities, the WPA's leadership and membership are multiracial.

Founded. 1974.

History. The WPA, which originally consisted of an alliance between four left-wing organizations, was formed as a pressure group in 1974. It constituted itself into a political party in 1979, and appealed for the formation of an alliance of opposition parties to replace the PNC administration by a "government of national reconstruction and unity".

Three of its leaders were arrested and charged with arson, and in 1980 one of them, Walter Rodney, was murdered, the government being widely suspected of complicity. Rodney's writings had been one of the main inspirations of the black power and new left nationalist movements that had sprung up in the Caribbean in the late 1960s. The charges against the other two leaders were dismissed the following year.

The WPA boycotted the 1980 elections, after its demands for measures to ensure their fairness were ignored by the government, but contested the 1985 elections, in which it was officially credited with 1.3 per cent of the vote and won one seat. It was a founder member of the Patriotic Coalition for Democracy (PCD) in 1986, set up to demand free elections but became increasingly critical of the People's Progressive Party (PPP) negotiations with the government, which increasingly undermined the PCD's effectiveness.

The WPA joined with other parties in criticizing the PNP's delaying of the general election in 1991 and opposed the extension of the current session of the National Assembly (see PNP; PPP).

It accused the government of refusing to relinquish its control of the voter registration machinery and proposed the formation of a caretaker government, including the PNC and opposition parties, until such time as free and fair elections could be guaranteed.

This led to frictions within the PCD, the PPP opposing the move. The party subsequently announced that it would stand alone in the coming elections unless a "superior arrangement" with another group emerged. The WPA boycotted the recalled Assembly, which in December 1991 voted to prolong its session to September 1992.

Publications. Dayclean and *Open World*, weeklies.
International affiliations. Socialist International (consultative member).

Minor parties

Al Muja Hodeen; formerly the Guyana United Muslim Party, Hoosin Ghania (l.).

Eligha Religious and Political Movement (ERPM); Mohammed Baksh (l.).

Democratic Labour Movement (DLM, Alexander and Robb Streets, Georgetown); Paul Tennassee (l.); a left-of-centre party founded in April 1982 by the Right-to-Work Association - Front for Democratic Unionism (RWA-FDU) which helped form the Patriotic Coalition for Democracy (see PCD) in 1986.

Guyana Labour Party (GLP), founded January 1992, N.K. Gopaul (l.), former president of the National Association of Agricultural, Commercial and Industrial Employees (NAACIE); the party had its origins in the "civic list" movement championed by the Guyanese Action for Reform and Democracy (see Guard).

National Democratic Party (NDP, Wismar, Linden, Georgetown); Joseph Bacchus (l.); formerly known as the National Democratic Front (NDF), a centrist opposition party founded in 1985 to contest the general election in which it won, according to government figures, 156 votes (0.05 per cent). In 1986, it was a founder member of the Patriotic Coalition for Democracy (PCD).

National Republican Party (NRP, National Republican Office, 238 Almond St, Queenstown, Georgetown); Max Mohammed (l.).

People's Democratic Movement (PDM, Croal St, Stabroek, Georgetown); Llewelyn John (l).; a centrist opposition party formed in 1973 and revived in 1985 by John. It gained a negligible share of the 1985 vote (according to government figures) and joined the Patriotic Coalition for Democracy in 1986, from which it was expelled in May 1991 (see PCD).

United Republican Party, (Croal St, Stabroek, Georgetown); Leslie Ramsammy (l.); formed in January 1987 in exile (in the USA) by Robert Gangadeen, formerly active in The United Front (TUF) and subsequently closer to the Coalition for Democracy (see PCD).

United Workers Party (UWP, Wellington St, Georgetown); Winston V. Payne (l.).

Haiti

Capital: Port-au-Prince **Population: 5,800,000**

The Republic of Haiti was declared the world's first Black Republic in 1804, the colonial power, France, finally recognizing the country's independence in 1825 after the payment of a large indemnity. Periods of great instability characterized the early 20th century due to intense political rivalries, financial insolvency and peasant uprisings. The US, who first intervened militarily in 1915, effectively administered the country until 1934. From 1957 to 1986, the country was run by the Duvalier family who used a mixture of patronage and terror to maintain their power. A return to democracy was delayed by the interference of the military (1986-90), factions of which vied for power.

The emphatic victory for the radical Roman Catholic priest Fr Jean-Bertrand Aristide in the December 1990 presidential election promised a clean break with the past and political and economic reforms. Aristide, however, was overthrown in a military coup on Sept. 30, 1991 and was forced into exile. A provisional government was established under President Joseph Nerette, a Supreme Court judge, and Prime Minister Jean Jacques Honorat which failed to receive international recognition. Economic sanctions were also imposed against the country. New elections, required by the Constitution to be held by January 1992, failed to take place despite the regime's use of constitutional arguments to prove that Aristide was barred from returning to office on the grounds that a President was prevented from succeeding himself. The Organization of American States (OAS) in October 1991 initiated a diplomatic process aimed at restoring democracy and effecting Aristide's return to the country.

Constitutional structure

Under the terms of the most recent Constitution, approved in March 1987, a bicameral Congress is made up of a 27-member Senate and a National Assembly of at least 70 members. Executive power rests with the President who appoints a cabinet.

The February 1984 general legislative election was the first congressional election since 1979. All but one of the 309 candidates for the 59 seats in the National Assembly were members of President-for-Life Jean-Claude Duvalier's Party of National Unity. The only independent candidate had to seek sanctuary in a convent.

In October 1986, a Constituent Assembly was elected to produce a constitution for consideration by a referendum in March 1987. Some 101 candidates stood for election to 41 of the Assembly's 61 seats; the remaining seats were filled by government appointees. Less than 5 per cent of the electorateparticipated as groups across the political spectrum boycotted the election either because they wanted an immediate return to civilian government or because they felt that all of the seats should have been filled by elected members.

Sequence of elections since 1990

Presidential election, Dec. 16, 1990

	% of vote
Jean Bertrand Aristide (FNCD)	67.48
Marc Bazin (ANDP)	14.22
Louis Pain (PAIN)	4.88
Hubert de Roncerary (MDN)	3.34
Sylvio Claude (PDCH)	3.00
René Théodore (MRN)	1.83
Thomas Desulme (PNT)	1.67
Volvick Remy Joseph (MKN)	1.30
Francois Latortue(MODEL/PRDH)	0.92
Vladimir Jeanty (PARADIS)	0.75
Fritz Simmons	0.62

National Assembly election, Dec. 16, 1990

	Senators	*Deputies*
National Front for Change and Democracy (FNCD)	13	27
National Alliance for Democracy and Progress (ANDP)	6	17
National Agricultural Industrial Party (PAIN)	2	6
Haitian Christian Democratic Party(PDCH)	1	7
Rally of Progressive National Democrats (RNDP)*	1	6
Movement for National Development (MDN)	-	5
National Party of Work (PNT)	1	3
Movement for National Reconstruction (MRN)	2	1
Movement for the Liberation of Haiti/Revolutionary Party of Haiti	2	
National Co-operative Movement (MKN)	-	2
Independents	-	5
Total	**27**	**81****

*The party of Leslie Manigat

**Two Deputy contests remained to be held.

The November 1987 presidential elections, marked by widespread intimidation against parties and candidates of the centre and left, and against members of the Electoral Council, were disrupted by violence by right-wing groups and the army and finally abandoned. The Electoral Council was dissolved and fresh elections were held in January 1988. These were boycotted by many candidates and parties and the ten candidates that did take part were all conservative and some with Duvalierist links. Leslie Manigat of the National Progressive Democratic Rally (RDPN) was judged the winner though massive fraud took place despite the low turnout of 5-10 per cent. Manigat was overthrown in a military coup in June 1988 led by Gen. Henri Namphy who was himself ousted in a counter-coup by another Duvalierist, Lt.-Gen. Prosper Avril. Avril survived two coup attempts before being forced to step down in March 1990 after sustained widespread protests and the pressure concentrated against him by a Unity Assembly, a body formed by the half dozen main political parties supported by some minor parties. Avril was replaced by an interim government headed by Supreme Court judge Ertha Pascal-Trouillot pending presidential elections, finally held in December. These were won by the electoral alliance, the National Front for Change and Democracy (FNCD) whose candidate Jean Bertrand Aristide won almost 67 per cent of the vote. Aristide's overthrow in the September 1991 coup left the country under provisional government without international acceptance.

In late 1991 and early 1992 the Congress had ceased to operate like a normal Chamber, genuine opposition politicians being thwarted by military intimidation and threats by Duvalierist gunmen.

Electoral system

The President is elected for a five-year term by an absolute majority by universal suffrage. If no candidate obtains an absolute majority, there is a run-off election between the two leading contenders. The Senate is elected for a six-year term and the National Assembly for four years.

Evolution of the suffrage

All adults over 18 years of age are allowed to vote; direct elections were not introduced until 1950, when the vote was also given to women.

PARTY BY PARTY DATA

Democratic Unity Confederation

Confédération d'Unité Démocratique (KID)
Leader. Evans Paul (l.).
Orientation. Centre-left.
Founded. 1986.
History. Paul was arrested and severely ill-treated along with three other opposition figures for allegedly plotting to kill Gen. Prosper Avril and was released in a February 1990 general amnesty following widespread protests.

He was briefly leader of the National Front for Change and Democracy (FNCD) in 1990, being replaced by Jean Bertrand Aristide, the future president deposed in the September 1991 military coup. Following the September 1991 military coup Paul, the mayor of Port-au-Prince, distinguished himself by his forthright opposition to the military and his attempt, at great personal risk to his person, to contact Aristide in exile.

Haitian Christian Populist Party

Parti Démocrate Chrétien Haitien (PDCH)
Leadership. Sylvio Claude (l.).
Orientation. Christian democratic, populist and centrist.
Founded. July 1979.

History. The founder, Claude, was harassed and endured spells of imprisonment during the Duvalier years but undeterred ran for the presidency in the November 1987 presidential election, aborted by violence of the military and Duvalierist *Tontons Macoutes* terror gang. Claude won 3 per cent of the vote in the December 1990 Presidential elections and subsequently tailed conservative opposition to Aristide's style of government and did not protest his overthrow in the September 1991 military coup.

Movement for the Installation of Democracy

Mouvement pour l'Instauration de la Démocratie en Haiti (MIDH)
Address. Port-au-Prince.
*Leadership.*Marc Bazin.
Orientation. Conservative and pro-Western and claimed to be in favour of moves by non-communist parties to secure a lasting democracy. However it did not denounce the September 1991 military coup that overthrew the democratically elected Aristide government. It subsequently backed the interim government.
Founded. 1986.
History. Bazin, a former World Bank official who had briefly served in 1982 as finance minister in a Duvalier cabinet, was from early 1987 regarded as the favoured presidential candidate of the US administration. In June of that year the MCDH joined with the National Progressive Party (RDPN), the National Agricultural and Industrial Party (PAIN) and the Popular National Party (PNP) in a coalition to oppose the new electoral law and demanded a stronger role for the Independent Electoral Council (CIE).

After the violent disruption of the November 1987 elections, the MIDH supported the early-December general strike, condemned army and Duvalierist violence and demanded the re-instatement of the CIE, dissolved on polling day, and the holding of fresh elections. It boycotted the January 1988 elections which it regarded as fraudulent. Already tainted by his past links to the Duvalierist regime and his reported current connections with Duvalierists, Bazin, along with Serge Gilles of the Revolutionary Progressive Nationalist Party (PANPRA) and Hubert de Ronceray of the National Democrats Movement (MDN) in July 1990 attacked as "adventurist" an effective ultimatum for the interim President Ertha Pascal-Trouillot to arrest Roger Lafontant, the ex-leader of the Duvalier's *Tontons Macoutes* secret police, and Gen. Williams Regala, a prominent supporter of the November 1987 coup, both of whom had recently returned from exile.

In 1989 MIDH joined with PANPRA to form the National Alliance for Democracy and Progress (ANDP) but its first rallies in September 1990 in the lead up to the December 1990 general election failed to attract popular support (see ANDP). Like other conservative politicians soundly defeated by Aristide, Bazin opposed the new government, claiming that Aristide had exceeded his powers by failing to consult with parliament. He did not publicly oppose the September 1991 military coup and was subsequently involved in manoeuvres aimed at guaranteeing a conservative presence in any future government. He was known to have formed a close alliance with René Théodore, leader of the Unified Party of Haitian Communists (PUCH) who, similarly, had been a bitter opponent of Aristide. In December 1991, with US backing, pro-regime politicians proposed that either Bazin or Théodore be appointed as the new Prime Minister with special powers as the price for Aristide's restoration to the presidency (see PUCH).

Rejected by his parliamentary colleagues, Bazin announced in January 1992 that he would not accept Théodore as Prime Minister unless Aristide, Théodore and Senate President Déjean Bélizaire accepted six "fundamental" conditions. These included the lifting of the OAS's economic embargo, a general amnesty and the retention in their posts of all armed forces personnel. In June, Bazin was elected as Prime Minister of the provisional government, despite the opposition of the USA and the organization of the American States (OAS).

National Alliance for Democracy and Progress

Alliance Nationale pour la Démocratie et le Progrès (ANDP)
Leadership. Marc Bazin, Serge Gilles (ls.).
Orientation. Conservative.
Founded. September 1990.
History. The ANDP was formed by an alliance of Bazin's Movement for the Installation of Democracy in Haiti (MIDH) and Gilles's Revolutionary Progressive National Party (PANPRA) to contest the December 1990 presidential and legislative elections. Bazin was a well-beaten second in the presidential race, with 15 per cent of the vote, but the ANDP gained a significant presence in the National Assembly, winning 16 seats. Following the overthrow of the Aristide government in September 1991 coup, the ANDP came out in support of the interim regime of Nerette and Honorat.

National Agricultural and Industrial Party

Parti Agricole et Industriel National (PAIN)
Leadership. Louis Déjoie (l.).
Orientation. Conservative.
Founded. 1986.
History. The PAIN was formed as the personal vehicle of Déjoie, the son of the candidate who lost the last comparatively free election in 1957 to the dictator, François ("Papa Doc") Duvalier. Following the February 1986 flight into exile of Jean Claude "Baby Doc" Duvalier, the PAIN emerged to campaign for free and open elections, violently denied in November 1987 by the army and the Duvalierist *Tontons Macoutes* who disrupted the poll. The PAIN called for the resignation of the subsequent military government and Déjoie was amongst other party leaders who in December called for a 48-hour general strike to further their demands for fresh elections.

The PAIN was one of four parties constituting the main opposition to Mirlande Manigat, leader of the National Progressive Democratic Party (RDPN) which served as an instrument for the military in the hastily reconvened elections of January 1988.

In the same month, Déjoie was briefly detained on returning from a foreign tour in the course of which he had appealed for outside intervention to restore democratic government. The PAIN, in tune with minor left-wing parties who were to compose part of the National Front for Change and Democracy (FNCD), warned outside monitoring agencies in August 1990, that a general election, then scheduled for November, should be delayed. In the presidential election held in December, Déjoie received 5 per cent of the vote.

National Committee of the Congress of Democratic Movements

Comité National du Congrés des Movements Démocratiques (Konakom)
Leadership. Victor Benoit (l.).
Orientation. Centre-left, a member of the National Front for Change and Democracy (FNCD).
Founded. January 1987.
History. Although officially becoming a party in 1989, Konakom originated in the amalgamation of an estimated 300 grassroots organizations who, at a founding congress in January 1987, called for broad political and economic reforms, including the demand for the recognition of creole and voodoo as part of the national language. Konakom played a key role in the *Group of 57* coalition who organized anti-government protests in mid-1987 and whose energy was channelled into supporting the presidential candidacy of Gérard Gourgue, the human rights leader, of the recently formed leftist National Co-operation Front (FNC) in the aborted elections of November 1987.

Benoit was briefly leader of the FNCD on its founding in June 1990 but was replaced by Evans Paul, the leader of the Democratic Unity Confederation (KID) who in turn gave way to future President Jean Bertrand Aristide. Following the military coup of September 1991, Benoit was one of the deposed Aristide's preferred choices to be the new Prime Minister as part of the Organization of American States (OAS) diplomatic effort to restore democracy.

National Democrats Movement

Mouvement des Démocrates Nationaux (MDN)
Leadership Hubert de Ronceray (l.).
Orientation. Centre-Right.
Founded. 1986.
History. In spite of holding ministerial and ambassadorial posts in the Duvalierist regime in 1971-81, de Ronceray later claimed that he had repudiated Duvalierism. Enduring a period of house arrest in May-September 1984, he formed the MDN and announced his candidature for the presidency within weeks of the fall of Jean-Claude "Baby Doc" Duvalier in February 1986. However, unlike the bulk of the opposition, the party involved itself in the January 1988 general elections stage-managed by the military and was adjudged to have come second to the equally collaborationist National Progressive Democratic Rally (RDPN).

De Ronceray, however, became one of the most outspoken critics of the dictatorship of Gen. Prosper Avril and was deported to the USA in 1990 and several prominent members of MDN were arrested.

However on his return, the MDN was one of several conservative leaders in the 12-party Unity Assembly who opposed the ultimatum of interim President Ertha Pascal-Trouillot for the arrest of leading Duvalierists, including Roger Lafontant, the leader of the *Tontons Macoutes*, the Duvaliers' much feared and hated private army.

Along with other conservative parties who performed poorly in the December 1990 presidential and legislative elections, the MDN condoned the military coup of September 1991 and supported the interim government of Nerette and Honorat.

National Front for Change and Democracy

Front National pour le Changement et la Démocratie (FNCD)

Leadership. Jean Bertrand Aristide (l.); Evans Paul (l.).

Orientation. A progressive, left- of-centre movement pledged to eradicate electoral fraud and official corruption, to limit the role of the army and to initiate a programme of social and economic reform. Previously, through Aristide in particular, it denounced the US government, the capitalist values it represented and its interference in Haiti's internal affairs. Once in office, however, a conciliatory stance was adopted to the US and international lending agencies.

Founded. June 1990.

History. Aristide, a member of the Salesian order and already known locally as a "liberationist" priest campaigning on behalf of the poor in the La Saline slum district of Port-au-Prince, came to international attention when in November 1987, he registered his candidacy, along with those of 25 others, for the presidency. The Duvalierist terror gang, the *Tontons Macoutes* disrupted the elections and in the process gutted Aristide's church and murdered 17 of his parishioners, seriously wounding 70 others. Rather than deter him, the massacre strengthened Aristide's resolve to oppose the Duvalierist controlled provisional government and the military. His continued outspokenness and high profile set him at odds with the leaders of his religious order, who encouraged by the conservative papal nuncio Paolo Romero, expelled him from the Salesians in late 1988 when he refused to obey an order to remain silent. The Haitian Roman Catholic hierarchy also suspended him from celebrating the sacraments.

The FNCD was founded on June 19, 1990, by a loose coalition of peasants, trade unionists and radical clerics and the Democratic Unity Confederation (KID) and National Committee of the Congress of Democratic Movements (Konakom) parties, but excluding the Unified Party of Haitian Communists (PUCH).

Aristide replaced Evans Paul of the KID as FNCD leader in October but remained opposed to the imminent presidential and legislative elections, arguing that the conditions did not exist for these to be free and fair. Such reservations receded as the UN and international observers promised to closely monitor the poll. Aristide won an emphatic victory, with 67 per cent of the vote, and was sworn in as President in February 1991. The FNCD however, in the legislative elections held in December 1990 and January 1991 failed to gain a majority in the Congress. This situation continued until August when the parties in the Congress split into four blocs, of which the FNCD, with 31 of the 81 seats, controlled the largest.

The US administration in particular, however, had endorsed the election result and this fact, coupled with the promise of resumed US economic aid, offered the Aristide government a degree of security from its opponents in the army and the congress. The army crushed an attempted coup attempt by the Duvalierist leader Roger Lafontant on Jan. 7, 1991, and the Congress offered the government leave to introduce a six-month economic emergency programme. This was sober and austere enough to win the support of the World Bank consultative group of aid donors in July. As part of a cost-cutting exercise, 5,000 of the 40,000 government employees had already been dismissed. The Congress, however, blocked Aristide's attempts to reform the judiciary, rejecting his nomination of five new supreme court judges.

Aristide's increasing reliance on a close group of advisors, known as the *Lavalas*, and his use of populist rhetoric emphasizing the urgent need for the redistribution of wealth from the rich minority to the poor, caused deep resentment among opposition parties in the Congress and unease among members of the FNCD. The temporary detention in April 1991 of the previous interim Prime Minister Ertha Pascal-Trouillot was also strongly criticized by the US, who also voiced unease about the Aristide style of government. An attempt by Congress to force the resignation of Prime Minister René Préval on Aug. 13 precipitated a violent demonstration of thousands of Aristide supporters outside the congress building. Préval was singled out for the government's poor economic performance and alleged lack of coherent perspectives after six months in office.

The Army, where profiteering and corruption was endemic, especially in its involvement in drug-trafficking, stood to lose from any government reforms to its structure. On the pretext that the government had adopted an autocratic style, had flouted the constitution and was inciting mob violence, it staged a successful military coup on Set. 30, led by Lt.-Gen Raoul Cédras, an Aristide appointee. Aristide himself barely escaped into exile in Venezuela and most of his cabinet sought sanctuary in foreign embassies. In successive sweeps by the army and members of the

Duvalierist *Tontons Macoutes*, an estimated 2,000 government supporters were killed.

In subsequent months, Aristide succeeded in attracting the support of the UN and its member governments for his peaceful return to power, a diplomatic task entrusted to a team representing the Organization of American States (OAS). By February 1992, the OAS had finally brokered an agreement between Aristide and the leaders of the Haitian Congress in Washington DC for the appointment of a compromise Prime Minster. This was René Théodore of the Unified Party of Haitian Communists (PUCH), a bitter critic of Aristide, who was given powers on a par with those of the President, including the right to negotiate jointly, with Aristide, the lifting of the current OAS economic embargo and other sanctions and the precise terms for the latter's return. In addition Théodore was jointly to appoint the Cabinet, have regularly policy meetings with Aristide whom in turn pledged himself to improve the moral and material conditions of the army and pay special attention to its professionalization. This was interpreted as meaning that he had finally agreed not to demand the removal from his post of coup leader, Lt.-Gen. Raoul Cédras. In late March, however, Aristide's continued insistence that Cédras be dismissed threatened his return to power, as had the refusal of the Congress on March 18 to endorse the February Washington DC agreement. The election of Marc Bazin of the Movement for the Institution of Democracy (MIDH) as the Prime Minister of the provisional government made the likelihood of Aristide's early return even more remote.

National Patriotic Movement

Mouvement National Patriotique (MNP)
Leadership. Déjean Bélizaire (l.).
Orientation. Centre-right.
History Blizaire, the President of the Senate, has been involved in negotiations with the OAS on Aristide's possible return to power.

Revolutionary Progressive Nationalist Party

Parti Nationaliste Progressiste Révolutionnaire (PANPRA)
Leadership. Serge Gilles (l.).
Orientation. Social democratic.
Founded. 1986.
History. Gilles had adopted a conciliatory approach to the military regime of Gen. Prosper Avril, despite being personally attacked by Duvalierist gunmen in January 1990 and then arrested. In 1989, he joined with Marc Bazin, leader of the conservative Movement for the Installation of Democracy in Haiti (MIDH) to form the ANDP which came a poor second in the December presidential election, with 15 per cent of the vote, but fared better in the legislative elections, coming a close second to the FNDC with 16 seats. The well respected PANPRA deputy Dully Brutus, a known supporter of the French Socialist Party who was elected President of the Chamber of Deputies in August 1991, was, following the September military coup, part of the congressional team which met with the Organization of American States (OAS) negotiators to lay the groundwork for Aristide's eventual return to power. This included the lifting of economic sanctions and the appointment of a new Prime Minister. Brutus, who was Aristide's preferred choice for the post, reportedly withdrew after US pressure; and the nomination then went to René Théodore, leader of the Unified Party of Haitian Communists (PUCH).
International Affiliation. Socialist International (consultative member party).

Unified Party of Haitian Communists

Parti Unifié des Communistes Haitiens (PUCH)
Leadership. René Théodore (s.-g.).
Orientation. Pro-Soviet before the collapse of the Eastern bloc and opposed to foreign, especially US, influence. Domestically, it has operated as a conservative force opposed to the progressive policies of Aristide.
Founded. November 1968.
History. Tracing its origins to the Communist Party founded by Max Hudicourt in 1930, the PUCH was the product of the 1968 merger of the People's National Party and the Popular Unity Party. It operated underground and in exile until the overthrow of the Duvalier regime in 1986.

Over the next few years, the party maintained a low profile as it organized cells in urban neighbourhoods and among industrial workers. During 1987 it was accused of infiltrating and taking control of opposition demonstrations organized by other groups. The Party fielded Théodore as its presidential candidate in the suspended election of November 1987 and boycotted the controlled elections of January 1988. After Gen. Avril's coup in November 1988, the PUCH became less critical of the military; Théodore met Avril and later expressed optimism about the country's future under the new military government, a view denounced by the main labour federation, the left-wing *Centrale Autonome des Travailleurs Haítiens*.

In the December 1990 presidential election Théodore polled only 2 per cent of the vote and seemed to be marginalized from mainstream events, although he remained a bitter critic of Aristide and his style of government.

However, as leader of the self-styled National Reconciliation Movement (MRN) Théodore returned to centre stage following the September 1991 military coup which he failed to denounce. Although nominally supporting the regime of Nerette and Honorat, he formed a close alliance with Marc Bazin, the right-wing leader of the Movement for the Installation of Democracy in Haiti (MIDH) in seizing the political initiative and formulated to the US and the Organization of American States (OAS) conservative conditions for Aristide's return to office. In January and February 1992, conservative parliamentarians, along with sections of the military leadership, provisionally accepted Théodore as a compromise Prime Minister with increased powers in a new Aristide administration. In March, however, after conservative politicians had boycotted a vote on Aristide's resumption of the presidency, Théodore still insisted that he would form a government of national consensus.

Structure. The party congress elects the Central Committee, which in turn elects the Political Bureau.

Membership. 350 (1989 estimate).

Publications. Boukan, published sporadically.

Honduras

Capital: Tegucigalpa **Population: 4,370,000**

The Republic of Honduras gained its independence from Spain in 1821. The country was ruled by the conservative National Party (PNH) from 1933 to 1957, a period which marked the political ascendancy of the army which used the party as a vehicle to legitimize its hold on power. A series of military coups, however, in 1956, 1963 and 1972, were needed to ensure this control was maintained. In an interlude of civilian government, a series of moderate social and political reforms were introduced by the Liberal Party (PLH), in office from 1957 to 1963, which included a programme of land reform and the establishment of the state social security system. The military ruled from 1963 to 1980, except for a short period under PNH government in 1971-72, before the PLH was returned to power in 1980. Even then, the military still wielded great influence. The PLH won the presidential election of 1985 but lost power to the PNH in November 1989.

Constitutional structure

Under the 1982 Constitution, there is a 130-member unicameral National Assembly. Executive power rests with the President.

Electoral system

The President is in theory elected for a four-year term by a simple majority of votes, although at the presidential and legislative elections on Nov. 24, 1985, the PLH candidate, who had received the most votes, was appointed President. The National Assembly is appointed on the basis of proportional representation.

Evolution of the suffrage

Men and women over 18 are eligible to vote and registration and voting are compulsory until the age of 60.

Sequence of elections since 1981

Presidential and Legislative

Date	*Winning party*
November 1981	Liberal Party (PLH)
November 1985	Liberal Party (PLH)
November 1989	National Party (PN)

Presidential elections, November 1989

	% of vote
Rafael Leonardo Callejas (PN)	50.97
Carlos Flores Facusse(PLH)	43.18
Enrique Aguilar (Innovation and Unity Party—PINU)	1.89
Efraín Díaz (Christian Democratic Party—PDC)	1.42
Others	2.5
Total	**100.00**

PARTY BY PARTY DATA

Christian Democratic Party

Partido Demócrata Cristiano (PDC)

Address. Colonia San Carlos 2, Avenida 204, Tegucigalpa, MDC.

Leadership. Rubén Palma Carrasco (pres.); Benjamin Santos (vice pres.).

Orientation. Christian democratic, with progressive and conservative wings.

Founded. 1980

History. The party performed poorly in presidential and legislative elections in 1981 and 1985, receiving less than 2 per cent in the presidential race and no more than two seats in the Congress.

In July 1986, the Party joined the Innovation and Unity Party (PINU), the Honduran Patriotic Front (FPH) and the Revolutionary Democratic Liberal Movement (MLDR or M-*lider*—see Liberal Party of Honduras) faction of the ruling PLH in an opposition coalition concerned particularly with promoting the neutrality of the country in the region's conflicts. In October 1986, Palma replaced the more conservative Efraín Diáz Arrivillaga as party president and this more moderate stance led the party in September 1990 to urge the PNH government to modify its IMF-approved economic austerity plan in order to avoid "confrontation between the public and the dominant class". A PDC member, Juan Ramón Martínez, was appointed to the Cabinet as Head of the National Agrarian Institute (INA), an agency in charge of agrarian reform.

Innovation and Unity Party

Partido de Inovación y Unidad (PINU)

Address. Apartado Postal No. 105, 2a Avenida Calle Real No. 912, Frente a Hiasa, Camayaguela, MDC.

Leadership. Enrique Aguilar Cerrato (pres.).

Orientation. Since 1986 has claimed to be social democratic and to have links with the German SPD.

Founded. 1970.

History. The party, whose support comes mainly from professionals and some rural workers' groups, was not afforded legal recognition until 1978. In 1981 it secured only 2.5 per cent of the vote and three of the 82 seats in the National Assembly, one of which was won by Julín Méndez, the first campesino (peasant) leader ever to sit in the legislature. Despite an enlarged Assembly, the party's number of seats fell to two in the 1985 general election and Aguliar gained only 1.6 per cent of the vote in the presidential race.

Liberal Party of Honduras

Partido Liberal de Honduras (PLH)

Address. Atrás Supermercado La Colonia, Colon Miramontes, Tegucigalpa, MDC.

Leadership. Carlos Roberto Flores Facussé (pres.).

Orientation. Split between conservative and more progressive wings both of which have been conservative in office.

Founded. 1890.

History. The oldest active party, the PLH has since 1970 been in effect a coalition of disparate tendencies, each with its own leadership and structure, overlaying the traditional divide between the conservative rural and the more reformist urban wings of the party. The party held power in 1929-33 and then in 1957-63 before being deposed by the military, an experience which did not prevent it in 1980 from being the main force in an interim government under the then military President Gen. Policarpo Paz Garcia. The party then won the subsequent November 1981 general election, winning an absolute majority in the National Assembly. Its leader since 1979, Roberto Suazo Córdova, a pro-USA right-winger and head of the conservative *rodista* faction of the party, was installed as President in January 1982, formally ending 18 years of almost uninterrupted military rule, although the armed forces retained extensive legal and de facto powers.

In January 1983 the PLH almost lost its legislative majority when Suazo Córdova's *rodistas* clashed with the Popular Liberal Alliance (ALIPO) faction of the party, led by the brothers Carlos Roberto and Jorge Arturo Reina, who were subsequently driven out and in February 1984 established the Revolutionary Democratic Liberal Movement (MLDR or M-*lider*). The *rodistas* in turn split in 1985, with competing factions backing Oscar Mejía Arellano and José Azcona Hoyo for the presidency. Azcona had resigned from Suazo Córdova's government in 1983 and subsequently accused the regime of corruption. Azcona won the presidency in alliance with ALIPO and after having agreed a power-sharing National Unity Pact (PUN) with the National Party (PNH) (the second since 1971), giving the PNH two cabinet posts and control of the supreme court and other important political and administrative posts.

While Azcona's government was pre-occupied with issues arising from the Nicaraguan conflict, not least the presence in the country of some 20,000 US-backed right-wing *contra* rebels, the battle for the PLH presidential election ensued, eventually won in December 1988 by Flores Facussé, a former minister in the Suazo Córdova government, who had forged a surprise alliance with the dissident M-*lider* movement. Flores Facussé, however, lost the 1989 presidential election but the party received two posts in the new PNH cabinet.

Structure. Party congresses elect the central committee.

Publications. The major newspapers *El Tiempo* and *La Tribuna* support respectively the social democratic and conservative factions of the party.

International affiliation. Liberal International (full member from 1986).

National Party of Honduras

Partido Nacional de Honduras (PNH)

Address. Case del Partido, Paseo El Obelisco, Camayaguela DC.

Leadership. Celín Díscua (pres.).

Orientation. A traditionally conservative party, now promoting neo-liberal economic measures.

Founded. 1923.

History. Traditionally the party of large landowners, the party has also been closely identified with the military. It held power from 1933 to 1957, including the dictatorship of Gen. Tiburcio Carías Andino (1939-49) and in 1971-72 and 1985-1987 when it participated with the PLH in short-lived National Unity (PUN) governments.

The PNH, like the PLH, is the product of various factions, including the Movement for Nationalist Democratization (MDN), the Movement for Unity and Change (MUC) and the Nationalist Labour Tendency (TNL). The ruling PLH government (1981-85) encouraged PNH in-fighting by using the then PLH dominated Supreme Court and the National Electoral Tribunal (TEN) to support the pro-government MUC in its claim to control the party. This decision was reversed by the military in 1985 when it supported the accession of the newly-created MONARCA faction led by Rafael Leonardo Callejas. The MONARCA won all 63 of the PNH's 134 seats in the 1985 general election and as part of the subsequent PUN government, where it controlled the Foreign and Labour ministry portfolios, forced the PLH to give it control of the Supreme Court, the TEN and an important role in the administration of the Legislature.

Callejas was the party's unopposed candidate in the 1989 presidential elections, which he won comfortably. On taking office, the government restored relations with the IMF and other creditors and implemented a package of IMF-approved neo-liberal economic measures which included the wholesale dismissal of thousands of public sector workers (many of whom were PLH supporters), the privatization of state-owned agencies, the abolition of price controls on basic essentials and the devaluation of the currency. The measures caused continuous and widespread social unrest throughout 1990-91 despite Calleja's periodic promises to increase social sector spending. Anti-government protest was increasingly repressed by the security forces and the armed forces leading to international protests at the high level of systematic human rights abuses.

International Affiliation. International Democrat Union (full member).

Minor parties

Communist Party of Honduras *(Partido Comunista de Honduras—PCH);* Rigoberto Padilla Rush (l.), returned from exile in January 1991; founded in 1927 and pro-Soviet before the collapse of the Eastern bloc. The PCH, together with the Communist Party of Honduras-Marxist-Leninist (PCH-ML) and the Socialist Action Party of Honduras (PASOH), founded the Honduran Patriotic Front (FPH) electoral alliance in 1981. This was constantly harassed and failed to win any seats. The PCH played a leading role in the United National Directorate (DNU).

Federation of the Xicaques Tribes of Yoro (FETRIXY); Dionisio Martínez Pérez and Rutilio Alberto Matute (ls.); an indigenist group, founded in 1987 and active in the Yoro region of Northern Honduras, to demand justice and land reform. Its internationally known agrarian reform leader Vincente Matute Cruz was murdered on Sept. 30, 1991, by gunmen known to be working for large landowners, the ninth FETRIXY leader to be assassinated.

Patriotic Renewal Party (Renovación Patriótica); formed by a number of left-wing politicians and labour leaders in March 1991; co-ordinating committee includes Communist Party of Honduras central committee member Pedro Brizuela. Based in the northern city of San Pedro de Sula, the party announced that its aim was to offer a "progressive alternative" to the neoliberal economic model "imposed" by the PNH and PLH in the forthcoming general election in 1993.

Major Guerrilla Groups

Unified National Directorate *(Dirección Nacional Unificada*—DNU); formed in 1983 as an umbrella organization in an attempt to co-ordinate the efforts of the militant left to form a single army under one command to conduct a guerrilla war and to "play an active part in the event of a regionalization of the Central America crisis". Founding members included the Communist Party of Honduras, the Social Action Party of Honduras, the Central American Workers' Revolutionary Party (PRTC, founded 1975), Wilfredo Gallardo Museli (l.), the Lorenzo Zelaya Popular Revolutionary Forces (FPR-LZ, founded by students at the National Autonomous University in 1980-81); the Revolutionary Unity Movement (MUR), the Cinchonero Popular Liberation Movement (MPL Cinchoneros, founded 1981), the Morazanista Front for the Liberation of Honduras (FMLH, founded in 1979). All members of the DNU took advantage of a general amnesty approved by the National Assembly in June 1991, although some rebels made it known that they intended to continue fighting. Four leaders of the Chinchoneros had announced their willingness to lay down arms in May 1991 and the FPR-LZ was the last group to disarm in October 1991.

United Popular Alliance *(Alianza Popular Unida)*; right-wing, Matias Funes (l.); thought to be behind the murder of at least two trade union leaders.

Jamaica

Capital: Kingston **Population: 2,396,000**

The former British colony of Jamaica became an independent state within the Commonwealth in 1962. Since independence Jamaica's allegiance has swung between the conservative Jamaica Labour Party (JLP) (1962-72 and 1980-89) and the social democratic People's National Party (PNP) (1972-80) although their policies were almost indistinguishable. In 1989 Michael Manley announced his commitment of the PNP to a more moderate set of policies in the 1990s.

Constitutional structure

According to the 1962 Constitution, the Head of State of Jamaica is the British monarch, represented by a Governor-General. He acts in almost all matters on the advice of the Cabinet. A six-member Privy Council advises the Governor-General on the exercise of the Royal Prerogative of Mercy and on appeals on disciplinary matters from the three Service Commissions. Executive power lies with the Prime Minister and the cabinet, of which he is a member. The Cabinet consists of not fewer than 12 ministers, not more than four of whom may sit in the Senate. The Prime Minister and Cabinet are responsible to a bi-cameral Parliament in which legislative power is vested. The Senate consists of 21 senators, 13 of whom are appointed by the Governor-General on the advice of the Prime Minister and eight on the advice of the Leader of the Opposition. The House of Representatives consists of 60 elected members of Parliament.

Electoral system

The 60 members of the House of Representatives are elected for a five-year term by universal suffrage, by simple majority in single-member constituencies. The Prime Minister, who is appointed by the Governor-General, is the leader of the majority party in the House.

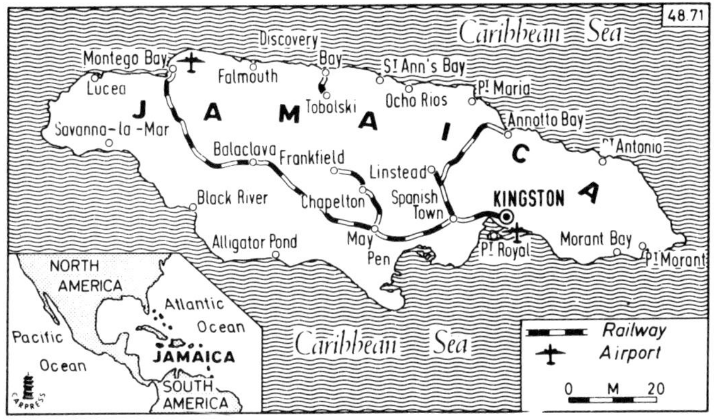
48.71
Caribbean Sea
Discovery Bay
Montego Bay
Lucea
Falmouth
St Ann's Bay
Pt Maria
Ocho Rios
Tobolski
J A M A I C A
Savanna-la-Mar
Annotto Bay
Pt Antonio
Balaclava
Frankfield
Linstead
Black River
Chapelton
Spanish Town
KINGSTON
Alligator Pond
May Pen
Pt Royal
Morant Bay
Pt Morant
NORTH AMERICA
Atlantic Ocean
Pacific Ocean
JAMAICA
SOUTH AMERICA
Caribbean Sea
Railway
Airport
0 M 20

Sequence of elections since 1980

Date	*Winning party*
Oct.ober 1980	Jamaica Labour Party (JLP)
Dec. 13, 1983	Jamaica Labour Party (JLP)
Feb. 9, 1989	People's National Party (PNP)

General Election Feb. 9, 1989

Party	*% of votes*	*Seats in House*
People's National Party (PNP)	55.8	45
Jamaica Labour Party (JLP)	44.1	15
Others	0.1	-
Total	**100.0**	**60**

PARTY BY PARTY DATA

Jamaica Labour Party (JLP)

Address. 20 Belmont Road, Kingston 5.
Leadership. Edward P. G. Seaga (l.); Peter Phillips (s.-g.).
Orientation. A conservative party which claims to be centrist, democratic and progressive, the JLP favours co-operation between capital and labour, privatization and foreign investment. It also favours republican status for Jamaica and non-alignment internationally, although it has always been pro-Western. It has traditionally been strong in rural areas.
Founded. July 1943.
History. The JLP was created by Alexander Bustamente as a conservative force to complement his right-wing Bustamente Industrial Trade Union (BITU), formed in 1938 and then allied to the People's National Party (PNP). BITU's opposition to the left in the PNP won the support of business interests.

The party won the 1944 legislative elections on the slogan "self government means slavery", winning 22 of the 32 seats, and narrowly retained power in 1949, only to lose it in elections in 1955 and 1959.

By 1962 it had reversed its position on sovereignty, leading the country out of the West Indies Federation to independence on the eve of the 1962 election in which it took 50 per cent of the vote and won by 26 seats to the 19 for the PNP. Bustamente was sworn in as the country's first Prime Minister and despite ill health and the devolvement of responsibility to an acting Prime Minister, saw the party returned to power in 1967 with 33 MPs out of 53. Hugh Shearer, the *de facto* head of the BITU, led the party from 1957 on Bustamente's retirement as leader.

In 1972 and 1976 the party won only 43 per cent of the vote and its share of seats in the legislature fell to 16 (out of 52) and then to 13 (out of 60), despite Shearer being replaced by the current leader Edward Seaga in 1974. Its dramatic recovery in 1980, when the JLP won 58.9 per cent of the vote and increased its representation to 51 MPs, was put down to strong US support and, according to the PNP and neutral observers, the effects of covert US destabilization methods. Seaga was named Prime Minister and in 1983 authorized the participation of Jamaica in the US invasion of Grenada. The PNP boycotted the general election, called two years early in December 1983, and the JLP claimed all 60 seats in the legislature.

In July 1986, the party was heavily defeated by the PNP in local elections owing to widespread discontent with the implementation of IMF-approved austerity policies at a time when the economy was seriously contracting and the cost of living rising.

In October-November, Seaga repeatedly threatened to resign as Prime Minister and party leader to silence intra-party opposition, especially to his autocratic style of government. During 1987, several prominent JLP members left the party. Seaga's successful appeal for international aid in the aftermath of the devastation wreaked by hurricane Gilbert in September 1988 restored some of his credibility only for this to be lost owing to allegations that relief had been preferentially channelled to JLP supporters. A serious rise in drug-related crime and violence from 1987 onwards, also seriously damaged the JLP's image as the party of law and order.

The party was heavily defeated in the February 1990 general election, winning only 44.1 per cent of the vote and 15 seats. It initially supported the policies of the new PNP government which continued the JLP's economic structural adjustment programme but began to capitalize on the growing public and private sector opposition, in particular to the abolition of foreign exchange controls and to the introduction of a new consumption tax in September 1991.

The JLP's active involvement in anti-government protests improved the party's standing in the polls, but Seaga refused to allow a candidate to stand in a mid-September by-election, causing a large degree of resentment in some quarters of the party. A rift in the leadership, which had first appeared between Seaga and a "Gang of Five" in June 1990, appeared to have been healed at the party's annual convention in July 1991. However, the "Gang of Five" were absent from a major anti-government demonstration in October which Seaga addressed and which one of them, Karl Samuda, had publicly opposed.
Structure. Party conventions, held irregularly, elect an executive committee. The JLP remains allied with the BITU, which has Shearer as its president and has a claimed membership of 100,000.
Publications. Voice of Jamaica (weekly).
International affiliations. International Democrat Union (full member 1985); Caribbean Democrat

Union (founder member, 1986); the JLP also has friendly relations with Christian Democratic parties.

People's National Party (PNP)

Address. 89 Old Hope Road, Kingston 6.
Leadership. Percival J. Patterson (l.); Ryan Peralto (s.-g.).
Orientation. Nominally democratic socialist but the party has promoted free-market and conservative economic policies since taking office in 1989.
Founded. September 1938.
History. The party was formed by Norman Washington Manley and was closely modelled on the British Labour Party. It unsuccessfully contested the 1944 and 1949 elections, being heavily defeated in the former and more narrowly in the latter by the Jamaica Labour Party (JLP). In 1952, Manley purged the party of its powerful left wing and launched the moderate National Workers Union (NWU) to accommodate and control the left's impressive grassroot support and mobilize it in time of elections.

The NWU played a key role in the party's victory in 1955 when it gained over 50 per cent of the vote and 18 seats, a position improved on in 1959 when in the enlarged 45-seat house, the PNP won 54.8 per cent of the vote and 29 seats. The party was defeated, however, in the 1962 election when the electorate backed the JLP in rejecting Manley's opposition to independence and continued status as a member of the West Indies Federation. The PNP suffered another defeat in 1967.

NWU leader Michael Manley succeeded his father as party leader in 1969 and became Prime Minister in 1972 when the PNP returned to power after winning 36 seats (out of 52) and 56.4 per cent of the vote. Under Manley, from 1974 onwards, the party projected a democratic socialist image both domestically, through nationalization policies, and internationally by championing the cause of the third world and of Cuba. As a result, the party, despite having aroused the hostility of the private sector, comfortably won the 1976 elections, taking 47 out of 60 seats being contested.

This position, however, was quickly reversed. Sustained pressure from a hostile US administration backing the JLP opposition, combined with weak attempts at reform and a fast deteriorating economy, led to the party's heavy defeat in the 1980 general election, the most violent in the country's history (with some 900 people killed), when it won only nine seats.

The scale of the defeat strengthened the hand of the party's conservative wing, and in 1981 the PNP expelled left-wingers and dissociated itself from the communist Workers Party of Jamaica (now defunct) in a bid to attract moderate voters. The party boycotted the 1983 elections, called at short notice by the JLP government and before a new official voters list had been completed, and lost all of its seats in the House of Representatives.

It then campaigned outside parliament, criticizing the new JLP government's IMF-backed austerity policies and attracted enough popular support to win 57 per cent of the vote in the July 1986 local elections. This tide of opposition carried the party to a resounding victory in the February 1989 general election when it took 55.8 per cent of the vote and 45 seats. Ironically, Manley, once more the Prime Minister, then committed his government to continue the JLP's economic restructuring programme, the terms of which he renegotiated with the IMF in June 1991 to guarantee continued credits from multilateral agencies.

The abolition of exchange controls and the subsequent devaluation of the currency, coupled with the introduction of a punitive consumption tax in September 1991, provoked widespread protest from trade unions and the private sector alike. According to party sources, the closed sessions of the annual party conference, held in September 1991, were tense as one faction justified the current policy while another argued forcibly that it was abandoning its social democratic platform.

Rumours that Manley was to step down were denied at the time, but in March 1992, he did so and was replaced as party leader and Prime Minister by another conservative, Percival J. Patterson, the former Deputy Prime Minister and Minister of Finance and Planning, dismissed from the government in December 1991 for his part in an import tax waiver scandal involving Shell Oil (West Indies) Ltd.
International Affiliation. Socialist International (full member party).

Minor parties

Republican Party (RP); Denzil Taylor (l.); planned to contest in a by-election the seat of former Prime Minister Michael Manley who resigned in March (see People's National Party).

Martinique

Capital: Fort-de-France **Population: 360,000**

Martinique is a French overseas department, becoming so in 1946, and in 1974 was given the status of a region. In 1983 the island obtained greater economic autonomy and control over taxation and local police.

Constitutional structure

France is represented by a Government Commissioner, who exercises powers not devolved to the 45-member General Council or the 41-member Regional Council. The island elects four deputies and two senators to the French National Assembly and two senators. Martinique is also represented at the European Parliament in Strasbourg.

Electoral system

Both General Council and the Regional Council are elected by universal adult suffrage for six-year terms, subject to dissolution—the General Council by majority voting in two rounds, and the Regional Council by proportional representation. The deputies to the National Assembly in Paris are elected directly and the two senators indirectly.

Sequence of elections since 1980

Date	*Winning party*
March 1985 (Gen.Council)	Combined Left
March 16, 1986* (Reg. Council)	Union of the Left
Sept-Oct. 1988 (Gen. Council)	Combined left
Oct. 14, 1990 (Reg. Council)	PPM-FSM-PCM

*annulled in 1990 because of a technicality

Regional Council Elections, Oct. 14, 1990

Party	*% of votes*	*seats*
Martinique Progressive Party/Socialist Federation of Martinique/Martinique Communist Party(PPM-FSM-PCM)	32.8	14
Union for French Democracy/Rally for the Republic (UDF-RPR)	22.3	9
Martinique Independence Movement (MIM)	16.5	7
Independent Left	11.7	5
Independent Right	9.7	4
Ecological/pro-independence list	5.2	2
United France (FU)	1.8	-
Total	**100.00**	**41**

Regional Council elections, March 22, 1992

Party	*seats*
Union for a Martinique of Progress (UMP)	16
Martinique Patriots (PM) (see MIM)	9
Martinique Progressive Party (PPM)	9
For a Martinique at Work (see PCM)	4
Socialist New Generation (NGS) (see FSM)	3
Total	**41**

PARTY BY PARTY DATA

Martinique Communist Party

Parti Communiste Martinquais (PCM)
Address. Rue Emile Zola, Fort-de-France.
Leadership. Armand Nicolas (s.-g.).
Orientation. Centre-left; as in other French overseas departments, the Communists' main concern in recent years has been the impact of European Community (EC) integration at the close of 1992. The PCM fears that Martinique will lose its protected markets in France and be swamped by EC imports. To discuss this problem, the party participated in 1988 in a meeting in Cayenne of socialist parties of Martinique, French Guiana, Guadeloupe and Réunion, which gave rise to the creation of the "Assemblage of Progressive Forces of the Antilles, French Guiana and Réunion". The PCM advocates autonomy for Martinique as a first step towards eventual independence, but condemns the use of terrorist methods.
Founded. 1957.
History. Formed in 1925 as a federation of the French Communist Party, the PCM received over 60 per cent of the vote in the 1946, 1951 and 1956 elections and returned two deputies to the French National Assembly, including the poet Aimé Césaire. Its influence declined, however, after Césaire resigned in 1956 and founded the Martinique Progressive Party (PPM), which many communists joined. The PCM became an independent party in 1957 and abandoned its former policy of assimilation for one of autonomy. Together with the PPM and the Socialist Federation of Martinique (FSM), it formed the Martinique National Front for Autonomy in 1975, but by 1980 this alliance had effectively collapsed. The three parties contested the 1983 Regional Council elections independently, and together obtained 21 seats, including four for the PCM. Césaire was elected President of the Council. He then formed a ruling bureau in which all three parties were represented. The PCM split in 1984, when two of the communist members of the Regional Council, Dany Emmanuel and Léandre Marimoutou, resigned from the party to form the Communist Party for Independence and Socialism (PCIS).

In the March 1986 French National Assembly elections, the PCM-PPM-FSM alliance gained 51.2 per cent of the vote and, on the basis of proportional representation, Césaire and an FSM candidate were elected as deputies. This success was repeated in the simultaneous Regional Council elections, when the Union of the Left, including the PCM-PPM-FSM won 21 of the 41 seats. Césaire remained Council President. The PCM-PPM-FSM alliance contested the September 1986 elections for two Martinique seats in the French Senate, and a PPM candidate won one of the seats.

In June 1988, the left took all four seats in the election to the French National Assembly, but the PCM's candidate was defeated and in the partial elections to the General Council in September and October, although the combined forces of the left won 23 of the 45 seats, the PCM won only two of them.

In October 1990 the PCM-PPM-FSM alliance again was the largest group after the Regional Council elections, but lost its absolute majority with only 32.8 per cent of the vote and its representation reduced to 14 seats because of the strong campaign mounted by pro-independence candidates. Césaire stepped down as President of the Council in favour of the PPM's Camille Darsiéres. In March 1992 Regional Council elections, the party, running under the name For a Martinique at Work (*Pour une Martinique au Travail*), won four seats. The PCM's Emile Capgras was elected President of the Council on a third ballot, and only then on the basis of being older, at 66, than Pierre Petit of the Union for a Martinique of Progress (UMP), who received, like Capgras, seven votes for and seven against his candidacy.
Structure. The PCM is organized in workplaces and residential branches. The congress, meeting every four years, elects the 33-member central committee, which in turn elects the 13-member political bureau and the four member secretariat.
Membership. Under 1,000 (1989 est.). A large percentage of the membership are teachers and civil servants.
Publications. *Justice* (weekly).
International affiliations. The PCM has close ties with the French Communist Party.

Martinique Independence Movement-Hear the People

Mouvement Indépendantiste Martiniquais-La Parole au Peuple (MIM)
Address. Mairie de Riviére-Pilote.
Leadership. Alfred Marie Jeanne (l.).

Orientation. The MIM is a socialist party advocating early and complete independence for the island.
Founded. 1974.
History. As the most radical of the pro-independence parties, the MIM declared in 1980 that it aimed to seize power through a revolution, with external assistance if necessary. It called for a boycott of the 1981 French general election, but contested the Regional Council elections in 1983, winning 2.9 per cent of the vote and no seats. However, in the October 1990 Regional Council elections, when pro-independence parties enjoyed a resurgence of support, the MIM won seven seats. Standing under the name Martinique Patriots (*Patriotes Martiniquais*) the party won nine seats in the March 1992 Regional Council elections.

Martinique Progressive Party

Parti Progressiste Martinquais (PPM)
Address. Rue de Tallis Clariére, Fort-de- France.
Leadership. Aimé Césaire (pres.); Camille Darsiéres (s.-g.).
Orientation. The party was historically divided between autonomists and a pro-independence-from-France wing. The former, under Césaire, won control of the party in 1982 and promotes the idea of autonomy as a stage in the transition to full independence and the final realization of "self managing socialism".
Founded. 1957.
History. The party developed from a split in the Communist Party (PCM) and inherited part of the PCM's large electoral following. The PPM's founder Césaire, a noted poet, was re-elected as a deputy in the French National Assembly in March 1986 (where he votes with the Socialist Party). Since 1975 the PPM has been allied with the PCM and the Socialist Federation of Martinique (FSM), an alliance which dominated the elections to the Regional Council in 1983, 1986 (as part of the Union of the Left alliance) and 1990 (see PCM); Césaire was its President from 1983-1988 when he relinquished the post to Darsiéres. In the March 1992 Regional Council elections, the party won nine seats.
Publications. Le Progressiste (weekly).

Rally for the Republic

Rassemblement pour la Republique
Address. BP 448, 97205, Fort-de-France.
Leadership. Stephen Bagoe (s.-g.).
Orientation A conservative, Gaullist, party.
Founded. 1976.
History. The largest single political formation, although it has remained in opposition to the combined forces of the left in the Regional Council in alliance with the Union for French Democracy (UDF); it lost control of the General Council in 1986. In the March 1986 election to the French National Assembly, the RPR-UDF alliance received 42.4 per cent of the vote and won one seat. In the simultaneous elections to the Regional Council the RPR-UDF, with 49.8 per cent of the vote, narrowly lost to the left, winning 20 seats to the latter's 21 seats. Right-wing parties fared better in the municipal elections in March 1989, winning 18 municipalities to the left's 16. In the October 1990 elections to the Regional Council, the RPR-UDF won 22.3 per cent of the vote and nine seats, losing ground due to the appeal of right-wing pro-independence candidates.
International affiliations. The party forms the departmental section of the metropolitan French party of the same name.

Socialist Federation of Martinique

Fédération Socialiste de la Martinique (FSM)
Address. Cité la Meynard, 97200, Fort-de France.
Leadership. Michel Yoyo (l.); Jean Crusol (s.-g.).
Orientation. Centrist.
Founded. 1971.
History. The party allied itself with the Communist Party (PCM) and the Martinique Progressive Party (PPM) in 1975, and this persuasive left electoral bloc went on to dominate the elections to the Regional Council in 1983, 1986 (as part of a broader Union of the Left) and 1990. In 1986, the FSM's Louise-Joseph Dogné won one of the island's four seats in the French National Assembly. Running under the name Socialist New Generation (*Nouvelle Génération Socialiste*) the party won three seats in the March 1992 Regional Council elections.
International affiliations. The FSM is the local branch of the French Socialist Party.

Union for French Democracy

Union pour la Démocratie Francaise (UDF)
Address. Fort-de-France.
Leadership. Jean Maran (l.).
Orientation. Centre-right.
Founded. 1979.

History. The party, a section of the metropolitan party of the same name, was in alliance with the Rally for the Republic (RPR) throughout the 1980s and posed the only real threat to the combined forces of the left (see RPR). In September 1986 its candidate was elected to the French Senate.

Union for a Martinique of Progress

Union pour une Martinique de Progrés (UMP)
Leadership. Pierre Petit (l.).
Orientation. Right-wing.
History. The party won the largest number of seats in the March 1992 Regional Council elections. Petit received an equal number of nominations for the presidency of the Regional Council but was forced to defer to the Martinique Communist Party (PCM), candidate Emile Capgras, because he was the older candidate.

Minor parties

Communist Party for Independence and Socialism *(Parti Communiste pour l'Indépendance et le Socialisme*—PCIS); Dany Emmanuel, Léandre Marimoutou (ls.); formed by dissidents who resigned or had been expelled from the Martinique Communist Party (PCM) in 1984 on the independence issue. The party advocates immediate independence from France and refuses to condemn violent activities aimed to further this goal.
Republican Party (*Parti Républicain Francaise*—PR); Jean Bally (l.); supported the right-wing Gaullist Union for French Democracy (UDF) in the 1986 Regional Council elections.
Socialist Revolution Group (*Groupe Révolution Socialiste*—GRS); Gilbert Pago (l.); a Trotskyist, pro-independence party founded in 1973, it joined with six other left-wing groups of the French Caribbean in 1980 to form the "permanent committee for the struggle against repression". As the *Liste Unitaire pour une Martinique Libre sans Oppression ni Exploitation* it won 2 per cent of the vote but no seats in the 1983 Regional Council elections.
United France (*France Unie*—FU); Emmanuel Argo (l.); won 1.8 per cent of the vote in the October 1990 Regional Council elections and no seats.

Mexico

Capital: Mexico City **Population: 88,600,000**

Mexico achieved independence from Spain in 1821. The iron rule of Porfirio Díaz, President from 1876 to 1911 (known as the *Porfiriato*), except for the period 1880-84, ended the political instability of earlier years but precipitated the violent revolution of 1910-20 which produced such leaders as Emiliano Zapata and Francisco "Pancho" Villa. Since 1929 one party, renamed the Institutional Revolutionary Party (PRI) in 1946, inherited the mantle of the revolution and has held political power ever since, although opposition parties have consistently accused the PRI of serious electoral malpractice. In addition, the PRI's vote in presendential elections has continued to decline, falling from 95 per cent in 1976 to 74 per cent in 1982 and 50.36 per cent in 1988 under the combined weight of the foreign debt burden, subsequent economic austerity policies, large scale corruption and human rights violations.

Constitutional structure

Under the 1917 Constitution (as amended) a bicameral Congress is made up of a 64-member Senate, elected every six years (two from each state and two from the Federal District), and a 500-member Federal Chamber of Deputies. Executive power rests with the President who appoints a Cabinet, including the governor of the Federal District.

Electoral system

The President is elected for a six-year term, known locally as the *sexenio*, as are the 64 senators. The 500 deputies are elected every three years, 300 by majority vote in single-member constituencies and the remaining 200 by proportional representation from minority parties' lists. Since 1989, any party obtaining 35 per cent of the votes in a general election is awarded an absolute majority in the Chamber of Deputies. Each state has its own constitution and is administered by a governor, who, with the exception of the Governor of the Federalist District, is elected for a six-year term.

Evolution of the suffrage

All elections, both national and state, are held on the basis of adult, universal suffrage. All Mexican citizens 18 years of age and older are required to vote, although the law is rarely enforced.

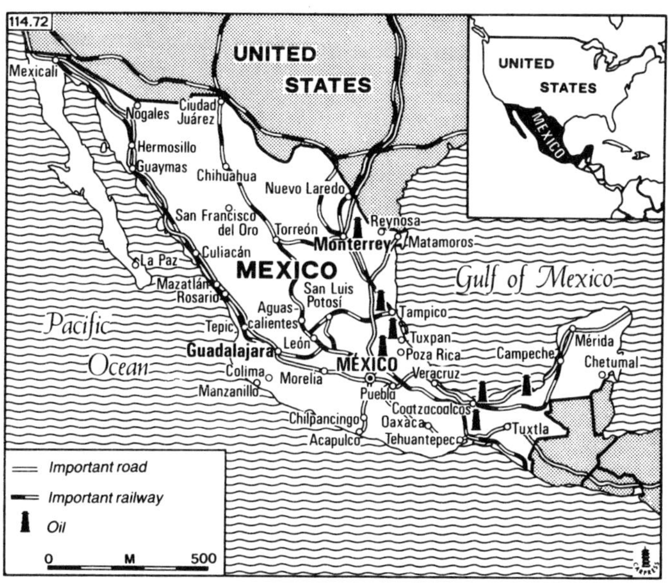
114.72
UNITED STATES
Mexicali
Nogales
Ciudad Juárez
Hermosillo
Guaymas
Chihuahua
Nuevo Laredo
San Francisco del Oro
Torreón
Reynosa
Monterrey
Matamoros
Culiacán
La Paz
MEXICO
Gulf of Mexico
Mazatlán
Rosario
San Luis Potosí
Aguascalientes
Tampico
Pacific Ocean
Tepic
Guadalajara
León
Tuxpan
Poza Rica
Campeche
Mérida
Chetumal
Colima
Morelia
MÉXICO
Veracruz
Manzanillo
Puebla
Coatzacoalcos
Chilpancingo
Oaxaca
Tuxtla
Acapulco
Tehuantepec
Important road
Important railway
Oil
0 M 500
UNITED STATES
MEXICO

Sequence of elections since 1982

Date	*Winning party*
July 1982 (presidential and legislative)	Institutional Revolutionary Party (PRI)
July 1985 (legislative)	PRI
July 1988 (presidential and legislative)	PRI
August 1991 (legislative)	PRI

Presidential elections July 6, 1988

Candidate	*Percentage of vote*
Carlos Salinas de Gotari (PRI)	50.39
Cuauhtémoc Cárdenas Solórzano (FDN)	31.12
Manuel Clouthier (PAN)	17.07
Rosario Ibarra de la Piedra (PRT)	0.42

Congressional elections, July 6, 1988

	Senate	*Chamber of Deputies*		
		direct	*PR*	*total*
PRI	60	233	27	260
FDN	4	29	110	139
PAN	-	38	63	101
Total	64	300	200	500

Congressional elections, Aug. 8, 1991

	Senate	*Chamber of Deputies*
PRI	61	320
PAN	1	89
PRD	2	41
PFCRN	-	23
PARM	-	15
PPS	-	12
Total	64	500

PARTY BY PARTY DATA

Authentic Party of the Mexican Revolution

Partido Auténtico de la Revolución Mexicana (PARM)
Address. Rio Nazas 168, México, DF.
Leadership. Jesús Guzmán Rubio (pres.); Carlos Cantú Rosa (s.-g.).
Orientation. Centrist; a vague ideological stance, centred on such intangibles as loyalty to the ideals of the 1917 revolutionary constitution, opposition to exploitation and injustice, and support for national sovereignty and civil rights, has given the party ample room for political manoeuvre.
Founded. March 1954.
History. Formed from a dissident faction of the ruling Institutional Revolutionary Party (PRI), the PARM provided a token opposition to the government in the 1960s and 1970s, its share of the congressional vote wavering between 0.49 and 2.6 per cent for a total of 10 congressional seats in 1979.

In 1982 it backed the PRI in the presidential race but won no seats in the Congress, subsequently losing its legal registration. This was restored in 1985 and a degree of political respectability was regained when the party gained nine seats in the 1985 congressional elections. In October 1987 the main opposition candidate Cuauhtémoc Cádenas Solórzano (see Party of the Democratic Revolution—PRD) accepted the PARM's offer to be its presidential candidate and the party joined the National Democratic Front (FDN) electoral alliance to promote his candidacy. In the August 1991 congressional elections, the party gained 15 seats in the Chamber of Deputies, none of which were directly won but allocated on the basis of proportional representation.
Structure. The party has an eight-member supreme presidium, a 21-member national executive committee, and state, district and municipal committees.
Membership. 191,500 (1984 claim).
Publications. *El Auténtico.*

Cardenista National Reconstruction Party

Partido del Frente Cardenista de Reconstrucción Nacional (PFCRN)
Address. Avd. México 199, Col. Hipódromo Condesa, 06170 México, DF.
Leadership. Rafael Aguilar Talamantes (pres.); Graco Ramírez Abreu (s-g.).
Orientation. Centre-left.
Founded. 1987.
History. The PFCRN emerged from the now defunct Socialist Workers Party (PST) which was a member of the National Democratic Front which supported the candidacy of Cuauhtémoc Cárdenas Solórzano in the 1988 presidential elections (see PRD). It subsequently chose not to join Cárdenas's newly formed PRD but remained part of the left-wing opposition in the Congress.

Following the August 1991 congressional elections, when it failed to get a single candidate directly elected, it was allotted a total of 23 seats in thc Chamber of Deputies on the basis of proportional representation.
Membership. 132,000 (1990 claim).

Institutional Revolutionary Party

Partido Revolucionario Institucional (PRI)
Address. Insurgnetes Norte 61, 06350 México, DF.
Leadership. Genaro Borrego Estrada (pres.); Rafael Rodríguez Barrera (s.-g.).
Orientation. The party inherited a general populist and symbolic tradition from the Mexican Revolution which gave it room to manoeuvre in practice, uniting disparate political tendencies from socialism and social democracy through to right-wing conservatism. Its current belief in a market-led economy and the conservatism of its foreign policy, points to a clear move to the right.
Founded. 1929 (as the National Revolutionary Party—*Partido Nacional Revolucionario*—PNR)
History. Following a period of violent revolutionary struggle between 1910 and 20, the PRI emerged to dominate the country's political life, first as the National Revolutionary Party, founded by President Plutarco Elías Calles, which was renamed the Party of the Mexican Revolution in 1938 before taking its present name in 1946.

Of the many PRI Presidents, the most radical and most influential was probably Gen. Lázaro Cárdenas (1934-40), whose re-organization of the party led to the PRI becoming a huge network for social control and patronage, incorporating labour and peasant unions and popular organizations for civil servants, professional groups and the army. Cárdenas nationalized thc oil industry in 1938 and introduced significant land reforms through the *ejido* common land system.

The authoritarian face of the party was shown most forcibly during the Presidencies of Gustavo Díaz Ordaz (1964-70) and Luis Echeverría Alvárez (1970-76) when student unrest was violently repressed. President José López Portillo (1976-1982) headed another conservative regime but in foreign policy it supported the 1979 Nicaraguan revolution and permitted the legalization of several left-wing parties.

President Miguel De la Madrid (1982-88), from the right of the party, gave effect to the party's anti-corruption rhetoric by bringing charges for corruption against the head of the state oil company and the Chief of the Mexico city police. His administration was dominated by the economic crisis which arose in 1982 from lower oil prices and the strain of servicing the vast foreign debt, and was worsened by the disastrous earthquake of 1985. Another feature of Madrid's *sexenio* was increasing domestic opposition, including National Action Party (PAN) protests over alleged fraud in federal, state and local elections in 1984-86, and internal dissent in the PRI. The number of the PRI's directly-elected members of the Chamber of Deputies fell from 299 in 1982 to 289 in July 1985.

During 1986 a new anti-authoritarian centre-left faction of the PRI, the Democratic Current (Corriente Democrática), campaigned for the selection of De la Madrid's successor. In 1987 the Current's leaders Cuauhtémoc Cárdenas Solórzano (son of the late President) and Porfirio Muñoz Ledo (a former president of the PRI) were expelled (see PRD).

The 1988 election victory of President Carlos Salinas de Gortari, by the smallest margin in the PRI's history, was one of the most controversial ever, opposition leaders being united in their claim that the PRI had been involved in widespread fraud. In July 1989 the PRI conceded victory to the PAN candidate in the governorship election in Baja California, its first electoral defeat in 60 years. PRI president Donaldo Colosio claimed that this was proof of the party's integrity although a simultaneous claim by the pro-Cárdenas Party of the Democratic Revolution (PRD) to have won the governorship of Michoacán was rejected.

Further controversy followed the PRI's emphatic victory in the August 1991 state and gubernatorial elections. Salinas was believed to have intervened personally to persuade the newly elected PRI governors for the states of Guanajuato and San Luis de Potosi, where there was evidence of systematic fraud, to stand down. The PRI governor of the state of Tabasco also finally resigned in January 1992, again reportedly at Salinas's request, in the face of sustained opposition charges of widespread electoral "irregularities". The opposition also accused Salinas of using the government's National Solidarity (pronasol) anti-poverty programme (with an estimated budget of US$1,700 million in 1991) to retain the allegiance of disaffected voters in areas where it was unpopular.

To restore its image at home and abroad, the PRI proposed electoral laws, passed by the Congress in July 1990, which the opposition PRD opposed, claiming that they would preserve PRI majorities in the Chamber of Deputies and the Senate. Internal unrest also surfaced within the PRI as dissidents in the Critical Current faction (*Corriente Crítica*) and the Movement for Democratic Change (*Movimiento por el Cambio Democratico*—MCD) objected to the lack of internal democracy and the continuation of the *dedazo* system whereby the party's elite hand-picked election candidates and delegates to the PRI's National Assembly. Rodolfo Gonzalez Gaviria, head of the Critical Current, resigned from the PRI in September claiming that the 14th congress of the party, despite passing several resolutions on increased internal democracy, had been "the worst sham in the PRI's long history".

The Salinas regime set out to improve the country's image and pledged itself to root out official corruption and to promote human rights. It established a pact for economic solidarity and growth (PECE) to contain wage and price increases in 1989 and initiated an ambitious programme to de-regulate and liberalize the economy and privatize the state sector, most notably state banks nationalized in 1982. Negotiations were also begun in 1990 to create a North American free trade agreement (Nafta) with the USA and Canada. This became the centrepiece of the government's strategy to modernize the country and extricate it from a decade of debt-ridden stagnation. Critics also contended that it was designed to salvage the PRI's hold on power.

In a final split with the republican and revolutionary past, Salinas in November 1991 proposed that the 1917 Constitution be altered to allow for the radical reform of the agriculture sector, the education system and that

official recognition, denied since the 1857 Constitution, be conferred on the Roman Catholic Church. The proposals became law in February 1992.
Structure. The PRI is composed of three sectors: labour, represented by the Confederation of Mexican Workers (CTM); peasant, in the National Confederation of Campesinos (CNC); and "popular", in the National Confederation of Popular Organizations (CNOC). However these traditional pillars are no longer seen as a sufficient basis for party support. Emphasis is now focused on the development of new territorial or "grass root" support networks, focused on local Solidarity (*pronosal*) committees (see above) which have directly benefited from government aid programmes. There is also a national membership structure (with local, district, state and federal organs) and a highly centralized leadership, formed by the national executive committee. Fourteen national assemblies have been held to date, the last in September 1990. It has a variety of support groups and affiliates, including a youth wing, the Revolutionary Youth Front (FJR).
Publications. La Republica, La Linea.

National Action Party

Partido Acción Nacional (PAN)
Address. Angel Urraza 812 esq. López Cotilla Colonia del Valle, 03109 México, DF, Mexico.
Leadership. Luis H. Alvárez (pres.).
Founded. 1939.
Orientation. A right-wing Social Christian party, with close associations with the Roman Catholic Church, which has highlighted human rights and social welfare abuses and advocated a government of national reconciliation.
History. Since its founding, the party has been the major opposition grouping and has stood against the Institutional Revolutionary Party (PRI) in congressional elections since 1943, in local elections since 1946 and most presidential elections since 1952. Internal disputes prevented it from presenting a presidential candidate in 1976. In 1982, its then leader, Pablo Emilio Madero, was accorded 16.4 per cent of the vote and the party won 55 seats in the Chamber of Deputies, reduced to 41 in the 1985 elections.

Together with the Authentic Party of the Mexican Revolution (PARM), the PAN was long regarded as a fairly benign opposition permitted to win a limited number of seats in order to give a pluralist credibility to a fairly monolithic system dominated by the PRI. However, during 1984-86, PAN supporters accused the PRI of blatant electoral fraud and were involved in numerous and occasionally violent protests, mainly in the relatively prosperous northern states where the party draws much of its support. Alvárez, who played a prominent part in the protests by staging a 40-day hunger strike, was narrowly elected party leader in 1987 as the representative of the northern radical conservative faction, the *neopanists*, opposed to the moderate traditionalist Madero grouping, the *Foro Democrático y Doctrinario* who were more disposed to work with the PRI. In July 1989, the party inflicted the first electoral defeat on the PRI in 60 years when the PAN candidate Ernesto Ruffo Appel won the governorship of the state of Baja California.

In August 1991, following complaints of blatant electoral malpractice, President Carlos Salinas de Gotari intervened and decided that the PAN's Carlos Medina Plascencia should replace the PRI hardliner Ramón Aguirre Veláquez as the governor-elect for the state of Guanajuato. The decision strengthened the hand of the party's leadership who were already disposed to a conciliatory approach to the government, especially in support of new electoral laws, a position endorsed by the national committee, which voted in September 1991 against the *Forista* faction who were opposed to such conciliation.

The change in mood was due in part to the tangible rewards that the PRI's liberal economic policies had given to some party members coupled with a growing belief throughout the party that a viable opposition movement to the government had diminished with the emphatic electoral defeat of the Party of the Democratic Revolution (PRD) in the August 1991 congressional elections, when the PAN's own total representation in the Congress was cut from 102 to 89 seats.
Structure. The supreme organ of the party is the national convention, and between conventions the national assembly. The convention elects a national council, which appoints a national committee. There are also state and district committees.

Party of the Democratic Revolution

Partido de la Revolución Democrática (PRD)
Leadership. Cuauhtémoc Cárdenas Solórzano (l.).
Founded. October 1988.
Orientation. Social democratic.

History. The PRD was established by a group of left-wing dissidents, led by Cuauhtémoc Cárdenas, the son of President Lázaro Cárdenas (1934-40) a revered figure in post-revolutionary history (see Institutional Revolutionary Party).

Cárdenas, as head of the Democratic Current faction (CD), was expelled from the PRI in 1987. He then accepted the presidential nomination of the Authentic Party of the Mexican Revolution (PARM) until he brought together several parties to form the electoral coalition, the National Democratic Front (*Frente Democrático Nacional*—FDN) to back his candidacy in the July 1988 presidential election. Including the PARM, these were the Popular Socialist Party (PPS), the Mexican Socialist Party (PMS), the right-wing Mexican Democratic Party (PDM) and the Socialist Workers Party (*Partido Socialista de los Trabajadores*—PST). During an often violent campaign, which included the assassination of a senior FDN co-ordinator Franciso Xavier Ovando Herández, the FDN organized the biggest demonstration for 20 years in the Zócalo, the main square in Mexico City against the economic crisis, political corruption and alleged intimidation by the PRI.

The FDN claimed that the subsequent PRI victory was a "massive fraud" and Cárdenas claimed that he had won a clear majority. The FDN parties, however, still managed to stun the PRI by taking over 31 per cent of the vote and receiving between them a total of 139 seats in the Congress owing to a low direct vote being boosted by seats awarded by proportional representation.

Of the FDN parties, only the PMS merged into the newly-formed PRD in October 1988 and the FDN itself became effectively defunct. The PRD disputed official results in the July 1989 elections for state legislators and mayors, providing evidence in the state of Michoacán that it had won 15 of the 18 electoral districts but had only been awarded six to the PRI's 12 seats. PRD supporters blocked several main roads in the state and occupied municipal buildings in protest.

The PRD was the most forceful opposition voice in its condemnation of electoral laws, finally passed by the Congress in July 1990, stating that they would preserve PRI majorities in the Chamber of Deputies and the Senate. One of the reforms had the effect of banning electoral alliances and coalitions, thus outlawing a future FDN-like electoral formation. Such opposition isolated them from former FDN allies who supported the reforms and provoked a split by a faction of militants led by Jorge Alcocer who had once belonged to the now defunct Communist Party (PCM).

The party participated, however, in the November 1990 state and local elections in the state of Mexico, winning no seats outright but being allocated eight by proportional representation. Along with the PAN, the PRD stated the elections had been a "scandalous fraud".

Leading party intellectuals who resigned at the end of 1990 argued that the leadership's continued questioning of the legitimacy of the electoral process, tied to its over-optimistic forecasts about the government's imminent collapse, was leading to the party's political marginalization. Such criticisms struck a chord because the PRD did not claim that its poor performance in mid-term congressional elections in August 1991 was solely based on government fraud. A national committee report cited the failure to have a single candidate directly elected, and only 42 seats awarded in the Chamber of Deputies via proportional representation, as proof of serious deficiencies within the party and the lack of systematic contact with the grass roots to guarantee the party's profile throughout the country.

The PRD expressed its vigorous opposition to the PRI's reform of the 1971 constitution in December 1991 but in late February 1992, Senator Porfirio Muñoz Ledo, considered as the party's second leading figure, stated the conditions existed for a dialogue between Cárdenas and Salinas. In state legislature and local government elections held in the state of Jalisco in February 1992, the PRD received 3.6 per cent of the vote, compared to 31.5 per cent for the PAN and 50.5 per cent for the PRI.

Popular Socialist Party

Partido Popular Socialista (PPS)

Address. Avenida Alvaro Obregón 185, Colonia Roma, 06977, México, DF.

Leadership. Francisco Ortiz Mendoza (l.).

Orientation. Centrist; prior to the collapse of the Eastern bloc, the party had pro-Soviet foreign policies and on the domestic front has cultivated a left of centre populist and nationalist image opposed to "North American imperialism and the oligarchic bourgeoisie".

Founded. June 1948 (as the *Partido Popular-PP);* known as PPS since 1960.

History. Although founded by the socialist trade union leader Vicente Lombardo Toledano, a close confidant of President Lázaro Cárdenas (see Institutional Revolutionary Party), the party consistently belied its left-wing credentials, being long considered a "loyal opposition" party, along with the PARM and PAN, and duly "rewarded" by the PRI with seats in the Congress. Between 1963 and 1985 it endorsed every PRI presidential candidate but saw its representation in the Congress increase from only 10 to 11 seats. Jorge Cruickshank, the party's secretary-general, sat in the Senate from 1976-82, as the only opposition senator elected since 1929.

The party broke with the PRI in 1988 over its choice of Carlos Salinas de Gotari as its presidential candidate and joined the National Democratic Front to support the candidacy of the PARM's Cuauhtémoc Cárdenas Solórzano (see Party of the Democratic Revolution). In the August 1991 congressional elections, none of its candidates were directly elected, but it received 12 seats in the Chamber of Deputies by proportional representation.

The party was not prominent in the opposition to the PRI's November 1991 reforms to the 1917 constitution, chief amongst which was the official recognition of the Roman Catholic Church. This contrasted with Ortiz Mendoza's protests during the Papal visit in May 1990 when he accused Pope John Paul II of making "political speeches" and recommended that he be expelled from the country and that governors who had welcomed him should be impeached for flouting the constitutional provision separating church and state.

Structure The party purports to be "democratic centralist" along Leninist lines. Its central committee and national officers are elected by a triennial national assembly. The party has a trade union affiliate, the UGOCMA, and a youth wing, the Popular Socialist Youth (JPS).

Publications. El Combatiente (weekly); *Nueva Democracia* (quarterly).

Minor parties

Mexican Democratic Party (*Partido Demócrata Mexicano*—PDM, Edison 89, 06030, México, DF); Victor Atilano Gómez (pres.); a right-wing conservative party founded in May 1971, modelled as a successor to the *Unión Sinarquista Nacional* (UNS), a neo-fascist and ultra-Catholic movement which had attracted a large popular following in the late 1930s. It received a total of 12 seats following the 1982 congressional elections, reduced to eight in 1985 and by the 1988 elections, when it joined the FDN (see Party of the Democratic Revolution), it had lost all congressional representation, and its current status. The party allied itself temporarily with the PAN in 1983 as the short-lived Democratic Action for Electoral Rescue (ADRE).

Revolutionary Workers' Party (*Partido Revolucionario de los Trabajadores*—PRT); José Manuel Aguilar Mora (s.-g.); Trotskyist, contested the 1982 presidential and congressional elections without success, but won six of the proportionally distributed seats in 1985.

Standing aloof from the FDN coalition in the 1988 elections, it received no seats. In April 1991 the PRT was reported to have joined the Revolutionary Socialist Current (*Corriente Revolucionario Socialista* (CRS), the People's Front (*Frente del Pueblo*) (FDP) and the Independent Democratic Alliance (*Alianza Democrática Independiente*) (ADI), to form the Socialist Electoral Front (*Frente Electoral Socialista*), leader, Raúl Jordan who said that the aim of the FES was to regroup in Mexico those who "still consider socialism a valid option".

Defunct parties

Mexican Socialist Party (*Partido Mexicana Socialista*—PMS); founded in March 1987, following a merger of various large and small left-wing groups, was at one time the third largest party until it was dissolved in May 1989 and merged with the PRD.

The PMS had been made up of the **Mexican Workers' Party** (*Partido Mexicano de los Trabajadores*—PMT); the **Union of the Communist Left** (*Unidad de la Izquierda Comunista*—UIC); **Trotskyist Workers' Revolutionary Party** (*Partido Revolucionario de los Trabajadores*—PRT); **Patriotic Revolutionary Party** (*Partido Patriótico Revolucionario*—PPR) and the **People's Revolutionary Movement** (*Movimiento Revolucionario del Pueblo).*

The largest PMS component was the **Unified Socialist Party of Mexico** (*Partido Socialista Unificado de México*—PSUM) which itself had been the product of a merger in November 1981 of the following parties: the **Mexican Communist Party** (*Partido Comunista Mexicano*—PCM), the **Popular Action Movement** (*Movimiento de Acción y Unidad Socialista*—MAUS), the **Mexican People's Party** (*Partido del Pueblo Mexicana*—PPM), the **Revolutionary Socialist Party** (*Partido Socialista Revolucionario*—PSR).

Illegal organizations

Army of the Poor (*Ejército de los Pobres*), Felipe Martínez Soriano (l.); armed wing of the **Party of the Poor** (*Partido de los Pobres*), active in the state of Guerrero in the 1970s against large landowners and their hired gunmen .

Montserrat

Capital: Plymouth **Population: 11,900**

Montserrat was part of the British colony of the Leeward Islands from 1871 to 1956, when it became a separate United Kingdom Dependent Territory.

Constitutional structure

Under the 1960 Constitution, amended in February 1990, Montserrat has an appointed Governor, who represents the British monarch. He is in charge of defence, internal security, external affairs and, since the 1989 financial corruption scandal, of offshore finance. Under the constitutional amendment, Montserrat obtained the right of self-determination in return for agreeing to the Governor's supervision of the financial sector.

The Governor chairs a seven-member Executive Council, which holds executive authority in most internal matters. The Executive Council has two ex officio members and four ministers drawn from the legislature, including a Chief Minister, the majority leader in the 11-member Legislative Council.

Electoral system

The Legislative Council consists of seven members elected by universal suffrage for a five-year term, two ex officio and two nominated members.

Sequence of elections since 1983

Date	*Winning party*
Feb. 25, 1983	People's Liberation Movement (PLM)
Aug. 25, 1987	People's Liberation Movement (PLM)
Oct. 8, 1991	National Progressive Party (NPP)

General election, Aug. 25, 1987

Party	*Seats*
People's Liberation Movement (PLM)	4
National Development Party (NDP)	2
Progressive Democratic Party	1
Total	**7**

General Election, Oct. 8, 1991

Party	*Seats*
National Progressive Party (NPP)	4
People's Liberation Movement (PLM)	1
National Development Party (NDP)	1
Independent	1
Total	**7**

PARTY BY PARTY DATA

National Development Party (NDP)

Address. Parliament St, Plymouth.
Leadership. Bertram B. Osborne (l.).
Orientation. Centrist.
Founded. November 1984.
History. On its formation, the NDP received the support of David Brandt, a member of the legislature who had in August 1984 resigned from the ruling People's Liberation Movement (PLM). In the 1987 election it won two seats, reduced to one in October 1991 when Bertram Osborne retained his southern constituency.

National Progressive Party (NPP)

Leadership. Reuben Meade l.
Orientation. Centrist.
Founded. September 1991.
History. Meade, a former head of the of the PLM government's Economic Development Unit, founded the NPP which won a surprise victory in the October 1991, winning four of the seven Legislative Council seats. Sworn in as Chief Minister, he promised "dedication and truthfulness" in government.

People's Liberation Movement (PLM)

Address. P.O. Box 495, Plymouth.
Leadership. John Osborne (l.).
Founded. November 1984.
Orientation. Conservative; the party favours eventual independence from Britain.
History. A dominant figure in recent Island political history, Osborne, a wealthy businessman, was a parliamentary representative of the Montserrat Workers' Progressive Party in 1966 and a founder member of the Progressive Democratic Party (PDP) in 1970. Following disagreements with PDP leader P. Austin Bramble, he formed the People's Liberation Movement in 1976. The PLM won all seven elective seats in the November 1978 general election, with 62.1 per cent of the vote and Osborne became Chief Minister. The party's representation fell to five seats in the February 1983 elections and to four in 1987.

The party lost power when it was defeated in the October 1991 election; it managed to win only one seat. Osborne failed to be re-elected and announced his resignation from politics.

The election had been forced following the resignation on Sept. 15 of the Deputy Chief Minister Benjamin Chalmers, who also held the portfolios of Communications, Works, Agriculture, Trade and Lands, who had rejected a freight landing bill from Osborne's Great Western Shipping Company. In retaliation, Osborne had tried to move him to another ministry. Chalmers subsequently resigned from the government and joined the National Development Party (NDP).

Progressive Democratic Party (PDP)

Address. P.O. Box 28, Plymouth.
Leadership. Eustace Dyer
Orientation. Social Democrat.
Founded. 1970.
History. The party superseded the Montserrat Labour Party, which had been the Island's majority party since 1948. In September 1973, the PDP won five of the seven elective seats in the legislature, PDP leader Austin Bramble subsequently becoming Chief Minister. In 1978, the party lost all of its seats to the People's Liberation Movement (PLM), led by PDP founder member John Osborne. Bramble regained one of two seats in the 1983 elections but lost his seat in the 1987 election when the party won only one seat. Bramble subsequently announced his retirement from politics.

Netherlands Antilles

Capital: Willemstad (on Curaçao) **Population: 191,000**

The Netherlands Antilles (then including Aruba) acquired separate status with full internal self-government within the Kingdom of the Netherlands in 1954, when the Kingdom's Charter came into force. Aruba achieved *status aparte* (self-government) in 1986, pending full independence, originally planned for 1996 but subsequently postponed indefinitely.

The federation of the Netherlands Antilles, more commonly known as the "Antilles of the five", consisting of the island communities of Curaçao, Bonaire, and the Windward islands (made up of St Maarten, St Eustatius, locally known as Statia, and Saba), under the 1954 Charter is an internally self-governing part of the Kingdom of the Netherlands. Aruba broke away in January 1986, and in the 1990 general election all the major parties on Curaçao were in favour of separation from the federation. The Dutch have also proposed a split federation of Bonaire and Curaçao and one made up of St Maarten, Saba and St Eustatius. No island, however, has expressed a wish for early independence from the Netherlands. An association with Aruba is maintained on some common economic matters.

Constitutional structure

Under the 1954 Charter, the islands are an autonomous part of the Kingdom, having their own 22-seat unicameral parliament *(Staten)*. A Council of Ministers, headed by a Prime Minister, is drawn from the *Staten* and exercises power in all areas save for Defence and Foreign Affairs; the latter areas are reserved to the Dutch government, represented locally by an appointed Governor, who in turn is assisted by an appointed Advisory Council.

Electoral system

The members of the *Staten* are elected by universal adult suffrage for four years, with the possibility of early dissolution. Each of the five islands, which are internally autonomous, forms an electoral district, with members of the federal *Staten* elected by proportional representation in the multi- member constituencies of Curaçao, Bonaire and Sint Maarten, and by simple majority in the single member constituencies of Saba and St Eustatius.

Evolution of the suffrage

Since 1954, provisions regarding suffrage passed by the Dutch parliament have also been introduced into the Netherlands Antilles. The minimum voting age is currently 18.

Sequence of elections since 1982

Date	*Winning party*
June 1982	New Antilles Movement (MAN)
November 1985	MAN

General Election, March 16, 1990

Party	*Seats*
Curaçao	
National People's Party (PNP-NVP)	7
30 May Workers' Liberation Front (FOL)*	3
MAN	2
Democratic Party (DP-C)	1
Nos Patria	1
Bonaire	
Bonaire Patriotic Union (UBP)	3
St Maarten	
Democratic Party of St Maarten (DP-SM)	2
St Maarten Patriotic Alliance	1
St Eustatius	
Democratic Party of St Eustatius (DP-SE)	1
Saba	
Windward islands People's Movement (WIPM)	1

** a member of the PNP-NVP ruling coalition.*

PARTY BY PARTY DATA

Bonaire Patriotic Union

Union Patriótico Bonairiano (UPB)
Address. P.O. Box 55, Kralendijk, Bonaire.
Leadership. C. L. R. (Rudi) Ellis (l.); C. V. Winklaar (s.-g.).
Orientation. Centrist; the UPB is concerned primarily with issues that affect the social and economic welfare of Bonaire.
History. The party first won the only Bonaire seat in the *Staten* in 1977, and held it in 1979 and 1982. It won four of the nine seats on the Bonaire Island Council in the local elections of April 1983. From late 1984 it supported a PNP-NVP coalition government, in which Ellis served as a minister.

Bonaire was given another two seats in the *Staten* as a result of the separation of Aruba from the "Antilles of the Five". In the first elections to the reformed assembly, in November 1985, the UPB won a single seat, with 41.9 per cent of the local vote (a little less than 1982). In the *Staten* election of March 1990, the party won three seats.
International Affiliations. Adherent party of the Christian Democrat Organization of America, which forms part of the Christian Democrat International.

Democratic Party (DP-C)

Democratische Partij (DP-C)
Address. Neptunusweg 28, Willemstad, Curaçao.
Leadership. Raymond Bentoera (l.).
Orientation. Centrist, with the long term aim of independence for the Antilles, with internal autonomy for each island.
Founded. December 1944.
History. The Curaçao DP, which is closely linked with the DPs on other islands in the federation, was in governing coalitions from 1958-73 and 1977-79, those from 1969 involving the PNP-NVP (see National People's Party). It lost much of its support after the resignation in mid-1979 of the coalition headed by its then leader Silvio Rozendal, and it held only three of the island's 12 seats in the *Staten* elections of June 1982, when it took 21.4 per cent of the island's vote. It was briefly part of the New Antilles Movement (MAN) coalition government of Domenico (Don) Martina from late 1981.

After the collapse of Martina's centre-left coalition in mid-1984, the DP-C supported the centre right PNP-NVP-led coalition of Maria Liberia Peters, with two DP members receiving ministerial posts. In November 1985, when the number of Curaçao seats was increased to 14, the DP-C again won three seats, with 17.9 per cent of the vote. In the ensuing centre-left MAN coalition, once again led by Martina, the party received two cabinet posts. In the March 1990 *Staten* elections, the party won only one seat.
Publications. The DP-C is supported by *La Prensa*, one of the main dailies on Curaçao.

Democratic Party (DP-B)

Partido Democratico Bonairiano (PDB)
Address. Kralendijk, Bonaire.
Leadership. Jopie Abraham (l).
Orientation. Centrist.
History. The DP-B, closely linked to the DP-C, won 47.6 per cent of the local vote in the 1982 *Staten* elections, but failed to win the single Bonaire seat. In April 1984, however, it won control of the Island Council, and in November 1985, it secured a slightly lower share of the vote but won two of the three seats then available for Bonaire in the *Staten*. Abraham was given a post in the MAN-led coalition government of 1986-88 and on its collapse the party received a cabinet post in the new PNP-NVP-led coalition government 1988-90 (see National People's Party). In the March 1990 *Staten* election, the party failed to win a seat.

Democratic Party (DP-SM)

Address. Philipsburg, St Maarten.
Leadership. Claude Wathey (l.).
Orientation. Centrist; the party has mainly concentrated on local issues on St Maarten, half of which, known as St Martin, is part of the French overseas department of Guadeloupe.
Founded. 1951.
History. The DP-SM, an English language party associated with the Papiamento-speaking DP-C, retained the sole seat allocated to the Windward Islands (including St Maarten and St Eustatius) in the elections to the *Staten* in June 1982. After the collapse of the MAN-led Martina government in mid-1984, the DP joined the centre-right PNP-NVP coalition led by Maria Liberia Peters, the DP-SM being given a cabinet post.

In November 1985, the Windward Islands representation in the *Staten* increased to five and the DP-SM won all three allocated to St Maarten, increasing its share of the local vote from 66.9 to 71.3 per cent. It then received a cabinet post in another MAN-led coalition in 1986 but withdrew its support in late 1987 after a serious disagreement between DP-SM leader Wathey and the MAN's Don Martina; Wathey had demanded greater autonomy within the federation for the Dutch half of the island of St Maarten and in early 1988 led a delegation to the Netherlands to ask the Dutch government about moves towards greater autonomy and eventual independence.

In the March 1990 *Staten* elections, the DP-SM won only two seats and in the April 1991 local council elections the party lost four seats to win only three of the nine council posts (see St Maarten Patriotic Alliance).

Democratic Party DP-SE

Address. Oranjestad, St Eustatius.
Leadership. Kenneth van Putten (l).
Orientation. Centrist; the party is mainly pre-occupied with social and economic issue affecting the welfare of the inhabitants of the island, one of the English-speaking and mainly Roman Catholic "Windward" group (in contrast with the mainly Protestant Dutch-Papiamento speaking-"Leewards", comprising Bonaire and Curaçao.
History. The fourth largest party in terms of size, the DP-SE won 53 per cent of the local vote in the 1982 elections when it was a subsidiary organization to the DP-SM. The departure of Aruba from the Antilles federation gave St Eustatius representation in its own right and in the November 1985 elections marking the transition the DP-SE won the single seat with 54.7 per cent of the vote. It received a cabinet post in the PNP-NVP-led centre-right coalition government in 1988-90 and in the March 1990 *Staten* elections retained its seat. In the Local Council elections of April 1991, the party defeated the St Eustatius Alliance and took three of the five seats.

Social Independent Party-Worker's Liberation Front

Social Independiente Frente Obrero Liberashon (SIFOL)
Address. Willemstad, Curaçao.
Leadership. George Hueck
Orientation. Socialist, for an independent federal republic.
Founded. 1990.
History. SIFOL superseded the May 30 Worker's Liberation Front (FOL) founded in 1973, which had grown out of labour disputes on Curaçao. The FOL had held three seats in the *Staten*, where it was in a PNP-NVP-led coalition government. After the elections of June 1977, the FOL staged a four-month boycott of the *Staten* to obstruct the new democratic Party government of Silvio Rozendal. It lost its seats in 1979 and in 1982 secured only 6.5 per cent of the local vote and no seat. In 1983 it held only one seat on the Island Council but gradually regained support, winning 11.1 per cent and returning to the *Staten* with a single seat in 1985. The withdrawal of the FOL was a deciding factor in the downfall of the MAN coalition government in 1988 and it received a cabinet post in the subsequent PNV-NVP coalition government (1988-90). In the March 1990 *Staten* elections, the FOL continued its recovery and won three seats.

National People's Party

Nationale Volkspartij (NVP) - Partido Nashonal di Pueblo (PNP)
Address. Casa di Pueblo, Penstraat 54, Willemstad, Curaçao.
Leadership. Maria Liberia Peters (l.).
Orientation. Social Christian and centre-right; it favours the eventual independence of the Antilles with a federal constitution.
Founded. 1945.
History. The PNP-NVP (formerly the NVP *unte*-NVPU or PNPU) is the largest single party in the Netherlands Antilles. It was in opposition until 1969 but held office for the following decade, in coalitions mainly involving the DP-C. In the late 1970s, it suffered a split, with its then leader, the former Prime Minister Juancho M.G. Evertsz forming *Akshon Social Kristian*, a short-lived Christian democrat party. The PNP-NVP representation in the *Staten* fell from five in 1973 to three in 1977 and two in 1979, recovering to three in 1982, when it won 33.6 per cent of the local vote.

Liberia Peters became Prime Minister in September 1984 at the head of a coalition government involving the Aruban People's Electoral Movement (MEP), the DP-C, the DP-SM, and the UPB. This government lost support as a result of austerity measures including a 10 per cent supplementary income tax, introduced mainly to offset the impact of oil refinery closures in 1985.

Following the elections of November 1985, in which the PNP-NVP won six seats with 41.3 per cent of the Curaçao vote, the coalition fell apart, with some of its members (but not the PNP-NVP) joining Don Martina's ensuing MAN coalition government.

Following Martina's resignation in 1988, Liberia Peters was invited by the Governor to form a new coalition government, which held office in 1988-90. In the March 1990 *Staten* elections the coalition strengthened its position, the party individually winning seven seats.

International affiliations. Christian Democrat International; Christian Democratic Organization of America (of which Liberia Peters is Vice-President).

New Antilles Movement

Movementu Antiyas Nobo (MAN)

Address. Landhuis Morgenster Marchena, La Plataweg 2a, Willemstad, Curaçao.

Leadership. Dominico F. (Don) Martina (l.); Angle Salsbach (s.-g.).

Orientation. Social Democrat, centrist; the party favours eventual independence.

Founded. April 1979.

History. The MAN arose from a split in the Worker's Liberation Front (FOL, see Social Independent Party), and rapidly gained electoral support, winning six seats in the Curaçao Island Council in April 1979 and, in the same year, four in the *Staten*. It then formed a centre-left coalition government under Martina, which survived crises in 1982 (in which year the MAN won another two seats) but fell apart in 1984 and was replaced by a PNP-NVP led centre-right coalition. In April 1983 the MAN had increased its share of Island Council seats.

In November 1985, the party's vote dropped to 28 per cent and it won four seats to the newly formed five-island *Staten*. It was again able to form a centre-left coalition, and Martina became Prime Minister in January 1986. His government was brought down by the departure of the DP-SM and the FOL and Martina was forced to resign in 1988. In the March 1990 *Staten* elections, the party won only two seats.

International affiliations. Socialist International (consultative member from 1980).

Windward Island's Progressive Movement (WIPM)

Address. The Level, Saba.

Leadership. Will Johnson (l.).

Orientation. The party seeks to represent the interests of the people of Saba and St Eustatius, the smallest of the five islands.

Founded. 1960s.

History. The WIPM won 77.4 per cent of the Saba vote in the 1982 *Staten* elections, but failed to win a seat. It secured four of the five seats on the Saba Island Council in May 1984, and won 93.6 per cent of the local vote and the single seat representing Saba in the *Staten* elections of November 1985. It did not participate in the ensuing Martina coalition government (see MAN). However it did join the centre-right PNP-NVP coalition government of Liberia Peters (1988-90) and received a cabinet post. In the March 1990 *Staten* elections, it retained the Saba seat and in the April 1992 local council elections defeated the incumbent Saba Democratic Labour Front, taking four of the five seats.

Publications. Saba Herald monthly.

International Affiliations. Adherent party of the Christian Democrat Organization of America, which forms part of the Christian Democrat International.

Minor Parties

Progressive Democratic Party (PDP); a split-off from the DP-SM, won two seats in the March 1990 elections to the St Maarten Council. A subsequent PDP-SPA (see below) coalition took office on July 12, 1991, with shared portfolios and a commissioner appointed by both parties to sit on the island's executive council along with the Lieutenant Governor Ralph Richardson. Both parties had reportedly reached an "understanding" on moves to limit the Lieutenant Governor's powers. On Aug. 27, however, the PDP withdrew from the coalition, citing "philosophical differences" with the SPA, and said it would try to form an administration with the DP-SM.

Saint Maarten Patriotic Alliance (SPA); Vance James (l.); it won one seat in the March 1990 *Staten* elections and increased its representation on the St Maarten Council from two to four seats in the April 1991 local elections.

Nos Patria; Chin Behilia (l.); won one seat in the March 1990 *Staten* elections.

Nicaragua

Capital: Managua **Population: 3,300**

The Republic of Nicaragua achieved independence in 1838 but was subjected to US military intervention in 1912-25 and 1927-33. The country was subsequently left in the control of the Somoza family until the overthrow of the right-wing dictatorship of Gen. Anastasio Somoza Debayle by a popular revolutionary movement, the Sandinista National Liberation Front *(Frente Sandinista de Liberación Nacional*—FSLN) in 1979. Far-reaching economic and social reforms were introduced despite attempts by conservative groups and US-backed right-wing *contra* rebels to destabilize the government. The FSLN won the national elections in 1984 with 67 per cent of the vote but lost the next election in 1990 to the National Opposition Union *(Unión Nacional Opositora*—UNO) alliance led by Violeta Barrios de Chamorro.

The November 1984 presidential and legislative elections were the first to be held in the country since 1974. Of the 1.55 million registered voters, an estimated 80 per cent turned out to elect Daniel Ortega Saavedra President and give an overwhelming majority to the Sandinistas in the National Assembly. A team of international observers described the elections as free of irregularities and fair but the United States government described them as a "farce".

War fatigue among the population and a decade of economic austerity were instrumental factors in the FSLN's unexpected and heavy electoral defeat in February 1990, although they remained the country's largest party. The victorious UNO alliance promised to end the civil war, promote national reconciliation and attract foreign aid and investment.

Constitutional structure

Under the 1987 Constitution a unicameral National Assembly is made up of 92 Representatives. Executive power rests with the President, who is head of state and Commander-in-Chief of the Defence and Security Forces and governs with the assistance of a Vice-President and an appointed cabinet.

Electoral system

National Assembly representatives (each with an alternative representative) are directly elected for a six-year term by a system of proportional representation and also elected are those unelected presidential and vice-presidential candidates (as representatives and alternates respectively) who receive nationally at least as many votes as the average winning percentages in each of the 143 regional electoral districts. Both the President and Vice-President are directly elected for a six-year term and consecutive terms of office are permitted.

Evolution of the suffrage

Men and women over 16 are eligible to vote.

Sequence of elections since 1984

Date	*Winning party*
November 1984 (presidential and legislative)	National Liberation Front (FSLN)
February 1990 (presidential and legislative)	National Opposition Union (UNO)

Presidential elections November 1984

Candidate	*% of vote*
Daniel Ortega Saavedra (FSLN)	66.9
Clemente Guido (PCDN)	14.0
Virgilio Godoy Reyes (PLI)	9.6
Mauricio Díaz (PPSC)	5.6
Others	3.9

Legislative elections November 1984

Party	*Seats*
FSLN	61
Democratic Conservative Party (PCDN)	14
Independent Liberal Party (PLI)	9
Popular Social Christian Party (PPSC)	6
Communist Party of Nicaragua (PCdeN)	2
Popular Action Movement-Marxist Leninist (MAP-ML)	2

Presidential elections Feb. 25, 1990

Candidate	*% of vote*
Violeta Barrios de Chamorro (UNO)	54.7
Daniel Ortega Saavedra (FSLN)	40.8
Moisés Hassan (MUR)	1.1
Erick Ramírez (PSC)	0.7
Others	2.7

Legislative elections Feb. 25, 1990

Party	*Seats*
UNO	51
FSLN	39
MUR	1
PSC	1

PARTY BY PARTY DATA

Democratic Conservative Party of Nicaragua

Partido Conservador Democrático de Nicaragua (PCDN)
Address. Costado Sur de la Diplotienda, Managua.
Leadership. Clemente Guido (l.).
Orientation. Right-wing, believes in a free market but supports the current government policy of achieving a national consensus for economic and social change. It has no delegate in the National Assembly but remains a respected party.
Founded. 1979.
History. The PCDN was formed by three factions of the traditional Conservative Party (PC), which had been the main legal opposition during the Somoza era. It inherited the radical middle class tradition of Pedro Joaquín Chamorro Cardenal, the anti-Somoza owner of the daily *La Prensa* newspaper and husband of the current President Violeta Chamorro de Barrios, who was assassinated in 1978. It supported the 1979 revolution but baulked at Sandinista reforms.

The party suffered a serious split in 1984 on the question of whether or not to participate in the general election. One wing opposed to participation, led by Miriam Arguello and Mario Rappaccioli, broke away to form the Nicaraguan Conservative Party (PCN—yet to receive legal status), which in turn joined the anti-Sandinista opposition grouping, the Nicaraguan Democratic Co-ordinator (CDN), which included business groups and two trade unions in favour of an electoral boycott. The remaining wing, the PCDN, fielded Clemente Guido for the presidency, won 14 per cent of the vote and, with 14 seats, emerged as the largest opposition party in the National Assembly. Another debilitating split within the PCDN led to the departure of Enrique Sotelo Borgen, whose PCDN "non officialist" faction forged a pact with the Independent Liberal Party (PLI).

Although Vice President of the National Assembly, Guido refused to sign the 1987 Constitution, although his deputy did so, along with 11 PCD delegates. This provoked a leading conservative Córdova Rivas to stage a week-long hunger strike in the name of party unity. Factionalism continued however, one led by Eduardo Molina and another by Hernaldo Zúñiga, who went on to form the Conservative National Alliance Party (PANC). The PCDN stood alone in the 1990 general election, with Molina as its presidential candidate. The PANC, still to be legally recognized, joined the victorious UNO coalition. Arguello's PCN itself split into the National Conservative Party (PNC) and Arguello's own Conservative Popular Alliance Party (PAPC). Both joined the UNO alliance and Arguello was elected leader of the National Assembly after the 1990 election.
International affiliation. International Democrat Union (associate member from 1987).

National Conservative Party

Partido Conservador Nacional (PNC)
Leadership. José Castillo Osejo (l.).
Orientation. Right-wing, believes in a free market and has five National Assembly delegates.
Founded. 1990.
History. A split from the PCDN (see above) and a member of the UNO ruling coalition, it submitted a controversial draft bill in June 1991 calling on the National Assembly to rescind the *piñata* laws 85 and 86 passed by the outgoing Sandinista government which had formalized the distribution of state property, mostly confiscated from their opponents, among their supporters. The laws were signed by UNO representative Antonio Lacayo Oyanguren, the Presidency minister, and Army Commander in Chief and former FSLN leader Gen. Humberto Ortega Saavedra on Mar. 27, 1991 as part of the transition agreements between governments.

Movement of Revolutionary Unity

Movimiento de Unidad Revolucionaria (MUR)
Leadership. Francisco Semper (l.).
Orientation. Left-wing and has disowned its one National Assembly delegate.
Founded. 1988.
History. The party was created in August 1988 by Moisés Hassan Morles, a former member of the Revolutionary Junta in 1979, an FSLN member for nine-years and former Mayor of Managua in a bid to group together left-wing opponents of the Sandinistas. Both the Nicaraguan Socialist Party (PSN) and the Communist Party of Nicaragua (PCdeN) were initially involved in the alliance, but quickly began co-operating with right wing parties, joining the UNO. Hassan's group remained independent and obtained legal status for the MUR in 1989. In the 1990

presidential elections Hassan obtained 16,751 votes and won a seat in the National Assembly. Hassan was subsequently expelled from the MUR on July 13, 1990, charged with having brought the name of the party into disrepute and was asked to give up his assembly seat.

He had voted to suspend the Sandinista's Civil Service Code, grant amnesty to ex-Somoza National Guardsmen and right-wing *contras* and had abstained from a vote to repeal the Sandinista Labour Code. Hassan claimed his expulsion from the party was a Sandinista-engineered plot.

National Opposition Union

Unión Nacional Opositora (UNO)

Leadership. Violeta Chamorro de Barrios (l.).

Orientation. a right-wing coalition with 51 delegates in the National Assembly, the majority of whom are opposed to the government's current policy of collaboration with the FSLN opposition.

Founded. 1988.

History. The US-supported UNO coalition was formed as an electoral bloc of 14 parties, including left-wing and right-wing parties hostile to the Sandinistas, to support the candidacy of Violeta Chamorro de Barrios in the 1990 presidential elections.

On taking power in April 1990, pre-electoral differences deepened and the UNO split into two factions, eight parties following Vice-President Virgilo Godoy's Independent Liberal Party (PLI) in opposing policies masterminded by Presidency Minister Antonio Lacayo Oyanguren. Chamorro's inner circle of advisors showed themselves to be astute and adept although lacking a strong political, economic and military base in a sharply polarized society. They had to rely on the support of a "pragmatic" FSLN leadership and the Sandinista People's Army (EPS) to maintain a modicum of political and military stability.

The government, however, managed to end the 11-year civil war and disarm and demobilize right-wing *contra* rebels while simultaneously working to create a national consensus for a radical free market reform programme. Such reforms were vigorously resisted by Sandinista mass organisations fighting public-sector cuts, privatizations and low pay. They were also criticized as insufficient by the hostile UNO right wing, supported by business groups, who accused the government of allowing the FSLN to dictate the pace of change. This UNO right-wing criticism reached a crescendo in September 1991 when Chamorro partially vetoed the decision of the National Assembly to nullify previous FSLN government laws granting property rights to Sandinista supporters.

Despite the fact that the country at times appeared to be ungovernable, the government used alternate policies of confrontation and conciliation to guarantee a gradual shift away from the legacy left by the FSLN. The resumption of hostilities between right-wing contra groups (*recontras*) and Sandinistas (*recompas*) was not expected to reverse this process.

Structure. The UNO is made up of the following parties who have seats in the National Assembly: Independent Liberal Party (*Partido Liberal Independiente*—PLI, founded 1944, Virgilio Godoy (l.); 5 seats); Democratic Party of National Confidence (*Partido Demócrata de Confianza Nacional*—PDCN, Agustín Jarquin (pres.); Adán Fletes (s.-g.); 5 seats); National Conservative Party (*Partido Nacional Conservador*—PNC, José Castillo Osejo (l.); 5 seats); Conservative Popular Alliance Party (*Alianza Popular Conservadora*—APC, Miriam Arguello (l.); 5 seats); Social Democratic Party (*Partido Social Demócrata*-PSD, Guillermo Potoy (pres.), Alfredo César (s.-g.); 5 seats); Constitutionalist Liberal Party (*Partido Liberal Constitucionalista*—PLC, Jaime Cuadra (pres.), José Ernesto Sommarriba (s.-g.); 3 seats); Neo-Liberal Party (*Partido Neo-Liberal*—PALI, José Luis Tijerino (l.); 3 seats); Nicaraguan Socialist Party (*Partido Socialista Nicaragüense*—PSN, Gustavo Tablada (l.); 3 seats); Communist Party of Nicaragua (*Partido Comunista de Nicaragua*—PCdeN, Eli Altamirano Pérez (l.); 3 seats); National Action Party (*Partido de Acción Nacional*—PAN, Eduardo Rivas Gasteazoro (l.); 3 seats); Nicaraguan Democratic Movement (*Movimiento Democratico Nicaragüense*—MDN, Roberto Urroz (l.); 3 seats); Central American Integrationist Party *Partido de Integración de America Central*—PIAC Alejandro Pérez (l.); 3 seats); Popular Social Christian Party - UNO Faction (*Partido Popular Social Cristiano*—PPSC-UNO, 2 seats); Conservative National Alliance Party (*Alianza Nacional Conservadora*—ANC, 2 seats); National Opposition Union-Yatma (*Unión Nacional Opositora-Yatma*—UNO-Yatma, Brooklyn Rivera (l.); 1 seat).

Sandinista National Liberation Front

Frente Sandinista de Liberación Nacional (FSLN)

Leadership. A National Directorate, elected in July 1991, is headed by former President Daniel Ortega Saavedra and made up by Henry Ruiz, Rene Nuñez, Victor Tirado, Sergio Ramírez, Jaime Wheelock, Luis Carrion, Tomas Borge Martínez and Bayardo Arce.

Orientation. Social-democratic.

Founded. 1961.

History. The FSLN, named after the national hero Agusto César Sandino, was founded by a small group of intellectuals, including former Nicaraguan Socialist Party (PSN) member Carlos Fonseca Amador and Thomas Borge Martínez, and began guerrilla activity against the US-backed Somoza regime in 1963. After suffering a series of defeats, it abandoned all military activity from 1970 to the end of 1974.

Fonseca, the FSLN's leading theoretician, was killed in action in 1976, and after 1975 disagreements on strategy split the movement into three factions. The Protracted People's War (GPP) group, led by Borge, favoured the creation of liberated zones on the Chinese and Vietnamese model, which would provide bases from which to attack towns; the Proletarian Tendency (PT), led by Jaime Wheelock, maintained that the FSLN should concentrate on winning the support of the urban working class; and the third way group (*terceristas*), led by Daniel Ortega Saavedra, advocated a combination of an armed offensive and broad political alliances with other opposition organizations, which would lead to a general insurrection.

A synthesis of all three strategies was finally agreed upon but with the *terceristas* the dominant tendency, and in March 1979 a national directorate was formed, consisting of the three main leaders of each faction. After intensified fighting, Gen. Anastasio Somoza Debayle was overthrown in the popular revolution of July 1979.

The FSLN's decisive role in the overthrow of the Somoza dictatorship inevitably made it the dominant political force after the revolution, although it shared power initially with anti-Somoza forces in the FSLN-led Patriotic Revolutionary Front (FPR) and with elements of the conservative middle class, in a Council of State. This Council was superseded in 1984 when Daniel Ortega was elected President and the FSLN secured a clear majority in a new National Assembly.

Initially, Sandinista measures to combat illiteracy and improve primary health care were very successful but eventually half the national budget came to be devoted to the war against US-backed right-wing *contra* rebels who had initiated in 1981 a guerrilla war to destabilize the government. US trade and investment embargoes led to greater reliance on Soviet-bloc aid, until 1987, when the Soviet Union began to scale down its oil supplies.

In 1987, the emphatic opposition of the FSLN to direct negotiations with the *contras* was modified when it welcomed peace plans devised by the Contadora group and by President Arias of Costa Rica which took shape in the Guatemala regional peace accords. The Sandinistas made major concessions to their critics in the hope of achieving peace; these included an end to the state of emergency, a readiness to talk to the contras, an amnesty of prisoners and an end to bans on the media. In December 1989, the FSLN signed a regional agreement calling for the demobilization of the Salvadoren guerrillas in the expectation that other governments would finally act to dismantle contra camps in Honduras.

After their surprise defeat in the 1990 presidential elections, the Sandinistas vowed to defend the "fundamental conquests of the revolution", such as nationalization of banks and foreign trade, state farms and the rights and freedoms contained in the 1987 constitution.

After the elections, however, the FSLN lost both its discipline and unity. Grass-root members became increasingly alienated from the leadership which was criticized for collaborating too much with the Chamorro government in the name of a responsible opposition. This gulf deepened when the leadership interposed itself between the UNO government and the mass Sandinista organizations during the 1990 strikes against cuts in jobs and services. Accusations that the FSLN leadership had personally benefited from laws allowing for the disposal of state property and land before the Sandinistas relinquished power (known locally as the *piñata* after a children's game where everyone rushes to grab what they can) also left their mark on rank-and-file supporters. However, when the UNO right-wing parties in the National Assembly repealed the laws in June 1991, which had also given land to campesinos (peasants), all 39 FSLN delegates withdrew from the Assembly indefinitely. Sandinista mass organizations rallied to their defence and in September Chamorro partially vetoed the Assembly's decision.

Structure. The National Directorship is accountable to the 105-member Sandinista assembly, but this has not met as regularly as the statutes stipulate (annually). The FSLN's first congress was held in July 1991, attended by 581 delegates and the next is due in 1995. It resulted in a victory for the "pragmatists", headed by the Ortega brothers, who advocated co-operation with the UNO government over the "radicals" led by Borge and Ruiz who considered conciliation with the government as a betrayal of Sandinista principles.

Popular Sandinista organizations, in stark contrast to the current stagnation in party structures, remain dynamic in the preservation of the perceived gains of the 1979 revolution and, as a result, have become more autonomous and democratic. These include the Sandinista Defence Committees (CDSs), the Sandinista Workers Central (CST), the National Workers' Front (FNT) and the Association of Rural Workers' (ATC).

Publication. Barricada, daily, 110,000 in 1988. Ceased to be the official organ of the FSLN in January 1990.

Affiliations. The FSLN retains close relations with the Cuban Communist Party and has been represented at congresses of the Socialist International, to which it formerly applied for membership in April 1992.

Independent Liberal Party

Partido Liberal Independiente (PLI)

Address. Ciudad Jardín, F29 frente a Óptica Selecta, Managua.

Leadership. Wilfred Navarro (pres.), Virgilio Godoy Reyes (l.); Ulises Somarriba (gen.-sec.).

Orientation. A focus of right-wing UNO opposition to any accommodation with the Sandinistas, with five delegates in the National Assembly.

Founded. 1946.

History. The PLI was formed by a dissident faction of intellectuals of Somoza's National Liberal Party who were opposed to the extension of the dictatorship's powers and who subsequently boycotted rigged elections. It welcomed the 1979 revolution and joined both the Revolutionary Patriotic Front and the Council of State. Godoy served as Minister of Labour in the Sandinista-led government. Opposed to restrictions placed on campaign activities, it called for a boycott of the 1984 elections shortly before the poll but won nine seats in the National Constituent Assembly. In March 1985 the PLI joined other centre-right opposition groups in the externally based Nicaraguan Democratic Co-ordinator (CON) alliance and was one of six opposition parties to campaign for new elections, a ceasefire in the civil war and the depoliticization of the army, a general amnesty and the return of seized lands to their original owners.

It refused to sign the 1987 constitution and joined the UNO alliance of parties which won the 1990 presidential election. Godoy was named Vice-President but quickly became a figurehead for the majority of UNO deputies, mayors of local councils, the organization of private business (Cosep) and the hierarchy of the Roman Catholic church, ideologically opposed to the government. Godoy demanded the resignation of the Presidency Minister Antonio Lacayo, the perceived architect of a policy of close collaboration with the Sandinistas, and the dismissal of Gen. Humberto Ortega Saavedra, the former Sandinista leader retained as Commander-in-Chief of the armed forces. He also called on Chamorro to honour her pledge of land and credits made to the *contras* before their demobilization in June 1990. These demands, which were ignored, were identical to those of re-armed *contra* rebels, known as *recontras.* Apart from a rising in November 1990 when right-wing mayors and supporters took temporary control of Region V of the country, the Godoy right-wing has had little political success.

Publications. Alternativa Liberal.

International Affiliation. Liberal International (since 1982).

Social Christian Party

Partido Social Cristiano (PSC)

Leadership. Erick Ramírez (pres.).

Orientation. A right-wing Christian Democrat party which has one delegate in the National Assembly.

History. Founded in 1957 and opposed to the Somoza dictatorship, it survived splits in 1976 and 1979. After the 1979 revolution it joined the Council of state which it resigned from in November 1980. It 1981 it was a founder member of the Nicaraguan Democratic Co-ordinator (CDN), a right-wing coalition of parties opposed to the Sandinistas. In November 1981 it expressed itself open to negotiations with the FSLN and did not follow other parties, such as the Nicaraguan Democratic Movement (MDN) and a right-wing PSC offshoot, the Christian Democratic Solidarity Front (FSDC), in establishing bodies supportive of the armed activities of right-wing contra rebels.

It was banned as a party by the FSLN government following its support of the CDN's boycott of the 1984 elections. Ramírez had opposed the decision and relations with other CDN parties became increasingly soured. In 1985 it co-founded a Costa Rican based alliance, the Co-ordinator of the Nicaraguan Opposition (CON) Nicaraguan Opposition alliance with the MDN, PSD, the Independent Liberal Party (PLI—see above) and the Democratic Conservative Party (PCD). In February 1987 it was one of five parties calling for a ceasefire and fresh elections. Internal strife ensued and in mid-1987 a right-wing faction led by PSC secretary-general Agustín Jerk Anaya and Eduardo Rivas Gasteazoro left the party. This faction subsequently subdivided itself into the National Confidence Democratic Party (PDCN-see UNO) and the National Action Party (PAN-see UNO)

In November 1987 Ramírez was one of eight members appointed by the FSLN to a National Reconciliation Commission established under the Arias peace plan for the Central American region. In the 1990 elections, the PSC joined the UNO opposition alliance, winning a single seat in association with an electoral ally, the Yatama, a right-wing *contra* rebel organization formed in 1987 from indigenous Atlantic coast political rebel groups. The Yatama disbanded along with other *contra* groups in mid-1990.

Structure. A seven-member National executive is elected by party conference held at roughly two-year intervals.

Publications. El Socialcristiano.

International affiliations. Member party of the Christian Democrat Organization of America, which forms part of the Christian Democrat International, a major PSC financial backer. The PSC has particularly close relations with the ruling Arena party of El Salvador, the Christian Democratic party (CDP) of Guatemala and the Christian Democratic Union (CDU) of Germany, the last of which provides it with funds estimated to be US$100,000 per year.

Minor parties

Parties not represented in the National Assembly: Independent Liberal Party of National Unity (*Partido Liberal Independiente de Unidad Nacional*—PLIUN), founded 1988, Eduardo Coronado (l.); Carlos Alonso (s.-g.); Popular Action Movement-Marxist Leninist (*Movimiento de Acción Popular-Marxista Leninista*—MAP-ML) founded 1972, Isidro Téllez (l.)); Social Conservatism Party (*Partido Socialconservadurismo*—PSOC), founded 1989, Fernando Aguero (pres.), José María Zavala (s.-g.); Popular Social Christian Party-Díaz faction (*Partido Popular Socialista-Mauricio Díaz*—PPS-Mauricio Díaz); Central American Unionist Party (*Partido Unionista Central Americana*—PUCA) Blanca Rojas (pres.); Giovani D'Ciofalo (s.-g.), Workers Revolutionary Party (*Partido Revolucionario de los Trabajadores*—PRT), founded 1984, Bonifacio Miranda (l.).

Nicaraguan Resistance for Civic Organization (*Resistencia Nicaragüense de Organización Civica*—RNOC), Oscar Sovalbarro (l.), Israel Galeano (s.-g.), founded in August 1990 by former members of the US-backed right-wing *contras* who have decided to enter the political mainstream.

Nicaraguan Democratic Party (*Partido Democrático Nicaragüense*—Padenic), Roberto Mayorga Kingland (l.); a Liberal party authorized by the Council of Political Parties in December 1991 and drawing its members from the Atlantic coast.

Major guerrilla groups

Democratic Force for National Salvation *Fuerza Democrática por la Salvación Nacional*; José Angel Moran Flores (alias *El Indomable*); Commanders Dimas, Campeo and Bigote de Oro (ls), founded 1991 from the ranks of 20,000 *contra* rebels who had demobilised in June 1990 after 10 years fighting the FSLN government with US support, renewed hostilities as *re-contras* (re-armed ex-contras), primarily in the north-western departments, particularly the mountainous Jinotega province. In tune with right-wing parties in the UNO coalition (see PLI), they accused the government of colluding with the FSLN and failing to guarantee them land and security. They demanded the removal of Presidency Minister Antonio Lacayo and of Army Commander-in-Chief and former Sandinista leader Humberto Ortego Saavedra, the break-up of the army, and a general purging of Sandinistas from the state security forces. In a communiqué of Dec. 14, 1991, they said they had withdrawn from peace talks and would conduct military operations throughout the country if the government did not respond constructively to their basic demands.

The *re-contras* renewed hostilities in January 1992 and fighting was still continuing in March 1992.

Revolutionary Alliance of Workers and Peasants (*Alianza Revolucionaria de Obreros y Campesinos*—Aroc) founded November 1991 as an umbrella organization with the aim of co-ordinating the actions of re-armed left-wing Sandinistas, *re-compas*, who were committed to fighting the *re-contras* and defending the social changes introduced by the 1979 Sandinista revolution. Known *recompa* groups include: Guerrilla Organization 91, Danto-19 ("death to the revengers"), the Altamirano Sandinista Movement, the Property Self Defence Group, the Armed Insurrectional Revolutionary Front, and the **Nora Astorga Front**, the last a group of 200 armed women, formed in March 1992 and active in the north and who were also campaigning against the government for child care programmes and free medicine.

Panama

Capital: Panama City **Population: 2,418,000**

The Republic of Panama seceded from Colombia in 1903. Its modern history has been marked by the considerable influence exercised by the United States on the country's internal affairs, especially in relation to the control of the Panama canal. Elected governments were overthrown in 1941, 1949, 1951 and 1968, usually after disputed elections, and there were serious constitutional crises in 1918, 1948, 1955 and 1968. In the 1972 and 1978 elections to the then National Assembly of Community Representatives, no candidate was allowed to represent a political party. A tentative return to democratic government in the early 1980s was overshadowed by the presence of the National Guard, whose commander, Gen. Manuel Antonio Noriega Morena, effectively ruled the country and annulled the result of the May 1989 presidential election which provoked the US military invasion in December of the same year. The current Endara government, judged to have been denied victory by Noriega, was then installed with US support.

Nicolás Ardito Barletta, the PRD winner of the May 1984 presidential election, had been favoured by the military and his election campaign was supported by a centre-right coalition of six parties, the now defunct **National Democratic Union** (Unade). He was forced to resign by the military in September 1985 when he announced that he would investigate charges that Noriega had ordered the killing of a political opponent, Hugo Spadáfora. Barletta's successor Eric Arturo Delvalle was forced to flee the country after an abortive attempt to dismiss Noriega but still claimed to be president from exile. An interim President, Manuel Solis Palma, was then appointed by the military.

Domestic and international pressure, especially from the US, for the removal of Noriega, who had also been implicated in drug smuggling, continued to mount. His attempt to deny the Civic Opposition Democratic Alliance (ADOC), victory in the May 1989 presidential and legislative elections, by annulling the result, led to his overthrow following the US military invasion in December. The results of the May elections which had been held in safe keeping by the Roman Catholic Church, were then declared valid on Dec. 27 but were incomplete and covered only 64 per cent of voters. Guillermo Endara Galimany was duly sworn in as "Constitutional President" to head a democratic government of reconstruction and national reconciliation (see ADOC below). Using the incomplete returns, 58 seats were confirmed in the Legislative Assembly. Fresh elections on Feb. 27, 1991, for the remaining nine seats resulted in three seats being won by the PRD, two each by the Christian Democratic Party (PDC) and National Liberal Republican Movement (MOLIRENA) and one each to the Liberal Party (PL) and the Labour Party (PALA).

Constitutional structure

Constitutional reforms adopted in April 1963 established a unicameral Legislative Assembly (which replaced the National Assembly of Community Representatives in 1984) consisting of 67 members. Executive power rests with the President, assisted by two elected Vice-Presidents, who appoints a Cabinet.

Electoral system

The President is directly elected by universal adult suffrage for a five-year term as are the two Vice-Presidents.

Evolution of the suffrage

All over 18 years of age are eligible to vote. Women gained the vote in 1946.

Sequence of elections since 1980

Presidential and legislative elections

Date	*Winning party*
May 1984	Democratic Revolutionary Party (PRD)
May 1989	Democratic Opposition Alliance (ADOC) (result annulled by military).

Presidential elections May 1989

Candidate	*Percentage of votes*
Guillermo Endara Galimany (ADOC)	62.0
Carlos Duque Jaén (Coalition for National Liberation—COLINA)	24.9
Hildebrando Nicosia (Panameñista Party—PP)	0.4

Legislative elections May 7, 1989

		No of seats
ADOC		
	PDC	28
	MOLIRENA	16
	PPA	7
	PLA	4
Total		**55**
COLINA		
	PRD	10
	PALA	1
	PL	1
Total		**12**

PARTY BY PARTY DATA

Arnulfista Party

Partido Arnulfista (PA)
Leadership. Guillermo Endara Galimany; Héctor Peñalba (s.-g.).
Orientation. Right-wing.
Founded. 1990.
History. The PA was established by a faction of the now defunct Authentic Panameñista Party (*Partido Panameñista Auténtico* (PPA) led by the late veteran politician Arnulfo Arias Madrid, President of Panama in 1940-41, 1949-51 and for an 11-day period in 1968 as the successful candidate of the five-party Opposition National Union (UNO) before being deposed in a coup d'état. The PPA itself had been launched in 1984 as the "authentic" "panameñista" party, as distinct from the renegade Panameñista Party (PP) set up by Alonso Pinzón and Luis Suárez to contest the 1980 legislative elections, against Arias's wishes.

The PPA, along with MOLIRENA and the Christian Democrat Party (PDC), joined the Civic Opposition Democratic Alliance (ADOC) to back Arias's fifth presidential campaign in 1984 against the military's choice, Nicolas Ardito Barletta of the National Democratic Union (Unade), whose victory they later claimed was fraudulent. The opposition also refused to accept the official results which gave ADOC only 27 of the 67 seats in the Legislative Assembly.

The PPA, which gradually lost the leadership of the ADOC to the PDC, itself split in August 1988 following Arias's death. One faction, again taking the party's original name (PP) and willing to collaborate with the military-backed regime, nominated Hildebrando Nicosia as their candidate in the May 1989 presidential elections. The other faction, however, received ADOC's endorsement of its presidential candidate, PA leader Guillermo Endara, who was judged to have won the election, despite the result being annulled by the military, but who nevertheless, following the US invasion of December 1989, was installed in office. To confirm a break with the past, Endara supporters then established the PA, which was legalized in May 1990.

The ruling ADOC coalition government weathered massive public opposition to its October 1990 austerity policies only to face sustained protests by the trade unions, especially public sector workers, in the new year. Internal divisions and evidence of official corruption and drug-related scandals, some involving Endara's own law firm, severely damaged Endara's reputation. In April 1991, he dismissed five PDC cabinet ministers who he accused of "disloyalty and arrogance", leaving the *Arnulfistas* without an assured majority in the Legislative Assembly. The PDC had 28 seats to the 16, seven and four respectively of the remaining ADOC members, MOLIRENA, the AP and the PLA.

Endara was also increasingly accused of sacrificing national sovereignty by being subservient to the US government, especially in his harsh public criticism of Cuba and most controversially in agreeing to the radical reform of the country's banking secrecy laws in July 1991, which critics said would do little to stop drug trafficking and drug laundering but would drain the country of foreign exchange. Critics, led by the PDC, also accused the government of fomenting military coup scares in order to keep the country in a perpetual state of emergency.

This, they alleged, allowed state security forces more effectively to quell opposition protest. Endara was also blamed for not pressing the US government for adequate compensation for the civilian victims of the December 1989 military invasion, and for not placing imprisoned military associates of Noriega on trial.

In September, Endara's choice for Legislative Assembly president was defeated when Marco Ameglio, a PLA member, aligned himself with the opposition.
Membership. 15,000 (1990 claim).

Authentic Liberal Party

Partido Liberal Auténtico (PLA)
Address. a/c Asamblea Legislativa.
Leadership. Arnulfo Escalona Riós (l.).
Orientation. Right-wing.
Founded. 1987.
History. The PLA was founded by Escalona, the former leader of the National Liberal Party (PLN) who resigned in 1987 in protest at the support offered by the party's president to Gen. Manuel Noriega. The PLN was a member of the ruling National Democratic Union (Unade) but the newly formed PLA joined the Civic Opposition Democratic Alliance (ADOC) and

supported a faction which backed Guillermo Endara, later leader of the PA (see above), who was subsequently adopted as ADOC candidate in the ultimately abortive presidential poll of May 1989. The PLA, individually, won four Legislative Assembly seats in concurrent legislative elections, finally confirmed in February 1990, and Escalona was named the Assembly's Vice-President.

However, association with the increasingly unpopular Endara government damaged the party and led to internal divisions. A PLA dissident, Marco Ameglio, sided with the opposition in September 1991 to defeat Escalona in the election for the presidency of the Legislative Assembly.

Civic Opposition Democratic Alliance

Alianza Democrática de Oposición Cívica (ADOC)
Orientation. Right-wing, free market
History. ADOC emerged from the earlier Opposition Democratic Alliance (ADO) established by the Christian Democrat Party, Authentic Panameñista Party and Nationalist Republican Liberal Movement whose candidate Arnulfo Arias Madrid (see Arnulfista Party) was widely felt by independent observers to have been denied victory in the 1984 presidential elections due to military interference. ADO then called for the removal of Gen. Noriega and the reform of the electoral system to eliminate fraud, a campaign which had its strongest resonance in the formation of the National Civic Crusade (CCN), a broad coalition of opposition groups committed to the demilitarization of the government. A serious split within the PPA in 1988 (see PA) over the choice of its presidential candidate transmitted itself to ADO.

Guillermo Endara Galimany, the leader of a PPA faction, retained the support of the PDC, MOLIRENA and the PLA, and together they reorganized politically to combine ADO with CCN support to create ADOC. Denied victory by Gen. Noriega in the subsequent May 1989 presidential and legislative elections, Endara was installed as head of an ADOC government following US military intervention in December and in February 1990 it was officially recognized as the largest grouping within the Legislative Assembly, with 51 seats, increased to 55 following the February 1991 partial legislative elections. However, the Alliance was severely weakened by the withdrawal of the PDC, the largest party with 28 seats, following a government crisis in April 1991 (see PCD).

Christian Democrat Party

Partido Demócrata Cristiano (PDC)
Address. Apartado 63222, Panamá 5.
Leadership. Ricardo Arias Calderón; Raúl Ossa (s.-g.).
Orientation. Centre-right.
Founded. 1960.
History. The PDC had its origins in the student National Civic Union (1957-1960), where the tradition of European Christian Democratic parties was assimilated. Middle-class professionals, intellectuals and students swelled its ranks but the Federation of Christian Workers (FTC) was also an early affiliate. The PDC contested the 1964 and 1968 presidential elections without much success and during the period when party politics were effectively banned by the military (1968-1978), the party reorganized itself, winning 20 per cent of the vote in the 1980 legislative elections and taking 19 of the 56 seats in the newly formed National Legislative Council (the other 37 being filled by nominees of a non-party National Assembly of Community representatives established in 1972). In 1984, the PDC was part of the Civic Opposition Democratic Alliance (ADOC) which lost the presidential and legislative elections following suspected widespread fraud by the military.

During 1987, the PDC became increasingly involved in confrontations with the government, openly campaigning through strikes (supported mainly by businesses rather than trade unions) and street demonstrations (which were violently suppressed) for the resignation and removal of Gen. Manuel Noriega who was accused of drug trafficking, electoral fraud, corruption and murder. The PDC was again part of the ADOC electoral alliance in May 1989 which supported the presidential candidacy of the Guillermo Endara (see Arnulfista Party—AP) and, following the official ratification of the results following the US military invasion in December became the largest party in the Legislative Assembly with 28 of the 67 seats. Its subsequent withdrawal from the ADOC coalition government in April 1991, when Endara dismissed five PDC cabinet ministers, caused a predictable political crisis. This had followed months of in-fighting and Arias Calderón had publicly described Endara's economic programme, which advocated severe austerity measures and the privatization of state enterprises, as "senseless". Although Arias Calderón was stripped of his Interior and Justice Ministry posts, he remained as one of the Vice-Presidents, a post he won in the May 1989 election annulled by Noriega.

In succeeding months, the PDC became the leader of the opposition, to such an extent that it was exerting strong influence within such organizations as the Civic Crusade, an organization from which Endara had drawn his strongest support and which in June called for a plebiscite to decide on the desirability of Endara remaining in office. In September 1991, the PDC was judged firmly to have secured its political influence on parliamentary committees as a direct result of facilitating the victory of a dissident PLA candidate in the election of a new President of the Legislative Assembly (see AP and PLA).

Membership. 35,785 (1985 claim).

International affiliations. Member party of the Christian Democrat Organization of America, which forms part of the Christian Democrat International.

Democratic Revolutionary Party

Partido Revolucionario Democrático (PRD)

Address. 35-02 Avenida 7a Central, Area del casino. apartado 2650, Panamá 9A.

Leadership. Carlos Duque Jaén (pres.); Gerado Gonzales, Alberto Aléman, Gabriel Altamirano Duque (ls).

Orientation. Originally populist and dedicated to the nationalist revolutionary ideals of Gen. Omar Torrijos Herrera, Commander-in-Chief of the National Guard who led a coup in October 1968 allegedly against imperialism and the oligarchy and in favour of a progressive and multi-class alliance to defend national independence and promote self-determination and integrity. The party subsequently in the 1980s became a vehicle for Gen. Manuel Noriega and is now characterized by its critics as the mainstay of the right-wing Noriega tradition.

Founded. September 1979.

History. The PRD was the product of the radical Torrijos years (1968-1979) dominated by extensive reforms, notably in land distribution, the creation of a non-party National Assembly of Community Representatives (est. 1972) to replace a dissolved National Assembly, and the signing, in 1977, of treaties whereby the US government agreed to hand over control of the Canal zone in the year 2000.

Formally created in 1979 by Torrijos supporters, who included businessmen, Christian Democrats and Marxists, the party retained its progressive image until the death of Torrijos in an air crash in July 1981. The military continued the tradition of Torrijos, albeit manipulating political power from the right of the political spectrum. By the time of the May 1984 presidential and legislative elections, the PRD-led National Democratic Union (Unade) coalition was a tool of the military and was duly declared the clear winner despite evidence of widespread fraud. The lack of PRD political autonomy was amply demonstrated when the Unade President Nicolás Ardito Barletta was forced to stand down by the military in 1985 after indicating his intention of investigating allegations that Noriega was implicated in the murder of an opposition candidate Hugo Spadáfora. Well-publicized allegations in 1985-1988 of Noriega's involvement in murders, drug-dealing, money-laundering, gun-running and espionage for and against the United States did not deflect PRD support for the military.

The party was a member of the Coalition of National Liberation (COLINA) alliance in the May 1989 presidential and legislative alliance and served as apologists for Noriega's annulment of the result until the US military invasion in December. Subsequently, in pursuit of a popular grass-roots base, it allied itself with domestic groups demonstrating for adequate compensation from the US government for civilians killed and property destroyed during the invasion, and with popular protests against corruption in the government and against its austerity policies. In July it opposed government moves to abolish the army, stating that it was needed to guarantee the security of the Panama Canal, and also spearheaded opposition to US demands that Panama's banking secrecy laws be repealed to assist in the detection of drug traffickers and money launderers.

Labour Party

Partido Laborista (PALA)

Address. a/c Asamblea Legislativa, Panamá.

Leadership. Juan Medrano, Azael Vargas, Jorge Federico Lee (ls).

Orientation. Extreme right-wing.

Founded. September 1982.

History. PALA was the product of several attempts by Vargas to establish a strong party on the extreme right. He split from the now defunct Agrarian Labour Party (PLA), co-founded the National Renovation

Movement (MNR) (which in 1982 became the Conservative Party, now defunct) before founding the PALA. The party's hostility to organized labour attracted the support of the country's ruling class, and PALA's then president Carlos Eleta Almarán was prepared to endorse the presidential candidacy of Gen. Ruben Darío Paredes, Chief of the National Guard, in 1984 but for the latter's withdrawal. PALA then joined the National Democratic Union (Unade) and supported its candidate Nicolás Ardito Barletta, whose subsequent victory was felt to have been heavily dependent on the military's ability to rig the results. PALA accepted three cabinet posts but its clientist relationship with the military hindered its further development, a factor behind the ousting of Eleta Almarán as a president who was known to favour a more independent line of development. A member of Unade's successor, the National Liberation Coalition (COLINA), which contested the abortive presidential and legislative elections of May 1989 and supported Gen. Noriega, PALA received one seat in the Legislative Assembly as a result of partial legislative elections held on Jan. 29, 1991, covering nine seats unaccounted for in the May 1989 results.

Liberal Party

Partido Liberal (PL)

Address. El Dorado, Apartado 7363, Panamá 6.

Leadership. Roberto Alemán Rodolfo Chiari (pres.); Jorge Riba, Rosamérica De Vasquez (vice-pres.).

Orientation. Centre-right, its avowal of democracy, national unity, the economic and social emancipation of the individual, peace and free enterprise has been at variance with its support for and presence in right-wing governments and alliances.

Founded. 1932.

History. The country's oldest party, the PL led the National Opposition Union (UNO) that won the presidency in 1960 and 1964. It lost the 1968 elections and was in opposition throughout the de facto rule of Gen. Omar Torrijos Herrera, 1968-1978. Having co-operated with military-backed governments since 1978, the PL joined the pro-government National Democratic Union (Unade) coalition judged by almost no one but those sympathetic to the military to have won the controversial 1984 presidential and legislative elections. In reward, the PL's then leader Roderick Lorenzo Esquivel was named Second Vice-President. On the forced resignation of President Nicolás Ardito Barletta, and the appointment of Erick Delvalle as his successor, Esquivel was promoted to First Vice-President. However, the PL's connection with the Unade government led to splits within its own ranks in 1987, with one minority faction loyal to Delvalle opposed to another opposition grouping around Esquivel, who had called for an inquiry into charges of murder and corruption against Gen. Noriega. A third faction left altogether to form the Authentic Liberal Party. Esquivel and his supporters left the Delvalle government and the Unade in October 1987, a decision subsequently challenged by the pro-government loyalists who won control of the party and replaced Esquivel with Chiari as leader in December. In January 1989 the PL joined the right-wing military-backed Colina electoral front, of which it remained a part despite the annulment of the May 1989 presidential and legislative elections by Noriega and following the US military invasion of December. In partial legislative elections in January 1991, the PL won one seat in the Legislative Assembly.

International affiliations. Member of the Liberal International (since 1982) and founder member of the Liberal Federation of Central America and the Caribbean (FELICA).

Liberty and Pro-Democracy Movement

Movimiento Pro-Democracia y Libertad (MPDL)

Leadership Arrigo Guardia (pres.); Miguel Antonio Berual (l.).

Orientation. Centre-left, populist and progressive.

Founded. March 1991.

History. The MPDL emerged out of the National Civic Crusade (CCN), formed in mid-1987 by labour, business and social organizations to stage anti-Noriega protests. The MPDL continued this populist tradition, only this time against the excesses of the government of Guillermo Endara which it accused of "corruption and nepotism". MPDL leaders stated that the new party was open to all "honest citizens", organized parties and labour groups committed to providing "an alternative to the ruling ADOC coalition movement and the existing opposition and ending the frustration gripping the country". Berual claimed that the government had retained the laws previously passed by the previous military regimes and continued to rule with the same "autocratic" conceptions. He stated that the MPDL wanted to establish a "functional and participative democracy" and would press for the convening of a National Constituent Assembly to lay the foundations for a new republic.

National Liberation Coalition

Coalición Nacional de Liberación (COLINA)
Leadership. Carlos Jaén Duque (l.).
Orientation. Right-wing.
Founded. 1989.
History. COLINA succeeded the Democratic National Union (Unade) coalition of parties which was discredited after winning the presidential and legislative elections of 1984, widely held to have been fraudulent, and then by close association while in government with the military under Gen. Manuel Noriega. The new grouping was composed of the Democratic Revolutionary Party (PRD), the Labour Party (PALA), the Liberal Party (PL) and the following parties, all of which are now defunct: the Republican Party (PR), the Revolutionary Panameñista Party (PPR), the People's Party of Panama (PPP) and the Democratic Workers Party (PDT). The military's blatant interference in the May 1989 presidential and legislative elections in favour of COLINA to prevent the victory of the ADOC opposition alliance and then the subsequent annulling of the result by Gen. Manuel Noriega, led to a storm of domestic and international protest. The annulment was revoked in December 1989 following the US military invasion that ousted Noriega. On the basis of 64 per cent of the returns, preserved by the Roman Catholic Church, Duque Jaén was placed second in the presidential race with 24.9 per cent of the vote to 62.0 per cent for the ADOC's Guillermo Endara Galimany. Incomplete returns for the legislative elections also showed that COLINA had only performed modestly, being allocated seven seats, although its position in the Legislative Assembly was improved to a total of 12 seats when the PRD won three seats and the PL and PALA one each in partial legislative elections for nine unaccounted seats held on Jan. 27 1991 (see ADOC).

Nationalist Republican Liberal Movement

Movimiento Liberal Republicana y Nacionalista (MOLIRENA)
Address. a/c Asamblea Legislativa, Panamá.
Leadership. Guillermo Ford.
Orientation. Right-wing free marketeer.
Founded. October 1981.
History. The party was established by breakaway groups of the now defunct Third Nationalist Party (TPN) and Republican Party (PR) and the Liberal Party (PL). Opposed to the military's hold on the country, it joined the Opposition Democratic Alliance (ADO) to contest the 1984 presidential and legislative elections and thereafter supported the campaign of the National Civic Crusade for the removal of the Commander of the Defence forces, Gen. Manuel Noriega. The party was a member of the Opposition Civic Democratic Alliance (ADOC) denied power by Noriega following the presidential and legislative elections of May 1989. Once the ADOC was installed in power following the US military invasion in December, the party received 15 seats in the Legislative Assembly. Ford was named as the Second Vice-President and Minister for Planning and Economic Policy. As such, he had a major say in defining the government's IMF-approved economic austerity programme and was the architect of a plan, presented in September 1991, for the wholesale privatization of the state sector, including, most controversially, social welfare agencies.

Guerrilla Groups

20th December Movement (*Movimiento-20 —M-20*), right-wing, formed to avenge the Dec. 20, 1989, US military invasion. It has claimed responsibility for several bomb attacks, including one that killed a US soldier in a Panama city night-spot in March 1990. It staged a machine-gun attack on the US embassy in June 1990, allegedly in response to the recent "execution" of its leader Angel Bénitez, who was a leader of Noriega's Dignity Battalions.

Defunct parties

The Electoral Tribunal of Panama in February 1991 dissolved the following parties because they no longer commanded the statutory minimum percentage of the national vote: the social democratic Popular Action Party (PAPO); the centrist Popular Nationalist Party (PNP), the Panamanian Revolutionary Party (PPR); the Authentic Panamanian Party (PPA); the Workers' Democratic Party (PDT); the National Action Party (PAN); the Republican Party (PR); the Panamanian People's Party (PPP).

Paraguay

Capital: Asunción **Population: 3,800,000**

Paraguay achieved independence from Spain in 1811. Its first constitution was introduced in 1844 in order to legitimize the power of Carlos Antonio López, one of the three consecutive dictators to rule Paraguay up to the end of the war of the Triple Alliance in 1870, in which Paraguay's population was halved. Political forces subsequently developed into the Colorado and Liberal parties who have dominated Paraguayan politics since 1876. A three-year period of military rule, albeit by reformist officers, followed the 1933-35 second Chaco war with Bolivia. A new constitution introduced in 1940 failed to build a state-dominated society and after a succession of unstable governments Gen. Alfredo Stroessner took power in a military coup in 1954.

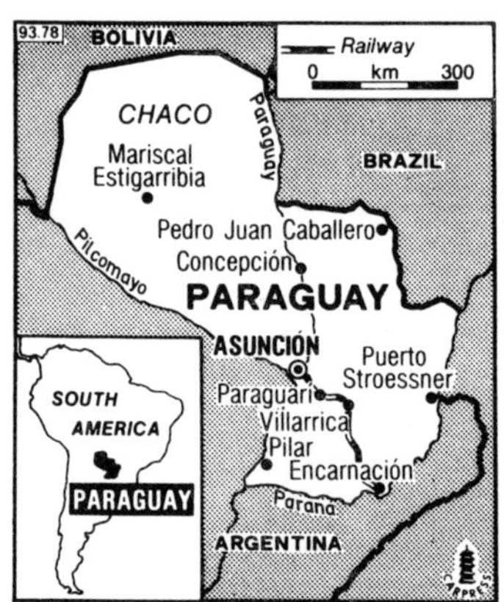

During Stroessner's 35-year rule Paraguay was under a permanent state of siege and all constitutional rights and civil liberties were suspended. The country's economic and political structure was nonetheless stabilized and its infrastructure greatly modernized. Stroessner was declared the winner of all eight elections which were held at five-year intervals. He was overthrown on Feb. 3, 1989, in a "palace coup" led by Gen. Andrés Rodríguez who was sworn in immediately as interim President. The subsequent presidential and congressional elections which took place on May 1, 1989, in which Rodríguez and the Colorado party won a sweeping victory, were considered to have been relatively free and open by international observers. Election to membership of the Group of Rio in October 1990 and entry into the Mercosur South American Common Market, with Argentina, Brazil and Uruguay, in March 1991 did much to restore the country's international credibility.

Constitutional structure

Under the 1968 Constitution executive power is vested in the President (who must be a Roman Catholic); he governs with the assistance of an appointed Council of Ministers. Legislative power, before the overthrow of Stroessner, was only nominally held by a bicameral National Congress comprising a Senate of at least 30 members and a 72-member Chamber of Deputies. A new constitution, in preparation and expected to come into force in 1992, is expected to curtail the previous powers of the President, which included the power to veto congressional legislation, to control foreign policy, and to declare a state of siege with the consequent suspension of all civil liberties.

Electoral system

The President is directly elected for a renewable five-year term. Both the Senate and the Chamber of Deputies are directly elected for five-year terms (subject to dissolution by the President). The party receiving the largest number of votes is allotted two-thirds of the seats in both houses, with the remaining seats being divided among other parties according to their electoral strength. A political coalition is not allowed currentlyto put forward a presidential candidate or participate in the elections.

Evolution of the suffrage

Voting is compulsory for all men and women of 18 years of age and older. Women have been allowed to vote since 1958

Sequence of elections since 1989

Presidential Election May 1, 1989

Candidate	*Party*	*% of vote*
Andrés Rodríguez	Colorado Party (ANR-PC)	74.2
Domingo Laíno|	Authentic Radical Liberal Party (PLRA)	18.0

Congressional election May 1, 1989

Party	*% of vote*	*Chamber*	*Senate*
Colorado Party (ANR-PC)	72.8	48	24
Authentic Radical liberal Party (PLRA)	20.1	19	10
Revolutionary Febrerista Party (PRF)	2.1	2	1
Radical Liberal Party (PLR)	1.1	1	1
Christian Democratic Party (PDC)	1.0	1	-
Liberal Party (PL)	0.4	1	-
Others	2.5	-	
Total	**100.0**	**72**	**36**

Constituent Assembly Elections Dec. 1, 1991

Party	*% of vote*	*Seats*
Colorado Party (ANR)	55.1	123
Authentic Liberal Radical Party (PRLA)	27.0	57
Constitution for All (CPT)	11.0	16
Revolutionary Febrerist Party (PRF)	1.3	1
Christian Democratic Party (PDC)	0.8	1
Others	4.8	-
Total	**100.0**	**198**

PARTY BY PARTY DATA

Authentic Liberal Radical Party

Partido Liberal Radical Auténtico (PLRA)
Address. a/c Congreso Nacional, Asunción.
Leadership. Juan Manuel Benítez Florentín (l.); Domingo Laíno (l.).
Orientation. Centrist.
Founded. 1978.
History. The PLRA was formed by Domingo Laíno, president of the Radical Liberal Party (PLR) and dissidents from the United Liberal Party (PLU—a splinter group from the PLR). The party was a founder member of the National Agreement (*Acuerdo Nacional—AN*), a coalition of four opposition parties with the aim of pressing for democratization and respect for human rights. Although the PLRA was the largest opposition party within Paraguay it was denied legal status. Under the Stroessner regime, it boycotted all elections and organized anti-government rallies. Many PLRA activists were arrested on these occasions and had to serve prison sentences. After four years of arrests and persecution for his open criticism of the regime, Laíno himself was deported in 1982 for "insulting" the memory of the former dictator of Nicaragua, Anastasio Somoza. He made numerous attempts to re-enter the country and in April 1987 was finally allowed to stay, after he made his way to Asunción accompanied by prominent politicians from Argentina, Brazil and Uruguay and a former US ambassador to Paraguay. He then suffered periodic arrests and beatings, treatment to which most PLRA leaders and activists were subjected.

In April 1988 the PLRA put forward a joint proposal with the "ethical" faction of the ruling Colorado Party (ANR-PC), demanding a transition to democracy by way of a provisional government in which both the Colorados and the PLRA would be involved.

The PLRA was legalized on March 8, 1989, a month after the military coup against Stroessner. The party unsuccessfully asked for elections to be postponed in order to give all opposition parties an opportunity to put their case and to draw up a new electoral register.

The PLRA convention of March 27 decided to participate in the May elections despite the short notice, but its attempt to form a National Accord coalition was outlawed by the authorities. Undeterred, Laíno stood as the PLRA presidential candidate and the party came second in both the presidential and congressional elections, winning the highest percentage of the opposition vote (although as expected its share of the vote was far smaller than that of the ruling Colorados). Laíno obtained 18 per cent of the votes and the PLRA won 20.1 per cent, giving it 19 seats in the Chamber and 10 seats in the Senate.

In the Constituent Assembly elections of Dec. 1, 1991, the PLRA again proved to be the strongest opposition party but ran a relaxed campaign, now convinced that the Colorados were a spent force. It won only 27 per cent of the vote and obtained 57 seats in the 198-seat Assembly.

Christian Democratic Party

Partido Demócrata Cristiano (PDC)
Address. Colón 871, Casi Piribebuy, Casilla 1318, Asunción.
Leadership. Jerónimo Irala Burgos (pres.)
Orientation. Centrist christian democratic, favours free enterprise.
Founded. 1960.
History. Formed by Luis Alfonso Resck, the party was illegal from the outset although it obtained the right to hold meetings. The PDC consistently called for a boycott of elections and in 1978 joined three other opposition parties in the National Accord alliance (AN). Resck was charged with subversion in July 1981 and after a hunger strike and imprisonment, during which he was tortured, he went into exile. As a result of pressure from the West German government, Resck was permitted to return to Paraguay in April 1986.

The PDC was legalized following the February 1989 coup which toppled Stroessner, and was allowed to participate in the elections of May 1, 1989. It obtained one seat in the Chamber (with 1 per cent of the vote). In the Dec. 1, 1991, Constituent Assembly elections, the party only won one of the 198 seats.
Publications. DC-CE (party organ); *Revolución* (youth organ).
International Affiliations. Member party of the Christian Democrat Organization of America, which forms part of the Christian Democrat International.

Constitution for All

Constitución Para Todos (CPT)
Orientation. An independent coalition supported by the Roman Catholic church and the CUT and CNT trade union confederations.
Founded. 1991.

History. The CPT grew out of the *Asunción para Todos—Apto* (Asunción for All), a new radical and progressive movement which won the May 1991 municipal elections in the capital, Asunción, with 35 per cent of the vote, beating the ruling Colorado party's candidate by seven per cent. Apto's victorious charismatic candidate Carlos Filizzola, was the president of the Association of Physicians and led a widely reported doctors' strike in 1986 which became a focus for the popular opposition to Stroessner.

The CPT, however, fared surprisingly badly in the Dec. 1, 1991, Constituent Assembly elections despite its important role in mobilizing popular support for constitutional reform. The CPT obtained only 11 per cent of the vote and 16 seats, suffering a set-back even in Asunción where it won only 23 per cent of the poll. The CPT's poor performance was attributed to a lack of experience in mobilizing voters, but was also put down to over-confidence and complacency stemming from the false belief that the Colorados were a spent political force, a mistake shared by other opposition parties.

Febrerist Revolutionary Party

Partido Revolucionario Febrerista (PRF)
Address. Casa del Pueblo, Manduvirá 552, Asunción.
Leadership. Euclides Acevedo (pres.).
Orientation. Social democratic.
Founded. 1936.
History. The PRF was founded following the radical nationalist coup of Feb. 17, 1936, which inspired the party's name. The new regime headed by Col. Rafael Franco was deposed in August of the following year and the PRF, which had supported Franco, was banned. In mid-1946 the *Febreristas* were invited to participate in the Colorado government but were expelled again in early 1947 for leading an anti-government rebellion. The uprising was joined by Communists and Liberals and developed into a civil war in which most of the rebel leaders were killed. The survivors went into exile and expelled most of the PRF's left wing. Nonetheless the PRF formed a short-lived guerrilla group, the *Vanguardia Febrerista* in 1959. In the same year the party also formed an alliance with the old Liberal Party (PL) and campaigned for absenteeism in the 1960 election. The party was legalized in the mid-1960s and participated in the 1967-68 elections in which it gained a seat in the Chamber of Deputies. However, because of blatant fraud, it boycotted all later elections and in 1978 joined three illegal opposition parties in forming the National Alliance coalition.

In 1983 the radical wing, led by Euclides Acevedo, gained control of the party and in February 1984 the PRF called the first demonstration against the government in 20 years. Although the centrist faction regained control of the party in 1985, the PRF continued to organize and participate in rallies, and its clear stance against the regime resulted in raids on its offices and arrests of PRF leaders.

The party participated again in elections after the coup against Stroessner in February 1989. Acevedo tried to persuade interim President Andrés Rodríguez to postpone the elections to enable opposition parties to organize their campaigns, but was informed that this would set a bad precedent and told to regard the elections as "training" exercise. The PRF nonetheless ran candidates in the May 1, 1989, general election, obtaining an overall vote of 2.1 per cent and was allocated two seats in the Chamber and one in the Senate. In the Dec. 1, 1991, elections to the Constitutional Assembly, the party gained only 1.2 per cent of the vote and one seat of the 198 seats.
Publications. El Pueblo (The People), weekly.
International affiliations. Socialist International.

Liberal Party

Partido Liberal (PL)
Leadership. Hugo Fulvio Celauro (l.).
Orientation. Centre-right.
Founded. 1961.
History. The PL is the successor of the 19th century party of the same name which held power, with Argentinian backing, from 1904 until 1936 and again in 1939 until it was dissolved by Gen. Higinio Moríngo in 1942. One branch of the splintered liberal movement joined the Febrerist Revolutionary Party (PRF) and provoked a revolt against Moríngo in 1947. In 1959 a further section of exiled liberal students formed the "14th of May" guerrilla group whose armed incursions into Paraguay in 1959-61 were crushed by the army.

After giving up the armed struggle, the liberal movement re-formed as the Liberal Party but suffered a split soon after. The small remaining PL rump became officially registered as a political party in 1963 under the name of the Renewal Movement. The party fielded unsuccessful candidates against Stroessner in the 1968, 1973, 1978, 1983 and 1988 presidential elections and its subsequent acceptance of a token representation in the Congress gave it the reputation of being subservient to the government, a charge amply proved by its dramatic collapse following Stroessner's overthrow in February 1989. In the May 1989 elections it won a mere 0.4 per cent of the vote, giving it one seat in the Chamber of Deputies, and its presidential candidate, Carlos Ferreira Ibarra, polled a negligible amount of votes. The party failed to win a single seat in the December 1991 Constituent Assembly election.

National Accord

Acuerdo Nacional (AN)
Leadership. Domingo Laíno (pres.).
Orientation. Centre-right.
Founded. 1978.
History. The AN was formed as an alliance of the four main extra-parliamentary parties, namely the Christian Democrats (PDC), the Popular Colorado Movement (MOPOCO), the Authentic Liberal Radicals (PLRA) and the Febrerist Revolutionary Party (PRF), the only legal party to be an AN member. The Accord co-ordinated the activities of its member parties which under Stroessner were mainly confined to campaigns for election boycotts, for the release of political prisoners and for the lifting of the state of siege.

Despite a process of democratization following the February 1989 overthrow of Stroessner, the AN, as a coalition, remained barred by the old constitution from fielding any candidates in the elections. By putting up their own candidates, member parties were therefore deprived from pooling their resources and, as a result, attracted far fewer votes than they could have expected to attract as a united front. The National Accord nonetheless continued to operate as an intermediary between the four member parties, and, dependent on constitutional reform, it expects to contest the general election of 1993.

National Republican Association-Colorado Party

Asociación Nacional Republicana (ANR-Partido Colorado)
Address. a/c Congreso Nacional, Asunción.
Leadership. Luís María Argaña (pres.).
Orientation. Right-wing.
Founded. 1887.
History. The Colorado Party originated in a conservative faction created by Gen. Bernardino Caballero (President of Paraguay 1882-91) and it took its name from the faction's red banners.

The Colorados were in power from 1887 until 1904, remained in opposition to Liberal governments until 1940 and opposed Moríngo's pro-Axis regime. A Colorado-*Febrerist* Revolutionary Party (PRF—*Febreristas*) coalition government was installed in 1946 after the USA put pressure on the regime. Moríngo expelled the *Febreristas* one year later and the Colorados thwarted them and their Liberal and Communist allies in the brief civil war which ensued. After a succession of coups and faction fighting between the *guionista* (extremist) and *democrático* (democratic) wings of the party, a democratic government was inaugurated in 1950 under Federico Chávez of the Colorado democratic faction.

The military coup of May 5, 1954, marked the beginning of Gen. Alfredo Stroessner's 35-year dictatorship. Then an army commander, he was officially elected President in July 1954. In 1956 Stroessner reorganized the party after exiling his main Colorado rival, Epifanio Méndez Fleitas. The 1958 elections were, like all six later elections held under his rule, completely stage-managed. To give a semblance of democracy, two opposition parties were permitted to take part and win some seats in Congress from 1968. The manipulated results invariably showed overwhelming support for Stroessner, despite the reality of exile, arrests, long prison sentences and torture being meted out to his political opponents.

While Stroessner was sworn in for an eighth term on Aug. 15, 1988, after winning 88.6 per cent of the official ballot the previous February, the Colorado party was beginning to reflect dissatisfaction with his dictatorship. The internal drive for increased democracy came mainly from the "ethical" faction (which had emerged in 1985 and was led by Carlos Romero Pereira) who signed a "democratic commitment" with the opposition Authentic Radical Liberal Party (PLRA) and in September put forward a joint proposal, together with the Popular Colorado Movement (MOPOCO), for a transition to democracy. More moderate arguments for change came from the larger "traditionalist" faction led by Gen. Andrés

Rodríguez, while the "militants" demanded a continuation of the status quo.

The violent coup of Feb. 3, 1989, which toppled Stroessner took place shortly before his former close ally, Rodríguez, was to be transferred from his top army position of First Army Commander to the passive role of Defence Minister. Rodríguez, as interim President, legalized most opposition parties and called a general election for May 1, 1989. As the Colorado's presidential candidate, Rodríguez won 78.18 per cent of the valid vote and the party polled 72.8 per cent of the vote in the congressional elections, giving it the two-thirds majority in Congress demanded by the Constitution. Despite suspicions of the size of the Colorado landslide and opposition accusations of widespread malpractice, the elections were considered by foreign observers to have been relatively free and open. Some of the party's electoral success was attributed to its wealth and organization, but a telling factor was Rodríguez's public pledges of democracy, reconciliation, and respect for human rights. He also restored good relations with the Catholic hierarchy, following violent and repressive attacks on the Church in previous years.

Rodríguez, promising that he would not stand for a second term, was sworn on May 15, 1989, and retained his interim Cabinet. The ensuing power struggle between the "traditionalists" and the newly formed "democratic" wing led, however to a severe rift in the party. A Colorado Party convention, dominated by "traditionalists", went ahead in early December 1989 despite a court injunction brought by the "democratic" faction, led by Blas Riquelme, and said to be supported by Rodríguez. This was followed on Dec. 11, 1989, by the resignation of the whole Cabinet. The leader of the "traditionalists", the Foreign Minister José María Argaña whose influence had grown considerably since the February coup, was dismissed in mid-August 1990 after his public statement that the Colorados would never give up power (contrary to Rodríguez's pledge to hold elections in 1993). The effects of such an internal struggle became clear in the May 1991 municipal elections, when the Colorado candidate Juan Manuel Morales lost Asunción to the popular Asunción for All Movement (Apto). After pressure from the army, who feared exclusion from the Constitutional reform process if the party failed to win a majority in the Constituent Assembly elections, a truce between the factions was imposed. The "traditionalists" duly won control of the party in the October internal elections.

The December 1991 elections for the Constituent Assembly produced a resounding victory for the Colorados, who won 55.1 per cent of the popular vote and 123 of the 198 seats.

Popular Colorado Movement

Movimiento Popular Colorado (MOPOCO)
Orientation. Centre-left.
Founded. 1959.
History. The party was crated by the former Colorado party leader Epifanio Méndez Fleitas, who was exiled by Stroessner in 1956, and anti-Stroessner dissidents from the Colorado Party (ANR-PC) who were exiled in 1959 after the Chamber of Deputies had condemned police and military violence. Although MOPOCO was formed in exile, the party nonetheless had a following in Paraguay. Attempts by one faction to re-establish links with the main Colorado party caused a split in 1973, with the breakaway group forming the (now defunct) ANR of Exile and Resistance. A year later about a thousand MOPOCO supporters were arrested for alleged guerrilla activity. In 1978 the party became a founder member of the National Accord (AN). Under pressure from the new democratic Argentinian government, 20 MOPOCO leaders were allowed to return to Paraguay in 1983 but any section of the media which aired their views, such as the Roman Catholic Radio Nanduti and the magazine *ABC Color*, was immediately closed down. Leaders and members of the party continued to be harassed and prevented from holding meetings and in 1985 its first and second vice-presidents were sent into internal exile. In September 1988 MOPOCO signed a proposal with the "ethical" faction of the ruling Colorado party for a transition to democracy. MOPOCO was legalized after the February 1989 overthrow of Stroessner, but unlike the other three National Accord members, it did not participate in any of the elections.

Radical Liberal Party

Partido Radical Liberal (PRL)
Orientation. Centre-right.
Founded. 1961.
History. The party was one of the two legalized opposition parties under the Stroessner regime. It was founded by a majority breakaway group from the Liberal Party (PL) and was given legal status in the

same year. It gained 28 seats in the constituent convention in 1967 and in the elections of 1968 and 1973 gained 16 seats in the Chamber of Deputies. From 1975 to 1977 the party was controlled by the reformist faction which was less compliant to the regime. The PLR split in 1977 when the conservatives regained the party leadership and the former party president Domingo Laíno, along with a large section of the party, left to form the Unified Liberal Party (which itself split in 1978 and became the Authentic Liberal Radical Party). The remainder of the PLR continued to participate in elections, winning 13 seats in the Chamber and six seats in the Senate in 1983 with 5.7 per cent of the poll. In the February 1988 general election, the PLR presidential candidate Luis María Vega, one of the two candidates permitted to stand against Stroessner, won 7.18 per cent of the official vote.

In the first relatively free elections on May 1, 1989, Aniano Denis Estigarribia was the PLR presidential candidate but attracted only a very small number of votes. In the simultaneous congressional elections the party won 1.1 per cent of the national vote which gave it one seat in each chamber. The PLR's political appeal declined further in the new democratic atmosphere and in the Dec. 1, 1991, elections for representation in the Constituent Assembly the PLR failed to gain a seat.

Publication. El Radical (weekly).

Minor parties

Humanist Party (*Partido Humanista*—PH); won 0.3 per cent or less in May 1, 1989, congressional elections.

Paraguayan Communist Party (*Partido Comunista Paraguayo*—PCP); has been illegal since its foundation in 1928 apart from short periods in 1936 and in 1946-47. Various attempts to mount a guerrilla resistance to the Stroessner regime from 1959 onwards were completely suppressed by 1966 and many of PCP leaders and members were believed to have been imprisoned without trial and tortured to death. Despite democratization following the overthrow of Stroessner in February 1989, the PCP was not permitted to participate in the May 1, 1989, elections. The party's general secretary Antonio Maidana, however, who was released from prison in 1978 to be expelled from the country, returned from exile in December 1989.

People's Democratic Movement (*Movimiento Democratico Popular*—MDP); led by Mercedes Soler, it was founded on Sept. 23, 1988. The MDP purports to be a democratic, popular, national and anti-imperialist political organization.

United Radical Liberal Party (*Partido Liberal Radical Unido*—PLRU) won 0.3 per cent of the vote or less in the May 1, 1989, congressional elections.

Peru

Capital: Lima **Population: 21,600,000**

The Republic of Peru achieved independence from Spain in 1826. In the post-independence era up to the present, periods of civilian government have frequently alternated with the rule of military dictatorships, the last holding power in 1968-1980. A move towards broad political alliances has characterized the recent activity of both left-wing and right-wing parties and the current President, Alberto Keinya Fujimori, had attempted to establish political consensus by forming a national unity government. Failing this, coupled with his deep distrust of the opposition and the judiciary, Fujimori staged an army-backed presidential coup in April 1992.

Constitutional structure

Under the 1980 Constitution, a bicameral National Congress is made up of a 180-member Chamber of Deputies and a Senate consisting of 60 elected members plus past presidents who can sit for life. Executive power rests with the President who appoints a Council of Ministers.

Electoral system

The President, together with the two Vice-Presidents and the Congress, is elected nationally by universal adult suffrage for a five-year term. If in the presidential elections no candidate obtains at least 36 per cent of the vote, a second round between the two leading candidates is contested. The president may not stand for a second term. The Senate is elected on a regional basis and the Chamber of Deputies, which can be dissolved by the president in exceptional circumstances, is elected regionally by party-list proportional representation, 40 members from the province of Lima and 140 representing the rest of the country.

Evolution of the suffrage

Men and women over 18 are eligible to vote and registration and voting is compulsory until the age of 60. Women gained the vote for the first time in 1956.

Railway
0 km 300
88.78
ECUADOR
COLOMBIA
Napo
Putumayo
Iquitos
Amazon
Talara
Piura
Marañón
Moyobamba
Chiclayo
Cajamarca
BRAZIL
Trujillo
Pucallpa
Chimbote
Huallanca
Ucayali
Cerro de Pasco
Pacific
La Oroyo
PERU
Callao
LIMA
Huancayo
Macchu Picchu
Huancavelica
BOLIVIA
Cuzco
Ica
Ocean
Lake Titicaca
Arequipa
Puno
PERU
Mollendo
SOUTH AMERICA
Tacna
CHILE
CARPRESS

Sequence of elections since 1980

Date	*Winning party*
May 1980 (presidential and legislative)	Popular Action
April 1985 (presidential and legislative)	American Popular Revolutionary Alliance-Peruvian Aprista Party
April 1990 (legislative)	Democratic Front
April/June 1990 (presidential)	Change 90

Presidential elections, 1990

First round, April	*% of votes*
Alberto Fujimori (Cambio 90)	24.62
Mario Vargas Llosa (FREDEMO)	27.61
Luis Alva Castro (APRA)	19.17
Henry Pease (IU)	6.97
Alfonso Barrantes Lingan (IS)	4.07
Second round, June	
Alberto Fujimori (Cambio 90)	56.53
Mario Vargas Llosa (FREDEMO)	33.95

Congressional elections April 8 1990

Party	*Senate*	*Chamber of Deputies*
FREDEMO	20	63
APRA	16	49
Cambio 90	14	34
IU	6	-
IS	3	-
FNTC	1	-
Other parties		34

Presidential elections, April 14, 1985

	% of votes
Alan García (APRA)	45.7
Alfonso Barrantes (IU)	21.3
Luis Bedoya Reyes (Democratic Convergence)	9.7
Javier Alva Orlandini (AP)	6.3
Others	2.6

Congressional elections, April 14, 1985

	Senate	*Chamber of deputies*
APRA	32	107
United Left (IU)	15	48
Democratic Convergence	7	12
AP	5	10
National Left	1	1
Independents	-	2

PARTY BY PARTY DATA

American Popular Revolutionary Alliance-Peruvian Aprista Party

Alianza Popular Revolucionaria Americana-Partido Aprista Peruano (APRA)

Address. Avda Alfonso Ugarte 1012, Lima 5.

Leadership. Alan García Pérez (s.-g.); Gilmer Calderón (party sec.).

Orientation. Centre-right. Pledges in the mid-1980s to promote democracy and human rights, improve general living standards and to resist IMF-imposed austerity programmes gave the party a populist image but were largely unfulfilled. Faced with spiralling inflation and mounting guerrilla activity, the APRA government imposed its own economic austerity measures and extended states of emergency around the country, conferring increased powers on the security forces.

Founded. 1924 (est. in Peru 1930 as the Partido Aprista Peruano).

History. APRA, the oldest and most dominant party in Peru, started as a continent-wide anti-imperialist movement by Víctor Raúl Haya de la Torre, a Peruvian Marxist in exile in Mexico. Its original purpose was politically to unite Latin America, obtain joint control of the Panama Canal and gain social control of land and industry. The Peruvian branch of APRA, the Peruvian Aprista Party *(Partido Aprista Peruano*—PAP) was founded in 1930 when Haya returned to Peru. As it became the sole surviving Aprista party, the PAP was increasingly referred to as APRA.

Haya unsuccessfully stood in the 1931 elections and following APRA-linked disturbances by urban workers and peasants, he was imprisoned from 1932-1933. The party was declared illegal in 1933 and remained so (barring a three-year legal period) until 1956. A coalition with the Social Christians and smaller parties in the National Front (*Frente Nacional*—FN) for the 1945 elections, in which José Luís Bustamente y Rivera of the Social Christians was elected with 45 per cent of the vote, allowed APRA to be legalized under the name of the Popular Party (*Partido Popular*—PP).

Bustamente rewarded APRA with 3 cabinet posts, but in 1947 the APRA ministers resigned after disagreements with the government. A year later, a military coup brought Gen. Manuel Odría to power, and APRA, then the largest party in Congress, was once more banned.

At the end of the Odría regime APRA re-emerged as a moderate force and supported the Peruvian Democratic Movement (MDP) of conservative ex-President Manuel Prado in the 1956 elections. Haya's authoritarian dominance of APRA produced the first split in 1960, when the opponents of co-existence with the right and a pro-Cuban faction left to form Rebel APRA (APRA Rebelde). In June 1962 Haya contested the presidential election, widely held to have been fraudulent, and marginally failed to win the necessary one-third of the valid vote. He withdrew in favour of Odría, the former dictator, who came third, before Congress could appoint a president. The army, nevertheless, staged a coup. In the fresh presidential and congressional elections of June 1963, Haya won 34.3 per cent of the vote but came only second to Fernando Belaúnde Terry of the Popular Action-Christian Democrat (AP-PDC) coalition. The party, however, gained 58 seats to form the largest bloc in the Chamber of Deputies and with the assistance of the right-wing National Odriíst Union (UNO) obstructed government legislation.

The 1968 military coup was welcomed by APRA and, despite the Aprista trade unions' anti-government activities, the party broadly supported the regime which lasted until 1980. In 1979 Haya, at the age of 83, was elected for the first time to a public office as President of the Constituent Assembly after APRA won 35 per cent of the vote and 37 out of 100 seats in the June 1978 constituent elections. He was also to be the APRA's candidate in the May 1980 presidential election but died nine months before they were held. His successor, Armando Villanueva del Campo, representing the left of the party which he led from 1978 to 1982, came second in the presidential race with 27.4 per cent of the vote. In 1981, a conservative faction led by Andrés Townsend Ezcurra split away to form the Hayista Base Movement (MBH), claiming that Haya's aims had been betrayed. Alan García Pérez,, took over as secretary-general in 1982 and led the party to victory in the April 1985 elections. APRA candidates won 107 seats in the 180-seat Chamber of Deputies and 32 gained seats in the Senate. García came first in the presidential elections but obtained only 21.3 per cent of the vote. However, his direct opponent Dr Alfonso Barrantes Lingánof the Socialist Left (IS) withdrew before the June run-off election.

García, the first Aprista to be elected President, and youngest ever to hold the office, was sworn in on July 25, 1985. His principal election promises were to halt the country's economic decline by devoting no more than 10 per cent of export earnings to service the huge foreign debt. In an attempt to address widespread and escalating guerrilla activity, he set up a Peace Commission. In June 1986, however, García ordered the quelling of mutinies in three different prisons, staged mainly by Shining Path guerrillas, as a result of which an estimated 254 guerrillas were murdered by the security forces. All the members of the Peace Commission resigned in protest. In addition accusations that the government was using the right-wing Comando Rodrigo Franco death squads to intimidate left-wing opponents dented APRA's liberal image. García, however, felt vindicated in his policies following APRA's resounding success in the November 1986 municipal elections, in which his party won 1,833 municipalities, including eight major cities. By 1987, however, the government was faced with a major labour unrest and the Prime Minister and Minister of Economy and Finance resigned in June. A month later, García announced his intention to curb the flight of capital from Peru by nationalizing all banks and privatizing financial and insurance institutions. In mid-1988 García imposed austerity measures to halt the severe economic problems. These did not curb inflation and led to widespread public discontent and heavy electoral defeat, foreshadowed in the November 1989 municipal election results.

In the April 1990 presidential and congressional elections, APRA won only 16 Senatorial seats and 49 seats in the Chamber of Deputies, and its presidential candidate and secretary-general Luís Alvaro (Castro), was beaten by two newcomers to politics, Mario Vargas Llosa of the Democratic Front (FREDEMO) coalition and Alberto Keinya Fujimori of Change 90. APRA supported the victorious Fujimori in the second round of the presidential election. The Aprista Armando Villanueva del Campo was given the post of President of the new Senate and Alvaro Castro became President of the new Chamber of Deputies. No APRA members were appointed to Fujimori's "national unity" cabinet, however, allegedly in response to right-wing allegations that Fujimori was being manipulated by APRA.

In the aftermath of the Fujimori's April 1992 presidential coup, García, elected secretary-general of the party in February, went into hiding from where he called for popular resistance to restore democratic rule. He had been released on corruption charges by the Supreme Court in February, a decision which had angered the government given the predominance of APRA supporters in the judiciary, which became one of the chief targets of the coup. Several prominent APRA politicians and trade unionists were briefly arrested and the main opposition news magazine *Carretas* was temporarily closed down.
Structure: The party president and political commission are appointed by the National Congress. APRA controls the Confederation of Peruvian Workers (CTP).
Membership. 700.000 (1985 est.).
Publications. Carretas, the weekly news magazine has been generally pro-APRA.
Affiliations. Associate Member of the Socialist International.

Change 90

Cambio 90
Leadership. Alberto Keinya Fujimori (l.); Guillermo Yoshikawa (s.-g.).
Orientation. Centre-right. A professed non-ideological and pragmatic response to the related problems of economic crisis and internal security was replaced by conservative policies of economic austerity and increased powers for the security forces. This culminated with the presidential coup of April 1992, when Fujimori dispensed with the Congress and began ruling by decree.
Founded. 1989.
History. Cambio 90 was formed by a group of independents to fight the April 1990 elections. Their campaign slogan was "hard work, honesty and technology" which promoted the apolitical image of *Cambio's* presidential candidate, the agronomist Alberto Fujimori. Support from the evangelical churches alienated the Roman Catholic Church, despite Fujimori himself being a Roman Catholic. This, however, did not deter many workers and rural migrants in towns and cities and peasants in the Andes who, disillusioned with the major political parties and fearful of the Democratic Front's (FREDEMO) promised "austerity programme", were attracted to *Cambio.* In the first round of the presidential election

held in April 1990, Fujimori came a close second with 24.6 per cent of the vote, forcing a second round. Supported by APRA and all the left-wing parties, he won the June run-off election with 56.3 per cent of the vote, defeating the FREDEMO candidate Mario Vargas Llosa. Fujimori became President in July and formed a "government of national unity" consisting of members from left-wing and right-wing parties, technocrats and members of the armed forces. The fact that *Cambio* was only the third-largest force in the Senate and Chamber of Deputies meant that Fujimori had to rely on the support of other parties. This was reduced as public opposition mounted to both the government's stern economic austerity measures, something which Fujimori had denounced during his election campaign, and the privatization of 230 of the 240 state-run companies. He also pledged to resume repayments on the foreign debt, halted since 1985. The more public resistance Fujimori met, the more he relied on an autocratic style of government. Fujimori took on the judiciary, which he accused of corruption, and forged close ties with the army, who were given a freer hand in the fight against internal subversion and drug trafficking. Reports of gross human rights abuses by the military rose alarmingly. In November 1990, faced with large-scale protests, Fujimori restricted, by decree, the right of public workers to strike. Other measures in 1990-91 included a controversial family planning programme, the reduction of import tariffs, the relaxation of restrictions on financial institutions and a plan to reform the taxation system. In September 1991, in recognition of the government's commitment to its austerity programme, loans from multilateral lending agencies, including the IMF, were resumed.

In the belief that the Congress and judiciary were wilfully opposing his economic restructuring programme and impeding the war against the *Sendero Luminoso* (Shining Path) guerrillas, Fujimori suspended sections of the Constitution in an army-backed coup in April 1992 and dissolved Congress and dismissed hundreds of judges. The coup, condemned internationally, struck, initially at least, a popular chord among the general public who had lost confidence in government institutions and wanted affirmative action at a time of extreme economic crisis and escalating violence. Fujimori promised plebiscites on his action and proposed constitutional reforms and announced that fresh congressional elections would be held by February 1993. However this popular support was expected to quickly drain away unless Fujimori eased the austerity programme and boosted public spending, something that would set him at odds with the multilateral lending agencies, who had already frozen credits to the government pending a return to democratic rule. Although opposition parties were not banned, there were widespread fears that Fujimori would try to weaken them by sharply curtailing their activities, with the army given a free hand to interpret what was a threat to state security in the context of an escalated war against the *Sendero Luminoso* guerrillas.

Structure. The party, very much an election vehicle for Fujimori, had its most organised members concentrated in the congregations of the evangelical churches. Its future was in doubt, however. Two prominent evangelicals, First Vice-President of the Republic Maximo San Román Cáceres and Second Vice-President Carlos García García opposed Fujimori's coup, and San Román was sworn in as the alternative "constitutional" president on April 21, 1992. San Román was expelled from the party as a "traitor" but it remained to be seen how many members would remain loyal to Fujimori.

Democratic Front

Frente Democrático (FREDEMO)

Leadership. Enrique Ghersi (deputy l.).

Orientation. A right-wing coalition supported mainly by the business community and the middle classes expounding free market policies and the minimum amount of state intervention.

Founded. 1988.

History. Formed by the Popular Action (AP), Popular Christian Party (PPC) and the small right-wing Liberty Movement (Movimiento Libertad) as a free marketeer opposition front, FREDEMO gained almost immediate success. In the November 1989 municipal elections the coalition won 37 per cent of the national vote, the largest percentage and 18 per cent more than the ruling APRA party. For the April 1990 general elections FREDEMO fielded the novelist and leader of the Freedom Movement, Mario Vargas Llosa, a clear pre-poll favourite. At the heart of his lavish campaign was the proposal to implement economic shock measures and place foreign debt repayments in abeyance. Vargas Llosa won the first ballot with 27.61 per cent of the vote but had to contest a second round. Although FREDEMO put a stop to ostentatious campaign spending, which was clearly unpopular in a time of marked hardship for most of the electorate, it could not allay popular fears about their proposed policies. Vargas Llosa obtained 33.92 per cent of the vote but failed to defeat Fujimori of the Change 90 (*Cambio*-90) movement. FREDEMO was completely excluded from power even though it won the largest share of seats in both the Senate (20) and Chamber of Deputies (63). Months after the elections Vargas Llosa pronounced the coalition dead, although there are plans to revive FREDEMO in the shape of a new Liberal Party.

Movimiento Libertad

Liberty Movement
Leadership. Luís Bustamante (l.); Miguel Cruchaga (s.-g.).
Orientation. Right-wing, believing in neo-liberal economic policies based on a free market economy.
Founded. 1987.
History. Libertad was formed by the internationally renowned novelist Mario Vargas Llosa in reaction to the APRA government's proposals to nationalize banks and other financial institutions. In early 1988 the organization joined forces with the Popular Action (AP) and the Popular Christian Party (PPC) and formed the Democratic Front (FREDEMO) with which Libertad won considerable successes but not the presidency. After the elections the coalition was disbanded and shortly afterwards its presidential candidate Vargas Llosa announced his resignation from Libertad on the grounds that he wished to devote more time to his writing. Vargas Llosa publicly denounced Fujimori's April 1992 army-backed presidential coup claiming that his pledges of constitutional reforms and fresh elections were the classic justifications of dictators used to legitimize their illegal actions. Bustamente stated that any reforms should be made in accordance with the 1979 constitution.
Publications. AMA - GI (a magazine; the name being a transliteration of the Sumerian word for freedom).

National Workers' and Peasants' Front

Frente Nacional de Trabajadores y Campesinos (FNTC or FRENATRACA)
Address. Avenida Colonial 105, Lima 1.
Leadership. Róger Cáceres Velásquez (pres.); Edmundo Huanqui Medina (s.-g.).
Orientation. Left-wing southern regional movement focused on demands for land reform.
Founded. May 12, 1968.
History. FRENATRACA originates in the Puno based Workers' and Peasants' Departmental Front (FDTC) which was successful in the municipal and congressional elections of 1963.

In 1978 FRENATRACA won four seats in the Constituent Assembly and in the general elections two years later it won four seats in the Chamber of Deputies and one in the Senate. The party lost its parliamentary representation in the 1985 elections but in the 1990 elections gained a seat in the Senate.
Structure. A biennial congress elects a 17-member national executive committee.

Peruvian Communist Party

Partido Comunista Peruano (PCP)
Address. Jirón Lampa 774, Lima 1.
Leadership. Jorge del Prado Chávez (s.-g.).
Founded. 1928.
Orientation. The collapse of east European Communist parties and the Soviet regime re-affirmed the moderate Eurocommunist stance of the party.
History. The Socialist Party of Peru (PSP), to which the PCP is a successor, was founded by José Carlos Mariátequi, a distinguished Marxist theoretician who attempted to adapt Marxism to Latin American conditions. Shortly after his death in 1930, the party split into two organizations, one which retained the original name while the other was renamed the PCP. The PCP joined the Third International and attempted to create a working class base, but the twin pressures of the growth of the populist APRA and the persistence of anarchist and libertarian socialist traditions among organized labour hampered its progress. Banned by the military regime in 1933, the PCP was legalized by President Prado during World War II, when its membership reached 30,000. In 1945, the PCP joined APRA in a Democratic Front supporting President Bustamente but was proscribed three years later following the overthrow of the government in the military coup led by Gen. Odría. It supported the mildly reformist government of President Belaúnde in 1965-68 and on his overthrow by the military, transferred its support, after some hesitation, to President Velasco's radical military regime.

The PCP split in 1978 into two factions, known as PCP-Unity and the PCP-Majority from the names of their respective newspapers, the former, which constituted the bulk of the party, inclining towards Eurocommunism, while the latter maintained a strongly pro-Soviet line. In the elections of the same year, the PCP-Unity obtained six of the 100 seats in the Constituent Assembly. For the 1980 elections, it allied with five other organizations to form the United Left (IU), Jorge del Prado Chávez, the PCP-Unity leader, being elected to the Senate. The 1982 party congress resulted in a victory for the pro-Soviet faction; a number of veteran party leaders were dropped from the central committee, and del Prado retained the general secretaryship only by a small majority. The reunited party again contested the 1985 elections as part of IU.

The PCP tried to keep the radical and reformist wings of the IU together by steering a middle course between them but failed to prevent the IU split in 1989. The party remains committed to an electoral strategy and has the best grass-roots level organization of any IU member.

Structure. The PCP is organized in cells, which are subordinate to local and regional committees. The national congress elects the 47-member central committee. The party's youth organization, the Peruvian Communist Youth, operates mainly in the universities, where it competes with Trotskyist and especially with the *Sendero Luminoso* guerrillas for support.

Membership. 4,000 (1989 estimate). The strongest support is drawn from the working-class areas of Lima. The party controls the General Confederation of Workers of Peru (CGTP), the principal trade union federation, which claims up to 70 per cent of union members.

Publication. Unidad (Unity), weekly.

Popular Action

Acción Popular (AP)

Address. Paseo Colón 218, Lima.

Leadership. Fernando Belaúnde Terry (l.); Edmundo Aguila (s.-g.).

Orientation. Right-wing and converted to free market policies in place of state-led reforms.

Founded. 1956.

History. The AP was founded in order to back Fernando Belaúnde Terry's candidacy in the elections of 1956, in which he came second. The party split almost immediately, with the breakaway section forming the Progressive Social Movement (MSP—now defunct). In 1962 Belaúnde again came second in the presidential elections, losing by a narrow margin, but used his influence within the armed forces to persuade the army to annul the result, even though the winning APRA candidate had withdrawn from the race. The fresh elections which took place in June 1963 provided a straight win for Belaúnde standing as candidate for the Popular Action-Christian Democrat alliance, with 39 per cent of the vote. The party itself won few seats in the Chamber of Deputies and Senate and therefore often had to form temporary alliances with right-wing and left-wing parties. Belaúnde's pragmatic government introduced moderate reforms but could not cope with internal unrest and economic crisis. In 1968 he was overthrown by a military coup led by Gen. Juan Velasco Alvarado and soon afterwards the AP suffered its second split. A minority grouping, led by the former Vice-President Edgardo Seoane Corrales was supported by the armed forces, while the group following Belaúnde was declared illegal. In 1976 the ban was lifted, but Belaúnde refused to participate in the 1978 constituent elections.

The May 1980 elections brought Belaúnde back to power; he won 45.4 per cent of the valid vote and the AP party obtained 98 of the 180 seats in the Chamber of Deputies and formed the largest bloc in the Senate. Belaúnde took office in July 1980 when the new Constitution came into force. The new government, which ruled in alliance with the Popular Christian Party (PPC) until 1984, introduced a drastic economic liberalization policy which accelerated the country's economic decline. Its inability to deal with the Shining Path (*Sendero Luminoso*) guerrilla group, which first emerged in 1980, contributed further to the unpopularity of his administration. This was reflected in a poor showing in the November 1983 municipal elections in which the AP won less than 6 per cent of the total vote and a further dramatic defeat in the 1985 elections.

AP had little impact in opposition to the APRA government, its seats having dwindled to 10 in the Chamber of Deputies and to five in the Senate. A renewed alliance with the PPC and the small Movimiento Libertad (ML) in the Democratic Front (FREDEMO), formed in early 1988, gave the AP a much needed boost. Although FREDEMO ultimately did not win the April 1990 elections, AP candidates took a large share of FREDEMO seats in both the

Chamber and Senate. Belaúnde gave instructions that no AP member should join the Fujimori government but instead his party was to present itself as a "constructive opposition". Consequently Juan Carlos Hurtado Miller resigned from the party so he could accept the post of Prime Minister and Economy Minister, resigning in February 1991 because of differences over economic policy. FREDEMO was dissolved in mid-1990, leaving the AP free to support new political initiatives, for example the 14-point agreement of the Socialist Left (IS).

Belaúnde Terry was among prominent politicians opposed to Fujimori's April 1992 army-backed presidential coup and was present to witness the swearing-in of Maximo San Román Cáceres as the alternative "constitutional" President.

Structure. There is a 70-member national plenum as well as national, departmental, provincial and regional committees.

Publications. Adelante.

Popular Christian Party

Partido Popular Cristiano (PPC)

Address. Avda Alfonso Ugarte 1406, Lima.

Leadership. Dr Luís Bedoya Reyes (l.).

Orientation. Conservative.

Founded. December 1966.

History. The party was formed by a splinter group of the Christian Democratic Party (PDC) led by the mayor of Lima, Dr Luís Bedoya Reyes. It kept a low profile during the period of military dictatorship, 1968-1980 but came to prominence once the democratic process was re-installed. The PPC obtained 25 out of 100 seats in the Constituent Assembly in the 1978 elections, but in the subsequent general election of 1980 the party won 10 seats in the Chamber of Deputies and six in the Senate. Bedoya came third in the presidential race with 9.6 per cent of the vote. The PPC nevertheless came to power by allying itself with the ruling Popular Action (AP) party. Participation in government caused a split in 1982, when a dissenting group formed the National Integration Party (PADIN), but the PPC continued to support the AP until April 1984.

The PPC contested the 1985 general elections as part of the Democratic Convergence (CODE), an alliance with the small Hayista Base Movement (MBH), after failing to interest AP in a joint campaign. Bedoya stood as the coalition candidate in the presidential elections and with 9.7 per cent of the vote once again came third. In the Chamber of Deputies the CODE won 12 seats and seven in the Senate. The alliance was dissolved soon after the elections and in Dec. 1986 the PPC underwent an internal reorganization which was to improve the party's electoral chances. Just over a year later the PPC joined the AP and the small Freedom Movement (Libertad) in the Democratic Front (FREDEMO) alliance.

Structure. A 15-member national political committee, a 21-member national executive committee and eight national secretaries supervise particular areas of work. There are 24 departmental, 152 provincial, 1,630 district and 514 zonal secretaries. The PPC controls the National Confederation of Workers (CNT).

Membership 120,000 (a 1985 estimate which is thought to be exaggerated).

Popular Democratic Unity

Unidad Democrática Popular (UDP)

Address. Plaza 2 de Mayo 46, Lima 1.

Leadership. Alfonso Barrantes Ligán (l.).

Orientation. Centre left—see Socialist Left (IS).

Founded. 1978.

History. A coalition of 18 Maoist and left-wing parties which in the 1980 general election won five seats in the Congress. In 1984 a more militant section broke away to found the Unified Mariáteguist Party (PUM). The UDP, a founder member of the United Left (IU) coalition in 1980, is now the major force in the Socialist Left (IS) alliance, also led by Barrantes.

Socialist Confluence

Confluencia Socialista

Founded. October 1991.

Orientation. A left-wing alliance formed by a breakaway group from the IU and made up of the Socialist Political Action (*Acción Política Socialista*—APS), the Socialist Action Movement (*Movimiento de Acción Socialista*—MAS), the Non Partisan Movement (*Movimiento No Partidarizado*—MNP) and the Revolutionary Mariáteguist Party (*Partido Mariáteguista Revolucionario*—PMR).

Socialist Left

Izquierda Socialista (IS)

Address. Plaza 2 de Mayo 46, Lima 1.

Leadership. Alfonso Barrantes Lingán (l.).

Orientation. Left-wing coalition seeking to play a more central political role promoting consensus rather than class conflict.
Founded. 1989.
History. The IS was formed by a group of parties who believed in offering critical support to the government of President Alan García Pérez of APRA. This led to a split with the left in the United Left (IU) coalition. Barrantes subsequently came fifth as IS candidate in the April 1990 presidential elections with a mere 4.07 per cent of the vote, but three IS candidates were elected to the Senate. IS support for Alberto Fujimori of Change 90 in the presidential run-off resulted in a small share of power, with the Energy and Mines portfolio being awarded to Fernando Sánchez Albavera. In late August 1990 Barrantes proposed to the government a 14-point economic "national agreement" which included suggestions for joint negotiation with labour and business organizations on wages and prices and a reform of the state to avert the turmoil and social upheaval of Peru's economic decline. The proposal was supported by the right-wing Popular Action (AP) and the Popular Christians (PPC).
Structure. The IS is dominated by Popular Democratic Unity (*Unidad Democrática Popular*—UDP) with several minor left-wing parties who also broke away from the IU.

United Left

Izquierda Unida (IU)
Address. Avda Grau 184, Lima 23.
Leadership. Gustavo Mohome (l.).
Orientation. Left-wing coalition advocating non-payment of the foreign debt, increased public ownership, nationalization of the US-owned copper mines, exchange controls, a ban on remittances of profits abroad and the greater distribution of wealth to narrow the gap between rich and poor.
Founded. 1980.
History. The IU was formed as a united left front in response to the poor results in the May 1980 general election caused by sectarianism among left-wing parties. Proof that a united left could be successful came almost immediately in the December 1980 municipal elections in which the IU captured six departmental capitals and came second in Lima.

In November 1983 IU president Alfonso Barrantes Lingán, a former APRA member and labour lawyer, was elected mayor of Lima and the IU gained 29 per cent of the national vote in the municipal polls. Barrantes stood as the IU's presidential candidate in the 1985 elections and came a close second with 21.3 per cent of the vote, withdrawing from the proposed run-off because he feared a heavy defeat. The IU gained 48 seats in the Chamber of Deputies and 15 in the Senate, despite its lack of a central secretariat and persistent internal disputes.

However, the conflicts between various IU parties and between Barrantes, who offered critical support to the APRA government, and those who opposed this policy, cost the IU several important cities in the November 1986 municipal elections, including Barrante's mayorship of Lima. Barrantes resigned from the IU soon after and formed the Socialist Left (IS) alliance with other breakaway parties. Despite the left being now officially split in two, the IU still managed to obtain 17 per cent of the national vote in the local elections in November 1989. In April 1990, the IU fielded Henry Pease as the coalition's presidential candidate. He won 6.97 per cent of the valid vote and came fourth. Like most left-wing parties, the IU encouraged its supporters to vote for Alberto Fujimori of Change 90 (*Cambio* 90) in the second round of the presidential elections. In return, President Fujimori appointed two IU members to his "national unity" cabinet, the teachers union activist Gloria Helfer (Education Minister) and Carlos Amat y Léon (Agriculture Minister). However, Amat y Léon resigned on Oct. 18, 1990, after disagreements with the Prime Minister and Finance Minister Juan Carlos Hurtado Miller who refused an emergency increase in agricultural credits.

IU leader Mohome joined with the rest of the opposition in opposing Fujimori's army-backed coup in April 1992 but suggested that a constituent Assembly be convened to draft necessary constitutional reforms followed by elections in April 1993.
Member parties. National Integration Party (*Partido de Integración Nacional*—PADIN) (see PADIN); Peruvian Communist Party (Partido Comunista Peruano—PCP) ; Revolutionary Communist Party (*Partido Comunista Revolucionario*—PCR); Revolutionary Socialist Party (*Partido Socialista Revolucionario*—PSR); Unified Mariáteguist Party (*Partido Unificado Mariáteguista*—PUM); Union of the Revolutionary Left (*Unión de Izquierda Revolucionaria*—UNIR); Workers', Peasants',

Students' and Popular Front (*Frente Obrero, Campesino, Estudantil y Popular*—FOCEP).

Structure. The IU is led by a national executive committee containing one or two representatives from each member party.

Minor parties

Christian Democratic Party (*Partido Demócrata Cristiano*—PDC, Avenida España 321, Apartado 4682, Lima 1); a centrist party founded in January 1956 which has been without representation in Congress since a split in 1966 which led to the formation of the Popular Christian Party (PPC). However, its leader Carlos Blancas Bustamente held the offices of Labour and Justice Minister under the Aprista government of 1985 -1990. Member party of the Christian Democrat Organization of America, which forms part of the Christian Democrat International.

Communist Party of Peru—Red Fatherland (Partido Comunista del Perú—Patria Roja—PCP-PR); led by Alberto Moreno (s.-g.) and Rolando Breña Pantoja (l.) the PCP-PR was formed in 1969 when it split away from what is now the PCP—Red Flag. Its orientation is nominally Maoist but it is effectively divided into a majority favouring the political parliamentary process and a minority group advocating guerrilla activity.

The party is a member of UNIR, which itself belongs to the United Left alliance (see IU above), and is influential in the Miners' Federation and the United Federation of Educational Workers of Peru.

Communist Party of Peru—Red Flag (Partido Comunista del Perú—Bandera Roja—PCP-BR); the PCP, formed in 1964 by Maoists who broke away from the Peruvian Communist party, split in 1969 into two sections taking their names from their respective periodicals *Red Flag* and *Red Fatherland.* In 1970, a Maoist group which was to later form the Shining Path guerrilla group (*Sendero Luminoso*) broke away from the Red Flag. Unlike other left-wing parties, the PCP-BR has refused to enter the IS, IU or UNIR and in recent years abandoned its pro-Chinese stance for a pro-Albanian one. Nominally pro-Albanian before the major political unrest in Albania in late 1990 and early 1991, the PCP-BR advocates but does not practise armed struggle.

Hayist Base Movement (*Movimiento de Bases Hayistas*—MBH, Pasaje Velarde 180, Lima); a right-wing party named after the founder of APRA, Víctor Raúl Haya de la Torre, it was formed in 1981 by Dr Andrés Townsend Ezcurra and other party dissidents after Townsend's expulsion from APRA. The MBH contested the 1985 elections with the Popular Christian Party (PPC) as the Democratic Convergence (CODE) on a platform of privatization and monetarism and jointly won 12 seats in the Chamber of Deputies and seven seats in the Senate. Since the dissolution of the alliance in 1986, the MBH has had only minor political impact.

National Integration Party (*Partido de Integración Nacional*—PADIN); a centre-left party which was founded in 1982 by a faction of the Popular Christian Party (PPC) which broke away in protest at the party's alignment with Popular Action (AP). Member of the United Left coalition.

Revolutionary Communist Party (*Partido Comunista Revolucionario*—PCR); formed 1974; originally Maoist but now more moderate.

Revolutionary Socialist Party (*Partido Socialista Revolucionario*—PSR); founded 1976; inspired by the policies of Gen. Juan Velasco Alvarado (president from 1968-1975) the PSR stresses a sustained programme of reforms to establish socialism.

Unified Mariáteguist Party$! (Peru)*& (*Partido Unificado Mariáteguista*—PUM); formed in 1984 by a merger of the Revolutionary Left Movement (MIR - Perú), the Revolutionary Vanguard (VR) and a section of the Revolutionary Communist Party (PCR), the PUM incorporates Maoist, Guevarist and Trotskyist traditions but is also influenced by the ideas of indigenous cultural revival championed by the founder of the Peruvian Communist Party (PCP), José Carlos Mariátegui.

Union of the Revolutionary Left (*Unión de Izquierda Revolucionaria*—UNIR); Brena Pantoja (pres.) national executive committee, formed in 1979 by the Breña faction of the Communist Party of Peru -Red Fatherland (PCP-PR see below), the National Liberation Front (FNI) and the Movement of the Revolutionary Left-Peru (MIR-Perú), the UNIR is nominally Maoist but participated in the 1980 and 1985 legislative elections; it claimed a membership of 50,000 (1987). Pantojo paid an official visit to North Korea in February 1992.

Workers', Peasants', Students' and Popular Front (*Frente Obrero, Campesino, Estudantil y Popular*—FOCEP); formed 1962 and legalised in 1978; nominally a Trotskyist alliance now operating as a single party.

Workers' Revolutionary Party (*Partido Revolucionario de los Trabajadores*—PRT); founded in 1978 by several small Trotskyist groups and led by the former guerrilla leader Hugo Blanco Galdós, the PRT contested the constituent elections of that year as part of the Labour, Peasant, Student and People's Front. In 1980 the party gained registration and in an alliance with two other parties it won three seats in the Chamber and two in the Senate in the elections. Hugo Blanco Galdós left the PRT before the 1985 elections and the party's influence has declined ever since.

Major guerrilla organizations

Comando Rodrigo Franco

Founded. 1988.

Orientation. A right-wing clandestine paramilitary force with close associations with the security forces.

History. It is known for sophisticated bomb attacks on trade union and human rights organizations' offices. The lack of action against the Comando Rodrigo Franco points to an apparent tolerance on the part of the government. The US State Department's 1989 "Country Reports on Human Rights Practices" accused extremist members of the then ruling APRA party and elements of the Interior Ministry of using the paramilitary group for political violence.

Communist Party of Peru-Shining Path

Partido Comunista del Perú-Sendero Luminoso (PCP-Sendero Luminoso); the party is now internationally known as the Shining Path group, which supporters claim is a pejorative term.

Founded. Early 1970s.

Leadership. Active leaders are Manuel Abimael Guzmán Reynoso (alias Comandante Gonzalo) and Julian García. Several others are in prison.

Orientation. Eschewing what they term as "parliamentary cretinism" and negotiations with the government, supporters claim that "*Guzmán Thought*" represents the "fourth sword" of communism after Marxism, Leninism and Maoism. *Sendero* holds to the classic Maoist dictum that peasant support bases must be formed in the countryside after which cities, where political and economic power is concentrated, can be surrounded and overwhelmed. In recent years, however, its operations have spread to urban areas, especially to the capital, Lima.

History. Shining Path originated among a small group of intellectuals at the state university of San Cristobal de Huamanga, Ayacucho, in the southern Andes, who in 1970 had split away from the PCP-Red Flag. In May 1980, it launched its "people's war" which has claimed the lives of more than 25,000 people, placed 40 per cent of the country under a perpetual state of emergency and has made *Sendero* a major threat to any government.

Despite army counter-insurgency measures, its scope of operations has spread from the southern to the central Andes and, critically, to the eastern Amazonian Upper Huallaga valley region where it finances its guerrilla operations by acting as an intermediary between peasant coca farmers and drug traffickers. Brooking no opposition to it, *Sendero* has regularly dealt out "revolutionary justice" to anybody or any community deemed to be collaborating with the state or failing to support one of its "armed strikes", a favoured tactic to close down a region. In numerous cases this has meant *Sendero* massacres in highland village communities which have previously been threatened by the military and dragooned into poorly armed peasant "self-defence" groups. That *Sendero* does not rely on popular support as such for its survival but compliance to its demands, was also demonstrated in February 1992 when it murdered Maria Elena Moyana, a popular and persuasive leader of Lima slum dwellers, who had opposed its call for an "armed strike".

The April 1992 coup of President Fujimori gave the army a free hand in combating Sendero, but critics believe that this would play into its hand of the guerrillas who have long seen themselves as the guardians of democracy against repressive government.

Structure. The party is highly authoritarian in style and very secretive, operating through clandestine cells.

Membership: 3,000 guerrillas on five fronts according to a 1987 US estimate, but far more active since. Committed supporters far outnumber activists and women are very prevalent in its ranks.

Publications. El Diario is a pro-*Sendero* newspaper published in Lima. Its editor Luís Arce Borja is currently in exile in Belgium.

Affiliations. Revolutionary Internationalist Movement (RIM), an obscure organization of communist groups, formed in 1980 out of the remnants of communist parties searching for a fresh identity in the wake of Mao, and given a major fillip by the Shining Path.

Main Shining Path overseas support groups are based in the United States and European capital cities.

Tupac Amarú Revolutionary Movement

Movimiento Revolucionario Tupac Amarú (MRTA)

Leadership. Víctor Polay Campos (alias Commander Rolando, arrested February 1989 but escaped in 1990); David Pereyra, who has also been reported as the group's leader, was arrested in August 1991.

Founded. 1983 (by groups who broke away from the Revolutionary Socialist Party—PRS).

History. Deriving its name from Tupac Amarú, the leader of the 1781 Indian revolt against Spanish colonial rule, the MRTA was formed by groups who broke away from the Revolutionary Socialist Party (PRS) in 1983.

Unlike *Sendero Luminoso*, it has been less hostile towards the rest of the left-wing movement. In late 1987, an original urban guerrilla strategy was changed for that of open rural warfare with a base of operations in the northern Huallaga region, the country's chief drug producing region where it is now in direct competition with *Sendero* in extracting protection money from drug-traffickers and peasant growers of coca to finance its military activities. Since September 1990 the MRTA has been interested in peace talks leading to eventual political integration.

Membership. 800-1,400 active guerrillas (1987 US estimate).

Puerto Rico

Capital: San Juan **Population: 3,359,000**

Puerto Rico was invaded by United States troops in May 1898 and has since been "a free state in association with the United States". Since 1928, there has been an active nationalist movement, which demands complete independence for the island and in 1950 organized an abortive insurrection. In recent years nationalist activities have been mainly confined to bombing incidents in the United States.

Constitutional structure

Under the 1952 Constitution, the island, with Commonwealth status, has internal autonomy but the US is responsible for its defence. Executive power is vested in the Governor and the bicameral legislature composed of a 27-member Senate and 51-member House of Representatives. The island also elects a resident commissioner as a delegate to the US House of Representatives, where he or she may vote in committee but not on the floor of the House. Puerto Ricans have all the obligations and rights of US citizens except that they are barred from voting in federal elections and do not have to pay federal income tax.

Electoral system

The Governor is elected for a four-year term by resident US citizens. Members of the Senate and House of Representatives are also elected for a four-year term. Of the House, 40 are elected in single-seat constituencies and 11 "at large", that is on a Commonwealth-wide basis. If two-thirds or more of the seats in either chamber are obtained by any one party, the number of seats may be increased by up to one-third to ensure the adequate representation of minority parties.

Sequence of elections since 1984

Date	*Party*
November 1984 (gubernatorial and legislative)	Popular Democratic Party (PPD)
November 1988 (gubernatorial and legislative)	Popular Democratic Party (PPD)

April 5, 1992 Puerto Rico US Primary Results

Democrats

Candidate	*Votes*	*Percentage*
Bill Clinton	60,611	95.6
Gerry Brown	1,012	1.6
Paul Tsongas	61	0.1
Uncommitted	1,714	2.7

Republicans

Candidate	*Votes*	*Percentage*
George Bush	251,937	99.1
Pat Buchanan	979	0.4
David Duke	972	0.4
Uncommitted	221	0.1

PARTY BY PARTY DATA

New Progressive Party

Partido Nuevo Progresista (PNP)

Address. P.O. 5192, Puerta de Tierra Station, San Juan.

Leadership. Baltasar Corrado del Rio (pres.); Rafael Rodriquez Aguayo (s.-g).

Orientation. Centre-right, the party favours the incorporation of Puerto Rico as a state within the USA.

Founded. August 1967.

History. The PNP broke away from the Popular Democratic Party (PPD) to contest the 1968 elections, in which it won the governorship and a majority in the house of Representatives. In opposition in 1972-76, it re-organized and won a majority in both chambers in November 1976, when its candidates were elected as Governor and delegate to the US House of Representatives. It narrowly lost its legislative majority in 1980, while retaining the governorship. After a split in 1983 and a further electoral defeat in 1984, its president and unsuccessful gubernatorial candidate, the former Governor Carlos Romero Barceló, resigned in September 1985, following more internal splits and scandals. He was succeeded by Corrado de Rio, a former Resident Commissioner and Mayor of San Juan. Del Rio was narrowly defeated in the gubernatorial elections in November 1988 and the PNP made little impression on the PPD's majority in both houses.

The PNP claimed that the referendum on Dec. 8, 1991, on Puerto Rico's future relationship with the USA was a defeat for the PPD government and kept alive the prospects of full statehood for the island (see PPD). In a 1967 plebiscite, 61 per cent had voted against statehood.

Popular Democratic Party

Partido Popular Democrático (PPD)

Address. Avenida Ponce de León 403, P. O Box 5788, Puerta de Tierra Station, San Juan 000906.

Leadership. Rafael Hernández Colón l.

Orientation. Centre-right; favours the retention of the island's present autonomous status and believes in free market economy and a measure of social provision for the poor.

Founded. March 1939.

History. Founded by Luis Muñoz Marín, it won half the seats in the 1940 elections, but only narrowly won control of the Senate. It won the 1944, 1948 and 1952 elections comfortably and was the ruling party when "commonwealth" status with the USA was introduced in 1950-52. Muñoz retired in 1965 after 16 years as governor and party leader and was succeeded by his deputy Roberto Sánchez Vilella. A subsequent dispute between them resulted in Sánchez Vilella's failure to win the party's nomination to stand for a second term as Governor in 1968. The party split, Sánchez Vilella running on a minority party platform, allowing the New Progressive Party (PNP) to win a majority.

The PPD regained a majority in 1972 and the party president Rafael Hernández Colón won the governorship in 1972 but lost it to the PNP in 1976 and 1980. In 1980 the party won a slim majority in both houses, although the governorship remained with the PNP until 1984, when Hernández was again elected. The party retained its control of the legislature.

In 1985, the party controlled 57 of the island's 78 municipalities and consolidated its position in power by winning 36 seats in the house and 18 in the Senate in the 1988 legislative elections. However, Hernández only narrowly hung on to the governorship.

The request of Hernández in January 1989 for a referendum on the island's future political status was endorsed by the US Senate in November. The referendum duly took place on December 8, 1991, with "no" voters rejecting by 53 to 45 per cent the PPD's "yes" platform which sought to maintain the island's autonomy. Hernández took the result as a personal defeat and announced on Jan. 2 1992, that he would not seek re-election as Governor in elections scheduled for late 1992.

This was despite the interpretation of the vote by analysts who claimed that it indicated that the majority of the population tended to support the continuation of the present "commonwealth" status with the USA rather than the radical options of full statehood, promoted by the PNP, or full independence as championed by the Puerto Rican Independence Party (PIP).

Puerto Rican Independence Party

Partido Independentista Puertoriqueño (PIP)

Address. Avenida Roosevelt 963, Puerto Nueva, San Juan 00920.

Leadership. Rubén Berrios Martínez (l.).

Orientation. Social Democrat and pro-independence. The party also calls for Puerto Rico to be designated a nuclear-free zone.

Founded. 1946.

History. The party was founded by Gilberto Concepción de Gracia following a split from the Popular Democratic Party (PPD). It campaigned for the full independence option which was supported by fewer than 1 per cent of voters in a 1967 referendum boycotted by pro-independence groups. In 1972, the current leader Berrios, who had succeeded Gracia on his death in 1967, came third in the gubernatorial elections. In 1976, the party's House candidates secured only 5.4 per cent of the vote and did little better in 1980, although in 1984 Berrios was elected to the senate and another PIP candidate to the House. In the 1988 legislative elections, the party won one seat in the Senate and two seats in the House. Its pro-independence position received a second resounding defeat in the December 1991 referendum on the island's future status with the USA (see PPD).

Minor parties

Puerto Rican Communist Party *(Partido Comunista Puertoriqueño*—PCP), Franklin Irrizarry s.-g.; founded in 1954, it dissolved itself in 1954 and was reconstituted two years later, on both occasions following the example of the Communist Party of the USA. In 1954, 10 of its leaders were prosecuted under the US anti-communist Smith Act. The party is opposed to the US military and political presence on the island, but has little popular support and did not present candidates in the 1988 elections.

Puerto Rican Socialist Party *(Partido Socialista Puertorqueño*—PSP), Carlos Gallisa s.-g.; founded in 1971, following the conversion into a political party of the Pro-Independence Movement established in 1959, it had one member in the House of Representatives in 1974-76. In the 1984 elections, the PSP received 0.3 per cent of the vote. In 1988, it supported the Puerto Rican Independence Party which finished a distant third.

Guerrilla organizations

Armed Forces of National Liberation (*Fuerzas Armadas de Liberación Nacional*—FALN); a separatist organization, believed to have no more than 20 active members, which has claimed responsibility for 120 bombing incidents in New York and other US cities between 1974 and 1983 in which five people were killed. Its then leader William Morales was arrested in Mexico City in 1983 after a gun battle in which two people were killed, and four of its members were convicted of seditious conspiracy in Chicago in 1985. The FALN was only sporadically active during the 1980s, as were other tiny groups including the Boricula Popular army (*Macheteros*), the volunteers for the Puerto Rican Revolution and the Armed forces of Popular Resistance.

Boricua Popular Army (*Ejército Popular Boricua-Los Macheteros*); the group was responsible for the shooting of several US soldiers and in 1981 destroyed nine military jet military aircraft at a US base in Puerto Rico. Believed to have been involved in an armed robbery in the USA in September 1983, 14 suspects were arrested in August 1985, although the main suspect, Victór Manuel Gerena, was thought to have escaped to Cuba. Several *Macheteros* were arrested along with members of the Dominican Popular Movement in the Dominican Republic in November 1985, accused of planning to assassinate prominent conservatives.

St Christopher and Nevis

Capital: Basseterre **Population: 41,000**

St Christopher and Nevis (usually abbreviated to St Kitts-Nevis) became an independent, federal state within the Commonwealth on Sept. 19, 1983.

Constitutional structure

The British monarch, represented locally by a Governor-General, is the head of state. Legislative power is vested in the unicameral National Assembly, consisting of 11 representatives elected for five years subject to dissolution and three appointed Senators, four if the Attorney-General is not an elected representative, plus a Speaker elected by the National Assembly. Executive power is exercised by a Prime Minister and a Cabinet, who are responsible to the National Assembly.

Nevis has its own legislature, the Nevis Island Assembly, which consists of five elected and three appointed members and has extensive local power. A premier leads the executive Nevis administration with two other members of the Assembly, while the monarch is represented on Nevis by a Deputy Governor-General. Nevis has the right to secede from the federation, subject to a referendum.

Electoral system

Representatives are elected to the National Assembly by simple plurality in single-member constituencies by universal suffrage of all adults over 18 years of age. For electoral purposes the state is divided into 11 constituencies, eight for the island of St Kitts and three for the island of Nevis.

Evolution of the suffrage

Universal adult suffrage was introduced by the British colonial administration in 1951. The age of voting was reduced from 21 to 18 years of age in 1980.

Sequence of elections since 1980

Date	*Winning party*
Feb. 1980	People's Action Movement/Nevis Reform Party
June 1984	People's Action Movement
March 1989	People's Action Movement
June 1992	Concerned Citizens Movement (CCM)

Election to National Assembly, March 21, 1989

Party	*Seats*
People's Action Movement (PAM)	6
Labour Party (LP)	2
Nevis Reformation Party (NRP)	2
Concerned Citizens' Movement (CCM)	1
Total	**11**

PARTY BY PARTY DATA

Concerned Citizens' Movement (CCM)

Address. Charlestown, Nevis.
Leadership. Vance Amory (l.).
Orientation. Centrist.
History. Formed by an alliance of four minor parties, the CCM broke the political monopoly exercised by the Nevis Reformation Party (NRP) on Nevis, by winning one seat from it in the March 1989 National Assembly elections. In the June 1, 1992, general election, it won three out of the five seats, unseating the Nevis Reformation Party (NRP).

Labour Party (Workers' League) (LP)

Address. Masses House, Church St, P.O. Box 239, Basseterre.
Leadership. Denzil Douglas, Jos N. France (s.-g.).
Orientation. Nominally socialist; the party has opposed what it regards as a disproportionate amount of power given to Nevis by the independence constitution, the terms of which were negotiated when the conservative People's Action Movement (PAM) depended on the political support of the Nevis Reformation Party (NRP) in the early 1980s.
Founded. 1932.
History. The St Kitts-Nevis Labour Party was founded by Robert Bradshaw, who led it until his death in 1978. It won all elections held under the British colonial regime between 1937 and 1975. Bradshaw's successor, Paul Southwell, was Premier of the then Associated State of St. Kitts-Nevis-Anguilla (from which the latter seceded de facto in 1971 and de jure in 1980, to remain a British colony) until his death in 1979, when he was succeeded by Lee L. Moore. The party lost power in the February 1980 elections, in which it won 58 per cent of the valid vote on St. Kitts and 16 per cent on Nevis, but held only four of the 19 elective seats in the House of Assembly (as compared with seven won in 1971 and 1975).

As the opposition party, it attempted unsuccessfully to delay the ruling coalition's plans for independence. disputing the terms of separation rather than the principle of independence which it had long supported. In the 1984 elections, its strength was further reduced to two of the 11 elective seats, both of which were on St Kitts, where it won 46 per cent of the vote. Moore lost his seat. In the March 1989 election, the party only managed to retain these two seats. Moore, who again failed to win a seat, resigned as party leader shortly afterwards and was succeeded by Douglas.
Structure. The party has a national executive, nine branches and a youth section. Its trade union affiliate is the St Kitts-Nevis Trades and Labour Union.
Publications. *The Labour Spokesman* (jointly with the union) twice weekly.

Nevis Reformation Party (NRP)

Address. Charlestown, Nevis.
Leadership. Simeon Daniels (l.); Levi Morton (s.-g.).
Orientation. Conservative and autonomist, the party's ultimate goal being independence for the people of Nevis; in practice it works within the state's federal system which gives Nevis considerable autonomy.
Founded. December 1970.
History. In the 1971 elections, the party won one of the two Nevis seats in the house of assembly of the then Associated State of St Kitts-Nevis-Anguilla (see LP). In local Nevis Council elections in 1971, the NRP won six of the nine seats, with Daniel becoming its Chairperson, and in 1975 it won all nine. In 1975, the NRP won both Nevis seats in the House, and in an unofficial referendum held in 1977 its policy of secession from St. Kitts was supported by 14,393 votes to 14.

In 1980, having held both its seats, the NRP formed a St-Kitts-Nevis coalition government with the People's Action Movement (PAM). In 1983, the NRP gained all five elective seats in the newly-created Nevis Island Assembly, and Daniel became the first Premier of St Kitts on Sept. 19, 1983, when the Federation of St Kitts-Nevis achieved independence. In the first National Assembly elections, in 1984, the party won all three Nevis seats, but lost the balance of power. The coalition nevertheless remained in office, with Daniel, Stevens and a third NRP representative in the ST Kitts-Nevis Cabinet.

In the March 1989 National Assembly election, the party lost one of its Nevis seats to the Concerned Citizen's Movement (CCM), giving it a total of two seats. The result revived speculation about the eventual secession of Nevis from the federation. In keeping with its role as a coalition government partner, the NRP had purposely not raised the issue during the campaign. In the June 1, 1992, elections the party lost

power to the Concerned Citizens Movement (CCM), winning only two seats.
Structure. There are five party officers and an executive committee.

People's Action Movement (PAM)

Address. P.O. Box 30, Cayon St, Basseterre.
Leadership. Kennedy Alphonse Simmonds (l.).
Orientation. Centre-right and pro-Western; the party promotes a model of economic growth based on free enterprise, agricultural diversification, tourism and foreign investment.
Founded. 1952.
History. The PAM, founded by William Herbert, entered the then House of Assembly in 1971, when it gained one of the two Nevis seats, subsequently losing it in 1975. Simmonds, who replaced Herbert as leader in 1976, won the seat back in a by-election on St. Kitts in 1979.

In February 1980, campaigning on a platform of early independence and the promised abolition of personal income tax, the party won three of the nine seats, and then formed a coalition government with the support of the Nevis Reformation party (NRP), with Simmonds as Premier.

This coalition led St Kitts-Nevis to independence on Sept. 19, 1983, when Simmonds became the first Prime Minister. In the June 1984 National Assembly elections (held a year early, and with the voting age lowered from 21 to 180, the PAM won an absolute majority but continued to rule in coalition with the NRP. Despite the poor performance of the economy, marked by a failure to attract sufficient foreign investment (and compounded by the devastation caused by Hurricane "Hugo" in 1989), and opposition allegations of official corruption, the party repeated its 1984 electoral performance by winning six seats in the March 1989 National Assembly elections.
Structure. The PAM's labour affiliate is the United Workers' Union, established by the party.
Publications. Democrat, weekly.
International affiliations. Member party of the Christian Democrat Organization of America, which forms part of the Christian Democrat International; International Democrat Union (since 1978); Caribbean Democrat Union (founder member, 1986).

St Lucia

Capital: Castries **Population: 147,000**

St Lucia has been an independent state within the Commonwealth since 1979.

Constitutional structure

Under its 1979 independence Constitution, the head of state is the British monarch, represented locally by a Governor-General. Legislative power is vested in the bicameral Parliament, consisting of a House of Assembly of 17 members (the Attorney-General, if not an elected representative, is appointed as an 18th member) and a Senate of 11 appointed members. Executive power is exercised by a Prime Minister, who is the majority leader in the House, and a Cabinet drawn from and answerable to Parliament.

Electoral system

Election to the House of Assembly is by simple plurality in single-member constituencies. The 11-member Senate is appointed by the Governor-General: six senators are nominated by the Prime Minister, three by the Leader of the Opposition, and two appointed in consultation with religious, economic and social groups.

Evolution of the suffrage

Universal adult suffrage of citizens aged 21 and over was introduced by the British colonial administration in 1951.

Sequence of elections since 1982

Date	*Winning party*
May 3, 1982	United Workers' Party (UWP)
April 4, 1987	United Workers' Party (UWP)
April 27, 1992	United Workers' Party (UWP)

General election, April 27, 1992

Party	*seats*
United Workers' Party (UWP)	11
St Lucia Labour Party (SLP)	6
Total	**17**

PARTY BY PARTY DATA

Progressive Labour Party (PLP)

Address. New Dock Rd, Vieux Fort.
Leadership. George Odlum (l. and ch.).
Orientation. Social democratic; the party advocates full employment, economic development, non-alignment and a serious North-South dialogue. It supported the left-wing New Jewel Movement in Grenada.
Founded. May 1981.
History. The party was formed by left-wing defectors from the centrist St Lucia Labour Party (SLP), including Odlum, who was deputy leader of the SLP and a government minister until a budget dispute in April 1981. The PLP's deputy leader, Michael Pilgrim, became Prime Minister in an interim government of national unity formed after the collapse of the SLP government in January 1982; in the May election of the same year, both he and Odlum lost their seats when the PLP gained 27.1 per cent of the vote but just one seat. In 1983, the conservative United Workers' Party (UWP) government accused the PLP of accepting money and guerrilla training from Libya.

The party performed poorly in the April 1987 general election, when its 12 candidates secured only 9 per cent of the vote and won no seats. When fresh elections were held at the end of the same month, the major parties increased their share of the vote at the PLP's expense, when it fought only four constituencies and received 6.1 per cent of the vote. An electoral commission subsequently overruled PLP and SLP charges that the elections had been fraudulent. In the April 1992 general election, the party contested only one constituency and received only 97 votes.
International affiliations. Socialist International.

St Lucia Labour Party (SLP)

Address. P.O. 64, Castries.
Leadership. Julian R. Hunte (l.); Peter Josie (dep. l.); Thomas Walcott (ch.).
Orientation. Centrist; the party has a declared commitment to full employment, social justice and an independent foreign policy.
Founded. 1946.
History. The party won the first elections held under universal adult suffrage in 1951 and held its majority in the then colony's Legislative Council until 1964. It then became the main opposition party and campaigned unsuccessfully for the holding of a referendum before the island achieved full independence from Britain in 1979. In the first post-independence elections, in July 1979, it won 12 of the 17 seats in the House of Assembly and formed a government with Allan F. L. Louisy as Prime Minister. On April 30, he was forced to resign after losing the support of SLP left-wingers led by his deputy, George Odlum.

A new centrist SLP government under Winston Cenac was formed but it collapsed in January 1982, having lost the support of the private sector and of public employees. Elections in May left the SLP with just 16.5 per cent of the vote and two seats in the house. Infighting between left-and right-wing factions resulted in the installation by the right in August 1983 of Neville Cenac (the younger brother of Winston) as the new party leader. Within a year, however, the leadership had passed to the centrist Julian Hunte, a former mayor of Castries. The party then regained much of its support over the following years, and in the general election of April 1987, it secured 38.1 per cent of the vote and eight of the 17 seats in the house. It increased its vote slightly, and held its seats, in the fresh elections held later in the same moth. In June 1987, Neville Cenac defected to the United Workers' Party (UWP), giving the latter a secure majority.

In the April 1992 general election, the party only managed to win six seats and it was felt that its future existence as an independent party, and that of its leader, were in doubt.
Structure. The SLP retains its traditional links with local trade unions.
Publications. Etoile.

United Workers' Party (UWP)

Address. 1 Riverside Rd, Castries.
Leadership. John G. M. Compton (l.).
Orientation. Conservative, anti-communist and pro-Western; despite its neo-liberal economic credentials, the party favoured some state assistance for the development of private enterprise.
Founded. 1964.
History. The UWP, which developed from the National Labour Movement and the People's Progressive Party of the 1950s, was in power from

1964 until July 1979, with Compton as Chief Minister of the colony in 1964-67, Premier of the Associated State in 1967-69, and Prime Minister of the independent state from February 1979. In 1974, the UWP won elections on a programme of seeking full independence, but in the first post-independence elections, in July 1979, it was defeated and went into opposition.

From January to May 1982, the UWP took part in a coalition government of national unity supported by all three major parties, cut short by the UWP's overwhelming victory in the general election on May 3, when it won 56.4 per cent of the valid vote and 14 seats (12 of them by absolute majorities) in the House of Assembly. Compton formed a government and in October sent a token force to participate in the US military invasion of Grenada.

In the general election of April 1987, the party secured 52.7 per cent of the vote but was reduced to nine seats, a majority of one over the St Lucia Labour Party (SLP). Fresh elections, called on April 30, produced a similar result, although the opposition accused the UWP of widespread fraud. In June the government recruited Neville Cenac, a right-wing SLP dissident, increasing its majority to three.

Compton, who had declared his intention of retiring from politics, nevertheless led the party into the April 1992 general election. The party increased its number of seats in the Assembly to 11, on an average national swing towards it of 6 per cent.

The campaign was dominated by the issue of which party was fit to manage the economy, most votes going to Compton whose leadership style was attacked by the SLP, and whom critics described as a "bencvolent dictator" well practised in the art of "clientist" politics. Compton hailed his victory as essential for the continuation of the process of political union with the three other members of the Windward Islands group, Grenada, St Vincent and the Grenadines, and Dominica.

St Vincent and the Grenadines

Capital: Kingstown **Population: 114,000**

St Vincent and the Grenadines became an Associated State of the United Kingdom in October 1969 before coming a fully independent member of the British Commonwealth since October 1979.

Constitutional structure

Under the terms of the independence Constitution, legislative power is vested in a unicameral House of Assembly, consisting of 13 elected members and six appointed senators (four chosen on the advice of the Prime Minister and two on that of the Leader of the Opposition). Executive power is exercised by the Prime-Minister (who is the elected Member of the House of Assembly who can best command the support of other elected members) and the Cabinet. Both the Prime Minister and the Cabinet are responsible to the Assembly.

Electoral system

Representatives are elected to the House of Assembly for a five-year term (subject to dissolution) by universal suffrage of all adults over the age of 18 by simple plurality in single-member constituencies. For electoral purposes the island of St Vincent is divided into 12 constituencies, with those of the Grenadine chain that belong to St Vincent forming the remaining constituency. A constitutional amendment passed in the House of Assembly in June 1986 allowed the number of elective seats to be increased to 15 for the next election.

Evolution of the suffrage

Universal suffrage of voters aged 21 and over was introduced by the British colonial administration in 1951. The age of voting was lowered to 18 in the 1979 constitution.

Sequence of elections since 1984

Date	*Winning party*
July 27, 1984 (general)	New Democratic Party (NDP)

General Election, May 16, 1989

Party	*Seats*	*Percentage of vote*
New Democratic Party (NDP)	15	66.2
St Vincent Labour Party (SVLP)	-	30.4
Movement for National Unity (MNU)	-	2.4
United People's Movement (UPM)	-	1.1
Total	**15**	**100.0**

PARTY BY PARTY DATA

Movement for National Unity (MNU)

Address. Melville St, Kingstown.
Leadership. Ralph Gonsalves (l.).
Orientation. Centre-left.
Founded. 1982.
History. Founded by Gonsalves as a more moderate political force than the left-wing United People's Movement (UPM), the MNU won only 1.9 per cent of the vote in the July 1984 election and 2.4 per cent in May 1989 and no seats.
Publications. *Unity* published on a weekly basis.

New Democratic Party (NDP)

Address. Granby St, Kingstown.
Leadership. James Mitchell (l.).
Orientation. Conservative; the party supports political union in the East Caribbean, social development and free enterprise.
Founded. December 1975.
History. Mitchell had been elected to the colonial Legislative Council as a member of the St Vincent Labour Party (SVLP) in 1966 and 1967, and became Minister for Trade, Agriculture and Tourism in the SVLP government. He was re-elected to the then House of Assembly as an independent in 1972, personally holding the balance of power between the SVLP and the People's Political Party (PPP), each with six seats, and being elected as the Premier of a PPP government. (The PPP (now defunct) was formed in 1952, and had held power until 1967.) In 1974, however, the PPP leader, Ebenezer Joshua, and his wife Ivy Joshua, who was also a member of the government, withdrew their support from Mitchell and allied with the SVLP, precipitating a general election easily won by the SVLP.

Mitchell, re-elected as an independent, was the only opposition representative but the SVLP government denied him the title of Leader of the Opposition, the empty honour being bestowed on Ivy Joshua. Mitchell then went on to form the NDP along with George Owen Walker who became its first secretary-general. The party boycotted a constitutional conference held in London in 1978 and also the House vote on the draft independence Constitution on Feb. 9, 1979. The general election in December 1979 gave the NDP 30 per cent of the vote and Calder Williams, one of its two elected MPs, became a credible Leader of the Opposition. Mitchell, however, lost his seat, but was returned to the House representing his old Grenadines seat in a by-election in June 1980. Meanwhile in March, Williams and two NDP senators had formed the short-lived Working People's Party (WPP) and the post of Leader of the Opposition went in mid-1981 to a SVLP defector. Mitchell and the NDP, however, continued to attract public respect and recognition as the main opposition force, despite its failure in 1982-83 to negotiate a merger with the United People's Movement. Mitchell supported the US military invasion of Grenada in 1983, but subsequently opposed US proposals that the Eastern Caribbean establish its own regional army, something which he considered not only wasteful but open to abuse and therefore potentially destabilizing for the region.

In the July 1984 general election, the party won an absolute majority of the votes and nine seats, and Mitchell became Prime Minister. In a by-election in February 1985 the party won a tenth seat and successfully defended a seat in a by-election in February 1987. This trend was amplified in the general election of May 1989, when the party won all 15 seats in the House.

An opposition movement National Council of Law and Order, supported by trade unions, the local Human Rights Association and by private citizens, was set up in July 1991 accusing the police, especially its commissioner Randolph Toussaint, of abusing power. Mitchell said that the campaign against Toussaint was part of a politically motivated campaign to destabilize the country and jeopardize economic development. However, the SVLP and the United People's Movement (UPM) demanded in July that Mitchell and his government resign following the seizure by the US authorities of the Vincentian ship *Lucky Star* on suspicion that it was being used in drug trafficking. The Cabinet had decided to prohibit public access to the ship's log, which provoked charges that the government was covering up for official involvement in drug-trafficking.
Structure. The annual convention elects a central committee.
Membership. 7,000 (1984 claim).
Publications. The *New Times*, nominally a weekly but published very infrequently.

International affiliations. International Democrat Union (since 1987); Caribbean Democrat Union (founder-member, 1986).

St Vincent Labour Party (SVLP)

Address. Halifax St, Kingstown.
Leadership. Vincent Beache (l.)
Orientation. Centre-right; the party advocates a mixed economy and a pro-Western foreign policy.
Founded. 1955.
History. The party defeated the People's Political Party (PPP—now defunct) by securing six of the nine seats in the Legislative Council elections in May 1967. The SVLP founder, R. Milton Cato, became the Chief Minister and, from October 1969 (when St Vincent became an Associated State), Premier. In 1972, it won only six of the 13 seats in what had become the House of Assembly, and it went into opposition to an independent-led PPP government (see NDP). In 1974, however, the SVLP won the support of the PPP leadership, and forced an election in which the SVLP won 69 per cent of the vote and 10 seats; the PPP held its two seats because the SVLP refused to contest them. Cato became Premier of an SVLP-PPP coalition government and led the country to independence on Oct. 27, 1979, when he became Prime Minister.

The party held power in elections in December 1979, with 53.5 per cent of the vote and 11 seats; the PPP winning only 2.4 per cent and no seats and later ceasing to exist). In 1981, the SVLP suffered internal splits over its controversial public order legislation. By July 1984, economic crisis and revelations of official corruption badly damaged the party and it lost the 1984 election; its vote fell to 41.4 per cent and it held only four seats. It went into opposition to the New Democratic Party (NDP) government. Cato later resigned the party leadership and his seat, which was won in February by the NDP. The SVLP leadership then passed to Hudson K. Tannis (the former deputy leader, who had lost his Assembly seat in 1984.) On his death in a plane crash in August 1986, Beache, the parliamentary leader, took over.

In the general election of May 1989, the party's share of the vote dropped to 30.4 per cent and it failed to win a seat in the House of Assembly. However, it has maintained itself as a credible opposition force capable of rallying extra-parliamentary groups in criticizing the government.
Structure. The SVLP has a trade union affiliate, the CTAUW, which with an estimated 3,100 members is the largest in the country.
Publications. The *Star,* nominally a weekly but published infrequently.

United People's Movement (UPM)

Address. Bay St, Kingstown.
Leadership. A. Saunders (l.).
Orientation. The party claims to accept scientific socialism adapted to St Vincent conditions, and rejects the label "communist". It was sympathetic to the Cuban, Nicaraguan and Grenadian revolutions.
Founded. August 1979.
History. The party was created under the leadership of Ralph Gonsalves as an electoral alliance encompassing the Youlou United Liberation Movement (Yulimo—f. 1974)), the *Arwee* rural left-wing group, and the People's Democratic Movement (PDM), a social democratic party formed in 1978.

In the 1979 general election, the UPM won 14.4 per cent of the vote but no seats. The (now defunct) PDM withdrew in 1981 and Gonsalves left the UPM in May 1982 to form the less radical Movement for National Unity (MNU). He was succeeded as UPM leader by Remwick Rose, who led unsuccessful merger negotiations with the (now defunct) Progressive Labour Party.

The UPM vigorously opposed the 1983 US military invasion of Grenada led by Oscar Allen and contested the 1984 general election, when its vote fell to 3.2 per cent. This downward trend continued and it gained only 1.1 per cent of the vote in the May 1989 general election. Under the leadership of Saunders, it has become an extra-parliamentary pressure group, combining on occasion with the SVLP.
Publications. *Justice* (weekly), *Advance* (quarterly); both have ceased to appear.

Surinam

Capital: Paramaribo **Population: 436,000**

Formerly Dutch Guiana, the Republic of Surinam achieved complete independence from the Netherlands in 1975. In February 1980 the government was overthrown in a military coup led by Sgt.-Maj. (later Lt.-Col.) Désiré "Desi" Bouterse, and after another coup in August a newly formed National Military Council (NMR) suspended the Constitution and dissolved the legislature in August 1981. An interim President and a predominantly civilian Council for Ministers (presided over by a Prime Minister) was appointed in 1982. Real power, however, remained with the army. A National Assembly, consisting of 31 nominated members, was appointed in January 1985 and in November of the same year the ban on traditional political parties was lifted. A new Constitution, approved by a national referendum, was inaugurated in September 1987. In January 1988, the Assembly elected Ramsewak Shankar as President. He was deposed in the December 1990 bloodless military coup, led by Bouterse's supporters in the army, and "passed" power to provisional President Johan Kragg, of the Surinam National Party (NPS), considered to be co-operating with military. In a promised general election, eventually held in May 1991, the opposition coalition New Front for Democracy (NF) won an absolute majority in the National Assembly but failed to win the necessary two-thirds majority to form a government. In the 817-member United People's Assembly, specially convened by the National Assembly in September 1991, Ronald Venetiaan of the New Front was elected President, receiving 645 votes which enabled him to form a government.

Constitutional structure

Under the 1987 Constitution, ultimate authority rests with a 51-member National Assembly which can amend any proposal of law by the Government. Executive authority rests with the President who is appointed by the party with at least 34 seats or is elected by the National Assembly for a five-year term. The President is head of state, head of government, head of the armed forces, chair of the Council of State and of the Security Council which, in the event of "war, state of siege or exceptional circumstances to be determined by law" assumes all government functions. The President is assisted by a Vice-President, who is also elected by the National Assembly, and a Cabinet appointed by the President.

Constitutional amendments, unanimously approved by the National Assembly on March 25, 1992, restricted the role of the army to national defence and combating "organized subversion". Serving members of the armed forces were restricted from holding representative political office but not denied personal involvement in political activity.

Electoral System

The 51 members of the National Assembly are elected by direct universal suffrage for a five-year term. To appoint a President a party has to have at least a two-thirds majority in the National Assembly, that is 34 seats. If none of the parties obtains such a majority, the National Assembly elects one of the parties' candidates. If there is still no consensus, the United People's Assembly, consisting of the National Assembly plus some 700 municipal and district councillors, have the final vote.

Evolution of the Suffrage

Universal suffrage for those aged 18 and over was introduced in 1953.

Ronald Venetiaan of the NF was elected President by a specially convened 817-member United People's Assembly on September 7, 1991, with 645 votes (80 per cent). The runners-up were Jules Wijdenbosch of the NDP with 120 votes (14 percent) and Hans Prade of DA-'91 with 52 votes.

Sequence of elections since 1987

General election Nov. 25, 1987

Party		*number of seats*
Front for Democracy and Development (FDO)		40
—VHP	16	
—NPS	14	
—KTPI	10	
National Democratic Party (NDP)		3
Bush Negro Progressive Party (PBP)		4
Progressive Labourers' and Peasants' Union		4
Total		**51**

General election of May 25, 1991

Party		*seats*	*% of votes*
New Front (NF)		30	54.2
—VHP	9		
—NPS	12		
—KTPI	7		
—SPA	2		
National Democratic Party		12	21.8
Democratic Alternative '91 (DA'91)		9	16.7
—Hindustani Reformed Progressive Party	3		
—Pendawa Lima	2		
—BEP	3		
—Alternative Forum	1		
Total		**51**	

PARTY BY PARTY DATA

Alternative Forum

Leadership. Gerard Brunings (l.).
History. The party won one seat in May 1991 election.

Brotherhood and Unity in Politics (BEP)

Orientation. Mainly *boschneger.*
History. The party won three seats in May 1991 general election.

Democratic Alternative '91

Democratisch Alternatief '91 (DA '91)
Leadership. Hans Prade (l.).
Orientation. Centre-left; anti-military; campaigns for a commonwealth relationship with the Netherlands, and for the constitutional exclusion of military from involvement the political process. It has taken a strong stand against corruption and claims not to co-operate with anyone involved in corruption.
Founded. March 1991.
History. The DA'91 consists of small anti-military parties, a coalition of dissidents who left the Front for Democracy and Development (FDO) critical of its alleged failure to curb the influence of the military. It contested the May 1991 general election, winning nine seats in the National Assembly with 16.7 percent of the vote. One seat was taken up by Winston Jesserun, brother of Artie Jesserun of the Surinam National Party (NPS) who lost his seat because two members of the same family, according to the Constitution, were not allowed to sit simultaneously in the Assembly. In the final vote for the presidency, staged by a 817-member United People's Assembly (specially summoned by the National Assembly) on Sept. 7, 1991, Prade won 52 votes.

Hindustani Reformed Progressive Party (HPP)

History. In the May 1991 general election the party won three seats, drawing its support from the Indian community.

National Democratic Party

Nationale Democratische Partij (NDP)
Leadership. Jules Albert Wijdenbosch (l.); Orlando Van Amson (ch.).
Orientation. Right-wing, backed by the army.
Founded. 1987.
History. The NDP was formed by *Standvaste,* the 25 February Movement under Lt. Col. Désiré (Desi) Bouterse. In the November 1987 general election the NDP was shunned by the electorate as being Bouterse's political mouthpiece. Wijdenbosch resigned in January 1991 as chairman of the NDP to take the posts of Vice-President and Prime Minister in the army-backed provisional government of Johan Kraag following the December 1990 military coup. The party, which dominated Kraag's government, against expectations increased its vote to 21.8 per cent in the May 1991 general election. Its number of seats in the National Assembly increased from three to 12, making it the joint largest single party with the Surinam National Party (NPS) and ensuring for it an influential role in the legislature. In the election for a new President in the 817-member United People's Assembly (specially summoned by the National Assembly), held in September 1991, Wijdenbosch came second with 120 votes.

New Front

Nieuwe Front (NF)
Leadership. Henck Arron (chair).
Orientation. A coalition of Indian, Javanese and mixed-race ethnic groups plus the Surinam Labour Party which seeks constitutional reform to reduce the involvement of army in internal affairs. It also seeks international military and technological aid to fight drug trafficking and advocates the renegotiation of bilateral links with the Netherlands and closer ties with Latin America and the Caribbean.
Founded. May 1987.
History. The New Front had its origins in the Front for Democracy and Development (*Front voor Demokratie en Ontwikkeling*—FDO) led by former President Henck Arron (toppled by Bouterse-led army in 1980). In November 1987 the FDO won the election with an overwhelming 85 per cent of the vote. Following the December 1990 military coup, dissident groups, critical of the NF's failure to curb military influence, left in March 1991 to form the Democratic Alliance (DA'91). The NF had its ranks swelled by the Surinam Labour Party (SLA) who joined shortly before the May 1991 general election which it convincingly won, taking 30 seats and 54.2 per cent of the valid vote. This victory at a national level

complemented the NF's control of a clear majority of local and regional councillors.

However, the party remained four seats short of the required two-thirds majority to win the presidency. Following four months of political wrangling, its presidential candidate Ronald Venetiaan was finally elected to be the new President by the 817-member United People's Assembly (specially summoned by the National Assembly) on Sept. 7, 1991, with 645 votes. The new government immediately began to draw up draft amendments to the constitution, a primary intention of which was to reduce the likelihood of another military coup by limiting the army's constitutional role to strictly that of defence, banning its members from active involvement in party politics and abolishing conscription.

In addition, the government pledged to co-operate with international initiatives, especially in the United States, to fully investigate the army's alleged long term involvement in gun running, cocaine processing, international drug trafficking, and money laundering. The Dutch government, which had suspended its development aid immediately after the December 1990 military coup, was sufficiently impressed by Venetiaan's pledges to agree in November 1991 to release NG 100,000,000 in development aid and NG 44,900,000 in transitional aid.

On March 25, 1992, after 12 hours of debate, the National Assembly unanimously approved the restriction of the army's role to national defence and combating "organized subversion", preventing serving members from holding "representative" public office but not banning individuals from participation in political activity.

Tension was apparent within the NF government by March 1992. The fresh appointment of Johan Sisal of the Party for Unity and Harmony (KTPI) as Internal Affairs Minister raised objections for member parties, as did that of Harry Kensmil as the Planning Minister, in replacement of the NPS's Eddy Sedoc, a move vetoed by the Progressive Reform Party (VHP) and Surinam Labour Party (SLP). There were also disagreements over the transitional economic programme, in particular the devaluation of the currency.

Coalition members: Suriname National Party (NPS); Progressive Reform Party (VHP); Party for Unity and Harmony (KTPI); Suriname Labour Party (SPA).

Party of Unity and Harmony

Kerukanan Tulodo Pranatan Ingil (KTPI)

Address. Weidestraat, Paramaribo.

Leadership. Willy Soemita (l.).

Orientation. The party has been the traditional protector and promoter of the interests of the Indonesian community and has switched its political allegiances to further this end.

Founded. 1947.

History. Formerly the Javanese Farmers' Party (*Kaum-Tani Persuatan Indonesia*), the KPTI was founded to represent the interests of the ethnic Indonesian community and is the oldest party in the country. In the 1970s, its leader, Willy Soemita, was convicted of corruption but made a successful comeback, the party being a founder member of the Front for Democracy and Development (FDO), later the New Front (see NF).

Following the May 1991 general election, its number of seats in the National Assembly fell from nine to seven. Soemita was appointed Minister of Social Affairs and Housing in the New Front (NF) cabinet and in March 1992 the KTPI's Soeratino Setrored was appointed to the portfolio of Agriculture, Animal Husbandry and Fishing, replacing party colleague Johan Sisal whose subsequent appointment as Internal Affairs Minister provoked opposition from other NF parties.

Pendawa Lima

Orientation. (see KPTI).

Founded. 1975.

History. The party was formerly within the Party of Unity and Harmony (KTPI) but contested the May 91 general election alone, winning two seats in the National Assembly.

Progressive Reform Party

Vooruitstrevende Hervormings Partij (VHP)

Address. Lim A Postraat, Paramaribo.

Leadership. Jaggernath Lachmon (l.).

Orientation. Leading left-wing party; Hindustani-based with its stronghold in Saramancca.

Founded. 1949.

History. A founder member of the Front for Democracy and Development (FDO), renamed for the May 1991 elections as the New Front, the party was the main loser in the elections, its representation in the national assembly falling from 18 to nine seats.

Jaggernath Lachmon is currently the Chair of the National Assembly.

Surinam Labour Party (SLP)

Leadership. Fred Derby (l.).
Orientation. Social Democratic
Founded. 1987.
History. The party, whose membership is predominantly Creole, joined the New Front just before the May 1991 general election and won two of its overall total of 30 seats.

Following the swearing-in of a New Front government in September 1991, the SLP was given the Defence, Labour and Transport portfolios in the new cabinet. The party has links with the C-47 trade union.

Suriname National Party

Nationale Partij Suriname (NPS)
Address. Wanicastraat, Paramaribo.
Leadership. Hans Breeveld (sec.); Artie Jesserun (dep. ch.).
Orientation. Creole; younger and more radical activists in ascendant.
Founded. 1946.
History. The party was a founder member of the Front for Democracy and Development (FDO) which changed its name to the New Front. Despite the NF's victory in the May 1991 general election, the NPS saw its representation in the National Assembly reduced from 13 to 12 seats; its deputy chairman Artie Jesserun giving his seat up to his brother Winston (see DA'91), because, according to the constitution, two family members could not simultaneously sit in the legislature, a check on the establishment of political dynasties.

The NPS's Eddy Sedoc was named Finance Minister in March 1992.

Minor parties

National Republican Party (*Partij Nationalistische Republiek*—PNR); founded in 1963, the party returned to political activities in 1987.

Progressive Bushnegro Party (*Progressieve Bosneger Partij*—PBP), founded in 1968; represents members of the "bush negro" ethnic group (the *boschneger* whose numbers are estimated at 50,000 and who inhabit the rainforests of the interior) and is associated with the Pendawa Lima (see above); the party resumed political activities in 1987 when it won four seats in the November general election. In May 1991 it lost all its seats.

Progressive National Party (*Progressieve Nationale Partij*—PNP), resumed political activities in 1987.

Progressive Workers' and Farm Labourers' Union (*Progressieve Arbeiders en Landbouwers Unie*—PALU); Ir Iwan Krolis (l.); founded in the late 1970s, the PALU, nominal socialist party which supported the Bouterse regime (1980-87) and in the November 1987 general election won four seats. It lost these in the May 1991 general election.

Surinamese Progressive People's Party (*Progressieve Surinaamse Volkspartij*—PSV); a Christian Democratic party founded in 1946 and which resumed political activity in 1987. Member party of the Christian Democrat Organization of America, which forms part of the Christian Democrat International.

Guerrilla Organizations

Surinamese Liberation Army (Jungle Commando - SLA)

Address. St Laurent du Maroni, French Guiana.
Leadership. Ronnie Brunswijk (l.); Johan "Castro" Wally (second-in-command).
Orientation. Centre-left, supports the rights of the Bush Negro community for self determination (see PBP above).
Founded. 1986.
History. Founded by Ronnie Brunswijk and Max Belfort, the SLA undertook guerrilla raids on police posts and important parts of the infrastructure, operating from bases in neighbouring French Guiana to avoid army counterattacks.

It signed a peace agreement in July 1989 with the Shankar government, the so-called "Kourou Accord" (because it was signed in Kourou in French Guiana), which was never implemented owing to pressure from the Army Commander in Chief, Lt. Col. Désiré "Desi" Bouterse.

Another preliminary peace accord was signed with Bouterse in March 1991 under which the SLA would be integrated into Suriname police force and given special duties within the army.

Progress towards a final peace agreement, however, remained stalled in April 1992, with the SLA remaining unwilling to be disarmed by the army, which it claimed was responsible for arming the Tucayana Amazonas, Mandela and Angula guerrilla groups.

Tucayana Amazonas based in Bigi Poika, founded in 1989, "Commander Thomas" (l.); Alex Jubitana, Chair of the Tucayana Advisory Group; An Amerindian insurgent group which objected to the July 1989 Kourou Accord between the government and the Surinamese Liberation Army (SLA).

Angula *(Defiance)* Carlos Maassi (l.); a Saramaccaner based "Bush Negro" clan group formed in 1990. The main guerrilla group, the Surinamese Liberation Party (SLA), accuses it of being a front for the military.

Mahabini—Dead or Alive, first emerged in November 1991 when the group claimed responsibility for an attack on a police post in Moengo in which one policeman died. The group is suspected of having links with dissenting members of the SLA unhappy with the peace negotiations with the army.

Mandela Bush Negro Liberation Movement (BBM), Leendert Adams (alias "Biko") (l.); founded in 1989 by members of the Mataurier "bush negro" clan; it is opposed to the agreement between the military and the Surinamese Liberation Army (SLA) and supports the Tucayana. The SLA accuses it of being in receipt of guns from the army.

Union for Liberation and Democracy (UBD) Kofi Ajongpong (l.); based in Moengo and founded in 1989 by radical elements of the Surinamese Liberation Army (SLA).

Trinidad and Tobago

Capital: Port of Spain **Population: 1,100,000**

Trinidad and Tobago became independent from the United Kingdom on Aug. 31, 1962. It had become a member of the Federation of West Indies in 1958 and in 1959 gained full internal self-government but had remained a British colony. It became the first Commonwealth country to join the Organization of American States (OAS) in 1967. Ten years later, a new constitution was passed and Trinidad and Tobago became a Republic. Tobago, which was joined with Trinidad as one political and administrative unit in 1888, obtained limited self-rule with the formation of the Tobago House of Assembly in 1980. Full internal self-government was achieved in early 1987. In 1986 the People's National Movement (PNM) lost power to the new opposition party National Alliance for Reconstruction (NAR) for the first time in its 30-year rule. The NAR government suffered an attempted coup on July 27, 1990 by the *Jamaat al Muslimeen* black Moslem group who held 47 people hostage, among them Prime Minister A. N. R. Robinson, who was shot in the leg, and several Cabinet ministers. Thirty people were killed in the five-day siege and 500 injured and widespread looting occurred. The rebels surrendered on Aug. 1 after obtaining a signed promise of an amnesty from the interim Prime Minister Emmanuelle Carter. Robinson, his government deeply unpopular, was heavily defeated by the PNM in the December 1991 general election.

Constitutional structure

Under the Constitution of Aug. 1, 1976, the nominally executive President is Head of State. Effective executive power lies with the Cabinet, which is presided over by the Prime Minister and is drawn from Parliament to which it is collectively responsible. Legislative power rests with a bicameral Parliament, which consists of a 36-member House of Representatives and a 31-member Senate. The Tobago House of Assembly has 15 members.

Electoral system

The President is appointed by an electoral college of members of both the Senate and House of Representatives for a five-year term. The President appoints the 31 Senators, 16 on the advice of the Prime Minister, six on that of the Leader of the Opposition and nine at the President's own discretion. The 36 members of the House of Representatives are elected for a five-year term by simple plurality in single-member constituencies (34 constituencies on Trinidad and two on Tobago). The leader of the party holding a majority in the House is appointed Prime Minister. The Tobago House of Assembly has 12 elected members and three chosen by the House of Assembly who hold office for a four year term.

Evolution of suffrage

Full universal adult suffrage was introduced by the British colonial administration in 1945. The voting age was reduced from 21 to 18 in 1976.

Sequence of elections since 1981

Date	*Winning party*
Nov. 9, 1981	People's National Movement (PNM)
Dec. 15, 1986	National Alliance for Reconstruction (NAR)
Dec. 16, 1991	People's National Movement (PNM)

General election December 16, 1991

Party	*Seats in House of Representatives*
People's National Movement (PNM)	21
United National Congress (UNC)	13
National Alliance for Reconstruction (NAR)	2
Total	**36**

Election to the Tobago House of Assembly Nov. 28, 1988

Party	*% of votes*	*Seats*
National Alliance for Reconciliation (NAR)	63.3	11
People's National Movement (PNM)	35.0	1
Independent	1.7	-
Total	**100.0**	**12**

PARTY BY PARTY DATA

National Alliance for Reconstruction (NAR)

Address. 71 Dundonald Street, Port-of-Spain.
Leadership. Herbert Atwell (l.).
Orientation. Belying its moderate left-wing origins, in office it adopted economic austerity policies and sharply cut public spending. It has accepted the autonomy demands of Tobago. In the December 1991 general election, it was mainly supported by Indo-Trinidadians in central Trinidad.
Founded. February 1986.
History. The NAR was first established in September 1985 as an electoral coalition of the Organization for National Reconstruction (ONR) with three parties of the Trinidad and Tobago National Alliance, namely the Democratic Action Congress (DAC), the United Labour Front (ULF) and part of the Tapia House Movement (Tapia). The ONR and the Alliance had already allied in 1983 for the local elections as the "Accommodation". The NAR was reconstructed as a single party when the constituent groups dissolved themselves in February 1986.

The ONR, generally regarded as a pro-business, was formed in April 1980 by Karl Hudson-Philips, a former minister in the People's National Movement (PNM) government who had been suspended from the PNM after criticizing the then Prime Minister, Eric Williams. In the 1981 elections it was accorded 22 per cent of the vote but no seats.

The Tobago-based centre left DAC was formed in April 1971 by the merger of the Action Committee of Democratic Citizens and a section of the Democratic Labour Party. It was led by A. N. R. Robinson, who had resigned in 1970 as the deputy leader of the ruling PNM of which he had been a founder member. The DAC campaigned initially on the issue of electoral reform, and in the elections of September 1976 and November 1981 it won both Tobago seats. In November 1980 it had won eight of the 12 seats elective seats in the Tobago House of Assembly, which it increased to 11 in elections in November 1984.

The democratic-socialist and East-Indian dominated ULF, led by Basdeo Panday (in the mid-1960s a leading member of the Workers and Farmers Party—WFP) was formed as a trade union alliance in February 1975 and became a fully fledged party in March 1976, drawing most of its support from Indian-descended sugar workers. Allied with some left-wing groups, the ULF won 10 seats in the 1976 elections and became the official opposition. In the 1981 elections, however, the ULF's parliamentary representation was reduced to eight seats.

The NAR had an impressive victory in the December 1986 general election over the ruling PNM, ending its 30 years in power by securing 33 of the 36 seats in the house.

Robinson was named Prime Minister but within months his government, faced with an economic crisis, had lost most of its popular support. The NAR's poor performance in office was publicly criticized by Tapia activists in mid-1987 and in early 1988, Robinson dismissed the ULF's Panday, then deputy leader of the NAR, and two other ULF members, from the Cabinet, a move which led to a period of intense dissension in the party. Those dismissed were finally expelled from the party at the October 1988 NAR annual convention accused of having disregarded the party's rules and constitution by forming the Club '88, a grouping which actively agitated against Robinson's style of leadership.

The popularity of the NAR, and of Robinson in particular, continued to wane during 1989 and 1990 as the economy continued to decline. IMF-approved austerity measures provoked growing social unrest, rising crime and severe unemployment and the IMF's insistence on tax reforms, including the introduction of value-added tax (VAT), was deeply unpopular. Robinson survived a coup attempt by Black Muslim *Jamaat al Muslimeen* in July 1990. Denied the popular following of the ULF, the NAR suffered a humiliating defeat in the Dec. 16, 1991, general election, receiving only three seats out of the 36 parliamentary seats. Robinson resigned as NAR leader a week later, having accepted full responsibility for the defeat.

People's National Movement (PNM)

Address. Balisier House, 1 Tranquillity Street, Port-of-Spain.
Leadership. Patrick Manning (l.); Lenny Saith (ch.).
Orientation. Nominally social democratic; mostly supported among urban Afro-Trinidadians.
Founded. January 1956.
History. The Party easily won every general election from 1956 to 1981 inclusive, each time taking an

overwhelming majority of the seats and all 36 of them in 1971.

The PNM was founded by Eric Williams, the noted historian of the West Indies, who attracted and encouraged young nationalist intellectuals determined to break with British colonial rule. Williams died in 1981 and was succeeded as Prime Minister and party leader by George Michael Chambers who led the party to its sixth consecutive victory, with 53 per cent of the vote and 26 seats, in the 1981 general election.

This success was dramatically reversed in the elections of 1986 when a jaded and corruption-ridden PNM was comprehensively defeated by the National Alliance for Reconstruction (NAR), winning only three seats. Patrick Manning, one of the three parliamentary survivors, replaced Chambers in December 1987 and surrounded himself with younger party members, provoking the resignation, amidst great personal bitterness, of a PNM founder member Murial Dowana-McDavidson, the country's longest serving parliamentarian.

Manning was the chief beneficiary of the mounting hostility to the NAR government. He was swept to power in the general election of December 1991, the PNM winning 21 of the 36 seats. On Dec. 17, Manning was sworn in as Prime Minister. In the election campaign the PNM, which had few policy differences with the NAR, exploited widespread fears that in agreeing to the temporary residence of 100 Haitian refugees, NAR Prime Minister A. N. R. Robinson was seeking to change the racial mix in a country where race relations had become a major political and social issue.

United National Congress (UNC)

Address. Churchill Roosevelt Highway and 5th Street, Barataria.

Leadership. Basdeo Panday (l.).

Orientation. Centre-left.

Founded. April 1989.

History. The party was formed by a group of former ministers, led by United Labour Front (ULF) leader Basdeo Panday, who had been expelled by the National Alliance for Reconstruction (NAR) government in October 1988. The UNC held its first annual convention on July 22, 1990, when Panday was elected unopposed as leader. It had the support of six members in the House of Representatives compared with three for the official party, the People's National Movement (PNM). In September the UNC decided to seek the status of official opposition, with Panday becoming parliamentary opposition leader, and the party nominated six appointees to the senate to replace the PNM senators. Prior to the party's internal elections in September 1991, the UNC's general-secretary Rampersad Parasram, a former NAR minister expelled with Panday, declined to stand for any party post.

He was reported to have had serious "ideological" differences with Panday, who welcomed the decision, stating that it would end party in-fighting and give the UNC a "real" chance in the December general election. In the election the party increased to 13 its number of parliamentary seats.

Minor parties

Communist Party of Trinidad and Tobago (CPTT) founded in 1979, was, prior to the political changes in Albania in 1990-91, a supporter of the Albanian communist regime.

February Eighteenth Movement (FEM) James Millett (l.); founded in 1972 and was represented at a pan-Caribbean socialist conference in Cuba in 1984.

Jammaat al Musilmeen Iman Yasin Abu Bakr (l.); a black militant sect that staged an abortive coup against the National Alliance for Reconstruction (NAR) in July 1990. In a series of co-ordinated attacks, the rebels seized control of the legislative building and captured NAR Prime Minister A. N. R. Robinson and several members of his Cabinet.

They demanded Robinson's resignation, the establishment of a coalition government (including Abu Bakr), the holding of national elections within 90 days and an amnesty for all who participated in the coup. Over five days more than 30 people were killed, 500 wounded and there was widespread looting. The rebels surrendered in early August. In November 1991, the Privy Council in London granted a right to an immediate hearing of the habeas corpus applications of 116 black Moslems to the Trinidadian courts for their release from prison.

The Privy Council agreed that the presidential pardon given to the Moslems by the then acting President Emmanuelle Carter in exchange for Robinson's release remained valid. Government lawyers had argued that the pardon was given under duress and therefore was invalid. There were unconfirmed reports in August 1991 that the group had re-formed and was involved in smuggling arms and ammunition.

Movement for Social Transformation (MOTION) 156 Henry Street, Port-of-Spain. The party is led by David Abdulah.

National Joint Action Committee (NJAC) 40 Duke Street, Port-of-Spain. The party leader is Makandal Daaga.

National Movement for the True Independence of Trinidad (NMTIT) Teddy Belgrave (l.); founded in 1974, the party is nominally Maoist and is linked with the Oilfield Workers' Trade Union.

People's Popular Movement (PPM) Michael Als (ch.); founded in 1981 and was represented at the Cuban pan-Caribbean conference in 1984.

In the 1986 general election the PPM contested only a few seats and lost its deposit in each case.

Tapia House Group (Tapia), 24 Abercromby Street, Port-of-Spain. Tapia is led by Michael Harris (see also National Alliance for Reconstruction).

It developed from a radical New World Group which split in 1968 into an activist Moko wing (which became the United National Independent Party, now defunct), and a more intellectual, Fabian-influenced, Tapia House Group (named after the local word for mud walls). The Group, four of whose members were appointed to the Senate in 1974, was reorganized as the Movement in May 1976. Led by Lloyd Best and Arnold Hood, it contested the 1976 and 1981 elections without success.

United Revolutionary Organization (URO) founded in 1971 and was pro-Soviet before the collapse of the Soviet Union and the Eastern bloc.

Workers' Revolutionary Committee James Poon (l.); founded in 1980 and was pro-Soviet.

Turks and Caicos Islands

Capital: Cockburn Town (Grand Turk) **Population: 13,000**

The Turks and Caicos Islands were a Jamaican dependency from 1859 to 1959, and became a separate United Kingdom Dependent Territory in 1962 after Jamaican independence. Ministerial government was suspended by the British government in 1986-88 while a public inquiry investigated allegations of official corruption.

Constitutional structure

Under the 1976 Constitution, amended in 1987 after a corruption scandal, the islands are ruled by a Governor who represents the British monarch. He is responsible for defence, external affairs and internal security and heads an eight-member Executive Council, a quasi Cabinet which includes the Chief Minister, and the 20-member Legislative Council.

Electoral system

Under the new electoral system introduced in 1987, 13 members of the Legislative Council are elected for four years by universal adult suffrage in five polling districts, with some constituencies being allowed to elect up to three representatives. The Legislative Council also has three ex officio members, three further members appointed by the Governor in consultation with the elected members and a Speaker, chosen from outside the Council. The same ex officio members serve in the Executive Council, which has also four ministers drawn from the elected members of the legislature.

Sequence of elections since 1980

Date	*Winning party*
1980	Progressive National Party (PNP)
May 29, 1984	Progressive National Party (PNP)
March 3, 1988	People's Democratic Movement (PDM)

General election March 3, 1988

Party	*seats*
People's Democratic Movement (PDM)	11
Progressive National Party (PNP)	2
Total	**13***

*seven further members of the Legislative Council are appointed.

General election April 23, 1991

Party	*seats*
PNP	8
PDM	5
Total	**13**

PARTY BY PARTY DATA

People's Democratic Movement (PDM)

Address. Cockburn town, Grand Turk.
Leadership. Oswald O. Skipping (l.).
Orientation. Centre-left; among the party's declared aims are internal self-government and eventual independence, although it is no longer a main feature of policy.
Founded. March 1976.
History. The party arose out of the *Junknoo Club*, a youth pressure group formed in 1973. It narrowly won the September 1976 elections to the Legislative Council, by six seats to five for the Progressive National Party (PNP), but later recruited the two independent councillors. A PDM member subsequently defected to the PNP, reducing its majority to one. In 1980, following the accidental death of its founder J. A. G. S. McCartney, the party lost the election, standing as it did on an explicitly pro-independence platform. It was reduced to three seats which it held in 1984.

Skipping was re-elected leader in 1985, succeeding Clement Howell who had taken over from him shortly before the 1984 election. A public inquiry held in mid-1986, following the conviction of corrupt government ministers (which included accusations that Skipping had been guilty of arson), declared the PDM leadership "unfit to hold public office". This did not prevent the party easily winning the March 1988 election with 11 seats, the first since Britain's restoration of constitutional rule following the imposition of direct rule in 1966. Skipping became Chief Minister. However, the party lost the April 1991 general election, receiving only five seats, its vote falling from 5,493 to 4,542.

Progressive National Party (PNP)

Address. Cockburn Town, Grand Turk.
Leadership. Washington Missick (l.).
Orientation. Conservative and anti-independence, committed to economic development through free enterprise.
History. The party was known until 1978 as the Progressive National Organization, which in the 1976 legislative elections had obtained four of the 11 elective seats. In 1980, however, the PNP won eight seats, with 59.1 per cent of the vote and Norman B. Saunders became Chief Minister.

The party won a second term in 1984, with 62 per cent of the vote and eight seats but Saunders was forced to resign as Chief Minister and party leader in March 1985 following his arrest in the United States, along with two government members, on drug trafficking charges.

He was succeeded by his deputy Nathaniel J. S. (Bops) Francis. However a July 1986 report of a public inquiry into corruption and arson instituted by the British government concluded that Francis and other ministers had acted unconstitutionally and were unfit for office.

Francis and his government were forced to resign, the executive council was dissolved and the governor was empowered to rule personally with an appointed advisory council, pending fresh elections and a return to ministerial rule (under a revised constitution) in 1988. The party suffered a crippling defeat on the 1988 election, winning only two seats.

Under the new leadership of Robert Hall, the party recovered to win the April 1991 election, taking eight seats and seeing its vote increase from 2,727 to 4,866.

United States of America

Capital: Washington D.C. **Population: 246,900,000**

The original 13 colonies of the USA declared themselves independent from Britain in 1776, and gave substance to the claim with a successful war of independence between 1775 and 1783. The current Constitution was adopted in 1787 and ratified in 1788, and by 1959 a total of 50 separate states had joined the union. After more than a century of isolationism, the USA emerged in the mid-20th century as a global super-power.

Although there are many political parties in the USA, the system is, in practice, based on two parties: the Republican and the Democratic Parties. Both are loose federations without clear ideological foundations. Both support American capitalism, although the Democrats tend to advocate a greater role for welfare services and federal government. Both parties pursue pragmatic policies and operate within a culturally and ethnically heterogeneous society where power is devolved to state, city and county. These factors ensure that Congressmen are highly susceptible to local or regional pressures and lobbying. The doctrine of the separation of powers also ensures a high degree of pragmatic compromise since there is no executive within the legislature to enforce strict party discipline.

The party system has endured in the last few decades a retreat from the levels of voter identification experienced in the 1940s and 1950s. Today's voter is more likely to switch allegiance between the two parties or to split ticket vote: to vote one way during congressional elections and another for the presidency. Increasing "voter volatility" has presented the parties with fresh challenges at the same time as their own structures have had to adapt to the growth of the media and to other changes within society. The oligarchical parties of the recent past have had to give way to calls for democracy, particularly the Democratic Party. Reform of the procedure for nominating presidential candidates has taken power away from the national conventions and resulted in the extensive use of primaries and candidate-centred campaigns. Instead of being a forum for selecting the candidate in "smoke filled rooms" the convention now tends to ratify a result determined by the exhaustive process of primaries and caucuses.

The increased use of primaries has also resulted in the development of candidate-centred campaigning, as has federal funding, available since 1974 to individual presidential candidates themselves rather than to the party organizations. Campaigns also tend to be run by political action committees (PACs) which owe their allegiance directly to a candidate. In recent years the national party organizations have been largely squeezed out from campaigning by these developments. Primaries have also been criticized for encouraging divisions within the parties, particularly as incumbant presidents such as Gerald Ford and Jimmy Carter were ultimately defeated having been damaged by strong challenges from within their parties during the primary process.

Constitutional structure

The USA is a federal republic of 50 member states which elect their own legislatures and governors. In accordance with the Constitution of 1778, the federal government is responsible for foreign affairs, defence, and the administration of the federal criminal justice system.

Legislative power is vested in a bicameral Congress consisting of a 100-member Senate and a 435-member House of Representatives, the lower house. Each state sends two Senators to the upper house, regardless of

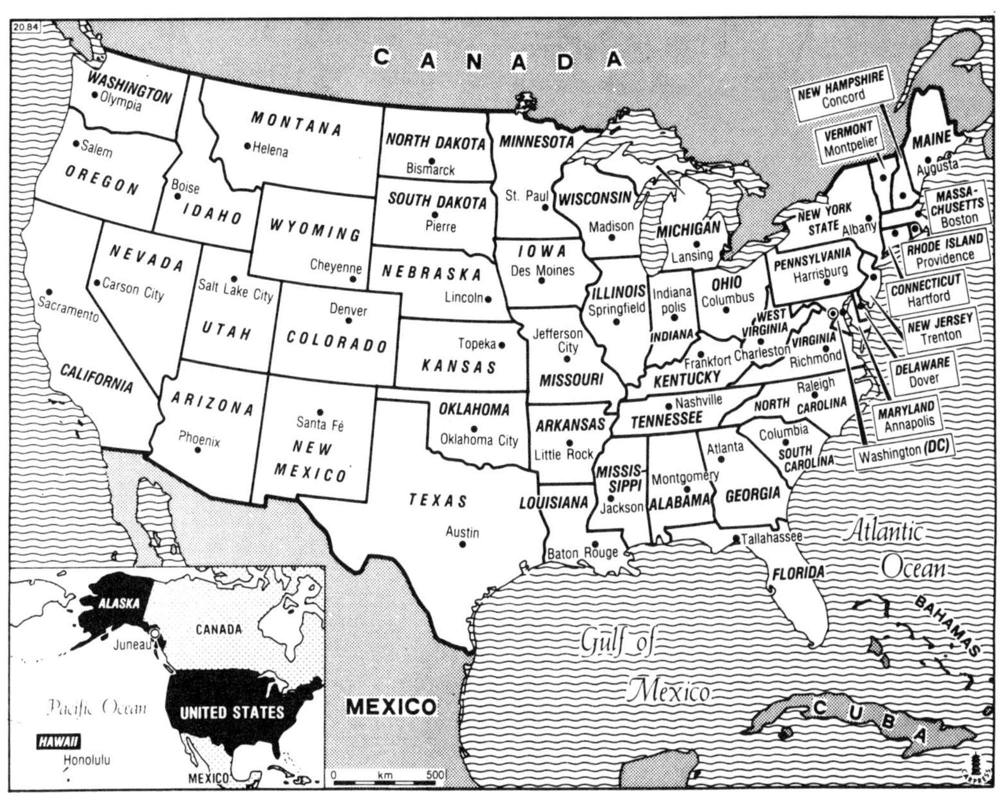
20.84
CANADA
WASHINGTON
Olympia
MONTANA
Helena
NORTH DAKOTA
Bismarck
MINNESOTA
NEW HAMPSHIRE
Concord
VERMONT
Montpelier
MAINE
Augusta
Salem
OREGON
Boise
IDAHO
WYOMING
SOUTH DAKOTA
Pierre
St. Paul
WISCONSIN
Madison
MICHIGAN
Lansing
NEW YORK STATE
Albany
MASSA-CHUSETTS
Boston
RHODE ISLAND
Providence
NEVADA
Carson City
Sacramento
Salt Lake City
UTAH
Cheyenne
NEBRASKA
Lincoln
IOWA
Des Moines
PENNSYLVANIA
Harrisburg
CONNECTICUT
Hartford
Denver
COLORADO
ILLINOIS
Springfield
Indiana polis
INDIANA
OHIO
Columbus
WEST VIRGINIA
Charleston
VIRGINIA
Richmond
NEW JERSEY
Trenton
CALIFORNIA
Topeka
KANSAS
Jefferson City
MISSOURI
Frankfort
KENTUCKY
DELAWARE
Dover
ARIZONA
Phoenix
Santa Fé
NEW MEXICO
OKLAHOMA
Oklahoma City
ARKANSAS
Little Rock
Nashville
TENNESSEE
NORTH CAROLINA
Raleigh
MARYLAND
Annapolis
Washington (DC)
Columbia
SOUTH CAROLINA
Atlanta
GEORGIA
MISSIS-SIPPI
Jackson
Montgomery
ALABAMA
TEXAS
Austin
LOUISIANA
Baton Rouge
Tallahassee
FLORIDA
Atlantic Ocean
BAHAMAS
Gulf of Mexico
CUBA
MEXICO
ALASKA
Juneau
CANADA
Pacific Ocean
UNITED STATES
HAWAII
Honolulu
MEXICO
0 km 500

Sequence of elections since 1948

Presidential elections 1948-1988

Date	*Winning Candidate*
1948	Harry S. Truman (Dem)
1952	Dwight D. Eisenhower (Rep)
1956	Dwight D. Eisenhower (Rep)
1960	John F. Kennedy (Dem)
1964	Lyndon B. Johnson (Dem)
1968	Richard Nixon (Rep)
1972	Richard Nixon (Rep)
1976	Jimmy Carter (Dem)
1980	Ronald Reagan (Rep)
1984	Ronald Reagan (Rep)
1988	George Bush (Rep)

Legislative elections

The Democratic Party has enjoyed unbroken control of the House of Representatives since 1955. During this same period the party has dominated the Senate apart from a brief period of Republican ascendancy in 1981-87.

Results of 1988 and 1990 Congressional elections.

Senate	*1988*	*1990*
Democrats	55	56
Republicans	45	44
House		
Democrats	262	267
Republicans	173	167

the size or population of the state. The Senate's powers include the right to ratify foreign treaties, to act as a court of impeachment, and to confirm senior appointments to the judiciary and to the executive. The number of representatives each state has in the House is determined by the population of the state.

The separation of powers embodied in the Constitution precludes party government in the accepted sense. The President and his Cabinet do not sit in Congress, resulting in loose party discipline and a strong sense of independence from the executive. As the President is elected separately from the legislature, it is not unusual for a President to be faced by a Congressional majority drawn from the other party. Many commentators suggest that the USA at times has a four-party system; executive Republicans and Democrats (when in office) and Congressional Republicans and Democrats. Although the powers of the executive have increased considerably in the twentieth century, even in recent years presidents have suffered some important legislative defeats even when their own party has been in control of both houses of Congress.

Political parties are not subsidised by the state although federal funding is available for presidential campaigns and for the cost of party conventions.

Electoral system

Elections for Congress and the presidency are held in early November. Senators are elected for a six-year term, one-third of them being re-elected every two years. The 435 members of the House of Representatives are elected for two years in single member constituencies.

Although the President is elected by an electoral college, in effect this amounts to a popular election. Each state contributes a number of delegates to the electoral college (in accordance with the size of its population) and, by convention, these delegates vote for the candidate who secured the largest number of popular votes in their particular state. It is possible for the candidate who wins most of the popular votes to lose the election because his rival accumulates a greater number of votes in the Electoral College—this occurred in 1824, 1876 and 1888—although this outcome has not occurred for more than a century. Also, members of the Electoral College are not legally bound to vote for the candidate who achieved greatest popular support in their particular state and, even in recent years, some have voted differently, but never in sufficient number to affect the outcome.

In the event of no single candidate achieving an overall majority in the Electoral College, the House of Representatives has the constitutional right to decide the issue, voting in state blocks with one vote each. This occurred in 1800 and in 1824.

Before submitting themselves to the popular vote, aspiring presidential candidates must first secure the nomination of their party, a contest ultimately decided at the party National Convention. Candidates from the same party compete in state elections or primaries. The victor of this popular vote, conducted under various rules in different states, secures the votes of the state's delegates to the party convention on a proportional or winner-takes-all basis. The larger the state, the more delegates it will send to the Convention.

Evolution of the suffrage

The principle of universal suffrage for white adult males was accepted by most states between 1800 and 1828. Despite the abolition of slavery in 1865 and the 14th and 15th Amendments to the Constitution guaranteeing their right to vote, most black males were disenfranchised throughout the 19th century by the use of devices such as "grandfather" clauses and literacy tests. In 1965 the federal government passed legislation enabling it to take over the registration of voters if there was evidence of unfair practises. This, together with the contribution made by the Supreme Court and the civil rights movement, ensured that for the first time in US history the black population was assured of the right to vote.

In 1920 the 19th Amendment guaranteed complete female suffrage. In 1971 the 26th Amendment reduced the voting age from 21 to 18 years.

It is an irony of American politics, with its emphasis on elections (judges and town officials such as sheriffs are often elected), that voter participation in primaries and presidential elections is very low. Turnouts in presidential elections in the 1950s and 1960s were historically high, 62.8 per cent in 1960, but have fallen to 50.1 per cent in 1988, 53.1 per cent in 1984, and 49.1 per cent in 1988. Turnout in the 1992 primaries has shown evidence of further decline. The New York primary in April 1992 revealed a 38 per cent fall compared with 1988. The decline in the number of black people voting is above trend; 40 per cent fewer blacks voted in primaries in Georgia and 61 per cent fewer in Louisiana.

PARTY BY PARTY DATA

Democratic Party

Address. Democratic National Committee, 430 South Capitol St, SE, Washington DC 20003.

Leadership. (National Committee) Ronald H. Brown (ch.); Kathleen M. Vick (sec.); Robert Farmer (treas.).

Orientation. The Democratic Party, one of the two major parties in the USA, can be broadly defined as a centre-left party which accepts the context of US capitalism. Traditionally, the party emphasizes labour and consumer rights, civil rights and greater government expenditure on welfare, health and social security.

Founded. 1800 (National Committee 1848).

History. The party is the oldest existing political party currently functioning in the USA. It originated in the form of the Republican Party founded by Thomas Jefferson, which later became the Democratic-Republican Party. The modern Democratic Party, however, is derived from the organization which fought the presidential election of 1828 on behalf of Andrew Jackson.

The period 1828 to 1860 was a period of Democrat ascendency; the party won all but two presidential campaigns, those of 1840 and 1848. After 1832 the main opposition came from the largely ineffective Whig party. In the 1850s, however, the issue of whether slavery should be extended into new states joining the union increasingly divided the party and even led to the fielding of two nominees for the presidential election of 1860.

The Civil War ushered in a disastrous era for the Democrats, with Abraham Lincoln's victory in 1860 marking the beginning of a period of Republican hegemony which stretched almost unbroken until 1932. Only Grover Cleveland in 1884 and 1892 and Woodrow Wilson in 1912 and 1916, managed to deny the White House to the Republicans. The Reconstruction period, however, saw the consolidation of the South's regional identity and its affiliation to the Democratic Party. White voters, incensed by black enfranchisement and Northern dominance, strengthened their commitment to the Democrats and created the "solid South" as a regional stronghold which lasted into the 1960s.

The Great Depression of the early 1930s marked the next major turning point in the fortunes of the party, for it shattered the reputation of the Republicans for economic competence and growth. The Democrats held the Presidency from 1933 to 1953, offering the country a "New Deal" to combat the depression, and leadership during World War II. The party owed its electoral success to a coalition consisting of organized labour in the North and Midwest, the immigrant community, and Southern whites. Franklin D. Roosevelt became the only President elected to four terms in office, winning the elections of 1932, 1936, 1940 and 1944. (After his death in 1945 the Constitution was amended to prohibit any individual from serving more than two terms).

Since 1952, however, the Democrats have won the presidency only in 1960, 1964 and 1976. The decline in the presidential fortunes of the party, which has not been matched at congressional level, has been due largely to a loss of support in the South. (The practice of split ticket voting in the Southern states—where voters vote Democrat on a local basis, but Republican for the presidency—has enabled the party to maintain its control over Congress).

The key reason for this decline was the advocacy of black civil rights by the national party in the 1960s, which brought local politicians into sharp confrontation with federal authorities under the control of a Democrat President. While achieving enormous benefits on issues such as school desegregation and black voter registration, the price paid by the party was the defection of many white

Southern voters to the Republicans, and an increasing tendency for the Democratic Party to be identified with minority interests.

Other factors behind the recent decline of the Democrats at the presidential level include the demographic drift away from the industrialised centres of the north-east, the "rust belt", to the "sunbelt states" of the South stretching from Florida to California. This demographic shift was fuelled by the economic decline of the northern cities (and concomitant worries about crime, drugs and urban decay), and the growth of "sunrise" hi-tech industries in the South.

Structure. The party is a loose coalition. Between conventions the business of the party is conducted by the national committee which consists of elected state representatives. The party includes several factions which lobby for particular programmes or points of view.

The most important of these include the Democratic Socialists of America (DSA). The DSA, founded in 1982, sees itself as the socialist wing of the Democratic Party, having around 40 chapters active within the Democratic Party, and is a member of the Socialist International. The Liberal Party is another faction which operates within the Democratic Party in the state of New York. The party is closely associated with New York Governor Mario Cuomo. Americans for Democrat Action, founded in 1947, is another tendency which seeks to protect the policies and philosophies of the New Deal.

Membership. While the Democratic Party does not have fee-paying or card-carrying members, millions of voters are prepared to demonstrate their allegiance to the party by registering themsleves on the electoral role as Democrats.

Republican Party

Address. (National Committee) 310 First Street, SE, Washington DC 20003.

Leadership: (National Committee) Clayton K. Yeutter (ch); Kit Mehrtens (sec); William J. McManus (treas).

Orientation: One of the country's two major political parties, the Republican Party is generally more conservative than the Democratic Party, although its conservatism tends to be pragmatic rather than ideological in origin. It is opposed to the over-centralisation of government power and emphasizes freedom of the individual. It advocates low taxes, a balanced budget and a strong military.

Founded. 1854.

History. Informally known as the Grand Old Party (GOP), the Republican Party originated from the Northern anti-slavery movement of the 1850s. Attracting supporters from the disintegrating Whigs, the Republican Party's first presidential candidate, John C. Fremont, carried 11 Northern states in 1856, but lost the election.

The period between the elections of 1860 and 1932 was a period of Republican hegemony, with the party winning 15 out of 19 presidential contests. During the same period the party also controlled the Senate for 54 years and the House for 50 years. It was weakened by a split between the Conservatives, who nominated William Howard Taft as the party's candidate for the 1912 election, and the Progressive faction of Theodore Roosevelt, who withdrew from the Republican Party and formed the Progressive or "Bull Moose" Party. But after Democratic victories in 1912 and 1916, the Republicans regained the presidency in 1920, and won again in 1924 and 1928. The party's hold on the White House was finally broken by the Great Depression of the early 1930s, which ushered in a period of Democratic ascendency.

The Republicans failed to make a breakthrough until 1946, when they won control of the two houses of Congress for the first time since 1928. Eisenhower's victory in 1952 was the first Republican presidential victory for 24 years, and was followed by a further win in 1956. However, Eisenhower had Republican majorities in both houses of Congress for only two of his eight years in office.

The party narrowly lost the presidential election of 1960 and that of 1964. Through Richard Nixon, however, the Republicans regained the presidency in 1968, and retained it with a comprehensive win in 1972. Following the Watergate scandal and the subsequent resignation of Nixon, the party was defeated by the Democrats in the presidential elections of 1976. The Republicans regained the White House in 1980, also gaining control of the Senate. The 1986 Congressional elections, however, saw the Senate fall to the Democrats, giving them control of both houses.

The Republicans held the Presidency in 1984 with the re-election of Ronald Reagan and in 1988 with the victory of George Bush, hitherto Vice-President. The success of the 1980s was largely based on the party's appeal to "Reagan Democrats"; the party succeeded in poaching from the Democrats that party's "natural constituency" of skilled manual and newly middle class voters, with its emphasis on incentives, low taxes, and personal freedom.

Structure. Like the Democratic Party, the Republican Party is a loose coalition of elements co-ordinated by the Republican national committee which consists of a chairman together with other executive officials and representatives from all of the states and territories of the federal union.

Membership. Although the Republican Party does not have fee-paying or card-carrying members, millions of voters are prepared to demonstrate their allegiance to the organization by registering themselves on the electoral role as Republicans.

Minor parties

American Federalist Party (POB 212, Batesville, MS 38606); founded in 1988, this small party is committed to policies designed to defend Northern European "white supremacy". It opposes firearms legislation and welfare rights. Leadership: R. A. Owens (man. dir.).

American Independent Party (8158 Palm St, Lemon Grove CA 92045); founded in 1968 to promote presidential candidate, George Wallace, the party embraces a right wing platform including opposition to abortion, communism and federal interference in local education policy. It also adopts conservative positions on disarmament and immigration. In the 1968 election Wallace received almost 10,000,000 votes (13.5 per cent of the popular vote), carrying five states and receiving 46 electoral college votes, although he failed to achieve his aim of forcing a deadlock in the electoral college. (He was shot and crippled during his campaign to secure the 1972 Democratic nomination. He failed in his attempt to win the nomination and, after failing again in 1976, retired from political life in 1987.) In 1969 the AIP split, with representatives from 38 states establishing the American Party of the United States. Both parties have fielded candidates for public office, including the Presidency, but neither has attained the success of the party under the leadership of Wallace. The AIP's presidential candidates achieved 170,673 and 41,268 votes in the presidential elections of 1976 and 1980. Currently the party is led by Eileen M. Shearer, and membership is estimated as 150,000 in California and 20-30,000 elsewhere.

American Party of the United States (POB 597, Provo, UT 84603); founded in 1969 as a split from the AIP, the party is currently led by Arly Pederson (nat. ch.) and Doris Feimer (sec.). In the 1976 presidential elections its nominee, Thomas J. Anderson, polled 160,600 votes or 0.2 per cent of the total.

American Populist Party (POB 1988, Ford City, PA 16226); led by John Couture (ch.) and Donald B. Wassall (exec. dir.), the party believes in "America First" policies and "the values and beliefs of middle class America"; founded in 1891 (reformed 1984), the modern party represents the remains of the agrarian populist party which was established in the late 19th century as a vehicle for agrarian and Western discontent. In the 1984 presidential election the Populist candidate won 66,336 votes. The party has 350,000 members and 42 state groups. Publications: the *Populist Observer* (monthly).

Archonist Club (682 Callahan Pl. Mendota Heights, MN 55118); founded in 1967, the party is a quasi-religious organization with Christian orientation which seeks to interpret the "divine will" in political affairs. It accuses US foreign policy of being "Zionist" and is critical of US policy towards Israel. It is currently led by William L. Knaus.

Citizens Party (1623 Connecticut Ave, NW, Washington DC 20009); founded in 1969 and currently led by Barry Commoner (ch.), the party describes itself as a progressive environmentalist and democratic party. Its policies include opposition to nuclear weapons, the phasing out of nuclear power and the adoption of tougher environmental standards. The party achieved 234,279 votes in the 1980 presidential election but this fell to 72,200 in 1984. The party has won local government seats. It has chapters in at least 30 states, and had 25,000 members in 1984. International affiliations: the party has links with West European Green parties.

Communist Labor Party (POB 3705, Chicago, IL 60654; founded in 1974, this Marxist group was formed by the merger of the Communist League, the League for Proletarian Revolution and the Motor City Labor League.

Communist Party USA (CPUSA, 235 West 23rd St. New York, NY 10011); led by Gus Hall (gen.sec.); founded in 1919, the party has sought to fulfil a vanguard role in US society, advocating a dictatorship of the proletariat. The CPUSA severed its connection with the Communist International in 1940, and ceased to exist in 1944, when it became the Communist Political Association. The party was reconstituted in 1945 but was harassed by the authorities, particularly during the McCarthyite period. Between 1947 and 1956 numerous party leaders were arrested and tried on various charges, and were seen as the agents of the Soviet Union. Persecution and prosecution of party members ceased after the Supreme Court ruled in 1964 that party membership was not of itself sufficient grounds for conviction under internal security legislation.

This breakthrough was followed by a further Supreme Court decision in 1965 which ruled that certain aspects of the Internal Security Act of 1950, requiring CPUSA registration with the Department of Justice, were unconstitutional. In 1957 a party convention decided to permit limited criticism of the Soviet Union and to allow a more flexible application of Marxist-Leninist principals.

The CPUSA has contested every presidential election since 1968, never achieving a significant percentage of the vote. In 1980 and 1984 the party's presidential candidate, Gus Hall, won 44,954 and 36,386 votes respectively. The party is active in 40 states, the basic unit of the organization being the party club. In the early 1980s it had a 73-member Central Committee and held four-yearly national conventions which elect a political bureau. It has a membership of 20,000. Publications: the *Daily Worker*, the party's organ for 30 years, ceased publication in 1957. The party publishes the monthly *Political Affairs*, a theoretical journal with a circulation of 20,000. The *Daily World*, a weekly Marxist newspaper, is another of its publications with a circulation of 100,000. International affiliations: the CPUSA was recognized by all the Communist parties of the former Soviet bloc.

Communist Party of the USA (Marxist-Leninist) (POB 6205 Chicago IL 60680); founded in 1978 and currently led by D. Weiss (sec.).

Communist Workers' Party (72 5th Avenue, Brooklyn, New York, NY 11215); founded in 1979, the party is currently led by Jerry Tung (gen. sec.).

Conservative Party (486 78 St. Ft. Hamilton Station, NY 11209); founded in 1962, the party operates exclusively within New York state where it has enjoyed local success. It advocates the promotion of individual liberty and limited constitutional government. Its current leadership includes Serphin R. Maltese (exec. dir.) and Michael R. Long (state ch.).

Constitution Party of the United States (Medina ND 58467); founded in 1952 as a vehicle to endorse and protect the original US Constitution as the supreme law of the land. The party is currently led by Clarence S. Martin (nat. ch.).

Expansionist Party of the United States (446 West 46th St. New York, NY 10036); founded in 1977, the party seeks annexation by the USA of areas willing to abide by the US Constitution as a prelude to world union. It is currently led by L. Craig Schoonmaker (ch.) and numbers around 600 members.

Green Committees of Correspondence (POB 30208, Kansas City, MO, 64112); founded in 1984 as an organization to protect the environment, it is also known as the American Green Movement and the US Green Network. The organization—which has 29 regional groups and 210 local groups—is currently led by Jim Richmond (co-ordinator).

Industrial Union Party (POB 80, New York 10159); founded in 1980, the IUP seeks to bring the US economy under the ownership and control of a government of industrial unions. It is currently led by Sam Brandon (gen.sec.).

Kach International (POB 16944, Encino, CA 91416); founded in 1985, the party supported Rabbi Kahane (recently assassinated) and encourages Jewish migration to Israel from the USA. It is currently led by Steve Smason (ch.), and has 125,000 members in 30 states.

La Raza Unida Party (483 Fifth St. San Fernando, CA 91340); founded in 1972, the party aims to achieve greater self-determination and representation for Latinos through the electoral process. Currently led by Xenaro G. Ayala (nat. ch.), the organization has 100 local groups and 4 state groups. Its publications include the monthly newspapers *El Sembrador* and *La Nacion*, and the quarterly *La Semilla*.

Libertarian Party (1528 Pennsylvania Ave, SE, Washington DC 20003); led by David Walter (ch.), D. Nick Dunbar (national dir.); founded in 1971, the party seeks election of libertarians to public office and opposes censorship, military conscription, and government regulation of personal matters.

The party favours the free-market economy and minimal regulation by government. It has a membership of 15,600. In the presidential election of 1974, the first the party had fought, the Libertarian

Party candidate, Roger MacBride, received 174,000 votes. In the 1980 presidential elections, the party attracted 921,188 votes (almost 1 per cent of the popular vote) but has since failed to live up to this achievement. In the 1984 contest its vote fell to 228,314.

In the 1982 Congressional elections the party fielded over 300 candidates for the House and 29 for the Senate, but none was successful. The party is organized in 19 regional groups, 51 state groups, 300 local groups. Publications: *Libertarian Party News* (bi-monthly newsletter, circulation 10,000).

Marxist-Leninist Party of the USA (Ontario St. Station, POB 11942, Chicago, IL 60611); founded in 1980, the party was the successor to the Central Organization of US Marxist-Leninists which had been created in 1973. It publications include the *Workers' Advocate* (monthly, in English and Spanish).

National Democratic Policy Committee (POB 17729, Washington DC 20041); founded in 1980, the party supports candidates for federal, state and local office. It also provides policy initiatives on issues such as defence and economics.

The committee has sponsored Lyndon LaRouche as presidential candidate (the committee's supporters are known as LaRouche Democrats). Currently led by Warren J. Hamerman (ch.), the organization—which is also known as the National Caucus of Labor Committees—has 12,000 members in six regional groups and 43 state groups.

National Determination Party (POB 5100, Charleston WV 25361); founded in 1975, this nationalistic right-wing party campaigns to prevent the domination of America by "Judae-fundamentalism". Currently led by Arnold Moltis (ch.), the party was formerly known as the American Majority Party. It publications include *Imperative News and Views* (monthly).

National Hamiltonian Party (3314 Dillon Rd, Flushing, MI, 48433); founded in 1962, the party is named after Alexander Hamilton (1750-1803) and advocates government by an elite of "aristocrats of the mind" and educated citizens.

The party is currently led by Michael Kelly (nat. ch.), and has a membership of around 1,000 in five regional groups and 47 state groups. Its publications include the *Hamiltonian* (periodical).

National Socialist Party of America (2519 West 71st St, Chicago, IL 60629); founded in 1970, this party advocates an "all white" America. It is organized into 11 state groups.

National States Rights Party (POB 4063, Marietta, GA 30061); founded in 1958 this party is a patriotic white racist order which advocates the repeal of all civil rights laws. It is currently led by J. B. Stoner (ch.), and has some 15,000 members. Its publications include a *Personal Newsletter* (monthly), and *Thunderbolt* (monthly).

National Unity Party (POB 106, Timonium, MD 21093); founded in 1983 by liberal Republicans who were disillusioned with the right-wing ideas associated with President Reagan, the NUP advocates relatively liberal social policies but a rather more conservative economic programme. It is currently led by Anne Lee (sec.).

Nationalist Socialist White People's Party (2507 North Franklin Rd, Arlington, VA 22201); founded in 1959 the party is currently led by Commander Matt Koehl and has 25 local groups.

New Federalist Party (POB 19908, Baltimore, MD 21211); founded in 1976, the party aims to promote the principles of George Washington and the federalist founders of the USA. It is currently led by Alexander Bora (nat. dir.), and has 38 state groups and 76 local groups. It produces a weekly newsletter, *New Federalist Papers.*

New Party (8319 Fulham Ct. Richmond, VA 23227); founded in 1978, the party advocates the adoption of a universal, publicly financed health care service for the USA. It is led by Jerome D. Gorman (sec.).

Peace and Freedom Party (POB 42644 San Francisco CA 94142); founded in 1967, the party advocates "world socialism " and includes amongst its objectives huge cuts in defence spending; centralized economic planning; abolition of the IRS and personal taxation; lowering of the voting age to 13; the legalization of most prohibited drugs; and the end of the use of nuclear power in the USA.

Curently led by Paul Kangas, the party has 150 local groups, and 70,000 members.

Progressive Labor Party (231 W. 29th St, RM. 502, New York, NY 10001); founded in 1962, this Marxist-Leninist party is currently led by Milton Rosen. Its publications include *Al Tahadi* (a bi-monthly newspaper in Arabic) *Challenge/Desafio* (a weekly newspaper in English and Spanish), *Le Defi* (a monthly newspaper in French), and *Progressive Labor Magazine* (quarterly in English and Spanish).

Prohibition National Committee (POB 2635, Denver, CO 80201); founded in 1869 the Prohibition Party opposes the manufacture, sale and consumption of alcoholic drinks and of drugs, as well as adopting a conservative position on social issues such as abortion, education, taxation and euthanasia. It champions "individual freedom". The party nominates candidates for presidential, congressional and gubernatorial elections. It is currently led by Earl F. Dodge (nat. chair.) and Margaret L. Storms (nat. sec.).

Social Democrats USA (SDUSA) (815 15th St, NW, Washington, DC 20005); founded in 1972 to succeed the Socialist Party (established in 1901), the party has 3,000 members and is led by Donald Slaiman (pres.) and Rita Freedman (exec. dir.). International affiliations: the SDUSA is a full member party of the Socialist International.

Socialist Labor Party of America (POB 50218, 914 Industrial Ave, Palo Alto, CA 94303); founded in 1877, this Marxist party was formerly the Workingmen's Party (1877).

From 1893 to 1976 the party unsuccessfully participated in every presidential election campaign, its candidate in 1976 being Jules Levin. It has 17 local groups and some 500 members. It is currently led by Robert Bills (sec.) and Genevieve Gunderson (Financial Sec.).

Socialist Party of the USA (1011 North 3rd St, Suite 232, Milwaukee, WI 53203); founded in 1973 the party has 10 state and 17 local groups and is currently led by Rick Kissell (nat. sec.).

Socialist Workers' Party (14 Charles Lane, New York, NY 10014); founded in 1938, this Trotskyist party aims to establish a government of workers and farmers which will abolish American capitalism. The party is opposed to US foreign policy and civil nuclear power and nuclear weapons. It is led by Jack Barnes (nat. sec.).

United States Pacifist Party (5729 S. Dorchester Ave. Chicago Il. 60637); founded in 1983, the party opposes military expenditure, civil nuclear power, and the death penalty, and advocates conventional and nuclear disarmament. It is led by Bradford Lyttl.

Workers' World Party; a small Trokskyist party formed in 1958 and led by Sam Marcy.

World Socialist Party of the USA (POB 405, Boston, MA 02272); founded in 1916, this small Marxist party is led by Ronald Elbert (sec.).

Major guerrilla groups

The most significant of the underground movements of the 1960s and 1970s are no longer operative.

These included black groups such as the Black Power Movement and the Black Panther Party; groups of the far right, such as the Minutemen, and of the left, including the Weather Underground. The only significant national grouping still in existence is the Ku Klux Klan.

Ku Klux Klan

Founded. 1865.

Orientation. The KKK is a clandestine, white racist paramilitary organization.

History. The KKK was founded in Tennessee in 1865 and rapidly spread throughout the defeated Southern states. Its primary aim was to terrorize the newly emancipated black population, and it was banned in 1871.

It re-emerged in Georgia in 1915 as a focus for violence against blacks, Jews, Catholics, trade unionists and other "anti-social" elements.

By the mid-1920s it had spread beyond the boundaries of the old Confederacy and had grown into a national movement with up to 5,000,000 members. Discredited by the war against Nazi Germany it was disbanded in 1944, but resurfaced once again in the 1960s in response to the campaign for black civil rights in the Southern states.

Although harassed by the federal and judicial authorities in recent years, the Klan has continued to be active, particularly in the South, and some of its members have been responsible for continuing attacks upon traditional targets such as blacks and left-wingers.

Uruguay

Capital: Montevideo **Population: 3,100,000**

The independence of the Republic of Uruguay was recognized in 1828 after a period in which its territory was the subject of a dispute between Argentina and Brazil. Internal politics has since been dominated by the struggle between the liberal Colorado (red) and the conservative Blanco (white) parties, giving rise to civil wars throughout the 19th century. The Colorados held power continuously from 1865 to 1958 before giving way to the Blancos. The illusion that Uruguay was the Switzerland of Latin America was shattered when in 1971 laws curtailing civil liberties were introduced to give the army a free hand in fighting the Tupamaro guerrillas, and two years later in 1973 the armed forces took power, dissolving Congress and replacing it with an appointed Council of State. Although by 1976 the military promised a return to democracy, their regime of terror continued, with an estimated 6,000 political opponents imprisoned and subjected to torture. With an eye on eventually transferring power to a civilian government, the military regime drafted a new constitution meant to assure the army a say in all national security matters. This was rejected by a plebiscite in November 1980. Amidst mass protests, demonstrations and strikes and an economic crisis, the military finally agreed in August 1984 to elections being held in November, subsequently won by the Colorado candidate Julio María Sanguinetti. His government was marked by the major controversy over whether a "Full Stop" *Punto Final* amnesty law be conferred on all military and police personnel accused of human rights infringements, which was finally approved in a referendum in April 1989. The first fully free elections since the coup were held in November 1989 from which the Blancos emerged as the winning party.

Constitutional structure

Under the 1966 Constitution the republic has an executive President and is assisted by a Vice-President and an appointed Council of Ministers. Legislative power is vested in a National Congress consisting of a 99-member Chamber of Deputies and a 31-member Senate. The Vice-President is also a member of the Senate who presides over Senate business but is also permitted to vote. Following the return to civilian rule in 1985 a National Constituent Assembly was installed on July 1, 1985, to draw up a series of constitutional reforms to be submitted to a plebiscite for ratification. An executive presidency was replaced with a nine-member collective leadership but was reintroduced in 1966.

Sequence of elections since 1984

Legislative elections

Date	*Winning party*
Nov. 25, 1984	Colorado Party
Nov. 26, 1989	National Party (*Blancos*)

Presidential elections November 26, 1989

Candidate	*Party*	*% of votes*
Luis Alberto Lacalle Herrera	National Party	37.0
Jorge Batlle Ibáñez	Colorado Party	30.0
Gen. Líber SeregniMosquera	Broad Front	21.0
Hugo Batalla	New Space	8.5
Rodolfo Tálice	Ecological Green Party	0.5
Others		3.0
Total		**100.0**

Legislative elections November 26 1989

Party	*Chamber of Deputies seats*	*Senate seats*
National Party	39	13
Colorado Party	30	9
Broad Front	21	7
New Space	9	2
Total	**99**	**31**

The simultaneous elections for the mayorship of the capital Montevideo were won by Tabaré Vásquez of the left-wing Broad Front (see FA).

Under Uruguay's referendum law, any citizen can start a petition to hold a referendum which has to be held if the petition contains signatures of at least 25 per cent of the electorate.

Electoral system

The President is elected for a five year term by direct universal suffrage and cannot be re-elected. The Vice-President, senators and deputies are also elected by proportional representation for fixed five-year terms.

Senators are elected from a national constituency and deputies from the 19 regional subdivisions. Under Uruguayan electoral law, the electorate votes for factions within each party itself. The winner of the presidential election has to win the largest number of votes within his party and come from the party which has secured a simple majority among the electorate.

Evolution of the suffrage

Voting is compulsory for all citizens who are 18 or older.

PARTY BY PARTY DATA

Broad Front

Frente Amplio (FA)

Leadership. Gen. Líber Seregni Mosquera (l.)

Orientation. Left-wing alliance; its election campaign demands in 1989 included the alleviation of social hardship, the reduction of unemployment and control of inflation; the Front is opposed to privatization.

Founded. 1971.

History. The coalition originally consisted of 17 parties of such diverse allegiances as the Christian Democratic Party (PDC) and the Communist Party of Uruguay (PCU), and various Colorado and Blanco factions. The Front's leader, Gen. Líber Seregni, who took early retirement in protest at the Colorado government's use of the army to break up strikes, stood as the Front's presidential candidate in the 1971 elections. He won almost 19 per cent of the valid vote, a record for a left-wing candidate. The FA also won five seats in the Senate and 18 seats in the Chamber of Deputies. Most member parties as well as the alliance itself were banned by the military junta which took over in 1973, and Seregni was imprisoned in 1973-4 and 1976-1984. Many of the Front's leaders and activists were imprisoned, forced into exile or tortured to death.

The Front was again allowed to operate legally from August 1984 and it participated in the general election the following November. Seregni himself, although allowed to participate in the negotiations between the military regime and the country's main parties, was prohibited from standing for President and was replaced by Juan José Crottogni who came third, with 20.4 per cent of the vote. In the congressional elections the Front won 21 of the 99 seats in the Chamber and 6 seats in the Senate, making it Uruguay's third political force.

A majority congressional block of the Front and the Blancos in September 1986 succeeded in blocking the Colorado government's first attempt to pass the *Punto Final* amnesty law releasing army and police personnel involved in human right abuses. The Front opposed its second passage but failed to stop it when the Blancos sided with the Colorado government in December. The Front thereafter joined forces with social and labour groups in the National Commission for the Referendum, which collected 634,702 signatures, well over the 25 per cent of the electorate required by the Constitution, in order to force a referendum on the amnesty law. The referendum on April 16, 1989, held after some delay by the government, approved the *Punto Final* law by 52.7 per cent. Despite this setback, Líber Seregni interpreted the result as the wish of the majority for democracy and peace and a fresh start to building a new society.

Internal divisions caused by former *Tupamaro* guerrillas joining the Front and over the nomination of a presidential candidate led to a serious split in March 1989, with the departure of the PDC, PGP and UC (who together formed New Space—NE). The Front nevertheless scored considerable success in the November 1989 elections; Líber Seregni, once more the presidential candidate, came third with 21 per cent of the valid vote. The Front also came third in the congressional elections with 21 seats in the Chamber and seven seats in the Senate. In the capital, Montevideo, it secured control of the city council and won 33.6 per cent of the vote for the House of Deputies. Tabaré Vázquez, a Socialist, became the first left-wing mayor of Montevideo with 35 per cent of the vote. Among his first measures, he announced in February 1990 a reduction in transport tariffs and a decentralization of the city's administration. On a national level, the Front supported a broad campaign against the Blanco government's privatization programme and in Congress voted against proposed austerity measures.

Membership. Advanced Democracy Party (PDA); Blanco Popular and Progressive Movement (MBPP); Communist Party of Uruguay (PCU); March 26 Movement (M26M); Left Liberation Front (FIDEL); Nationalist Action Movement (MAN); National Liberation Movement (MLN); Pregón Group; Uruguayan Socialist Party (PSU).

Christian Democratic Party

Partido Demócrata Cristiano (PDC)
Address. Colonia 1131-33, Montevideo.
Leadership. Juan Guillermo Young (pres); Carlos Vassallo (s.-g.).
Orientation. Centre-left.
Founded. 1962.
History. The party was formed as a successor to the Civic Union of Uruguay, a progressive party founded in 1872. The majority decision to join the Broad Front in 1971 caused a more conservative section to split away and form the Civic Union (UC). Like all Broad Front parties, the PDC was banned after the coup in 1973 but was legalized again in July 1984.

In 1988 the Christian Democrats opposed the inclusion of the former *Tupamaros* guerrillas (see MLN) in the Broad Front. Soon after the party had further disagreements with the more left-wing members of the Front when the candidacy of Hugo Batalla, (leader of the Front of the Party for the Government of the People—see PGP) was not approved for the 1989 presidential elections. The Christian Democrats, together with the PGP and the UC, withdrew from the Broad Front in March 1989 and together formed the New Space alliance which came fourth in the November 1989 general election.
International Affiliations. Member party of the Christian Democrat Organization of America, which forms part of the Christian Democrat International.

Colorado Party

Partido Colorado (PC)
Address. Vásquez 1271, Montevideo.
Leadership. Américo Ricaldoni (l.).
Orientation. Nominally liberal; its electoral base is in the urban middle and working classes.
Founded. 1836.
History. The Colorados emerged from the 1836-38 civil war and were named after the liberals' red flag. The party came to power first in 1865 and governed Uruguay uninterruptedly for 93 years. The party was dominated by the Batlle family—one of whom, José Batlle y Ordóñez, during two terms as President (1903-07 and 1911-15) introduced a wide-ranging social welfare system, and *Batllismo* became synonymous with welfarism and industrial development. Having lost the collective leadership (which replaced the presidential system from 1951-66) the Colorados regained power in the 1966 elections which gave them 50 of the 99 seats in the Chamber and re-introduced the presidency.

The party shifted to the right under the President Jorge Pacheco Areco (1967-71), a period marked by industrial disputes, rampant inflation and guerrilla activity. His successor, Juan María Bordaberry Arocena, who took office in March 1972, gave the army free reign in the repression of the Tupamaros guerrillas, which subsequently led to a military coup against his government in June 1973 which he assisted. His proposals radically to reform the constitution led to his own dismissal by the military in 1976. Opposition to the military led the Colorado party leadership, in the early 1980s, to transfer its allegiances to the more liberal "Unity and Reform" and "Freedom and Change" factions.

The Nov. 25, 1984, elections which marked the end of Uruguay's military rule was narrowly won by the leader of the Colorado "Unity and Reform" faction, led by Julio María Sanguinetti with 38.6 per cent of the vote. The party, however, secured only 41 seats in the 99-seat Chamber and 13 in the Senate, and on taking office on March 1, 1985, Sanguinetti included members of other parties, acting in a personal capacity, in his government. Sanguinetti's first task was to find solutions to the economic decline. His economic strategy, however, provoked a large number of strikes culminating in a general strike in October 1989 in opposition to expected widespread redundancies in the public sector following World Bank conditions for a new structural adjustment loan. Sanguinetti's most controversial policy was the *Punto Final* (Full Stop) law granting amnesty and immunity from prosecution to military and police officers accused of gross human rights violations during the military rule of 1973-85. Although widely opposed, the need to mollify the military was uppermost in the government's mind and the amnesty law was passed by Congress in December 1986 with the assistance of the Blancos. A referendum on April 16, 1989, initiated by the National Commission for the Referendum, approved the amnesty law with 57 per cent of the vote. This result was interpreted by President Sanguinetti as the country's desire for unity, a rejection of the divisions of the past and the final stage in the country's transition to democracy.

In the internal selection in May 1989 for the party's main presidential candidate in the November 1989 elections, Sanguinetti's Vice-President and preferred choice Enrique Tarigo was beaten by the neo-liberal Jorge Batlle Ibáñez. The other two candidates were the centrist Labour and Social Welfare Minister Hugo Fernández Faingold and the right-wing former president Jorge Pacheco Areco. Batlle's campaign promises centred on the lowering of inflation and erasing the foreign debt by selling the country's gold reserves. He came second with 30 per cent of the national vote and the Colorado Party went into opposition with 30 seats in the Chamber and nine seats in the Senate. The party suffered an even greater set-back in the simultaneous mayoral elections for Montevideo, where the two main Colorado candidates together polled 25.5 per cent of the votes and came only third.

As the second largest party in Congress, the Colorados signed an agreement with the new Blancos government pledging support for the government economic reform in return for four ministerial posts (Industry and Energy, Health, Tourism, Territories and Environment). The Health Minister, however, was forced to resign when in late May 1991 Sanguinetti's Foro Batllista faction withdrew his support from the government over its privatization strategy. The move reflected general Colorado opposition to direct negotiations by the government with potential buyers rather than putting up state assets for competitive tender.

Structure. The Colorado Party has four main factions: Independent Batlleist Current (CBI), Manuel Flores Silva (l.); Freedom and Change (LyC), Enrique E. Tarigo (l.); Unity and Reform (UyR), Jorge Batlle Ibáñez and Julio María Sanguinetti (l.); Colorado Batlleist Union (Pachequist), Jorge Pacheco Areco (l.).

Publications. The various factions of the party are supported by a number of newspapers, including the daily *El Día*.

Communist Party of Uruguay

Partido Comunista del Uruguay (PCU)

Address. Rio Negro 1525, Montevideo.

Leadership. Jaime Pérez (s.g.).

Orientation. Left-wing; the party is the main force in the Broad Front, Uruguay's second strongest opposition group (see FA).

Founded. 1920.

History. The party originally was the Socialist Party, whose delegates to the 1920 party congress voted by a large majority to join the Communist Third International. Despite initial opposition from the party leadership the party nevertheless joined and changed its name, registering as a legal political party the following year. Unusually for a Latin American communist party, the PCU remained legally recognized for 52 years and regularly had candidates elected to Congress.

The party also has had a strong representation in the trade union movement throughout its history. Together with some small left-wing parties the PSU formed the Left Liberation Front (FIDEL) in 1962, which won several seats in Congress.

Although denouncing the armed struggle and rejecting any links with the Tupamaros guerrillas (MLN), the party became a target for army harassment at the end of the 1960s and early 1970s; on one occasion nine militants were shot dead outside party headquarters. In 1971 the PSU set up the Broad Front (FA) in conjunction with 16 other left-wing and centre-left parties and groups, and in the general election of the same year the Communist Party won two of the 18 FA seats in the Chamber.

As a result of the 1973 military coup the PSU was banned and fiercely persecuted. The party's secretary general, Rodney Arismendi, was permitted to go into exile in the Soviet Union in 1975 but many others continued to be subjected to torture in prison. Maintaining its distance from the guerrillas, the PSU joined forces with the Colorados, Blancos and some Socialist parties in organizing popular resistance to the military regime. The PCU was barred from participating in the 1984 elections but managed to campaign through the legalized Broad Front under the name "Advanced Democracy" and won 6 per cent of the national vote. Arismendi returned from exile at the end of 1984 and in March 1985 the PCU regained legal status. The PCU continued to be the dominant left-wing force in the Broad Front and took a major part in the campaign for a referendum on the *Punto Final* amnesty law and contributed to the Front's success in the Nov. 26, 1989, general election in which 21 Broad Front deputies and seven senators were elected. As part of the FA, the third political force in Uruguay, the PCU has remained an active opposition party.

Structure. The party leadership is made up of a 16-member Executive Committee and a Central Committee

Membership. 42,000 (estimate)

Publications. La Hora (The Hour); *El Popular.*

National Liberation Movement

Movimiento de Liberación Nacional (MLN)

Leadership. José Mújica (s.-g.).

Orientation. Left-wing; the former guerrillas campaign for rural reforms and say that although the MLN is intent on defending and deepening democracy, people should not renounce the right to defend themselves when known coup-mongers remain in the army

Founded. 1962.

History. The MLN was founded by Raúl Sendic Antonaccio as the *Tupamaros* guerrilla group (named in honour of the 18th century Peruvian Indian leader Tupac Amaru). Originally concentrated in rural areas, sparked off by the plight of the sugar cane cutters (whom Sendic had helped organize in the strikes of 1961-62) and attempts to "strike the local oligarchies" without using violence against the person, the group switched its attention to the cities in 1966. *Tupamaros* activities included robberies (which financed the distribution of food and money among the poor), occupations of radio stations and theft of company ledgers to prove the governments involvement in corruption. However, with the increasing economic and social tensions in the late 1960s the guerrillas' tactics became more violent. The MLN became responsible for the killing of the head of intelligence and a US adviser to the police force in 1970 and kidnappings.

Following the army offensive launched against them in 1972, and the ensuing military dictatorship, the MLN was virtually annihilated. Those guerrillas who were captured underwent torture and were held for years before being placed on trial. Raúl Sendic was captured in 1972 and was given the death sentence which was commuted to 45 years' imprisonment. On the return to democracy, most guerrillas were released in an amnesty in 1985, Sendic announcing that the MLN would now be working within the democratic political system. While piloting the MLN towards parliamentary involvement, Sendic founded a movement to promote rural reform. Although at first excluded from the Broad Front, the MLN was finally permitted to join in late 1988. In May 1989 it obtained legal recognition as a political party, Sendic dying the same year from a serious neurological condition which was a legacy of harsh treatment during his 13 years in prison. Since the departure of the centrist PDC, PGP and UC, the MLN has become an influential part of the Broad Front alliance.

Publication. The MLN has a bi-weekly newspaper and operates a radio station in Montevideo.

National Party

Partido Nacional (Blancos) (PN)

Address. 18 de Julio 2338, Montevideo.

Leadership. Carlos Julio Pereira (ch.); Alberto Zumarán (s.g.); J. E. M. Parsons (sec. of national directorate).

Orientation. Conservative, believes in neo-liberal economic policies, including the complete privatization of the state sector.

Founded. 1836.

History. The Blancos, who derive their name from the conservatives' white flag in the 1836-38 civil war, were founded by large landowners to defend their interests in the civil wars. The National Party was for a long time the permanent opposition party and only turned to parliamentary politics after the unsuccessful

1904 uprising. It focused mainly on the rural constituencies and did not win national power until 1958 when the Blancos obtained six of the nine seats on the National Executive Council. The party retained a majority in this collective national leadership in the elections of 1962. However, in 1966, when the presidential system was re-installed, the PN lost the elections to the Colorados. The party leader, Wilson Ferreira Aldunate, won the most votes of any single candidate in the 1971 presidential elections, but lost the election under the aggregate party vote system. He was forced into exile after the 1973 military coup and was imprisoned for six months on his return in 1984. Other reformist PN members who had remained in the country suffered persecution and imprisonment.

Ferreira, who had intended to stand for the November 1984 presidential elections, was replaced as the party's main candidate by Alberto Sáenz de Zumarán, who came second with 32.9 per cent of the vote. The party, however, won 35 seats in the Chamber and 11 in the Senate, thus making it the largest opposition bloc in Congress. As such, and because the victorious Colorado Party lacked a working majority, the Blancos obtained two Cabinet posts in return for their co-operation.

The PN, with the support of the Broad Front (FA) nevertheless exercised their power to block or alter government proposals, most notably in September 1986 when the opposition block threw out a bill proposing full amnesty for military and police accused of human rights violation. By December, however, the PN sided with the Colorados to pass the controversial *Punto Final* amnesty law.

For the presidential elections of Nov. 26, 1989, the party selected Luis Alberto Lacalle Herrera, representing the right wing, as its main candidate. The other two Blanco candidates were Sáenz de Zumarán standing for the Blancos's centre and Carlos Julio Pereyra representing the left wing. Lacalle's campaign was concentrated on the need for national reconciliation and the necessity of free market policies to reverse economic decline. He won the presidency with only 37 per cent of the ballot and the party did not perform well in the Congressional elections, taking 13 seats out of the 30 in Senate and 39, only just over a third, in the House of Deputies. In the important elections for the mayorship of Montevideo, held simultaneously, the main Blanco candidate Carlos Cat came second with 27 per cent of the vote.

In early 1990 Lacalle resigned the leadership of the Blanco Party and his presidency of the national executive committee of the party's "Herrera Movement" faction in order to be able to take up his post as President of Uruguay. In his inauguration speech to Congress on March 1, 1990, Lacalle requested a 100-day "social truce" between business, trade unions and political parties in order that state accounts could be put in order. He reiterated election promises of gradual privatization of state-owned companies, the renegotiation of the foreign debt, the reduction of government spending and the creation of a climate for increased foreign investment, the promotion of exports and growth of off-shore banking. He also kept his pledge to form a coalition government, made necessary given the PN's lack of an absolute congressional majority. He signed a "National Convergence" agreement with the Colorados, giving them four Cabinet posts in return for their support for his economic programme.

Despite this search for national consensus, the Lacalle government met with sustained opposition from the Inter-Union Workers' Assembly-Workers' National Convention (PIT-CNT), who staged numerous general strikes between 1990 and 1992 against the government's austerity programme, but also from sections of the Colorado Party and even a faction of the Blancos. The government was forced to link wages to inflation following the seven general strikes in 1990, a year in which it managed to pass only one of its economic reform bills through a deeply divided Congress. The May 1991 bill to sell off whole or part of state assets, including the state airline, the telephone company (Antel), the national ports administration and the insurance, alcohol, gas and electricity sectors, received the backing of only 13 Senators, with three of the Blancos *Movimiento Nacional de Rocha* faction abstaining. A large budget deficit, rising inflation and an ailing economy also damaged confidence in the government.

By 1992, the business sector was turning against Lacalle in protest at higher corporate income tax and social security contributions along with the removal of tax concessions and protection for the car industry.

Structure. The party has the following main factions: National Herrerista Council (*Consejo Nacional Herrerista*) led by Francisco Ubilles; White Badge (*Divisa Blanca*), conservative, led by Eduardo Pons Etcheverry; Rocha National Movement-Popular

Nationalist Current (*Movimiento Nacional de Rocha-Corriente Popular Nacionalista*) led by Carlos Julio Pereira and Juan Pivel Devoto; National Party-Barrán (*Partido Nacional-Barrán*); Sector for the Fatherland (*Sector por la Patria*) led by Alberto Zumarán.
Publication. *La Democracia* (weekly); various other newspapers support the party, including the daily *El País*.

New Space

Nuevo Espacio (NE)
Orientation. Moderate left-wing.
Founded. 1989.
History. This electoral alliance was formed by the Christian Democratic Party (PDC), the Party for the Government of the People (PGP) and the Civic Union (UC) after the PDC and PGP left the Broad Front (FA) in March 1989 following disagreements over the presence in it of the former *Tupamaros* guerrillas, its policies and the choice of presidential candidate for the forthcoming elections.

The New Space alliance backed the moderate campaign of Hugo Batalla, the leader of the PGP, who came fourth in the Nov. 26, 1989, elections with 8.5 per cent of the national vote. The alliance altogether won nine seats in the Chamber and two seats in the Senate.

Party for the Government of the People

Partido por el Gobierno del Pueblo (PGP)
Address. Calle Ejido 1480, Montevideo.
Leadership. Hugo Batalla (l.).
Orientation. Centrist.
Founded. 1970.
History. The party was founded by members of the Colorado Party's *Lista 99* created eight years earlier. The faction broke away in 1970 in order to become a founder member of the Broad Front (FA). The PGP was banned by the military regime which took over in 1973 and in May 1976 the party's leader Zelmar Michelini was kidnapped and assassinated by special agents in Argentina. The party re-emerged in 1984 under the leadership of Hugo Batalla and participated in the general election of that year as part of the Broad Front. The PGP, together with the Christian Democrats (PDC), split from the FA in March 1989 when the PGP's leader Hugo Batalla was not selected as the Front's presidential candidate. The two parties formed an new alliance, New Space (NE), which was joined by the small Civic Union (UC), and won two seats in the Senate and nine seats in the Chamber in the general elections of Nov. 26, 1989, Batalla coming fourth in the presidential race with 8.5 per cent of the vote.

Minor parties

Advanced Democracy Party (*Partido de Democracia Avanzada*—PDA) founder member of the Broad Front (FA); communist.
Blanco Popular and Progressive Movement (*Movimiento Blanco Popular y Progresista*—MBPP) a moderate left-wing party, A. Francisco Rodríguez Camusso (l.); originally a faction within the National Party (Blancos) which split away to join the Broad Front (FA) in 1971.
Civic Union (*Unión Cívica*) Río Branco 1486, Montevideo; Juan Vicente Chiarino and Humberto Cigando (ls.); originally a centre-right faction of the Christian Democratic Party (PDC) which split away when the PDC joined the Broad Front in 1971. The Civic Union was suppressed under the military regime but was allowed to operate again from 1981. It won two seats in the Chamber of Deputies in the November 1984 general elections and its presidential candidate Vicente Chiarino came fourth with 2.3 per cent of the vote. He subsequently joined the Colorado government as Defence Minister. In 1989 the Civic Union joined the Christian Democrat-led New Space alliance (NE).
Ecological Green Party (*Partido Verde Etoecologista*—PVE) an environmentalist party, led by the 90-year old Rodolfo Tálice who was the party's candidate in the presidential elections of Nov. 26, 1989, obtaining 0.5 per cent of the national vote.
March 26 Movement (*Movimiento 26 de Marzod*—M26M), Durazno, 1118 Montevideo; Eduardo Rubio (pres.), Fernando Vazquez (s.-g.); a socialist party founded in 1971 and founder member of the Broad Front (FA).
Left Liberation Front (*Frente Izquierda de Liberación*—FIDEL); Adolfo Aguirre Gonzáleza (l.); a socialist party founded in 1962. FIDEL won one seat in the Senate and three in the Chamber in 1962 and in the 1966 general election increased its representation in the Chamber to five. It became a founder member of the Broad Front (FA) in 1971 which it rejoined after 11 years of underground activity during the military regime. The party remains active in the Front.

Nationalist Action Movement (*Movimiento de Acción Nacionalista*—MAN) José Durán Matos (l.); a "progressive conservative" group which was a tendency within the National Party (Blancos) before joining the FA in 1971.

Nationalist Liberation Alliance (*Alianza Libertadora Nacionalista*—ALN); Osvaldo Martínez Jaume (l.); an extreme right-wing party. Martínez was one of the candidates who fought the presidential elections of Nov. 26, 1989. He obtained only a small fraction of the vote.

Pregón Group (*Grupo Pregón*); a left-wing liberal member party of the Broad Front (FA), formally a faction of the Colorado Party.

Righteous Party (*Partido Justicialista*—PJ) Bolívar Espíndola (l.); a far right party.

Uruguayan Socialist Party (*Partido Socialista del Uruguay*—PSU), Casa del Pueblo Soriano, 1218 Montevideo; José Pedro Cardoso (pres.), Reinaldo Gargano (s.-g.); founded in 1910 by Emilio Frugoni and reorganized after the majority split away to form the Communist Party (PCU) in 1921. The PSU moved to the left in 1959 and became a founder member of the Broad Front (FA) in 1971 and one of its leaders, Tabaré Vázquez, became the first left wing major of Montevideo in the November 1989 elections (FA).

Workers' Party (*Partido de los Trabajadores*—PT) Juan Carlos Vital Andrade (l.); a far left-wing party founded in 1984. Andrade stood as the party's presidential candidate in the 1984 and 1989 elections but obtained only a very small number of votes. The party failed to win any congressional seats.

Venezuela

Capital: Caracas **Population: 18,500,000**

The Republic of Venezuela achieved full independence from Spain in 1830. It was mostly ruled by *caudillos* ("strong men") and the military until 1945, when Gen. Enisaías Medina Angarita was removed by a coup led by progressive young army officers and supported especially by an ambitious middle class. An interim revolutionary junta was established and a new Constitution introduced which for the first time provided for the election of the President and Congress by universal suffrage. The first President elected under the new Constitution, Rómulo Gallegos, was deposed by a military coup in 1948, however, and a period of military rule followed. Gen. Marcos Pérez Jiménez, who proclaimed himself President in 1952, alienated all sections of opinion by his corrupt and repressive rule, and was overthrown in 1958 by a popular uprising. The two strongest parties, Democratic Action (AD) and the Social Christian Party (COPEI), have since alternated in office, the former holding power from 1958 to 1968, 1973 to 1978 and since 1983. The AD's Carlos Andrés Pérez, who had been President from 1973 to 1978, again won the presidential elections for the AD in 1988. Harsh economic austerity measures, introduced in 1989, subsequently provoked major social unrest throughout the country which were repressed by use of the army, resulting in the loss of more than 600 lives and the detention of 7,000 people. The continuation of these policies, and the reluctance of sections of the army to be used again as a social pacifier, culminated in a serious coup attempt against Pérez in February 1992 which resulted in 14 deaths and the detention of over 1,000 rebel soldiers.

Constitutional structure

Under the 1961 Constitution executive power is vested in the President, who is assisted by and presides over an appointed Council of Ministers. The President may not be re-elected within 10 years of completing a term. Legislative power is exercised by a bicameral National Congress, the Senate having 44 elected members and as life members the ex-presidents of constitutional governments, and the Chamber of Deputies having 201 members. The 20 Venezuelan States, two Federal Territories and one Federal District are autonomous and each have a Governor and an elected assembly. Since December 1989 Governors are also directly elected.

Electoral system

The President and National Congress are directly elected for concurrent five-year terms.

Evolution of the suffrage

Adult suffrage is universal and nominally compulsory.

79.78
Caribbean Sea
Fijo
Maracaibo
Pto.Cabello
CARACAS
MARGARITA
Cabimas
Cumaná
Barquisimeto
Valencia
Maracay
Barcelona
TRINIDAD
La Solita
El Tigre
Maturín
Palacio
Mérida
San Silvestre
Ciudad Bolívar
Ciudad Guayana
Apure
San Cristóbal
San Fernando
Ciudad Piar
Guri Dam
VENEZUELA
COLOMBIA
Caroní
GUYANA
Puerto Ayacucho
VENEZUELA
Sta. Elena
Majanajanaña
Orinoco
Pan-American Highway
Railway
Piedra Lais
Pipeline
SOUTH AMERICA
Oilfield
BRAZIL
0 km 300
CARPRESS

Sequence of elections since 1983

Date	*Winning Party*
Dec. 4 , 1983	Democratic Action (AD)
Dec. 4, 1988	Democratic Action (AD)

Presidential elections, December 4, 1988

Candidate	*Party*	*% of vote*
Carlos Andrés Pérez	Democratic Action (AD)	52.91
Eduardo Fernández	Social Christian Party (COPEI)	40.42
Teodoro Petkoff	Movement to Socialism-Left Revolutionary Movement (MAS-MIR)	2.73
Others		3.94

Congressional elections, December 4, 1988

Party	*Seats in Senate*	*Seats in Chamber*
Democratic Action (AD)	23	97
Social Christian Party (COPEI)	22	67
Movement to Socialism-Left Revolutionary Movement (MAS-MIR)	3	18
New Democratic Generation (NGD)	1	6
The Radical Cause (LCR)	-	3
Others	-	10
Total	**49**	**201**

PARTY BY PARTY DATA

Communist Party of Venezuela

Partido Comunista de Venezuela (PCV)

Address. Edificio Cantaclaro, esq. San Pedro, San Juan, Caracas.

Leadership. Alonso Ojeda Olaecha (s.-g.).

Orientation. The party was pro-Soviet and its support seriously dwindled prior to the collapse of the Soviet Union and the eastern bloc.

Founded. 1931.

History. The country's oldest existing party, it operated underground until 1942 and to 1945 as the Venezuelan Popular Union (UPV), a legal front. The party then temporarily split into the PCV, which favoured co-operation with the then Medina government and was legalized by it, and the UPV which opposed this policy.

Re-united, apart from a UPV faction which broke away to form the Revolutionary Party of the Proletariat (PRT), the PCV won three seats in 1946 in elections to a Constituent Assembly. Banned by the military regime in 1950, the PCV joined Democratic Action (AD), the Democratic Republican Union (URD) and the Social Christian Party (COPEI) in 1957 to form the Patriotic Junta, which organized a popular revolt against President Pérez Jiménez in the following year. Legalized once more, the party won two seats in the Senate and seven in the Chamber of Deputies in the 1958 elections. In 1960 its membership reached a peak of 30,000.

At the 1960 Moscow conference, the PCV was one of a few Communist parties to support China in the Sino-Soviet split. Under the influence of the Cuban revolution, a number of younger communist leaders, most notably Douglas Bravo and Teodoro Petkoff, joined activists of the Movement of the Revolutionary Left (MIR) in forming the Armed Forces of the National Liberation which began guerrilla activities in 1962 with Cuban assistance. In 1963 the PCV was again banned, the parliamentary immunity of its congressional delegates was lifted and many senior communists were arrested. After two years of internal controversy, the party abandoned its support for the guerrilla struggle in 1967, and Bravo and his followers, who advocated its continuation, were expelled. As a result of its participation in the guerrilla war the party's membership fell heavily and it lost almost all of its influence in the trade union movement.

The party was allowed to contest the 1968 elections under the name Union for the Advance, winning two seats in the Chamber and in 1969 was legalized under its own name. It lost the bulk of its membership and many of its leaders in the following year, however, when Petkoff and Pompeyo Márquez formed the Movement Towards Socialism (MAS), and in the 1973 elections it retained only one seat in the lower house. A fresh split in 1974, when a group under Eduardo Machado broke away to form the Unitary Communist Vanguard (VUC), further weakened the party, and the PCV candidate in the 1978 presidential election received only 0.54 per cent of the vote. The party fought the 1983 elections as part of the Alliance for the Unity of the People and increased its parliamentary representation from one to three seats in the Chamber.

For the 1988 elections, the PCV formed an alliance with the People's Electoral Movement (MEP), performing so poorly that it needed to re-register its membership in order to qualify for participation in future elections. In 1988, the MAS had also turned down PVC overtures for a common presidential candidate, although there was some co-operation between the two in the concurrent State Assembly and national congressional elections.

The party's leader, Hector Mujica, resigned in August 1991 in protest at the position adopted by some sections of the party which celebrated the attempted coup d'etat against the then Soviet President Mikhail Gorbachev.

Membership. 4,000 (1989 est.).

Structure. The Congress elects a 65-member central committee, which elects a politburo of seven members plus three alternate members.

Publications. Tribuna Popular (People's Tribune) weekly; *Canta Clara* (Plain Talk) monthly.

Democratic Action

Acción Democrática (AD)

Address. Edificio Azul y Blanco, Av. Libertaor, La Campiña, Caracas 1050.

Leadership. Humberto Celli (pres.); Luis Alfaro Ucero (s.-g.).

Orientation. Nominally social democratic but has promoted deeply unpopular conservative economic policies in office.
Founded. 1936.
History. The party was formed by Rómulo Betancourt under the name of National Democratic Party (Partido Democrático Nacional—PDN) and was registered as a legal party under its present name in 1941. Its grass-roots support came mainly from organized labour. The AD came to power in 1945 when Betancourt was the beneficiary of a successful army coup mounted by progressive officers, installed with a large majority in the Constituent Assembly which introduced a new Constitution providing for democratic elections for the first time in Venezuela's history. The AD won both the 1946 and 1948 presidential elections, the latter by Rómulo Gallegos who, however, was overthrown by the military the same year. The AD was persecuted during the 10-year period of the Jiménez dictatorship that followed but re-emerged victorious in 1959, when Betancourt was elected President with 49.9 per cent of the vote. In 1960 the left-wing faction of the AD broke away to form the Revolutionary Left Movement (MIR) which took up arms against the Betancourt government. His successor Raúl Leoni won the presidency in 1964 with 32.8 per cent of the poll. After losing the 1969 election to the main opposition Social Christian Party (COPEI), the AD candidate Carlos Andrés Pérez won the presidency in 1974 with 44.8 per cent of the popular vote. Despite the first Pérez administration's emphasis on economic advancement based on heavy government investment in industry and agriculture and the nationalization of sectors crucial to Venezuela's economy, especially oil, the AD nonetheless lost the 1978 elections.

In December 1983 the AD candidate Jaime Lusinchi won the presidential elections with an absolute majority of 56.8 per cent of the ballot, and the party won control of the congress. Popular support for the AD was again confirmed in the municipal elections of May 1984 despite the government's austerity programme. In order to revive a deteriorating economy, accelerated by reduced revenue from petrol exports, President Lusinchi in 1986 introduced a 21-point financial package of fiscal and foreign investment incentives. Popular protests became more frequent with the deepening of the recession and drug smuggling became more commonplace, which the Lusinchi government tried to tackle in a common agreement with Colombia. Lusinchi also initiated a "national crusade" against official corruption, although after his term had ended Lusinchi himself came under suspicion of embezzlement and only avoided being investigated by his successor's controversial intervention (see below).

Control of the AD in late 1987 went to the faction supporting the charismatic populist and former President Carlos Andrés Pérez and opposed to Lusinchi's austerity policies. Pérez was subsequently selected to fight the December 1988 presidential elections which he won with 52.91 per cent of the vote. The party, however, won only 97 seats in the Chamber and 23 in the Senate and thus lost control of Congress. After his inauguration in February 1989, Pérez introduced an IMF-approved austerity programme which was followed by days of mass protest, rioting and supermarket looting throughout the country. The intervention of the military, on Pérez's order, resulted in the death of some 600 people in Caracas alone and the imprisonment of around 7,000 people (according to a parliamentary commission), many of whom claimed that they had been tortured.

Despite regular popular protests and opposition from within the party, Pérez refused to alter his neo-liberal economic policies. He introduced a wide-ranging privatization programme, including that of the state airline Viasa in August 1991, which attracted criticism from the business community for being too sluggish. Furthermore, Pérez was highly criticized from all sides for devoting more of his time to international affairs than to national problems. He also attracted hostility from the opposition for shielding government officials and AD politicians from corruption investigations during the period of the Lusinchi government, with the exception of the former minister José Angel Ciliberto, who in 1989 was charged with embezzlement and abuse of public funds.

As opposition to Pérez mounted within the party, the AD became increasingly dominated by the "orthodox" faction supporting ex-President Lusinchi. This was confirmed in the September 1991 internal party elections when the pro-Perez "renewalists" won only 44 per cent of the votes. In the party leadership elections at the party convention on Oct. 6, 22 of the 26 posts on the national executive committee went to the "orthodox" wing as did the presidency of the party. Strong opposition to Pérez also came from the AD youth movement and the major CTV labour confederation (to which the AD is affiliated) who were demanding a change in his economic strategy with more emphasis given to social legislation in tune with public opinion. The November general strike against cost of living increases and widespread student protest led conservative opposition deputies to warn of a military coup unless emergency measures were taken. These warnings were amply fulfilled when, on Feb. 3 and 4, 1992, rebel army units tried to take over the government palace and presidential residence in an attempt to assassinate Pérez. He narrowly escaped and in a television broadcast rallied loyal troops who put down the uprising.

Under renewed pressure from within the AD, as well as from the opposition, to alert his government's economic policies, Pérez reshuffled his Cabinet but nevertheless left his economic team almost intact and insisted that he would continue with his austerity programme, softening the blow with a price freeze on electricity, petrol and basic foodstuffs and a promise of a US$4,000 million welfare programme. He also pledged a referendum on constitutional reforms and the convening of a Constituent Assembly to implement them. His request to opposition parties to join a "political" Cabinet to help draft policies for the following two years was initially rebuffed, but in March, the Social Christian Party (COPEI) accepted two portfolios in a "Cabinet of National Unity". Unrest within the AD failed to subside, however, and in late March two senior party members were expelled for criticizing the continuation of the economic austerity programme. COPEI withdrew from the government in June 1992.

Membership. 1,450,000 (1986 est.).

International affiliations. Socialist International.

Democratic Republican Union

Unión Republicana Democrática (URD)

Address. Quinta Amalia, Avenida Páez, El Paraíso, Caracas.

Leadership. Jóvito Villalba (l.).

Orientation. Centrist.

Founded. 1946.

History. Originally opposed to the dominance of the Democratic Action (AD) when it came to power following a progressive military rebellion in 1945, the URD initially supported its overthrow in the military coup of 1948. It then opposed the junta headed by Gen. Marcos Pérez Jiménez and contested the 1952 Constituent Assembly elections with the support of the AD, then illegal, only to be denied power by a front party, the FEI, loyal to Jiménez and consigned to second place with 20 out of the 104 seats. Subsequently repressed by Jiménez along with other political parties, the URD joined the Revolutionary Patriotic Front which actively participated in the popular movement which ousted him in 1958. The party then signed a pact, the *Punto Fijo*, which made it a part of the freely elected government of the AD's Rómulo Betancourt. It gained 34 seats out of a total of 133 seats in the Congress. However, it withdrew its ministers in 1960 in opposition to Betancourt's growing anti-communism. The URD's leader, Villalba came third with 17.5 per cent of the vote in the 1963 presidential elections and the party won 29 out of 179 seats in the Congress. Its congressional representation declined rapidly thereafter to 14 out of 188 in 1968 and five out of 203 in 1973. In 1978 the URD had only three congressional deputies who sat with the Social Christian Party (COPEI) opposition bloc. In the 1983 elections, it supported the New Alternative (NA) and won eight seats in the Chamber and two in the Senate. Since then, it has made no electoral impact, whether standing on its own or in alliances.

Movement Towards Socialism

Movimiento al Socialismo (MAS)

Address. Edificio Los Tribunales, Piso 2, esq. Parajitos, Caracas, 1010.

Leadership. Teodoro Petkoff Maleo (l.); Pompeyo Márquez (pres.); Freddy Múñoz (s.-g.).

Orientation. Democratic socialist.

Founded. 1971.

History. The MAS was formed by the bulk of the membership of the Communist Party (PCV), a majority of Communist trade union leaders, and almost the entire PCV youth movement, following a split in 1970. The split had occurred after the expulsion of PCV leader and former guerrilla leader Teodoro Petkoff for his open condemnation of the 1968 Soviet invasion of Czechoslovakia and his rejection of both Soviet and Eurocommunist models for the development of Venezuelan socialism. In the 1973 elections MAS won two seats in the Senate and nine in the Chamber of Deputies and emerged as the strongest of the left-wing parties. The party supported the independent candidate José Vicente Rangel in the simultaneous presidential election. The MAS backed Rangel again in the 1978 election in which he came third with 5.1 per cent of the vote while the MAS's representation in the Chamber was increased to 11 deputies. The party's growing success, however, was hampered in the run-up to the 1983 election when it split into supporters of Petkoff and those who, backing Rangel as the representative of a broad left alliance, broke away from the party. Petkoff, with the support of the Movement of the Revolutionary Left (MIR), won 4.2 (as opposed to Rangel's 3.3 per cent) but the MAS's representation in the Chamber of Deputies fell to 10 seats and to only two in the Senate.

The two parties formed an alliance in 1988 when Petkoff once more stood for the presidency in the December elections, although one sector of the party wanted to support the Democratic Action (AD) candidate Carlos Andrés Pérez in order to concentrate the alliance's efforts on the congressional elections. Petkoff came third with 2.73 per cent of the presidential vote, as did the MAS-MIR alliance which obtained 18 seats in the Chamber and three in the Senate. Because the ruling AD failed to retain its congressional majority the MAS gained considerable influence as part of the congressional opposition block.

After the attempted military coup in early February 1992 (AD), the MAS leadership was invited by President Pérez to take part in a "cabinet of national unity" to draft policies for last two years of his term. Aware of the compromising position in which this would place the party, the MAS rejected the offer. In March and April, it supported anti-government protests, demanding the restoration of constitutional rights and Pérez's resignation.

Structure. The MAS is governed by a 15-member Executive Committee and a 45-member National Directorate.

Membership. 220,000 (1990).

Publications. El Ojo del Huracán (The Eye of the Hurricane); *Punto*; *Foco Internacional*

Movement of the Revolutionary Left

Movimiento de Izquierda Revolucionaria (MIR)

Leadership. Héctor Pérez Marcano (pres.); Moisés Moleiro (s.-g.).

Orientation. Left-wing.

Founded. 1960.

History. The MIR was set up by members of a large left-wing dissident group which split away from the ruling Democratic Action (AD) and included among its ranks 13 Deputies and most of the AD's student section. The party's ideology was inspired by the Cuban revolution and in 1962 began guerrilla operations mainly in rural areas. MIR members were being arrested for "subversion" in 1960 and it was completely banned in 1962. A section of the membership renounced violence in 1965 but the main group, led by Américo Martín and Moisés Moleiro, continued the armed struggle until 1969. In that year MIR accepted the Caldera government's offer of an amnesty and was legalized soon after.

The party participated for the first time in an election in 1973 and won one seat in the Chamber of Deputies. In 1978 the MIR fielded Martín as its presidential candidate, who won only 0.98 per cent of the vote, although the party increased its representation in the Chamber to four seats. The party suffered a severe split in 1980 when Martín headed a non-Leninist breakaway group and in 1982 formed the New Alternative (NA). Moleiro's faction was awarded the right to retain the MIR name in 1982 by the Supreme Court, which ruled that its Marxist-Leninist principles better represented the ideas of the original party.

In the 1983 presidential election the MIR supported the candidate of the Movement Towards Socialism (MAS) but stood alone in the congressional elections in which the party won only two seats in the Chamber as a result of the 1980 split. Like the MAS, the MIR became much more pragmatic during the 1980s and in 1988 the two parties joined forces. The electoral alliance won 18 seats in the Chamber and three in the Senate and the MAS-MIR presidential candidate Teodoro Petkoff won third place with 2.73 per cent of the vote.

Social Christian Party

Partido Social Cristiano (COPEI)

Address. Edificio COPEI, Av. Fuerzas Armadas y Panteón, Esquina de San Miguel, Caracas 1010.

Leadership. Eduardo Fernández (s.-g.).

Orientation. Centrist, Christian Democratic.

Founded. 1946.

History. The party was founded by Rafael Caldera as the Organizing Committee for Independent Electoral Policy (*Comité de Organización Política Electoral*

Independiente), whose acronym COPEI is still in use despite the party's change of name. It won second place with 19 of the 160 seats in the Constituent Assembly elections in 1946. In the presidential elections of December 1947 Rafael Caldera also came second with 22 per cent of the popular vote. COPEI supported the military coup against the Democratic Alliance (AD) government in 1948 but then opposed the junta. After Col. Marcos Pérez Jiménez was overthrown in 1958, COPEI joined the AD, the Communist Party (PCV) and the Republican Democratic Party in an alliance to preserve the newly restored democracy. COPEI won 19 of the 133 seats in the Chamber of Deputies in the elections which took place the same year. In the presidential elections of 1963 Rafael Caldera, with 20.2 per cent of the poll, lost again against the AD candidate. The party increased its representation in Congress to 40 seats. Caldera was finally elected in 1969 with 29.1 per cent of the vote, although COPEI won only 50 of the 188 seats in the Chamber and had to form an alliance with independents to form a government.

COPEI lost the 1973 elections despite its candidate winning 36.8 per cent of the vote and its congressional representation rising to 64 deputies. In 1978 the party's candidate, Luis Herrera Campíns, was elected President with 46.6 per cent of the vote, and the party allied in Congress with the Democratic Republican Union (URD) and other minor parties. In the municipal elections of 1979 COPEI won an absolute majority of the vote.

Rafael Caldera was again selected to fight the December 1983 election but, after a particularly vitriolic campaign in which the AD attacked the Herrera government on economic and personal grounds, lost to the AD's candidate Lusinchi with 34.6 per cent of the vote. The party obtained only 60 seats in the Chamber and 16 in the Senate. In December 1988 the COPEI put forward Eduardo Fernández as its presidential candidate but with 40.42 per cent of the vote once more lost the election to the AD. Its representation in the Chamber, however increased to 67 seats and in the Senate to 22, making it the dominant party in the majority opposition block in Congress.

Following the unsuccessful February 1992 military coup (see AD), the COPEI, along with the Movement Towards Socialism (MAS), declined President Pérez's request to the main opposition parties to join a "political Cabinet" of ministers without portfolio to draft policies for the next two years. They characterized the move as a "cosmetic" operation which would not lead to any significant changes in the government's economic policies. However, in early March two COPEI Ministers joined a "Cabinet of National Unity", one of whom, Humberto Calderón Beti, was named as the new Foreign Minister. Pérez stated that this provided evidence of COPEI's "sense of responsibility" in agreeing to "demonstrate its solidarity with the Venezuelan democratic government". It also produced a split within the party, with one faction still determined to oppose the government and insisting that Pérez resign. However, COPEI withdrew from the government in June 1992.

Structure. A National convention normally meets every two years and a national directorate annually. A national committee is elected at alternate conventions. There are other national, state, district, municipal and branch structures and a trade union affiliate, the Venezuelan Confederation of Autonomous Trade Unions (Codesa).

Membership. Variously put at between 400,000 and 800,000.

International affiliations. Member party of the Christian Democrat Organization of America, which forms part of the Christian Democrat International.

The Radical Cause

La Causa Radical (LCR)

Address. Casa del Partido Causa R, Calle Valencia, URB, Las Palmas, Caracas 1050.

Leadership. Noé Acosta (l.), Pablo Medina (s.-g.).

Orientation. Independent left-wing.

History. The party controls the 17,000-member union of the steel company Sidor and has its main support base in the Guayana industrial region. The LCR joined the New Alternative (NA) in the 1983 elections but in the 1988 elections stood by itself and won three seats in the Chamber of Deputies, attracting votes away from traditional left-wing parties. The party leader and presidential candidate Andrés Velásquez came fifth and in the 1989 gubernatorial elections won the governorship of Bolívar. Opposed to the ruling Democratic Action (AD) and its austerity policies, the LCR openly expressed sympathy for rebel officers who tried to depose President Carlos Andrés Pérez in February 1992 (see AD). Its leader Noé Acosta was arrested on Feb. 6 in the city of Maracaibo. In March the LCR characterized Perez's appeal for a "Cabinet of National Unity" as a farce and joined with the Movement Towards Socialism (MAS) in supporting a one-day strike against the government on April 8.

Minor parties

National Integration Movement (*Movimiento de Integración Nacional*—MIM, Edificio José Maria Vargas 1, esq. Pajaritos, Caracas 1010); Gonzalo Pérez Hernández (s.-g.); a nationalist party, founded in 1977, which won a single seat in the Chamber of Deputies in 1983.

New Alternative (*Nueva Alternativa*—NA, Edificio José María Vargas, esq. Pajaritos, Apdo 20193, San Martín, Caracas 1010); Guillermo Garcia Ponce (s.-g.); an alliance of democratic left-wing parties founded in 1982. Its founder members comprised the Martín faction of the Movement of the Revolutionary Left (see MIR), the Unitary Communist Vanguard (VUC), the People's Revolutionary Movement (MRP) and the Movement of the Socialist Fatherland (MPS). The member parties have since acted as one in the New Alternative. The NA won two seats in the Chamber of Deputies in the 1983 elections but in 1988 failed to obtain any representation in Congress. Its presidential candidate Leopoldo Díaz Bruzual, a former Social Christian Party (COPEI) member and ex-president of the Central Bank, was widely criticized on the left and received a negligible numbers of votes. Secretary-general Ponce was among other left-wing leaders to meet with a delegation from the Korean Workers Party (KWP) in the Ecuadorian capital Quito, in April 1992.

New Democratic Generation (*Nueva Generación Democrática*—NGD; Centro Andrés Bello, Torre Oeste, Piso 12, Oficina 122-0, Las Palmas, Caracas 1050); Vladimir Gessen (s.-g.); originating from the right-wing New Generation (NG) founded in 1977 by Gen. Arnaldo Castro Hurtado which did poorly in the 1983 elections. However, in 1988 the NGD won seven congressional seats.

National Opinion *Opinión Nacional*—Opina, Pájaro a Curamichate 92-2, Caracas 1010); a centre-right party founded in 1961 to promote its own version of "collective integralism", it won a seat in the Chamber of Deputies in 1978, when it endorsed the COPEI presidential campaign. Its own candidate won only 0.5 per cent of the poll in 1983 but won three seats in the Chamber.

People's Electoral Movement (*Movimiento Electoral del Pueblo*—MEP); Luis Beltrán Prieto Figueroa (pres.), Adelso González (s.-g.), Jesús Paz Galarraga (vice-pres.); the MEP split from Democratic Action (AD) in 1968 and initially was based mainly in the Confederation of Venezuelan Workers (CTV). It achieved some success through alliances, chiefly with the Communist Party (see PCV). In 1988 its presidential candidate, Edmundo Chirinos, former rector of the Central University of Venezuela, was supported by the PCV and the Independent Moral movement but won less than 1 per cent of the vote and its congressional representation fell to two deputies. In 1989 an MEP candidate, Ovidio González, supported by a broad "anti-corruption" front including the Social Christian Party (COPEI), won the governorship of Anzoátegui.

British Virgin Islands

Capital: Road Town (Tortola) **Population: 12,197**

The British Virgin Islands, consisting of around 60 islands, are a British Crown Colony.

Constitutional structure

Under the 1977 Constitution the Governor, representing the British monarch, is in charge of defence, security and external affairs. The Governor chairs the six-member Executive Council which includes the Chief Minister. The Executive Council is responsible to the Legislative Council which consists of 12 members.

Electoral system

Nine members of the Legislative Council are elected for four years by universal adult suffrage in single-seat constituencies. Additionally the Council has one ex officio member, one member nominated by the Governor and a Speaker chosen from outside the Council. The Executive Council has one ex officio member and four ministers drawn from the elected members of the legislature.

Sequence of elections since 1983

Date	*Winning party*
Nov. 1983	United Party (UP)
Sept. 30, 1986	Virgin Islands Party (VIP)

PARTY BY PARTY DATA

Independent People's Movement (IPM)

Leadership. Omar Hodge (l.).
Founded. 1989.
History. The IPM was founded by Omar Hodge, who was dismissed on March 16, 1988, as Deputy Chief Minister for attempting to use a court action to delay the report of an inquiry into allegations of bribery made against him. A co-founder of the party was the director of the Tourist Board, Allen O'Neal, who resigned from the post.

United Party (UP)

Address. P.O. Box 253, Road Town, Tortola.
Leadership. Conrad Maduro (l.).
Orientation. Centrist.
History. The UP won three of the then seven elective seats on the Legislative Council on Sept. 1, 1975, but in November 1979 it failed to win any seats on the enlarged Council. In 1982 the leader of the UP, Oliver Cills, left to join the Virgin Island Party (VIP) government. He was succeeded as leader by Willard Wheatley, a former independent councillor who was Chief Minister in 1971-79.

In 1983 the UP won four of the nine elective seats and returned to power by allying with an independent, Cyril B. Romney, who became Chief Minister with Wheatley as his Deputy.

It held only two seats in 1986; Wheatley lost his seat but Romney was returned as an independent, despite the fact that the elections were precipitated by allegations concerning his involvement in drug money laundering. After Ralph O'Neil left the UP for the VIP, before being appointed Deputy Chief Minister in March 1989, Conrad Maduro was appointed Leader of the Opposition.

Virgin Islands Party (VIP)

Address. P.O. Box 263, Road Town, Tortola.
Leadership. H. Lavity Stoutt (l.).
Orientation. Centre-right.
Founded. 1970.
History. Stoutt was Chief Minister from 1967 to 1971 and Deputy Chief Minister as an independent in 1975-79. In 1979 the VIP increased its representation in the enlarged Legislative Council from three elective seats out of seven to four out of nine (with five seats going to independents), and Stoutt again became Chief Minister.

The VIP held its four seats in the November 1983 elections, but went into opposition to a coalition formed by the United Party (UP) and an independent MP. In 1986, however, the VIP regained control, winning five seats, the first-ever outright majority. Stoutt again became Chief Minister. On March 16, 1989, the Deputy Chief Minister, Omar Hodge, was dismissed from office (see IDP) and was replaced by the UP Leader of the Opposition Ralph O'Neal, who defected to the VIP. Hodge subsequently joined the UP and then went on to found the Independent People's Movement in 1989 (see IPM).

United States Virgin Islands

Capital: Charlotte Amalie **Population: 109,105**

The islands were sold to the USA by the Dutch government in 1916 for US$25,000,000. US citizenship was granted in 1927 and in 1931 a civil administration succeeded that of the Navy department and control passed to the Department of the Interior.

Constitutional Structure

The islands are administered under an Organic Act of 1936 (revised in 1954) as an "unincorporated territory" of the United States. Due to fears of increased taxation, several offers of greater autonomy have been rejected in referendums. Executive power is vested in a Governor, assisted by a Lieutenant-Governor, and there is a unicameral legislature (Senate) made up of 15 senators with limited powers. Since 1972 the islands have been allowed a non-voting deputy in the US House of Representatives.

Electoral system

The Governor is elected for a four-year term. The senators are elected in multi-seat districts for a two-year term by universal suffrage of resident US citizens, along with the island's non-voting delegate to the US House of Representatives.

Recent elections

Senate elections November 1990

Party	*No of seats*
Democratic Party	6
Independent Citizens Movement	2
Independents	3

PARTY BY PARTY DATA

Democratic Party of the Virgin Islands (DPVI)

Leadership. Winston Hodge (l.); Marlyn Stapleton (ch.).
Orientation. Centre-right; the party is affiliated to the US Democratic Party.
History. In the 1988 legislative elections, the party won 10 seats in the Senate.

Independent Citizen's Movement (ICM)

Leadership. Virdin Brown (l.).
Orientation. Centrist.
History. The ICM was formed by a breakaway group from the Democratic Party (DPVI), and one of its members, Cyril King, was elected Governor in November 1974. He died in 1978 and was succeeded by his deputy, Juan Luis, an independent who was elected to the office in 1982.

Republican Party of the Virgin Islands (RPVI)

Leadership. Charlotte Poole-Davis (l.).
Orientation. Right-wing; the party is affiliated to the US Republican Party.
Founded. 1968.
History. The party convincingly won the 1986 elections and Alexander Farrelly was elected governor. It only won two seats in the 1988 legislative elections.

Index of names

C

D

E

F

M

N

O

P

Q

R

S

T

Index of parties

B

C

D

E

F

G

H

N

T

U

V

W